BE UPDATE AND FACE TO FACE WITH INDIAN REPUBLIC

BE UPDATE AND FACE TO FACE WITH INDIAN REPUBLIC

Rajkumar Singh

KALPAZ

ISBN : 978-93-5128-028-6
₹ 985

First Published 2014

Published by

Kalpaz Publications
C-30, Satyawati Nagar,
Delhi-110052
Ph. : 9212142040
E-mail: kalpaz@hotmail.com

Laser Typesetting : Sanya Computers, Delhi
Printed at : G. Print Process, Delhi

Cataloging in Publication Data—DK
Courtesy: D.K. Agencies (P) Ltd. <docinfo@dkagencies.com>

Singh, Raj Kumar, 1958-
Be update and face to face with Indian republic / Rajkumar Singh.
p. cm.
Includes bibliographical references (p.) and index.
ISBN 9789351280286

1. India—Politics and government—1947- 2. Constitutional law—India. I. Title.

DDC 320.954 23

Dedicated to

Dr. D.N. Mallik

My Most Revered Teacher

Contents

PART-II: INS AND OUT OF INDIAN REPUBLIC

Preface

The work *Be Update and Face to Face with Indian Republic* entails gradual dramatic events with analysis from different angles that have largely shaped the current impass in Indian politics and society. On 26 January, 1950, the Constitution of independent India declared it to be a Republic who's Head of the State – single or collective is always elected for a prescribed period. Now our Republic is not only sovereign and democratic but socialist and secular too. It ensures all the citizens of India—justice, liberty, equality and fraternity in the entire social, economic and political spheres of human activity. Meaningfully it has been made a democratic republic whose democracy is not direct but through the Parliament of India. The parliamentary democracy, is of course, a representative democracy and the people of India are to exercise their sovereignty in electing their representatives for Central and State legislatures. Democracy cannot function without the system of representation, and elections cannot be contested without the political parties and their leaders. It is based on the active and intelligent interest of the people in their national affairs and in the elections that result in the formation of governments. Heavily relying on governments of political parties the national state was made an instrument of development and social transformation. The Indian Republic had showed the courage to two major innovations of historical significance in nation building and social engineering: first, to build a democratic and civil libertarian society among an illiterate people and second, to undertake economic development within a democratic political structure. Political system, when understood as the state, is characterised by an ensemble of institutional patterns and political organisation. In general the state is distinguished from other organisations in society by its capacity to monopolise the legitimate use of violence within a given territory. In a land of immense regional, linguistic, ethnic and religious diversity national unity had to be strengthened by recognising and accepting multiple identities and by giving various sections an adequate space in the Indian union. Diversities exist and the Indian republic moves forward with multiparty system and a federal structure of the Constitution along with a non-partisan attitude with all religions. However, it was too good to last long but a crack appeared after two decades when a clear shift recorded in socio-political perspectives.

For the positive change of socio-political milieu, also affected by the ongoing economy of the nation, basics of the Indian Constitution and world environment of the day should be given a large part of credit. The political rights of citizens as enshrined in the Constitution played a vital role in increasing awareness of the meaning of franchise and the efficacy of the vote. Although democracy in India has not solved the problems of the poor, it has not provided them food and shelter, but it has given them a space to fight for their dignity, rights and entitlement. Their participation in electoral process is growing and assertively reaffirms their faith in democracy. Unlike the decades of 1950s and 1960s when the Congress was an umbrella organisation representing a bloc of classes and interests, the decade 1990s onwards revealed the formation and rise of post-Mandal and post-Hindutva forces and as a result democracy in India is no longer dependent on the guardianship of the elite. Today a large group of "common people" has emerged to protect, with necessary reforms, the established political system of the Indian republic. Now it has enabled the unprivileged to transcend their social location; gave them a sense of power that they never experienced in social life.

I wish to thank the institutions and individuals for their encouragement, cooperation and good wishes that I received and staff of the central libraries at New Delhi and other places where I got a lot of information and analytical/ critical views of different subject experts. They all concerned deserve cordial thanks.

I am deeply grateful to several persons and colleagues. Among teachers Dr. D.N. Mallik, Dr. Kirtyanand Singh, Dr. R.N. Kumar and Dr. M.R. Kazami, retired Professors of the University Department of Political Science, BRA Bihar University, Muzaffarpur, have been constant source of guide and encouragement at every stage. Colleagues Dr. Dhirendra Narayan Singh, Department of Political Science MLT College, Saharsa, Dr. Chandra Prakash Singh, Department of History, Dr. Kumar Jyotivardhan, and Dr. Usha Sinha Department of Hindi, Dr. Ram Naresh Singh, Department of Maithili, West Campus P.G. Centre, Saharsa and departmental colleagues, Dr. Bijay Kumar Verma and Dr. Pawan Kumar are thankful for their cooperation and goodwishes. Eldest brother late Suryanath Singh, elder brother Bhuvneshwar Prasad Singh, father-in-law Shri Ramanand Singh, retired Professor and Head, University Department of Physics, BRA Bihar University, Muzaffarpur, deserve deep sense of gratitude for their sincere goodwishes. I am no less grateful to Rajeev Ranjan who performed the painful task of composing the book, and to colleagues and staff of the B.N. Mandal University, West Campus, P.G. Centre, Saharsa.

I would be failing in my duty if I do not record my honest goodwishes and gratitude to the family members including my wife Dr. Hemlata Singh, son Aditya Priyadarshi and Apurv Adarsh in the completion of the book.

However, for the facts, analysis, views and misjudgements contained in the book I alone am responsible.

6th February 2013 **Rajkumar Singh**

Glossary

Absolutism	a system in which authority is absolute and unchecked
Accountability	exercise of powers and discharge of duties properly
Administration	process of implementing decisions and organising the government of a country
Amendment	a change made to a bill, law, constitutional provision or regulation
Assemblies	collections of people who either directly comprise, or represent, a political or social entity
Authority	right to give an order, such that the command will be obeyed with no question as to that right
Ballots	votes cast in an election
Behavioural	applied to certain schools of thought in the social sciences
Bourgeois	one who lives in a town
Bureaucracy	a way of organising the activities of any institution
Cabinet	the name for the small body of senior politicians responsible for directing the administration of a country
Cabinet Government	a form of government in which responsibility for directing the policies of the country lies in the hands of a small group of senior politicians
Capitalism	any economic system where there is a combination of private property, a relatively free and competitive market
Centralisation	the concentration of government and political authority
Civic Culture	one in which the political ideas and values of the citizenry are attuned to political equality and participation

Civil Disobedience	a protest strategy, invented and popularised by Mahatma Gandhi
Civil Rights	those rights protected constitutionally or legally as fundamental rights
Civil Society	the organised society over which the state rules
Coalition	grouping of rival political unit in the face of a common enemy
Cold War	the state of extreme hostility between the super powers
Colonialism	the treating of another country as colony
Congress	a meeting of representatives or official for debate and discussion
Constitution	a set of rights, powers and procedures that regulate the relationships
De Facto	a position to control and order some political system
De Jure	entitlement to give legitimate orders
Democracy	a rule by the demos, the people or mob
Détente	a policy process mainly an easing of tension
Dictatorship	a form of government in which one man has sole and complete political power
Diplomacy	an entire method of resolving international conflicts
Direct Democracy	Direct participation of citizen in decision making and passing of laws
Discrimination	the practice of singling out usually for unfavourable treatment
Due Process	procedural fairness
Election	a method of choosing amongst candidates for some post or office
Electoral System	a method used to translate the votes for candidate in an election
Equality of Opportunity	a basic social justice by all ideologies in the modern world

Executive	the part of a governmental system which takes decision as opposed to making laws
Federalism	a loose alliance or union of states for limited purposes
Feudalism	a particular form of medieval government
Franchise	another name for the eligibility to vote.
Heads of Government	a person appointed to head a government
Heads of State	the person who exercises a number of formal and ceremonial powers and responsibilities
Ideology	the overall perception one has about the working of the world
Initiative	a method whereby a group of citizens can put a legislative proposal before the electorate
Interest Group	associations formed to promote a sectional interest in the political system
Judicial Review	a method whereby a superior judicial body decides whether an executive or legislative action is constitutional
Judiciary	the body of judges in a constitutional system
Justice	fair trials, equality before the law, and so on
Law	a system that govern the behaviour of citizens or political actors
Law and Order	the provision of a strong police force and a concern with reducing crime and vandalism
Leadership	the ability of a person or a group of persons to persuade others to act according to one's proposed course of action
Legislature	the official rule-making body of a political system
Liberal Democracy	a form of representative democracy
Local Government	a system of administration for small political units-town, counties and rural districts
Majority System	a system in which a full arithmetic majority of voters (50%+1) are required
Mandate	vote in a fixed way on some particular issue

Maoism	the thoughts of Chairman Mao-Tse-tung
Militant	some one who is very strongly committed to some cause or other
Minorities	those who are not in a majority in some sense in a political system
Modernisation	the capacity of countries to develop the economic and political capacity
Monarchy	rule by a single individual who is seen as royal
Multi-Party System	a political system in which there is more than one political party contesting elections
Nationalisation	the policy of taking firms, enterprises or whole industries into public ownership
Neutrality	state of non-involvement in international conflict
Opposition	a political grouping, Party or loose association of individuals who wish to change the government and its policies
Parliament	elected assemblies with the duty of checking, controlling and sometimes electing the executive power
Parliamentary Government	a system of government in which the Executive is responsible to an Assembly or Parliament
Participatory Democracy	an alternative label for 'Direct' as opposed to 'Representative' Democracy
Party	an organised group of people sharing common policy preferences, a general ideological position
Plebiscitory Democracy	a system for allowing the whole of an electorate directly to give their opinion on some political question.
Police State	a political system where those in power use naked force by police, secret police, military to control the population
Political Culture	the totality of ideas and attitudes towards authority, discipline and other related issues
Political Science	title for the academic study of politics and political behaviour

Power	the ability of A to make B do something B would not choose to do
President	a person in a Republic who can represent, legally and symbolically the entire state
Pressure Group	a voluntary organisation formed to defend and promote interest in society
Ratification	the formal approval required by many constitutions
Representation	a system in which the interests or beliefs of many are represented
Representative Democracy	a form of indirect rule by the majority of the electorate
Republic	a system of government that does not entail Monarchy
Revolution	a violent and total change in a political system
Secular State	a secular state is one which has no official ties to any religion.
Separation of Powers	a classic doctrine of liberal politics
Socialism	a politico-economic system where the state controls the basic means of production
Sovereignty	the right to own and control some area of the world
State	the whole fixed political system, the set up of authoritative and legitimately powerful
Third World	the less industrialised, non or under-developed world
United Nations	the United Nations is an international organisation founded in 1945 after the Second World War by 51 countries committed to maintaining international peace and security, developing friendly relations among nations and promoting social progress, better living standards and human rights
Voting	an act of choice amongst a set of alternatives, by a free individual, and is at the heart of modern democracy

Welfare State	a social system whereby the state assumes primary responsibility for the welfare of its citizens, as in matters of health care, education, employment, and social security, the general idea that misfortunes that have financial consequences to those unable to manage should all be dealt with by the state
Zamindari	landowner's estate

Abbreviations

AIADMK	All India Anna Dravida Munnetra Kazhagam
AICCCR	All India Coordination Committee of Communist Revolutionaries
AGP	Awareness Generation Programme
APC	Armoured Personnel Carrier
ASEAN	Association of South East Asian Nations
BJP	Bharatiya Janata Party
CEDAW	Convention on the Elimination of all forms of Discrimination Against Women
CFD	Congress for Democracy
CMP	Common Minimum Programme
CPC	Communist Party of China
CPI (M)	Communist Party of India (Marxist)
CPI (ML)	Communist Party of India (Marxist Leninist)
CRPF	Central Reserve Police Force
CSW	Commission on the Status of Women
CTBT	Comprehensive Test Ban Treaty
DIA	Defence of India Act
DMK	Dravida Munnetra Kazhagam
DWID	Division of Women in Development
ECI	Election Commission of India
EU	European Union
FDI	Foreign Direct Investment
FTAs	Free Trade Agreements
GAD	Gender and Development Approach
GIDP	Gender in Development Programme
GNP	Gross National Product

HVP	Haryana Vikas Party
IGOs	Inter Governmental Organisations
IIPO	Indian Institute of Public Opinion
IJPS	Indian Journal of Political Science
IMF	International Monetary Fund
INC	Indian National Congress
INGOs	International Non-Governmental Organisations
JMM	Jharkhand Mukti Morcha
JP	Janata Party
KMPP	Kisan Mazdoor Praja Party
LJPS	Lok Jana Shakti Party
LPG	Liberalisation Privatisation and Globalisation
LTTE	Liberation Tigers of Tamil Eelam
MCCI	Maoist Communist Centre of India
MISA	Maintenance of Internal Security Act
MNCs	Multi-National Companies and Multi-National Corporations
MRTP	Monopoly and Restrictive Trade Practices
NAM	Non-aligned Movement
NDA	National Democratic Alliance
NORDA	Norwegian Development Agency
OPEC	Oil-producing European Countries
PGN	Practical Gender Needs
PLA	People's Liberation Army
POTA	Prevention of Terrorist Act
PSP	Praja Socialist Party
PWG	Peoples War Group
RJD	Rashtriya Janata Dal
RSS	Rashtriya Swayam Sevak
RTI	Right to Information
SAP	South Asia Politics
SAARC	South Asian Association for Regional Cooperation

SC	Scheduled Castes
SGN	Strategic Gender Needs
SP	Samata Party and Samajwadi Party
SS	Shiv Sena
ST	Scheduled Tribes
STEP	Support to Training and Employment
TDP	Telugu Desham Party
TMC	Trinamul Congress and Tamil Maanila Congress
UF	United Front
UNDP	United Nations Development Programme
UNDFW	United Nations Development Fund for Women
UPA	United Progressive Alliance
VHP	Vishva Hindu Parishad
WID	Women in Development
WMD	Weapons of Mass Destruction
WTO	World Trade Organisation

PART-I
INDIAN REPUBLIC BETWEEN HOPE AND DESPAIR

1 Introduction

The Republic Day is the people's day in many ways and the Constitution of India stands fundamentally for the aspirations of the common man, the "aam admi". The freedom struggle was not just for political freedom. It was not merely to dislodge foreign rulers and install our own. It was also for social and economic change and for a life of peace and dignity to all citizens. While India witnesses rapid economic growth, there are still vast numbers of people in the country who face grave problems of illiteracy, disease and poverty.[1] All is not well with Indian democracy. In the whole system of governance the political parties have acquired most important position on whose conduct, failure or success the system of Parliamentary democracy depends. A responsibility also falls upon the political parties to see and ensure that malpractices which are often heard of are not resorted to. Holding on to the power unethically may not be conducive to the successful functioning of Parliamentary democracy. The concept of democracy is different from mere majoritarianism. It is based on higher values and pluralism, not a game of numbers only.[2] Over time, democracy has become essentially an instrument of winning power and there is a danger of falling deeper into a "democratic trap" if we confuse a democratic mandate with democratic values.[3] Only in recent years it has been felt that democracy has become a part of the problem and cannot therefore be part of the solution. The protest is, therefore, moving closer to the borders of revolt. History teaches us that this is the point at which the state usually begins to crumble.[4] However, there is still time for our Central and State leaders to remember that no society that has lost its sense of justice and its moral legitimacy, has not survived for long.

1.1 India at Independence

The name India, officially the Republic of India (Bharat Ganarajya), is derived from Indus, which originates from the old Persian word Hindu. The term 'Hindu' stems from the Sanskrit word Sindhu, which was the historical local appella for the Indus River. The ancient Greeks referred to the Indians as Indoi, which translates as "the people of the Indus". The geographical term 'Bharat', which is recognised by the Constitution of India is an official name for the country and is used by many Indian languages in various subtle guises. The eponym of Bharat is Bharata, a mythological figure that Hindu scriptures describe as a legendary emperor of ancient India. By area it is the seventh largest country of the region, the second most populous country with over 1.2 billion people and the most populous democracy in the world. Bounded by the Indian Ocean on the south, the Arabian Sea on the South–west, and Bay of Bengal on the south east, it shares land borders with Pakistan to the west; China, Nepal and Bhutan to the north–east; and Burma and Bangladesh to the east. In the Indian Ocean, India is in the vicinity of Sri Lanka and the Maldives; in addition, India's Andaman and Nicobar Islands share a maritime border with Thailand and Indonesia. Four world religions–Hinduism, Buddhism, Jainism and Sikhism originated here, whereas Zoroastrianism, Christianity, and Islam arrived in the 1st millennium CE and also helped shape the region's diverse culture. Gradually annexed by and brought under the administration of the British East India Company from the early 18th century and administered directly by the United Kingdom from the mid–19th century, India became an independent nation in 1947 after a struggle for independence that was marked by non–violent resistance led by Mahatma Gandhi.

Historians consider India's modern age to have begun sometime between 1848 and 1885. The appointment in 1884 of Lord Dalhousie as Governor General of the East India Company rule in India set the stage for changes essential to a modern state. These included the consideration and demarcation of sovereignty, the surveillance of the population and the education of citizens. Technological changes among them, railways, canals, and the telegraph were introduced not long after their introduction in Europe. The victor of India was a modern nation which had abolished feudalism in its own country and created, in its place, modern bourgeois society. It was the rule by a people who had already overcome feudal disunity of their country based on feudal economy and integrated themselves into a modern nation through the rise and expansion of capitalism.[5] A capitalist nation is socially, politically, economically and culturally stronger than a feudal people. Since capitalism is based on higher technique of production than feudalism, a capitalist nation is economically more powerful than a feudal people. A capitalist nation has a high sense of patriotism and nationalism since, unlike the feudal people, who are physically separated, socially disunited and politically unamalgamated, it is socially, economically and politically highly integrated, living under one political regime and a single economic system.[6] But on the other disaffection with the Company also grew during this time, and set off the Indian Rebellion of 1857. Fed by diverse resentments and perceptions, including invasive British style, social reforms, harsh land taxes, and summary treatment of some rich landowners and princes, the rebellion rocked many regions of northern and central India and shook the foundations of the Company. Although the rebellion was suppressed, it led to the dissolution of the East India Company and to the direct administration of India by the British government. Proclaiming a unitary state and a gradual but limited British–style Parliamentary system, the new rulers also protected princes and landed gentry as a future safeguard against future unrest. After World War I, in which around I million Indians participated a new period began. It was marked by British reforms but also repressive legislation, by more strident Indian calls for self rule, and by the beginnings of a non–violent movement called non–cooperation, of which Mohandas Karamchand Gandhi was the leader and the enduring symbol. During the 1930s, slow legislative reform was enacted by the British; the Indian National Congress (INC) won victories in the resulting elections. The next decade was beset with crisis: Indian participation of World War II, the Congress's final push for non-cooperation, and an upsurge of Muslim nationalism. All were capped by the advent of independence on 15 August 1947, but tempered by the bloody partition of the subcontinent into two states: India and Pakistan.

At independence India felt that the national progress can neither lie in a repetition of the past nor in its denial. New patterns must inevitably be adopted but they must be integrated with the old. Of the two views– traditional and modern, the Indian modernist occupied an intermediate but quite half-way position between the modernists and the critical traditionalists. For all practical purposes they accepted the modernist assessment of traditional India and stressed the need for comprehensive modernisation.[7] The political change that took place in 1947 began to move with the existing social structure on the basis of give and take. The new institutions and the new leadership offered economic opportunity, administrative patronage, and positions of power which drew the articulate sections of society into the modernist network. In return, the political elite were provided with a basis of support that was already structured and endowed with, symbols of identification and experiential meaning. It was felt that as India is a multicultural country its society needs to find ways and means to accommodate diversity without losing its cohesiveness and unity. In the process they avoided the approach of assimilation and unbounded multiculturalism. Assimilation requires minorities to abandon their own distinctive institutions, cultures and values to merge into the prevailing culture. This way is sociologically unlikely to succeed and is morally untenable in view of the people's deep adherence to normative values such as religion. Likewise, the unbounded multiculturalism which entails giving up the concept of shared values and identity in order to privilege ethnic and religious differences presuming that a nation can be replaced by a number of diverse minorities is also unacceptable. Such a course of action usually results in an undemocratic backlash, support for extremist parties and anti–minority policies. It is morally unjustified as it does not accept the values and institutions upheld by society at large. In this background the Constitution of India ensures that all citizens have equal rights and should have an equal opportunity. In particular, the principle of secularism enshrined in our constitution is the best method to accommodate religious diversity and could be emulated across the globe. In a multicultural society, the state cannot be identified with any religious or cultural group and it should either be neutral or even–handed in its approach to all such groups. This makes it possible to survive as a nation and to move ahead as the largest democracy in the world.

Prior to the complete transfer of power on 15 August 1947 a Constituent Assembly had been set up in order to draw up a constitution for India. The Constitution enacted by the Constituent Assembly conformed the principles laid down in the 'Objective Resolution' which included, after due discussions, the word 'Republic'. It was a controversial word that was put in and withdrawn, at least thrice. The word 'Republic' first figured in the Objective Resolution moved by Pandit Jawaharlal Nehru in the Constituent Assembly on 13 December 1946. He observed, 'The Resolution states that it is our firm and solemn resolve to have a sovereign Indian republic. We have not mentioned the word republic till this time; but you will well understand that a free India can be nothing but a republic. India is bound to be sovereign, it is bound to be independent and it is bound to be a republic. It must inevitably be a republic. In reference, to the displeasure of Rulers of Indian States he added, 'I want to make it clear personally and the House knows that I do not believe in the monarchical system anywhere, and that in the world today monarchy is a fast disappearing institution.[8] On the other, several members of the Constituent Assembly including Sir Alladi Krishnaswami Ayyar and Sir B.N. Rau suggested the substitution of the word 'Republic' for 'State'. The general complain about the use of the word republic was that while it is suggestive of the citizens' share in the government of the country it does not necessarily connote a democratic form of government. To fill the gap, as M.R. Masani also felt that there was the need to qualify the word 'Republic' by the word 'democratic' specifically, otherwise, the republic might degenerate into an authoritarian government.[9] Pandit Nehru also supported the view of Masani and observed while speaking on the Objective Resolution pointed out that this resolution is based on democracy and that all our past bears witness to the fact that we stand for Democracy and for nothing else.[10] With the interposition of words the draft constitution finally used the 'Sovereign Democratic Republic' in the Preamble of the constitution.

Thus our founding fathers resolved that we, the people of India, constitute ourselves into a Sovereign Democratic Republic where all sovereign powers vested in the people with no superior internal or external, and where the people were their own masters and governed themselves through their representatives under a system they choose. The variant of democratic system chosen for us by the framers of our Constitution is that of representative parliamentary democracy where under the Legislature and the Executive are not separate centers of power. They intermingle and merge. The executive government or Council of Ministers comes out of Parliament, remains part of it and responsible to the House consisting of directly elected representatives of the people.[11] The President of India is the Head of State and is elected indirectly by a national electoral college for a five year term. The Prime Minister of India is the head of government and exercises most executive powers. The executive branch of the Indian government consists of the President, the vice-President and the Council of Ministers–the cabinet being its executive committee–headed by the Prime Minister. In the Indian Parliamentary system, the executive is subordinate to the legislature. The legislature of India is the bicameral Parliament. It operates under a Westminster – style Parliamentary system and comprises the Upper House called the Rajya Sabha or Council of States and Lower House called Lok Sabha or House of the People. India has a unitary three – tier independent judiciary that comprises the Supreme Court, headed by the Chief Justice of India, 21 High Courts, and a large number of trial courts. The Supreme Court has original jurisdiction over cases involving fundamental rights and over disputes between states and the centre; it has appellate jurisdiction over the High Courts. It has the power both to declare the law and to strike down union or state laws which contravene the constitution. The Supreme Court is also the ultimate interpreter of the constitution. Indian democracy is best understood by focusing on how power is distributed.

India is a caste–based society with deep–rooted social hierarchies. Here people are shaped in intensive ways through ethnic, religious and social groups. In the situation the civic culture as evolved by Almond and Verba which conceives that in a modern democracy the element of unity is dominant over the element of conflict exists merely in a rudimentary form.[12] The evolution of consensus over questions of national concern is difficult because of the heterogeneity of the society and the multitude of apparently irreconcilable interests. In the context J.P. Nettle has rightly pointed out that cleavages based on highly divisive structures almost invariably influence the basic commitment and orientation of those who are mobilised in the electoral process.[13] In India's case the ethnological peculiarities excluded more or less the possibility of erecting a unitary state. The diversity in population could be accommodated only in a federal state and therefore the founding fathers of the constitution wanted the same, consistent with a strong government at the Centre. In addition, there was a host of princely states enclaves and exclaves whose integration was conceivable only if granted provincial autonomy.[14] The Constitution is held flexible so that there is wide scope for the play of power–politics between the Centre and the States. The system established naturally followed the multiparty system with periodic election, secular spirit of the state and representative democracy to keep the heterogeneous country together as a nation and move ahead with a prosperous life with togetherness.

Elections in a democracy can be defined as a process through which the political opinion or will of the people is shaped. They help people to crystallise their interests and to give expression to them. In the elections, it is decided who shall govern and who shall have the control over the government. The right to govern is acquired in competition with other parties. The basic theme of popular sovereignty as enshrined in the Preamble has been reaffirmed in several places in the Constitution but particularly in the chapter dealing with elections. Article 326 declares that 'the elections to the House of People and to the Legislative Assembly of every State shall be on the basis of adult suffrage'.[15] As a result the formed Governments derived their authority from the people who choose their representatives for Parliament and the State Legislatures at regular intervals. Further Section 61 of the Representation of the People Act 1951 deems that every person whose name is on the electoral rolls has the right to vote. In the representative democracy of our country this formal equality lies in the inclusion in the Constitution of universal adult franchise, with the *raison d'etre* that man or woman, rich or poor, upper or lower caste, the voter was brought through the electoral roll on to a common platform. Through this provision the age – old inequalities were, at one stroke, sought to be eliminated, or at least substantially diminished, by conferring political equality. This among other measures, reflected an enlightened and bold vision, while in many countries different groups especially women, had to struggle hard and long to obtain franchise.[16] This precious right in their hands, which ensures the democratic ideal of "one man, one vote, one value", irrespective of his wealth, education, social status and "importance" has, in fact, enhanced their self–respect as citizens of a democratic India.

True to the spirit of political system and multi–religiousness of India the framers of the Constitution made the declared country secular one although the world 'secular' was not initially incorporated in the Preamble. They denied any special treatment or preference for a particular religion and laid stress on equal approach towards all the religions of the land. Unlike the Western concept of secularism which means a total separation between the religion and the state, secularism in India is not opposed to religion as such it is opposed rather to use the religious institutions and religious motivation in the legal, political and educative processes. So long as religion does keep its own sphere secularism is religiously natural, it neither endorses nor disapproves of religiousness.[17] Under our constitution secularism has been safeguarded by providing several restrictions on the religious chauvinism and separatism as M.P. Jain writes, India is a country of religions. There exists multifarious religious groups in the country but the constitution stands for a secular state of India. No one is disabled to hold an office on the ground of religion. The essential basis of the Indian constitution is that all citizens are equal and that the religion of a citizen is irrelevant in the matter of his fundamental rights. The constitution ensures equal freedom for all religions and provide that the religion of the citizen has nothing to do in socio–economic matters.[18] Further the secular objective of the state has been specifically expressed by inserting the word 'secular' in the Preamble by the constitution's 42nd Amendment Act 1976 and now secularism is a part of the basic structure of the constitution.[19] Again in 1976 the meaning and content of secularism was clarified which meant that the state shall not make any discrimination whatsoever on the ground of religion or community against any person professing any particular form of religious faith.[20] Thus, the republic of India established in 1950 is the home of Hindus, Buddhists, Jains, Sikhs, Christians, Zoroastrians, Jews and Muslims living together under the protection of a secular constitution which guarantees, by law, the absolute equality of different faiths. Secularism does not mean that one cannot practise one's religion. It means that religion is a private affair unconnected with the state, which will have no religion.[21] And secularism is the only policy which can hold our country together and take it to the path of prosperity.

Thus, after independence the strategy of nation-building in India commenced on the basis of; the making of consensus and accommodation, secularism, Parliamentary democracy, federalism, democratic decentralisation and others that could make Indian republic effective and purposeful. Democracy is both a system with norms, procedures and a set of institutions; and actors, functionaries and officials who work these procedures and institutions. For the people, democracy is also a pattern of experiences. The experience of its two facets is at sharp variance. The impressions derived–from its abstract side, like the norms, values, or procedures; and the concrete experiential side, like those in charge of giving these a shape, or who work them–are contrary.[22] The difference was, perhaps, due to the societal character of India at the time of independence. In the pre-modern society that India was, and largely exists—caste, religion and language are strong factors fostering sub–national identities. Horizontal and vertical cleavages have made it difficult for the civil society to develop the size and cohesion necessary to interact as an equal with the political and economic power of the state. Unless the size of the civil society enlarges to encompass most of the Indian citizenry, the psycho–cultural idea of the nation and the politico–legal concept of the state are unlikely to reinforce one another.[23] Like the plural societies of the United States, Canada, Belgium and Holland, from the very beginning, party organisations in India have had a base of support that cuts across the horizontal dispersal of caste groups, further subdivided by the sentiment of village, lineage and kin group neighbourhood, compelled the competing party organisations to build support structures for themselves across their divisions. But the Indian experience different from that of Western democracies was in the fact that, so far as social organisation was concerned, the ethnic groups in the former stood in a hierarchical relationship.[24] This difference indicated a corresponding gap in economic, political and educational attainments, particularly in the lower strata of society, which remained handicapped in their exercise of electoral choice in initial years following the independence of the country.

Each developing society like India which is struggling to modernise itself politically, registers its own peculiar, complex, and often internally self–contradictory processes. When we go in search of their 'revolutionary universal', in advance of sufficient knowledge of those processes, in the end it may prove to be a barren exercise.[25] Similar to many the Indian citizen is born to ethnicity, makes his living, by and large, in the class of his birth, and shares the perspectives of his generation. In contrast to this inherent instinct, electoral processes, party organisations, mass movements and the search for better economic returns induce or force him to take up a position and make secular decisions on issues which lie outside the primary groups to which he belongs. While he continues to live his social life within the primary groups to which he was born, the constraints imposed by such groups, on his thinking and movement, tend to become increasingly weaker in the face of his need to act effectively in conjunction with others.[26] The new challenges faced by him forced him to take a position, other than the established pattern of behaviour. The established system had hardly any match with the then shattered social, economic and cultural life of the Indian people. The introduction of Western rationalist education in India bifurcated the society's common sense and divided Indian culture in a radically different and unprecedented fashion. Traditionally, the Indian culture, which was marked by great internal inequality and distance, various inflections and articulations by divergent groups, was identified by a single common sense. The new European education was largely responsible for the ruination of this integral single common sense of traditional culture. It was done by inducting a new kind of common sense based on rationalist premises common in nineteenth century Europe. It created a strange dichotomy of inside and outside of the home and the world, of the rationalist world of politics and the sentimental one of domesticity created essentially by generalising upon the experience of the middle class.

In general political parties are institutions of the civil society rather than the state. But they link the power structure in society with the state. The party system reflects the historical conditions of struggle in each country and is a good indicator to test this idea. It is the only one component of the political system. The others are the state structures or government institutions and the state process that links the government to the society. This interaction between state and society has three dimensions; coercive, responsive and legitimative.[27] Coercive function of the state is exercised by the police and the army and also through a framework of laws and rules to obtain obedience of the citizens. The responsive functions to the positive actions that the state takes to meet people's demands. No modern state can carry on without being responsive to social needs voiced from time to time. But coercive and responsive functions may not be adequate unless the state takes specific measures to acquire moral and voluntary support of a large number of people. Such legitimation is secured through symbolic propaganda, patriotic mobilisation and a variety of political and economic activities. The party system of a modern state is particularly relevant to the latter two functions of the state namely, responsive and legitimative. As for coercion, the state agencies are directly authorised to carry out these functions and enforce law.[28] In India the dominant social forces operate through the major political parties in managing state power.

At the time of independence and long thereafter, the establishment of the system of Parliamentary democracy has privileged the Congress organisation at the expense of other institutions of post–colonial state. While the Congress as the premier political party was undoubtedly the main player in the new dispensation, its ability to frame a constitution and enforce central authority over diverse provinces and hitherto nominally independent princely states owed much to civil bureaucracy the military and police. Without these institutional legacies of colonialism, even an organisation like the Congress might have bulked at the tasks confronting India in the initial years of independence. Working in close concert with the Congress, these institutions engaged in a process of state consolidation where legitimacy gained from the formalization of regular elections had frequently to be supplemented with authoritarian methods in the name of preserving law and order in the different regions.[29] The partnership between the Congress and the non–elected institutions, the civil bureaucracy and the police in particular, facilitated the establishment of a formal democracy within the barely modified structures of British India's unitary state system. The holding of regular elections lent legitimacy to a multi party system dominated by the Congress. General elections at five yearly intervals gave Indian voters the inestimable power to freely choose and depose governments.[30] With the widening of the electoral base, this is a power which a discerning Indian electorate has exercised effectively to oust discredited governments, both at the centre and states. But on the other, persistence of massive magnitude of poverty, gross social inequalities and regional disparities showed that the bulk of the Indian population was deprived of some basic human rights. Thus, initially people's anger was held in check by their faith in the democratic system. They therefore, gave vent to their demand for accountability in the state by turning out to vote in ever larger numbers and regularly overthrowing incumbent governments.

However, to meet the economic challenges of the time, by independence, India had developed an independent economic base from which to attempt a take off into independent industrialisation.[31] India's polity had been conceptually built by Mahatma Gandhi and Jawaharlal Nehru but promotion of socialism was essentially a Nehruvian project. As the concept of socialism developed in India, the welfare facet got discarded and the central planning facet got emphasised. The 1948 industrial policy prepared the foundations for a mixed economy. The First Five Year Plan (1951-56) struck a good balance between the needs of the society and the state. It emphasised agriculture, irrigation, power and transport and its performance was impressive. The Second Plan (1956-61) was more ambitious, industry-oriented and state–centric.[32] In the year 1956 the vision of an egalitarian social order was further emphasised by Nehru and the

Congress adopted the aim of ushering in a socialistic pattern of society with equitable distribution of wealth and income. In doing so it was only reiterating the instructions contained in Article 38 (2) and 39 (c) of the Constitution. Article 38 (2) prescribes, 'The State shall, in particular, strive to minimise the inequalities in income and endeavour to eliminate inequalities in status, facilities and opportunities not only amongst groups of people residing in different areas or engaged in different vocations.'[33] In the period rising capital intensity and worsening total factor productivity were ignored. Also ignored were the reality that agriculture must prosper and its productivity increase if it were to support industrialisation. The aims and objects of Third Five Year Plan (1961-66) faced a more fateful fortune due to 1962 war with China and 1965 war with Pakistan. In mid–1960s the country had become substantially dependent on food and financial aid from the West. Meanwhile, politics began to dominate and economic thinking became derivative. The interests of the political class and bureaucracy became the pre–eminent consideration. For democracy to be actually a system of self-governance, the substantive rights of people, that is the socio–economic rights along with political rights must be realised.

There is no doubt that Nehru felt deeply and passionately for the people; his sway over the masses was immense as was his capacity to communicate with them, to sense their feelings and to win their vote, affection and trust. It was his belief that measures like Zamindari abolition and public sector development would reduce inequalities in independent India and that through education and technological development Indian society would move in the direction of equality. Electoral politics through universal adult franchise would facilitate every individual and each group to pursue their rights. These were special safeguards in legislature and bureaucracy for representation of the most deprived sections of Indian society–the Scheduled Castes (SC) and Scheduled Tribes (ST). This was the design of socio–political change envisaged in the Indian Constitution. But Nehru's own model of development and social transformation depended on active pressure from below by the deprived, the exploited and the dominated. Such active popular participation in politics alone would enable parliamentary democracy to serve as an instrument of nation building, social change and equity.[34] And Nehru failed to help create any institutions or structures or agents through which the people or even the lower–level cadres of his own party could be mobilised and activised and politically educated. The only form of mobilisation was his extensive tours through which he communicated with the people, educated them and created popular support for his policies.

In addition, Nehruvian period did not witness greater participation by the people in the political processes except in the form of elections. Actually after independence, there was a gradual demobilisation of the people, weakening over time of the link between politics from below and the national leadership in power and also between politics and social work. He neglected party–building even after he acquired full control over it in 1951. He had never been a builder or organiser of the party before independence, but situation deteriorated after Mahatma Gandhi and Sardar Patel left the scene and Nehru became its sole leader. As a result Congress was increasingly weakened as an organisation and began to lose its role as an instrument for social change or the implementation of government policies or even education in the party ideology.[35] Mere electoral verdicts in and of themselves have not sufficiently empowered the Indian voter when it has come to shaping the states social or economic development policies. Political privilege has been far too entrenched at various levels of the polity to permit the elimination of caste, class and gender–based discrimination. In the sense political processes in India have fallen well short of the democratic ideal and may even have served to disguise the authoritarianism inherent within the Indian political economy and state structure. Ruling configurations at the centre have been content with securing support from regional elites who are inclined to further entrench their own political and economic interests, not advance the process of democratisation.[36] With only inadequate implementation of the fundamental right provisions of the Indian constitution, the removal of widespread social inequalities and injustices has remained an unrealised ideal.

In sphere of foreign policy under the leadership of Nehru, who was the great statesman, India raised to a pedestal higher than her economic or military strength could take her,[37] but in the period the country had become heavily foreign–aid dependent during the first two decades of independence. The policy of non–alignment played the same critically decisive role. It enabled a relatively weak India to deal with the West on the basis of self–respect and equality. On a superficial view, the policy appeared to be directed against the West. In reality it was nothing of the kind Nehru was interested not in hurting the West but improving his country's status vis–a–vis the United States and its European allies. His emphasis on rapid industrialisation, too was part of his effort to reinforce India's search for autonomy.[38] Perhaps right in his view, he stated before the Constituent Assembly on 4 December 1947 that, 'foreign policy is the outcome of economic policy and until India has properly evolved her economic policy her foreign policy will be rather vague.'[39] As a consequence, by the late 1950s, India had become the biggest aid recipient not only from the US, but also from the US–dominated World

Bank. In comparison to economic interests, India's politically focused foreign policy hurts its security interests even more. A major foreign policy study conducted after 1962 and 1965 wars considered politically conceived non–alignment, unsupported by strategically structured economic and security designs responsible for the deterioration of India's ability to network globally from the late 1960s. Thus the policy of non–alignment failed to recognise the unique configuration of world politics after the Second World War.

It all resulted in Nehru increasingly relying on government administration and bureaucracy for implementing his policies. Even the Community Development Programme and the Panchayati Raj, the two great efforts to involve the people in their own development, ended up under bureaucratic control; and the village level social worker, the kingpin in rural reconstruction, became a cog in the bureaucratic machine. He never attacked vigorously through mass mobilisation and mass educational campaigns on aspects of social structure, such as the caste system, male domination, kinship networks, economic dependence of the rural poor on the rural rich and growing corruption, which were bolstering the existing socio–economic system. While strong opposed to political opportunism and manipulation, he could replace these only with *ad hoc* political and administrative measures. This often left the field open to the manipulators. This weakness was heightened by the fact that he was a poor judge of men and women. Nehru could see the process of the political manoeuvres taking over, but could do little to counter it. He observed and denounced the corruption, careerism, bureaucratisation, and the many other emerging ills of a developing ex–colonial society but was unable, apart from exhortations, to take the necessary concrete steps to control them. Thus, the working of Indian republic for about two decades since independence had tarnished its image, in practice. The large areas of neglect which covered a wide range of subjects in this period, assumed monstrous proportions in coming years. As one of Nehru's bio–graphers, Geoffrey Tyson has said, 'If Nehru had been a different kind of man, India would have become a different kind of country.'[40] But despite all these India's success in working a system of Parliamentary democracy, has, over time, greatly assisted the mobilisation of ever larger segments of the populace in all walks of life which decided the future course of action in Indian politics and society.

1.2 Changing Perspectives of Indian Republic

The first three general elections of Indian Republic registered an easy overwhelming majority for Jawaharlal Nehru–led Indian National Congress. In post–independence phase the Congress was converted into not just a ruling party, but a dominant framework institutionalising the whole process of power. The party system that emerged from such a framework was somewhat distinctive and served Indian democracy well during the years of consolidation and consensus making. Although Congress became an active organisation in the cause of national freedom it soon led to frustration due to its narrow social base and its ultra–modern idiom of communication.[41] Although our Constitution has provided sufficiently for multi–party system the initial years were dominated with the concept like the "Congress System" and it suggested that the Congress had a method of representing a range of diverse demands and reconciling them into formulation and implementation of consensus policies.[42] Since all possible interest groups could operate within and through the INC, no outside opposition could grow in any substantial manner in the early years after independence. The Congress system provided the peripheries with channels to operate at the centre. Rightists and leftists, Hindu nationalist and secularists all found their place in Nehru's Congress– which has often been described as such because it was the dominant party and all other parties were in near permanent opposition. In this phase our party system could not develop an alternative to the Congress government. The party system did not work as a system of alternating party government; there was the complete absence of a potential democratic alternative to the party in power.

The test of entire edifice's reality was held in the First General Election held in 1951-52. It was an exciting event for all parties and a test of their political strength. About 77 parties and thousands of independents participated in the elections,[43] but the Socialists who had organised themselves into the Socialist Party and into the Kisan Mazdoor Praja Party (KMPP), as well as the Communists lashed out against Nehru's Congress. Many local parties existed only on paper, others tried to fight organised parties in their supposed domain by using cultural and traditional symbols of the region.[44] The outcome of the results was overwhelmingly in favour of the Congress party and disintegrated opposition was punished for not combining against the Congress. The Second General Election held in 1957 confirmed the structure of the party system. Again the Congress Party won an absolute majority in the Lok Sabha and it appeared as if this party was born to rule. The Congress Party had reached its climax, whereas the opposition parties had literally stood still in the development. Neither the Socialists nor the Communists succeeded in building up their position against the Congress. Although the Third General Election took place in 1962 witnessed more candidates contesting on the part of opposition parties including the newly founded Swatantra party.[45] It was again only the Congress Party which presented itself as a potential majority party. This time the opposition parties indulged in cut–throat competition against each other. They were not only concerned with the defeat of the Congress Party, but each of them wanted to enter the Lok Sabha as the strongest opposition party. In the election results the Congress Party remained dominant in the Lok Sabha, its share of votes decreased slightly. Materially the Congress suffered slight losses but one impression was created in 1962 that fortune had turned against the Congress.[46] Even at the time it appeared to many observers that a 'third force' had entered in Indian politics which offered an alternative to the Socialism of the Congress and to the pure Socialism of other parties. It gave an alarm to consolidate the party system by the integration of regional parties and groups and it can be considered the most positive aspect of results.

As a result of the deteriorating social, economic, political and defence conditions of the country the Fourth General Election held in 1967 proved an 'electoral miracle' which exerted a far–reaching impact on the Indian political scene. After holding its first national elections in 1951-52, India achieved the status of the world's largest liberal democracy with universal suffrage. Dr. Ambedkar and the other founding fathers believed this to be a necessary pre–condition, although India's literacy level in 1947 was abysmal. But from the first election onwards, the Election Commision of India (ECI) helped illiterate electors to identify candidates during voting, by alloting a symbol to each.[47] Once seen against a backdrop of illiteracy and social tensions, the evolution of the electoral process has involved the vitality of greater and more broad–based participation. In encompassing traditional values and newer integration processes, confronting social tensions with innovative measures to help constructively resolve them, the focus has been to bring different strands into the electoral mainstream. The right to vote has emerged not only as a fundamental right, but as an instrument of political awakening.[48] It resulted in the assertion of the Backward and Scheduled Castes in several states which had a direct bearing on the changes of Indian political situation. The ruling configurations that had dominated the Congress had been vigorously challenged by the newly empowered middle and lower castes and classes, with serious consequences at least in states. Each successive election saw a broadening of the political base, placing the organisational machinery under greater pressure from newly mobilised social groups. Thus, it was clear that the deinstitutionalisation of the Congress was already well underway before the setback registered in the fourth general elections in 1967.

Politically using the carrot and stick approach in dealing with his own party leaders, Nehru showed considerable ingenuity and skill in leading the

Congress to victory in three successive general elections. Even though each election underscored the limitations of the party bases of support, Nehru neglected to initiate the kind of reforms that might have offset the processes of organisational disintegration within Congress. Nehru's failure to reform the party proved fatal and it continued as a legacy after his death under the Premiership of Lal Bahadur Shastri. Without the necessary organisational reforms, its limited social support base was turning into a liability, not the asset as it had been in pre–independence period. About the time there were serious divisions in the party organisation at the lower levels which helped fuel a slow but steady downward leakage of power and initiative. Under increasing pressure from members of the Congress state bosses, known as the syndicate, Shastri sought refuge among the notables of the higher civil services.[49] Rule by the Congress state bosses came to an abrupt end with their failure to deliver the vote banks in the 1967 general elections. While scraping through at the centre, the Congress was ousted from power in several states. Challenge of regionalism was now plainly coming from political forces outside the pale of Congress. A simple partnership with the civil bureaucracy was no longer sufficient to maintain Congress hegemony or central authority. The dynamics of centre–state relations had begun shifting the focus of power away from the parliament towards executive authority residing in the hands of the prime minister. They prevented the genuine democratisation of the state and the premier political party.

In 1966, Indira Gandhi became the Prime Minister of India after the sudden demise of Lal Bahadur Shastri. It was the time when the country was surrounded by a variety of problems and everything appeared in a transitional phase. The negative side of earlier governance began to show its limits in the late sixties despite Mrs. Gandhi's initiatives in spheres of party organisation along with economic reforms. In post–1967 period discerning Congressmen realised that substantial steps had to be taken to reverse the process and rejuvenate the party and the government and that mere manipulation would not work. Although the party had got a clear majority in 1967 elections at the centre her worry was due to organisational problems and fast recede of the traditional vote bank of the Congress. Her support base one time consist the SC, ST, women and minorities. After the split in the party in 1969 she even attempted land reforms in the 1970-72 periods, but soon she retreated from structural change and instead concentrated on strengthening her personal power base. At the time intermediate castes and classes especially big farmers and middle to richer peasants, had been providing the principal power base of the opposition to the Congress at the state level in most regions. But there were more radical challenges in the states of West Bengal and Kerala, where left–wing coalitions came to power. The late 1960s also witnessed the Maoist Naxalite movement involving poor peasants and militant students in West Bengal as well as parts of Andhra Pradesh and Bihar. Faced with a variety of challenges, Indira Gandhi set about trying to link the top and bottom layers of agrarian society through renewed efforts to woo the high–caste, old landed elites and advocating the interests of subordinate castes and classes cutting across local and regional arenas.[50] Her populist anti–poverty programme was designed to get the Congress substantial electoral support from scheduled castes and tribes, who also happened to form the bulk of the rural poor. Mrs. Gandhi's socio–economic programme captured by the ringing slogan 'garibi hatao' helped her in getting resounding success in the general elections of March 1971 and also in the 1972 elections to the state assemblies. All this turned into euphoria with the defeat of Pakistan in the war and the creation of Bangladesh out of the erstwhile Pakistan province of East Pakistan.

However, the crushing success of Indira Gandhi one after another presented a momentous challenge to the Indian state. Her success in restoring the Congress Party's sagging electoral fortunes with her brand of populism came to be seen as a threat not only by dominant rural groups but also paradoxically, by the bearers of the central state authority. Her alliances with populist leaders in the states had only delivered the votes. They had not succeeded in vanquishing, the old rural power structures dominated by the syndicate bosses with whom she had parted company. Although they lost the elections, the erstwhile Congress bosses could rely on their middle to richer peasant supporters–many of whom were strategically located in the state police and civil services–to foil a centrally orchestrated populist challenge. Opting for more democracy entailed reorganising the Congress Party to consolidate the gains, of the new and broader–based electoral alliances. But this meant strengthening popular regional leaders at the expense of the centre, a reversal of fortunes that was untenable without substantially modifying both the party and the state structure. It also meant to extract greater concessions for their constituents and, more dangerously, provide them with ammunition to blast their way into power at the centre. As this was anathema to Indira Gandhi, she reacted by scrapping any semblance of inner party democracy within the Congress. In the circumstances she preferred to appoint her own loyalists as state and local leaders. The state, which was going through a process of rapid centralisation of power ever since Indira Gandhi effected a split in the party in 1969, met all such challenges increasingly with sharp authoritarian measures. More people were arrested during this period and more died in police firing than at the time of Quit India movement.[51] It culminated in the darkest chapter in the history of independent India the jettisoning of democracy and the imposition of internal emergency in June 1975. Authoritarianism, which was sporadic and *ad hoc* in Indian politics till then, became institutionalised.

Thus, by imposing emergency Indira Gandhi attempted to ward off both sorts of regional challenges and made centre the sole repository of supra–local and supra–state populist programmes. Aided by the non–elected institutions of the state, the resort to overt authoritarianism aimed at augmenting central power's against the regions. A workable enough strategy in the short–run, it lacked legitimacy and could not for long withstand concerted opposition from an array of political forces. Democracy as a system of governance, or a mode of organising power, or a space for struggles, after its long journey through turbulent times, stands independent, valued for its own sake. It does not any longer require crutches in the shape of powerful leaders–as guardians of democracy and as trustees of the people in order to survive. It was Nehru's commitment, or Indira's populism, which provided democracy with the cushion to survive in what was considered an inhospitable environment. But emergency, changing all this, showed the people what it means to lose freedom. They learnt retrospectively that it is possible to fight for liberty, and also realised how precious is the possession of freedom. Ordinary people were always subjected to institutionalised violence, oppression and terror in Indian society, apart from exploitation, which is normal in every class–divided society. Earlier with the exception of exploitation, all other oppressive measures were *ad hoc* and sporadic in nature. Emergency made it systematic and pervasive to the extent that the privacy of the person, though little, was daily invaded by the lumpen elements of the ruling party and agents of the state.[52] Since then criminalisation of politics became a regular feature of Indian politics.

Apart from this the over–centralisation of the polity under the Indira Gandhi regime led to regional assertions and alienation of people in many parts of the country. The rise of the Telugu Desham Party (TDP) in Andhra Pradesh, consolidation of DMK vs. AIADMK politics in Tamil Nadu, the autonomy movements in Jammu and Kashmir, north–east India and Punjab were consequences of over centralisation. Growth of regional disparities, persistence of poverty and under development has continued to give birth to many new regional parties. This political process has finally forced the Congress and the BJP to take federalism seriously and support decentralisation of power. At the time the Indian National Congress failed to grapple with the class–caste dynamics which came from the backward-class leader Charan Singh in the late sixties. Thereafter, this challenge took many other forms leading to parties such as the Samajwadi Party of Mulayam Singh and Rashtriya Janata Dal (RJD) of Laloo Prasad Yadav.[53] The period also witnessed in Indian politics the rapid popular reversal of moods. The electoral process and the outcomes of elections, as well as the structuring of political responses between them were breached. The same people who voted the governments in with huge mandates soon turned against their own government, and the Indian state was under constant popular assaults. The Janata government which followed the defeat of the Emergency regime and which restored democracy faced the same situation of popular agitation. Once in power, the Janata with its regional base confined to the north Indian Hindi heartland fell prey to its own internal contradictions. The same was the case in 1980 and 1984. This is an important indicator of the unresponsive nature of the ruling class vis–a–vis the problems of the people, and the lack of adequate accountability of the government of the day. This phase of politics devalued the leaders, political parties and certain institutions which lost their autonomy and were converted into mere instruments of powers.

The decade 1980s exihibited the declining strength of Congress's claim to power at an effectively unitary all–India centre and therefore, the Party substituted its populism with implicit, if not explicit, to religious majoritarianism. Communalism against regionalism was a well tried formula of the colonial state. Its implementation in this period must be placed squarely in the context of the many powerful regional challenges to central authority. As ideologies of secularism and socialism lost credibility the Congress regime turned implicitly to region–based majoritarianism to meet regional threats. Earlier in 1970s and 1980s several regional political parties, such as TDP, in Andhra Pradesh. Akali Dal in Punjab and others in different parts of the country claimed to have achieved national status and some of them, especially more extreme elements of the Sikh religious community launched a violent campaign for the attainment of a separate Sikh homeland called Khalistan. It culminated in the brutal assassination of Indira Gandhi in October 1984 by her Sikh bodyguards and her son Rajiv Gandhi registered a record–breaking victory in the 1984 elections with the help of sympathy wave and Hindu card. Viewing Indian society through the colonial lens that revealed a majority and a minority community based on the religious distinction, the new regime took a couple of decisions. On the one hand Rajiv Gandhi's government opened the doors of the Ayodhya mosque to Hindu worshipers. On the other, in a curious and ill–advised attempt to placate Muslim opinion after India's judicial system has awarded alimony to Shah Bano, he railroaded through Parliament a deeply conservative Muslim women's bill. The new steps appeared to give a new lease to the continued exercise of central authority by the Congress.

The politics of majoritarianism brought a new twist in Indian politics and society as well. By doing so the Congress, at least, paved the way for the more ideologically committed and organisationally cohesive forces of Hindutva–the BJP, the RSS and the VHP to emerge as a major forces on the Indian political scene and the most controversial /emotional symbolic issue of temple–mosque came to the fore. Some extremist Hindu groups, the VHP in particular, began demanding that the Babri Masjid be pulled down and a mandir to Ram built in its place. The demand was based on the claim that Rama, the mythical hero of the great Hindu epic Ramayana, was born exactly on the spot where the mosque stands. On the eve of 1989 elections to the Lok Sabha it along with the corruption charges against Rajiv Gandhi determined the further path of Indian politics. It has rightly been said, 'Nehru ignored corruption when he took no action against some corrupt leaders, Indira Gandhi encouraged corruption when she described it as a global phenomenon and Rajiv Gandhi allowed himself to get besmirched by corruption in the wake of the Bofors scandal.[54] This innings of Mrs. Gandhi's premiership had changed the earlier role of religious figures as she began to rely on appeal to specific category of voters. She drew Hindu religious figures into the lime light through her patronage of religious institution and played the Hindu card against the minorities.[55] From other side was VHP, itself a religious organisation, took a prominent position and emerged into a powerful interest group along with a major player in national politics. This adoption of religious symbolism in political mobilisation was one of the factors that led to huge increase in BJP's vote share and Lok Sabha seat. The anti-Congress and pro-religion forces the BJP, Janata Dal and the Communists also aggressively carried on propaganda of pseudo–secularism of the Congress, which in practice, is the policy of appeasement of minorities in order to exploit them as their vote–banks.

The general elections of 1989 took place in a religious environment. This time it was not the Congress but the Bharatiya Janata Party which was poised to do best on the issue of a Hindu Rashtra. On the eve of elections the BJP took part in the transportation of 'holy bricks' to Ayodhya and a foundation – laying ceremony for a temple to Ram near the mosque. The Congress government afraid of losing some Hindu votes, did not stop the ceremony from taking place. There was a miracle victory and increase of seats for the BJP and it supported the Janata Dal led by V.P. Singh to form second non-Congress government at the Centre. With the support from both the BJP and the Communists the electoral verdict spelled the beginning of the end of the Nehru Gandhi dynasty and represented the most decisive success of certain groups influential at the regional level in exercising state power directly from the centre.[56] In less than a year the government of V.P. Singh decided to implement the recommendations of the Mandal Commission to reserve jobs at the centre for backward castes in August 1990. All political parties of the time including the BJP adopted that blank to seek the votes of this largest caste conglomerate. The scheme appeared designed to divide the Hindu community by caste and thereby undermine the BJP's electoral project of mobilising support by playing the Hindu majoritarian card. In response, the Hindu movement led by the BJP and others, such as RSS, VHP and Bajrang Dal became active and left a decisive effect on party system. Its leader L.K. Advani responded by undertaking a *rath yatra* and threatened to arrive in Ayodhya and start building the temple. It resulted in the polarisation of Indian politics on communal line. By doing this the BJP had taken on not only its political rivals but had also challenged one of the main ideological foundations of the Indian state. In coming years the dynamics of this trend has been fully played up in course of the fragmentation of the parties in the nineties. It is in conjunction with other issues – economic, secular, federal that these forces have played a substantial role in Indian politics. However, in this brief period the nature of state and its dealing with issues remained unchanged. The Janata Dal had little option and it settle down to working within the established parameters of the compromise between formal democracy and covert authoritarianism. The incidents, taking place severely damaged the secular facade of the Indian state. We do need religious values but certainly not politicisation of religion.

The campaign and blind wave of religion finally led to demolition of the Babri Masjid in the presence of the leaders of the BJP, the RSS and the VHP on 6 December 1992, setting off some of the worst attacks on the Muslim community in many parts of India. The Bharatiya Janata Party from seventies onwards sincerely executed its two pronged policy. Especially after the dramatic success of the Rath yatras its own agenda was rewritten in a retrograde direction but it also adhered to its more secular constituency. From the advertising tactics it continued to appeal to the constituency of modernist groups but on the other it persisted with its blatantly communal propaganda aimed at the more traditional Hindu groups. But once again the political economy of India took a turn when Congress Party formed the government with a working majority after 1991 elections under the premiership of P.V. Narasimha Rao. The new regime began economic reforms – privatisation of public sector units, liberalising of rules allowing freedom for investors and globalisation of flow of capital and consumer goods and services. The initial impetus for the economic reforms came as a result of an acute balance of payments crisis in mid-1991, making it necessary to seek a loan from the International Monetary Fund (IMF) and accept certain terms of a stabilisation and structural adjustment programme. However, the economic reforms pursued by the Congress government addressed only the first part of a two-pronged problem facing Indian economic development. The reforms concentrated on addressing the negative effects of over–intervention by the state in certain sectors and removing the more stiff bureaucratic controls on industry. They moved tardily to rectify state negligence of critical social sectors, notably, health and education. The political costs of pursuing a lop-sided reform process contributed to the defeat of Congress in 1996 elections.

As a result of the general elections held in 1996 two successive governments were formed led by H.D. Devegowda and I.K. Gujral respectively. It enabled the longforgotten intrinsic values of development to re-enter the discourse. It received the support of several regional and left – wing parties and displayed deep taints of localism and agrarianism with a rich farmer bias while proclaiming solidarity with the poor and disadvantaged majority. As any successful realisation of the idioms of equitable development requires the appropriate instruments, both economic and political, the failed institutions of state could not easily be imaginatively refashioned.[57] On the other even though the anti- BJP forces acquired strength for some time, in this election the BJP emerged as the largest political party. In this election the BJP's election manifesto clearly adopted the theory of 'cultural nationalism' and noted, 'our nationalist vision is not merely bound by geographical or political identity of India, but defined by one ancient cultural heritage. From this belief flows our faith in cultural nationalism which is the core of Hindutva'.[58] But soon the BJP's electoral politics and desire to remain in power led it to forge alliances with other known secular parties. Till then the 'Hindu nationalist BJP had been regarded as politically untouchable by regional parties, the further decline of the Congress Party in the general elections of 1998 and 1999 created the conditions for the formation of BJP-led coalition governments at the centre. In the 1999 elections, it formed the National Democratic Alliance (NDA) with 22 parties in it and came to power at the centre. The NDA's agenda of governance set aside such contentious issues as building Ram temple in Ayodhya, abrogating of Article 370 of the Indian Constitution which gave special status to Jammu and Kashmir, and framing of a uniform civil code for citizens which would mean that the Muslim would not be governed by the Shariat law on civil matters. Once again, the debate on the issue of defining Indian nationalism goes on among the parties within and outside the NDA. While BJP pursues the Hindu Rashtra agenda, the rest of the parties stressed the pluralist, multi–religious, multi–cultural character of the Indian polity.

In approach and content the coalition partners – BJP and others remained poles apart. During election campaigns regional parties emphasised local issues and sought more autonomy for the states and a legitimate share of power at a more federal and less unitary centre. Surprisingly the regional parties were able to get more than 250 seats out of 537 with limiting the BJP on 182 and the Congress on just 112 seats. The major regional parties on the side of ruling included Telugu Desham, Dravida Munnetra Kazhagam, Samata Party and Trinamool Congress while the opposition bench consisted Samajwadi Party and Bahujan Samaj Party (BSP). The general elections of 1999 dented the all India, national pretentions of the Congress and BJP alike, a string of defeat in state election led the BJP to fall back on its hard Hindutva line. The incident of 2002 in Gujarat occurred despite the personal view of the NDA Prime Minister Atal Bihari Vajpayee that in a country as diverse as India it would be patently undemocratic to have a single–Party government. Politicisation of religion in our democracy has already done enough damage.

Unfortunately, in India politics has not only been politicised but also commercialised. Religious leaders identify themselves with one or the other politician or political parties. They have amassed wealth by exploiting religious beliefs of people and lead a life of luxury. They enter into profitable bargains with powerful politicians and politicians go to them for money and votes. Both together they thus exploit religious belief of common people.[59] A state should never priorities one religion over the other, particularly in a secular country like India. But most of our politicians while paying lip service to secularism grossly misuse religion for political purposes. The irony is that these politicians take oath for secularism while filing their nominations but having filled that beg for vote openly in the name of religion and caste. In addition, religion in our society has also become the greatest obstacle for any meaningful change. Religion, unfortunately identified with status quo. Most of the religious leaders oppose any change as violation of religious beliefs. This attitude does not arise from religious beliefs per se but by the interest associated with status quo. Every religion in the world brought social change and a truly religious person would always fight against status quo and try to change society to make it more just and meaningful.[60] Religion is basically a transcending force and fights against all sorts of vested interest. Unlike others, the religion in India has promoted vested interests to gain short–term selfish mottos–power, wealth or anything else. If even formal democracy in India has been a success it is not because of religious ethos but owing to its secular credentials.

In this era of globalisation only a partial number of population has been benefitted from the economic reforms initiated in early 1990s by the P.V. Narasimha Rao's government. While the other larger part of people still remain in poverty, destitution, illiteracy and misery, the benefitted lot operates the state as well as the party system to carry on further economic reforms to enhance their own interests. Now the beneficiaries of reforms, the rich peasants and the bourgeoisie have linked to global capital, use state power to manage the economy and generate surplus. The electoral system is used to legitimise this process. Thus, contradictions continue to grow in Indian society and are often manifest in various kinds of social violence. Autonomy movements including separatist and militant movements, tribal movements, dalit movements as well as workers and peasant movements– constitute a whole range of political action distinct from party politics. The Indian state apparatus responds to these movements in a variety of ways. Whenever, challenges has taken place the form of armed struggle, state repression seems to have been the main policy of successive governments. However, repression has failed to curb these movements for they have popular support in most cases and raise basic structural issues such as land reforms, poverty eradication, right to land and demand for autonomy, which the dominant political parties have failed to highlight in their preoccupation with electoral politics. In this turbulent situation counter – politics has given rise to large scale corruption and criminalisation. Thus, Indian polity at the turn of the century, experienced these trends in the development of a multi-party system, a range of social movements and outbreak of violence in society.

1.3 The Current Impass

Once a republic takes birth , it is the leaders who produce the institutions. Later, it is the institutions which produce the leaders. The success story of independent India has been its secular, federal and multi–party system. These systems have strengthened India politically, economically and emotionally. Jawaharlal Nehru played a very significant role in order to strengthen political institutions under the framework of the Indian Constitution. The adoption of the Constitution in its secular spirit during the years of strife and communal tension was itself a dashing step taken under his leadership.[61] The Indian state as it developed in the Nehruvian era, concentrated all powers of patronage in its hand. It had quickly created a progressive constitutional framework and possessed an enlightened political leadership. While the constitution and the state structures based upon it have remained essentially intact, the quality of political leadership steadily deteriorated. The inability of the state to use its political capabilities effectively, accommodating the moderate and isolating the militant, has contributed more to the spread of insurgencies in the various parts of the country.[62] Even in case of Pandit Nehru there was a clear decline in his effectiveness and glamour in comparison to pre–independence leadership, but his departure from the scene in May 1964 marked the end of an era in Indian society and politics. In the post–Nehru phase the political system of the country felt itself stressed and registered an overall decline in public morality, political leadership. Political parties were held responsible for the chaotic condition of the system. Consequently, India had ceased to be a stable society that it was in the fifties and the early sixties.

At the time Mrs. Gandhi took over, the political system of the country was in deep crisis from economic points in view, in particular. It was an additional tension on the prevailing system as it had been sick politically even earlier. Hard pressed by this array of hostile economic forces, large sections of the population stepped up their demands on the system at the very moment but it was least able to meet them. It is only when relatively stable societies are sought to be changed rapidly and profoundly that they begin to undergo ferment. As a remedy to these all Emergency was declared, but this approach brought rapidly diminishing returns in terms of 'discipline', 'order' and stability. Social conflict could not forever be held in abeyance, public opinion could not forever be manipulated and regulated, popular resentment could not forever be contained. At a later stage, the social ills that posed a direct threat to the political system of the country were rated high, resulting in the worsening of the quality of political management, indisputably the standards of public life have declined sharply. Our political system is the system of election and a keen observer of the Indian political scene argued that the way things are going today, it is quite possible that India might become a paradox of successful elections and a failed democracy.[63] Despite the conduct of so many elections so far, the actual exercise of power in the country has yet to reflect true democracy. This has largely been because, unlike the elites and middle class, the poor in India are unable to generate pressure. It has rightly been said, 'The very conditions which inhibit the masses from effectively organising to push their own interests, namely, their poverty, ignorance and isolation, and the hierarchical power structure of the Indian society, have made it possible for India to hold general elections based on universal suffrage, with endangering political stability.[64] The democracy in India has lagged behind in its sacred responsibility of promoting and protecting public good.

From the mid–1960s onwards after the break of single party rule particularly in states, a beginning of political awareness was registered by the regional forces and oppressed class/caste for promotion and protection of their interests. As a result from this time the ruling establishment has shown a strong propensity to take recourse to authoritarian means to handle popular pressure. Even the declaration of internal emergency failed to mitigate the stress on system and democracy in India survives due to their pressures for a democratic polity. Simultaneously, the problems have become more pronounced with the slow erosion of the support for the Congress in post – Emergency period and its sudden decline after the 1989 Parliamentary elections. The danger to democracy comes not from the self – mobilisation of ordinary people; the threat lies in the emerging elite lacking the skill to manage to democratic institutions. There is a propensity in them to violate the rules of the game and to pay scant regard to the procedural aspects of democracy. In their haste to be empowered, they break the rules and jump the queue, indeed an unseemly sight for any established order. They also have not yet learnt to regulate, in a durable fashion, the relationship between themselves either in the social sphere or, more importantly, in the political realm.[65] Thus, unlike the earlier ritual participation, struggle is now a key form of taking part in community life for the lower castes as it always was for the working class. However, the implementation of Mandal Commission recommendation and reassertion of Hindutva ideology at the close of 1980s acted as a trigger, upsetting the ground equations of power and domination. Thereafter, groups formed around privileges and it resulted in an altogether peculiar decomposition of the consciousness of the established middle classes formed out of the upper castes. These factors remained in active consideration of Indian voters in the years to come. In the period Indian republic passed through a tough experience of coalitions and minority governments working within the traditional parameters of state without any forward movement in the direction of substantive democracy.

It is a time for the Indian republic to choose between majoritarian principles and substantive democracy. In general the failure of post–colonial states to assure equal citizenship rights and to deliver on the promise of redistributive justice has brought these entities into some disrepute. As secularism and socialism have resorted to majoritarian ideologies, religiously or ethnically defined, in attempt to prevent their own structures from being undermined. In today's polity instead of the unbending insistence on the singular loyalty of the citizen to the state, the time is overdue to rethink the relevance of multiple and shifting social identities for the cause of democracy. If it happens so it can be a boon and not a threat to democratic values and practice. The multiple identities can only flourish within a political and state system based on layered and shared sovereignties.[66] The rise of Hindu majoritarian 'nationalism' in India is tied to the defence of centralised state authority against a variety of regional as well as class based challenges, even though it has not succeeded in dislodging the formal secular ideology of the Indian state. But over the years the social character of the BJP, as distinct from its class composition, has therefore undergone a rapid change. From a party of traders and other hidebound petty bourgeoisie, it has grown into a representative party of dominant sections of Indian society, including the ruling classes. A notable feature of the rise of rightwing militant Hindu nationalism and the assumption of power by the BJP-led alliance in 1998 and 1999 elections, is the materialisaion of a new alignment between the ruling classes and the social basis of political power.

While the 1990s witnessed the phenomenal growth of the BJP, the Congress registered a steady decline. The Indian National Congress–long emblematic of the ruling classes–represented a diverse social constituency earlier; consisting as much of the Dalits, and the poor and oppressed of various communities, as of the richer sections of society. It has now become more a party of the disprivileged sections of society, with the privileged moving into the BJP. In the period the vote for Congress among the rich sections of the upper castes is as low as 26.3 per cent, while the BJP boasts 57.2 per cent. Surprisingly the Congress vote 26.5 per cent was lower than that of the BJP 40.8 per cent among the rich sections of Dalits. Apart from this the Congress has also lost heavily among all sections of the Muslims and the Dalits in the Gangetic belt. The rule provided by the BJP–led alliance represents a specifically ruling–class bloc–a unification of the ruling-class interests under bourgeois leadership and bourgeois aspirations among the various strata in society. However, in a Parliamentary rule based on party competition, it is important how the social bases of support are structured. The political responsiveness of a government is partly conditioned by the social support it depends on. And in the similar class character of the two parties, their parliamentary rule cannot make any difference to the interests of the peasantry or the working class but it would have a definite setback to the democratic interests of the masses particularly in Indian context where democratic gains have been so slow and so little.

Only at this point lies the basics of Indian state–a unique situation in which the birth of our republic took place. The state became congealed in its present form in the wake of independence; in fact, the first few years were of crucial importance. It began its trajectory of consolidation by facing mass upheavals; popular struggle the like of which India never saw again. On the face of this, the state had two choices. One, it could have used the popular upheavals to start altering or restructuring its institutions. Alternatively, it could continue to rely on the inherited colonial bureaucracy, and, a host of other repressive institutions and law to subdue the popular movements. At the juncture out of fear of popular struggles, the ruling leadership chose the second alternative–a case of historical short sightedness. This choice had long term consequences as it allowed the state institutions to become insulated from popular pressures and the need for accountability, as well as gave them permanence as necessary intermediaries to the state's exercise of power. The fluidity of the early period could have been utilised in moulding the state institutions as truly democratic structures. Given the alignment of forces in the political establishment as a whole, the first option would have had short-term destabilising consequences. But it may also have had long term beneficial results more responsiveness to popular aspirations, anti–feudal and transformational measures such as participatory grassroots–level institutions freed of bureaucratic control, self–initiative and local mobilisation in planning and handling of poverty, health, literacy etc. Such open–ended options would surely have helped in breaking the power of the narrow–minded elite.[67] The state in India thus failed in living up to its inheritance of the values, inspirations and aspirations of the anti–colonial national movement. The state failed to materialise as the site of structural possibilities of changing social relations, of institutional initiatives, of involving people, and of normative impulses for justice and equity. Instead it pursued a narrowly conceived, western capitalist inspired modernisation under the charge of a bureaucracy that had foreclosed possibilities of an emancipatory transformation based on popular impulses.

As a result of this after more than 60 years and 15 national general elections, India's Parliament is nowhere close to being truly representative. Since the adoption of the Constitution, India has moved decisively towards a multi–party system, with laws such as the one to prevent defection restricting inner–party dissent even while curbing horse trading. Power is still concentrated in the hands of a few, with the role of the public limited to voting in governments every five years or so.[68] While the strength of Indian democracy has withstood the decades of social, economic and political developments, there are numerous challenges to democratic governance. The social and economic progress achieved by the deepening of democracy in many societies has been shaped by their efforts to successfully protect the rule of law. Despite various attempts to enforce and institutionalise the rule of law in Indian society, the intended results have not been achieved. While the normative framework of constitutional governance is established through the Constitution of India and the various institutions established under it, deeply embedded values constitutionalism have not taken roots in the Indian society.[69] In between the period, huge social expectations have been generated by institutions that are responsible for checking abuse of power. But given that the capacity for dealing with abuse of power is disproportionate to the demands imposed upon them by the sheer size and magnitude of the country, there have been numberous unfulfilled promises. Urgent steps are needed to establish a rule of law society in India, without which our fundamental credentials as a democracy will seriously be undermined.

Even the national general elections held in 2004 and 2009 failed to make an impression quite different to the earlier, it however, registered a voting structural adjustments contrary to the decade of 1990s. The verdict of the 2004 Parliamentary elections showed that Indian democracy is not just the largest in the world, it is also becoming one of the most vibrant. The defeat of the BJP is not only a mark of the vibrancy of Indian democracy, it also removed a major paradox from politics. It brought a much closer correspondence between the social forces which took shape in the 1990s and political power. As such, this lends greater coherence to Indian politics, and in this there is an opportunity for democratic forces to strength the secular and pluralist foundations of Indian republic as cherished by the framers of Indian Constitution. In 2004 elections there was a subtle shift in the social profile of voters. By the late 1990s the Congress had become a party whose support base was a mirror image of its opponent in different parts of the country. The party did not have a vote of its own and was excessively dependent upon the residual support it got from the marginal sections of society. This time the Congress regained something of its famous rainbow coalition. It has improved its standing among the urban middle classes and educated voters. It has done so while retaining the bottom of the pyramid that constitutes its core voting bloc.[70] In the last three elections the seat /vote multiplier for the Congress has gone up from 0.74 in 1999 to 1.01 in 2004 and 1.34 in 2009 and every one per cent of the vote gave the Congress four seats in 1999, 5.5 seats in 2004 and 7.2 seats in 2009.[71] Though there was nothing like a national wave, strong or mild, there appeared to be a nationwide trend working to the Congress' advantage.

On the other in both these elections the BJP posted its lowest vote share since it first exploded in 1989. This is the third successive election that its support base has shrunk since the high watermark of 1998. The BJP's rise to power through the 1990s involved three kinds of expansions, all of which faced reversal in 2009 elections. First of all it involved extending the party's support base to new States. The big strides that the party made in the South and East in the early 1990s soon came to a point of stagnation. Secondly, the BJP expanded its bandwidth on the political spectrum by acquiring new allies. The NDA of 1999-2004 represented the pinnacle of the BJP's political expansion. Since then it has been downhill for the party. From the peak of 41.1 share of the national vote, the NDA slipped to 35.9 per cent in 2004 and has fallen to just 24.1 per cent in 2009. Thirdly, The BJP attracted new social groups during its phase of expansion. It expanded from urban to the rural areas. From being an upper caste party, it cultivated a major base among the lower OBC's. It took major strides towards capturing the adivasi vote in middle India and started securing some vote among non–Hindus. In 2009 election, the BJP's hitherto upward trend among adivasis and Muslim voters has been reversed and its expansion among the lower OBC's halted.[72] It suffered a negative swing in nearly every State. It needs to reflect not so much on the election campaign and strategies as on its overall political direction.

In totality the recent trends of election results and experiences show that the underprivileged and vulnerable people have displayed an unanticipated capacity to exercise their voting power against the privilegensia's insensitiveness to their sufferings and misery. These are the people who make the economy work and therefore feel they ought to have right to say that some investments should directly benefit them so that they come to possess some assets, get enhanced opportunity for credit, secure employment, and have access to education and health. The formation and consolidation of this section of society is not in haste, but ever since the anti–Emergency wave of 1977, people have learnt to mobilise themselves in terms of their experiences. It also appeared that in these elections, emotional issues and primordial sentiments were set aside. The everyday life of ordinary people with their myriad small problems became foregrounded. The everyday life that is lived in different contexts is also a reflection and expression of the religious, cultural, social and regional diversities of Indian society. The vote, therefore, in essence, is also for the plural traditions and the secular way of life of Indian society. Separation of religion and politics is the means to make politics autonomous of substantive commitments and fulfil the unfulfilled desires of Indian republic.

The due time for 16th national general election is the year 2014 but the post–2009 general elections phase in India continued to remain a crucial one. It witnessed the anger in the minds of the people which was steadily built up as scams of huge proportion burst one after another; the 2-G spectrum scam, Commonwealth Games scam, Aadarsh Society scam in which high level politicians, civil servants and military officer were found to be involved with government looking the other way failing to take swift and decisive action, and moving only under the direction of the Supreme Court. Public confidence in the willingness and ability of government to act against corruption was shaken and India came to be known as one of the most corrupt countries in the world.[73] The large scale all pervading corruption compelled Anna Hazare to launch fast in April 2011 at Jantar Mantar, New Delhi. At the time the people were so outraged by scandals after scandals of large proportion coming out, that they responded in a big way when Anna and his associates gave a call for fight against corruption. Corruption exists at the 'culturing edge level' the-day-to-day engagement of people with lower level of administration as also big corruption at the highest level.[74] There is no doubt that the entire political system and public life including government needs to be cleaned. It is a deeply–entrenched, systemic problem that is corroding the nation, widening the gulf between ordinary citizens and those with access to power and privilege, and under-mining the faith of people in democratic institutions.[75] However, President Pratibha Patil in her Republic Day address on 26 January 2012 warned the reformers not to shake the tree of state so hard in their drive to remove bad fruit that the tree itself is brought down. In the context nobody can disagree with the idea that India's democratic system must be safeguarded while introducing reforms in its political institutions.

In the forthcoming general elections to the members of Lok Sabha the ruling Congress Party and the main opposition Bharatiya Janata Party with their allies and associates is likely to face each other in a straight way. In the election if the Congress party wants to worm its way back into middle class respectability, it has to raise its own decency index. At the very minimum, the country needs to see for itself that the Congress has respect for constitutional and political institutions. As the oldest and the most responsible political party, it is the Congress's historic burden to inculcate good manners in the polity.[76] On the other is the BJP and its associates, but equally for both, winning the coming elections in India is not easy. The Party's enthusiasm in the BJP's third consecutive triumph in Gujrat's 2012 state assembly elections is understandable. It has, at large, began to think this victory in terms of national context and with analysis, it is hopeful about the prospect of 2014 Parliamentary election. In party's expectations the viability of Chief Minister Narendra Modi as a Prime Ministerial candidate and the electoral appeal of Hindutva is rated high. For the past decade, most observers of Indian politics have believed the electoral appeal of Hindutva to be on the decline. In the current electoral strategy the party is not sure whether the continuing decline of Hindutva can be a arrested, or even reversed or the Party can only succeed by emphasising claims of "development" and "good governance."[77] In any case the BJP should avoid easy generalisations about Hindutva advocacy in facilitating the party's dominance. As per general assumption Modi's success has accrued from a "post – Hindutva" strategy based on "development". However, the central problem for the Congress and the BJP would be to face regional parties in which most have taken the form of dynasty. Each one of those now has a strong, proprietary votebank and total ownership of its party. In earlier elections these regional parties had been the greatest game changer in our politics. Each one has learnt the art of leveraging his regional power to grab a share of the national pie.[78] These regional parties may be limited by geography but cannot be challenged by a national party.

Today the people are in a mood which comes rarely in the life of a country. They are looking forward starry eyed, to a new direction, a new era, a life. Despite the conduct of so many elections so far, the actual exercise of power in the country has yet to reflect real democracy. To the extent that democracy in India has lagged behind in its sacred responsibility of promoting and protecting public good, it has certainly failed. It is the state that needs to accommodate the interests of different stakeholders on important issues by building political consensus and by being transparent in the way it functions. The tardy functioning of democracy since independence has produced in India a vast college of political leaders at various levels but there has been a failure to develop political capabilities to deal with expanding pressures in empowering society, to broaden the social base of nationalism, and to find political cover for pragmatic actions. The government will certainly have to do a lot more in achieving sustainable, socially equitable growth. For that, the country needs a strong popular movement that puts pressure on the administration. If the Indian republic is to flourish and prosper, it cannot be left to the mercy of politicians alone. The national conscience has to be aroused to such a degree that it would cease to tolerate falsehood and dishonesty in public life. India's people need to be an active part of the political process before they can be the agents of change, and the masters of their own destiny.

References

1. Eduardo Faleiro, 'Reflections on the Republic Day', *South Asia Politics*, Vol. 11, No. 10, February 2013 (New Delhi: 2013), p. 3.
2. Justice Brijesh Kumar, 'An Appraisal of the Working of the Indian Constitution', *Ibid.,* Vol. 11, No. 7, November 2012 (New Delhi: 2012), p. 5.
3. Hassan Suroor, 'Looking Beyond Ballot – box Democracy', *The Hindu* (Madras), 22 August 2007.
4. Prem Shankar Jha, 'Overcome by a Sense of Betrayal', *Ibid.,* 15 January 2013.

5. A.R. Desai, *Social Background of Indian Nationalism* (Bombay : Popular Prakashan, 1948), p. 33.
6. Dr. Rajkumar Singh, *India and Pakistan – Social, Political and Military Perspectives* (New Delhi: Regal Publications, 2009), p. 20.
7. *Ibid.,* pp. 33-34.
8. K.C. Markandan, *The Preamble – Key to the Mind of the Makers of the Indian Constitution* (New Delhi: National Publishing House, 1984), pp. 109-10.
9. *Ibid.,* p. 114.
10. *Constituent Assembly Debates,* Vol. 1, 15 December 1946. p. 93.
11. Subhash C. Kashyap, 'Democratic Governance – Space for the Under - Privileged', *South Asia Politics,* Vol. 7, No. 8, December 2008 (New Delhi: 2008), p. 6.
12. Gabriel A. Almond and Sidney Verba, *The Civic Culture* (Princeton: 1963), p. 5.
13. J.P. Nettle, *Political Mobilization: A Sociological Analysis of Methods and Concepts* (Newyork: 1967), p. 271.
14. Durga Das Basu, *Introduction to the Constitution of India* (Calcutta: 1966), p. 38.
15. M.V. Pylee, *India's Constitution* (Bombay: Asia Publishing House, 1974), p. 19.
16. Navin Chawla, 'Towards a Level Playing Field', *The Hindu,* 5 January 2012.
17. M.V. Pylee, *Our Constitution Government and Politics* (Delhi: Universal Law Publishing Co. 2000), p. 53.
18. M.P. Jain, *Indian, Constitutional Law* (Agra: Wadhwa & Company, 2000), p. 9.
19. Bommai Vs. Union of India, AIR, 1994, SC. 1998, as quoted in Ganesh Prasad and Anand Kumar, 'The Concept, Constraints and Prospect of Secularism in India', *The Indian Journal of Political Science,* Vol. LXVII, No. 4, October – December 2006 (Meerut: 2006), p. 795.
20. *Ibid.,* p. 794.
21. Markandey Katju, 'Rid Our Body Politic of Communal Poison', *The Hindu,* 11 October 2012.
22. Javeed Alam, *Who Wants Democracy – Tracts for the Times* (New Delhi: Orient Blackswan, 2012), p. 12.
23. Verghese Koithara, *Society State and Security: The Indian Experience* (New Delhi: Sage Publications, 1999), p. 28.

24. Dr. Rajkumar Singh, *India and Pakistan – Social, Political and Military Perspectives*, p. 33.

25. Talcott Parsons, 'Political Development: Times Sequences and Rates of Change', in Finkle and Gable (eds.), *Political Development and Social Change* (New York: 1971), p. 456.

26. A.H. Somjee, *The Democratic Process in a Developing Society* (Delhi: 1979), p. 6.

27. Manoranjan Mohanty, 'The Contemporary State', *Teaching Politics*, Vol. VIII, Nos. 1-2, 1992.

28. Manoranjan Mohanty, 'Party and Polity', in G.P. Deshpande and Alka Acharya (eds.), *50 Years of India China - Crossing a Bridge of Dreams* (New Delhi: Tulika Publications, 2001), p. 136.

29. Sugata Bose and Ayesha Jalal, *Modern South Asia – History, Culture, Political Economy* (New Delhi: Oxford University Press, 2004), p. 169.

30. *Ibid.,* p. 170.

31. Aditya Mukherjee and Mridula Mukherjee, 'Imperialism and the Growth of Indian Capitalism in the Twentieth Century', *Economic and Political Weekly*, 12 March 1988.

32. Verghese Koithara, *Society, State and Security: The Indian Experience*, p. 43.

33. As quoted in Vivek Katju, 'Herald a National Vision That Little Resembles the Old', *The Hindu*, 16 November 2012.

34. Bipin Chandra, Mridula Mukherjee and Aditya Mukherjee, *India After Independence 1947-2000* (New Delhi: Penguin Books, 2002), p. 182.

35. *Ibid.,* p. 183.

36. Sugata Bose and Ayesha Jalal, *Modern South Asia – History, Culture, Political Economy*, p. 170.

37. S.K. Sinha, 'Nehru – Gandhis in Indian Politics', *The Hindustan Times*, 30 June 1991.

38. Girilal jain, 'Gandhiji And Mr. Nehru – Two Different Moral Universes', *The Times of India*, 16 November 1980.

39. Verghese Koithara, *Society, State and Security – The Indian Experience*, p. 61.

40. Geoffrey Tyson, *Nehru: The Years of Power* (London: 1966), p. 173.

41. Moumita Ghosh, 'Democracy in India – Background and Emerging Challenges', *South Asia Politics*, Vol. 9, No. 5, September 2010 (New Delhi: 2010), p. 32.

42. Rajni Kothari, *Politics in India* (Delhi: Orient Longman, 1970), as quoted in Manoranjan Mohanty, 'Party and Polity', p. 141.

43. *The Eastern Economist* (New Delhi), 30 December 1966.
44. S.V. Kogekar and Richard L. Park (eds.), *Reports on the Indian General Elections 1951-52* (Bombay: 1956).
45. Election Commission, *Report on the Third General Elections in India'*, 1962, Vol. 1 (Delhi: 1966), p. 51.
46. *The Eastern Economist*, 1966 as quoted in Horst Hartmann, *Political Parties in India* (Meerut: Meenakshi Prakahan, 1971), pp. 157-58.
47. Navin Chawla, 'Towards a Level Playing Field.'
48. *Ibid.*
49. Sugata Bose and Ayesha Jalal, *Modern South Asia – History, Culture, Political Economy*, pp. 174-75.
50. *Ibid.*, pp. 175-76.
51. Javeed Alam, *Who Wants Democracy – Tracts for the Times*, pp. 15-16.
52. *Ibid.*, pp. 17-18.
53. Manoranjan Mohanty, *'Party and Polity'*, p. 142.
54. S.K. Sinha, *'Nehru – Gandhis in Indian Politics'*.
55. Virginia Van Dyke, 'Religious Mobilisation and Sadhus' in Politics: The Idealised Versus Realpolitik', in Paul R. Brass and Achin Vanaik (eds.), *Competing Nationalism in South Asia* (New Delhi: Orient Longman, 2002), p. 144.
56. Sugata Bose and Ayesha Jalal, *Modern South Asia – History, Culture, Political Economy*, pp. 187-89.
57. *Ibid.*, 189-90.
58. A.G. Noorani, 'Anti – Consensus, Pro-Hate, *The Hindustan Times*, 21 January 2003.
59. Zenab Banu, 'Religion in Indian Politics: Need to be Value Oriented, Not Power Oriented,' *IJPS*, Vol. LXX, No. 3, July – September 2009 (Meerut: 2009), p. 714.
60. *Ibid.*, p. 715.
61. Dr. Akhileshwar Singh, *Political Leadership of Jawaharlal Nehru* (New Delhi: 1986), p. 266.
62. Verghese Koithara, *Society, State and Security – The Indian Experience*, p. 307.
63. Dr. Rajkumar Singh, *India and Pakistan – Social, Political and Military Perspectives*, pp. 71-74.
64. Gunnar Myrdal, *Asian Drama: An Inquiry into the Poverty of Nations* (London: 1968), p. 295.

65. A.K. Sen, *Inequality Reexamined* (New Delhi: Oxford University Press, 1995), as quoted in Javeed Alam, *Who Wants Democracy – Tracts for the Times*, pp. 43-44.

66. *Ibid.*, pp. 204-05.

67. *Ibid.*, pp. 106-14.

68. *The Hindu* (editorial), 15 May 2012.

69. C. Raj Kumar, 'Democracy and the Rule of Law in India', *Ibid.*, 21 September 2007.

70. *Ibid.*, 26 May 2009.

71. *Ibid.*

72. As quoted in *Ibid.*

73. P.R. Dubhashi, 'Hazare's Fast and its Aftermath', *South Asia Politics*, Vol. 10, No. 1, May 2011 (New Delhi: 2011), p. 11.

74. P.R. Dubhshi, 'End of Anna Team's Fast and its Aftermath', *Ibid.*, Vol. 11, No. 5, September 2012, pp. 17-18.

75. *The Hindu* (editorial), 28 January 2012.

76. Harish Khare, 'Time for House – cleaning in the Congress,' *Ibid.*, 4 April 2012.

77. Tariq Thachil, 'Can Hindutva Win Votes?', *The Indian Express*, 25 February 2013.

78. Shekhar Gupta, 'One Dynasty Dimming', *Ibid.*, 23 February 2013.

2 Perspective Post-mortem of Indian Republic

2.1 Foundation

With 21 guns salute and the unfurling of the Indian national flag by Dr. Rajendra Prasad heralded the historic birth of the Indian Republic on January 26, 1950. The transition of India from a British colony to a sovereign, secular and democratic nation was indeed historical and its journey started around two decades ago with the conceptualisation of the dream in 1930 to its actual realisation in 1950. The seeds of a republican nation were sowed at the Lahore session of the Indian National Congress at the midnight of 31st December, 1929. The session was held under the Presidency of Jawaharlal Nehru and those present in the meeting took a pledge to mark January 26 as 'Independence Day' in order to march towards realising the dream of complete independence from the British. It was also decided that January 26, 1930 would be observed as the Purna Swaraj (Complete Independence) Day. India achieved independence from British rule on 15 August, 1947 following the Indian independence movement noted for largely peaceful nonviolent resistance and civil disobedience led by the Indian National Congress, but vital to India's self-image as an independent nation was its constitution, completed in 1950, which put in place a sovereign, secular, and democratic republic. After many deliberations and some modifications, the 308 members of the Constituent Assembly signed two hand-written copies of the document, one each in Hindi and English on 24 January, 1950. Two days later, it came into effect throughout the nation.

On this day India became a totally republican unit and it finally realised the dream of Mahatma Gandhi and numerous freedom fighters who fought for and sacrificed their lives for the independence of their country. Two days earlier on 24 January, 1950, the Secretary of the Constituent Assembly, H.V.R. Leugar, who was also the Returning Officer of the election of President of India, declared in the Assembly that Dr. Rajendra Prasad was duly elected to the office under sub-rule (1) of rule 8 of the rules for the Election of the President. Among others Jawaharlal Nehru and Sardar Patel congratulated Dr. Prasad on the great honour conferred on him and said that he had been elected as the Head of the State by the unanimous will of the representatives of the nation. However, speaking of the solemnity of the occasion and heavy responsibility placed on him, Dr. Prasad remarked, 'I have always held the time for congratulation is not when a man is appointed to an office, but when he retires, and I would like to wait until the moment comes when I have to lay down the office which you have conferred on me to see whether I have deserved the confidence and the goodwill which have been showered on me from all sides and by all friends alike.[1]

In fact, while Nehru and Prasad had always had the highest personal regard and affection for each other, the two had somewhat different intellectual and ideological orientation. Nehru was a Harrow-Cambridge educated Western-oriented modern liberal. On the other hand, Prasad even though a brilliant intellectual, was deeply rooted in the Indian soil. He was a religious-minded person with a healthy conservative approach to life. He represented all that was best in the traditional Indian culture and ethos as Dr. Radhakrishnan once said he was, 'the suffering servant of India…who incarnates the spirit for which the country stands'. The sharp difference between Nehru and Prasad surfaced in coming years after the Republic began its journey. Even Dr. Prasad objected to January 26 being fixed as the day for the Constitution taking effect because he said, it was not an auspicious day. This enraged Nehru who said: 'National programmes cannot be fixed according to astrology, and if people want it, let them elect astrologers to govern the country. And if they believe in astrology out of ignorance let us combat it.'[2] Despite this, Nehru and Prasad understood each other well. The two had been comrades-in-arms during the national struggle for freedom. Both were prepared to yield, to give and take, to compromise and to cooperate. In the context the thoughts that strike us most compulsively are that Nehru and Prasad were human, all too human, that both in their own ways, were great and among the finest of men and patriots, that their differences were not a question of the personal prestige of Prasad or Nehru being at stake but that through these conflicts of views the shape and future of Indian polity was being determined. Having the experiences of the republics of Vaishali and Lichavi and the ideals of Dharma-ruled kings from Vikramaditya to Shivaji, we were ready to move ahead.

Since then every year the date of 26 January is celebrated as the Republic Day with patriotic fervor of the people and is one of the three national holidays in India. It marked the true spirit of Independence and by applying the constitution gave the citizens of India the power to govern themselves by choosing their own government. After being declared Dr. Rajendra Prasad, the first President of India, took oath at the Durbar Hall in the Government

House and in the Irwin Stadium he unfurled the National Flag. Like the United States of America, India, has an elaborate flag code which carries a number of restrictions. The British are very careless about the way they treat their flag and so are the Japanese. The French get upset only if their flag is reviled during a public ceremony when the Republic is all dressed up. Sweden and Norway are easy about the flag. While Denmark advocates that care be taken so that the flag does not trail on the ground, the German balance their laws against flag desecration with the right to freedom of expression. Ireland has no established norms on how the flag should be treated, but only advises that it should be handled with care and respect.[3] But in India we are different.

Establishment of Republic in India was hailed largely in the country and abroad and Dr. Rajendra Prasad, in his first special message to his country men, on the birth of the Indian Republic said, 'We must re-dedicate ourselves on this day on the peaceful but sure realisation of the dream that had inspired the Father of our Nation and the other captains and soldiers of our freedom struggle, the dream of establishing a classless, cooperative, free and happy society in his country. We must remember that this is more a day of dedications than of rejoicing – dedication to the glorious task of making the peasants and workers the toilers and the thinkers fully free, happy and cultured'. Likewise C. Rajagopalachari, His Excellency the Governor-General in a broadcast talk from the Delhi Station of All-India Radio on 26 January, 1950 said : 'On the eve of my laying down office, with the inauguration of the Republic, I should like to tender my greetings and best wishes to the men and women of India who will henceforth be a citizen of a republic. I feel deeply thankful for the affection showered on me by all sections of the people which alone enabled me to bear the burden of an office to the duties and conventions of which I had been an utter stranger'.

At the time of the emergence of Indian Republic Sir Anthony Eden, the Prime Minister of the United Kingdom (April 1955 to January 1957), said, 'Of all the experiments in government, which have been attempted since the beginning of time, I believe that the Indian venture into Parliamentary government is the most exciting. A vast continent is attempting to apply to its tens and thousands of millions a system of free democracy... It is a brave thing to try to do so. The Indian venture is not a pale imitation of our practice at home, but a magnified and multiplied reproduction on a scale we have never dreamt of. If it succeeds, its influence on Asia is incalculable for good. Whatever the outcome we must honour those who attempt it.[4] A more meaningful opinion was expressed by Granville Austin, an American Constitutional authority, who wrote that what the Indian

Constituent Assembly began was 'perhaps the greatest political venture since that originated in Philadelphia in 1787.' He also described the Indian Constitution as 'first and foremost a social document'... 'The majority of India's constitutional provisions are either directly arrived at furthering the aim of social revolution or attempt to foster this revolution by establishing conditions necessary for its achievement'.[5]

The term 'Republic' which India had declared itself to be on 26 January, 1950 as a follow up of the Constitution, derived from the Latin words *res publica*, public affair or thing. That concept was in turn loosely equivalent to the classical Greek *ta koinonia*, common things or property, a term originally applied in the early city-state to the city's treasure, the public funds, and then by analogy coming to symbolise and denote the common interests. It is a term denoting (i) a state not ruled by a monarch or emperor, generally a public interest and not a private or hereditary property; (ii) a state where power is not directly in the hands of or subject to complete control by the people, in contrast with a democracy; (iii) more loosely, any regime where government depends actually or nominally on popular will.[6] During the later middle ages there were established some brief-lived local republics, consequent on revolt. But it was in certain city states of Italy that the republic re-emerged as a meaningful designation and form of government. In modern usage of republic which derived the dual ideas, absence of monarchy, and some degree of avowed concern for the common welfare of the state and for public control or participation.

The concept of republic witnessed several ups and downs as a result of the changed contexts. As a combined idea of absence of monarchy, a realm of public affairs and popular consent or participation first emerged, generally as temporary phenomena in the 17th and 18th centuries. Further during the 19th century the moral significance of the republican idea declined in Europe, where monarchies continued and republics remained the exception. Constitutional government spread in the monarchies, and by the early 20th century the term republic no longer connoted the substance and content of political institutions and practice. After World War II, moreover, the term had still less relevance. In essence the basic classification of government was into constitutional government and dictatorships, a division which corresponded in ethos to the former opposition of republics and monarchy. But gradually contemporary ideas on the issue, Montesquieu in particular gave the idea of democracy as direct and small scale and insisted that democracy was impossible in a larger state which could be at best a representative republic. These and other related were studied and combined by a number of the founding fathers, and especially by James Madison, who used the term republic (i) as a technical designation for representative government as opposed to direct democracy and (ii) to insist on the necessity for a system of checks and balances against the dangers of straight majoritarian decision in a legislature elected by majority on a single principle of representation.[7] The insistence that republic is not synonymous with democracy either as direct democracy or as absolute majoritarian democracy, but rather is synonymous constitutional democracy, is correct in the specific US context.

India is a federation with a parliamentary system governed under the Constitution of India, which serves as the country's supreme legal document. It is a constitutional republic and representative democracy, in which majority rule is tempered by minority rights protected by law. Federalism in India defines the power distribution between the federal government and the states. The government abides by constitutional checks and balances. The Constitution of India, which came into effect on 26 January, 1950, states in its preamble that India is a sovereign, socialist, secular, democratic republic. The framers of the Constitution were conscious of our social problems and hoped that democracy would solve them. Dr. Rajendra Prasad, the first President of Indian Republic, said, 'We have communal differences, caste differences, language differences, provincial differences and so forth. It requires men of strong character, men of vision, men who will not sacrifice the interests of the country at large for the sake of smaller groups and areas and who will rise over the prejudices which are born of these differences. We can only hope that the country will throw up such men in abundance.[8] Earlier the colonisation of India had changed the social categorisation which had a deep social impact. Middleton, the superintendent of the 1921 census, said, 'We pigeonholed everyone by caste and community. We deplore its effect on social and economic problems but we are largely responsible for the system we deplore. Government's passions for labels and pigeonholes has led to crystalisation and fragmentation'.[9] This is why both Nehru and, much more clearly, B.R. Ambedkar realised that India did not exist as a nation. What they were promoting was a vision of nation-in-the-making, a new formation shaped by republican ideals and cast in the mould of a modernistic Constitution.[10] Ambedkar made it more clear when he wrote on the eve of drafting the Constitution, 'In believing that we are a nation, we are chasing a great delusion. We can only attempt to become a nation-in-the-making. Under the new republic India had to be invented. But the invention has to be, first and foremost, of an ideal for Indians. The ideal can only be equity, participation, plurality, etc.

2.2 Parliamentary Democracy

The Constituent Assembly drafted the Constitution in which the system of Parliamentary democracy was clearly provided and it began to take a concrete shape in independent India. The adoption of democracy had never been in doubt and as early as 1936, Jawaharlal Nehru as President of the Indian National Congress, declared that India's ultimate objective was the "establishment of a democratic state", a sovereign state which would promote and foster "full democracy" and usher in a new social and economic order.[11] In independent India state power was to be exercised in the public domain: be it a policy difference, or an ideological dispute, or political disagreement, all were to be anchored in the public interest. The thrust of new India was meaningfully noted by Jawaharlal Nehru on August 15, 1947 : 'It must be clearly understood that the interests of our long suffering masses must come first and every entrenched interests that come in their way must yield to them.[12] The same theme was voiced by Nehru in the Constituent Assembly when he argued, 'We have given the content of democracy in this resolution and not only the content of democracy but the content, if I may say so, of economic democracy.[13] Thus, it was with this larger national objective that a democratic polity based on Parliamentary system was established. Our founding fathers perceived that such a system would respond effectively to the problems arising out of our diversity as also to the myriad socio-economic factors that we were faced with when we achieved freedom through a people's movement after centuries-long humiliation of being a slave nation.

Democracy, which has been implemented in India through the parliamentary system, is a philosophy of life, art of living, way of thinking, method to organise an egalitarian society and essence of world peace. It meets the needs of a civilised, aware and assertive society.[14] Political life of a majority of the countries of the world are influenced and governed by democracy. Modern political scientists viewed democracy with varied angles and expressed their perception accordingly. Elitist theory of democracy, propounded by Mosaka and Parretto emphasised upon the fact that important decisions are taken by few influential people only.[15] While J.A. Schumpeter argued that political leaders in democracy cannot enjoy unlimited power as it is restricted, by the choice of people in elections.[16] On the other believers of participatory democracy emphasise upon participation of common citizens in democratic process. People act as watch dog to activities of rulers and prevent misuse of power. But there is no denying fact that democracy is desired destination for the political system due to its many positive traits and it is the only accepted form of rule in today's global world.

Unlike British model, the Indian Parliamentary form of government works under a republican framework with multiparty system. Though the word Parliamentary democracy has nowhere been used in the Constitution of India, there is absolutely no doubt that India has accepted Parliamentary system of government. For all practical purposes the British constitutional system is based on Parliamentary form of government but it functions under constitutional monarchy. As against this, the Indian Parliamentary system works under a republican framework wherein the constitutional head is an elected President and not a hereditary king as in the case with Britain.[17] Likewise as against the concept of direct democracy which is a 'single tier institution of governance constituted and operated by all the eligible willing citizens of the country, India has chosen representative democracy which provides absolute and unconditional equal opportunity, liberty and right to vote to every eligible citizen of the country. The concept of 'vote' in essence and spirit inherently constitutes personal choice of an individual participating voter of the constituency/electoral college.[18]

However, exercise of absolute and unconditional equal opportunity, liberty and right to vote includes three inseparable and interdependent democratic sub-functions which every participating voter of the constituency/ electoral college has to perform at the election. They are: (i) to evaluate the candidature of every participating voter including self, of the constituency/ electoral college; (ii) to select the most suitable voter out of all the participating voters of the constituency/electoral college; and (iii) to express his/her choice/selection/nomination through ballot paper or any other media.[19] As such, an individual participating voter inherently is an 'evaluator-cum-nominator. In other words, democracy does not imply merely casting ballots into the ballot box. It envisages that the decision to vote would be made on the basis of merit alone, with utmost discretion and prudence, unswerved by demagoguery and exhortations, and undeflected by considerations; caste, colour, creed, or any other extraneous factors. Enlightened, informed and vigilant citizenry is a prerequisite to effective functioning of a vibrant democracy.

The decision to adopt the British Parliamentary system was not taken in a vacuum. The Lok Sabha and the Rajya Sabha, as envisaged in the Constitution, were new. But a bicameral central legislature had functioned for 30 years during the British Raj. Adult suffrage was new. But the elective principle had been introduced more than half a century earlier. Our Constitution was framed on the basis that our citizens, including the best, would be willing to take a continuous and considered part in public life. Democracy depends upon habits of consent and compromise which are attributes only of mature political societies. The lawful government by the majority, under the rule of abiding law, and with freedom of opposition and dissent is, both geographically and historically, an exceptional human achievement rather than the normal way of organising nations.[20] Not only that the adopted form of government was largely defended by Dr. B.R. Ambedkar in the Constituent Assembly on November 4, 1948, when he said, 'The Parliamentary system differs from a non-Parliamentary system inasmuch as the former is more responsible than the latter but they also differ as to the time and agency for assessment of their responsibility. Under the non-Parliamentary system, such as the one that exists in the USA, the assessment of responsibility of the Executive is periodic. It takes place once in two years. It is done by the electorate. In England, where the Parliamentary system prevails, the assessment of responsibility of the Executive is both daily and periodic. The daily assessment is done by Members of Parliament, through Questions, Resolutions, No-confidence motions, Adjournment motions and Debates on Addresses. Periodic assessment is done by the electorate at the time of the election, which may take place every five years or earlier. The daily assessment of responsibility which is not available under the American system is far more effective than the periodic assessment and far more necessary in a country like India.'[21] Thus, India embarked on the path of democracy to have a viable and vibrant political system which could fight against country's backwardness, poverty, economic dependence and exploitation, lack of unity and poor level of consciousness among the masses.

However, in spite of this, at the time the Constitution was framed, many considered Parliament to be an alien institution unsuited to India. The member of the Constituent Assembly who moaned that instead of the music of veena and sitar the constitution was blaring forth the "music of a British band".[22] In fact our constitution makers were constrained not to follow the advice of Lord Bryce who said', do not give to a people institutions for which it is unripe in the simple faith that the tool will give skill to the workman's hand'. In regard to the universal adult franchise, the founding fathers knew full well that the majority of the population was poor and illiterate and vulnerable to influences like caste, community, bribery and intimidation. Had all the weaker sections been denied the right to vote, democracy would have lost in meaning. But contrary to this was a reality that our electorate at the time was largely illiterate and not in a position to take an objective or critical view of the promises and performances of different political parties. Just as it is not enough to import the latest technology if a country lacks the scientific temper and skills to harness it, so the parliamentary system too can become arid if members of Parliament, on both sides of the political divide, continue to display a lack of democratic temper. To some extent even Dr. B.R. Ambedkar was doubtful about the men who were engaged in the task and while piloting the Constitutional Bill he said, 'I feel that, however good the Constitution may be it is sure to turn out bad if those called upon to work it happen to be bad lot. However bad a Constitution may be, if those who are called upon to work it happen to be good lot, it will turn out to be good.'[23] Sachchidananda Sinha, the Provisional Chairman of the Constitution also laid emphasis on people's role in making the constitutional provisions a success, 'that it all may perish in a hour by the folly corruption or negligence of its only keepers, the people.'

In the circumstances it was the considered opinion of Mahatma Gandhi that our democracy has to be evolved from the bottom and it should be people-centric not institution-centric and leader-centric. He had no faith in the state. In fact, he had developed apprehensions about the state. That is why he insisted that people should have power to resist if state worked against the interests of the people. In the new structure state machinery was made the main instrument that would correct the ills of society through government-sponsored schemes and programmes. It was the thought of the day that indigenous science, technologies, medicines and community practices have to be improvised and improved. The reconstruction proposal through evolutionary process would consume longer time to reach its fullness and maturity. Hence an improvised hybrid model was thought of and as a result, the representative democracy modeled on the West was introduced. At the point to quote Gandhi, 'Democracy must in essence mean the art and science of mobilising the entire physical economic and spiritual resources of all various sections of the people in the service of the common good of all'.[24] Inspite of this it was cautioned by Mahatma Gandhi that the state machinery would ultimately control the society and people cannot establish their control over the state machinery. It is normal expectation that state will be generous and benevolent and it would provide better service. But in reality it is not so. As long as the state is vigilantly monitored by the citizens, it would work effectively. When citizens are weak, the state will exert control over the citizens.[25] Knowing fully well the attitude and behaviour of the people, Gandhi advised to build a people – centric institution. John Stuart Mill, a celebrity of representative form of government although argued that the representative democracy is one of the finest instruments for governance evolved by human society but added that its applicability and utility is limited as it requires high maturity on the part of the society.

Thus independent India has been a large scale experiment in democracy. Unlike many other nations that gained independence from colonial rule but descended into dictatorships and military rule, India has opted democracy despite its size and diversity. Earlier our people were mobilised for freedom struggle and we won freedom but they were not mobilised for democratic governance. Only the elite were oriented in democratic governance. In contrast, in the West, representative democracy was evolved over a period of time and the people grew with the system for which they had struggled over centuries. After a long struggle only they got Parliamentary democracy and franchise for the citizens. But in India, democracy and franchise were given all of a sudden; people were not prepared to take up the challenges. They were not mobilised for governance or participation in governance.[26] The famous scholar Lord Acton, after a profound examination of historical processes came to the conclusion that the fate of every democracy, of every government based on the sovereignty of the people, depends on the choice it makes between these opposite principles: absolute power on the one hand, and on the other the restraints of legality and the authority of tradition. It must stand or fall according to its choice, whether to give the supremacy to the law or to the will of the people; whether to constitute a moral association maintained by duty or physical one kept together by force.[27] The picture of Indian republic which the preamble envisages is democratic not only from the political but also from social standpoint.

As a result due to mismatch between adopted parliamentary democracy and overall actual position of Indian society democracy is never treated as a culture. From the beginning democracy in India began to revolve around elections and electoral politics. Our politics had not moved beyond elections. This tendency provided opportunity to keep an individual as a leader for many decades in the political system and in the party structure in the feudal mode. This enabled them to act as a ruler and not as leaders. The initiated electoral politics looks at people as always voters or beneficiaries. Others look at people as dole receivers. Consequently people have been reduced as an object or subjects or receivers of benefits. The Constitution is not a structure of fossils like a coral reef and is not intended merely to enable politicians to play their unending game of power. In fact democracy should enable the society to achieve development. But in India democracy survives at the cost of development. Rajni Kothari lays out the empirical basis of why India remained democratic : first, by analysing elements of Indian tradition that are democratic; second, by showing how the leaders of India's anti-colonial struggle operated and institutionalised a democratic polity in the first few decades after independence; and third, by reviewing recent strains and stress, as well as new possibilities and prospects.

Article 12 of the Indian Constitution defines the term 'State' which includes the Government (Executive) and Parliament of India and the Government and the Legislature of each of the States and all local and other authorities within the territory of India or under the control of the Government of India.[28] Since the process of decolonisation the institution of state has emerged as an important focus of study among political scientists and political economists. Different interpretations and theories offered to analyse the nature and role of the state in newly independent countries. Often the two major approaches – Liberal and Marxist interpreted the nature of postcolonial state according to their respective position to the state. While Marxists interpret the state as an instrument of class domination and an executive committee for managing the affairs of the bourgeoisie, the liberal approach considered the state as an instrument of modernisation – socio – economic, political and cultural. The process of modernisation in the West was the outcome of Industrial Revolution but in developing countries, it was the product of decolonisation. The prime motive of the overall modernisation process was to recover from the underdevelopment created by colonialism.[29] Hence the postcolonial state focused all developmental efforts towards the fulfilment of the objective of modernisation – through an effective process of national reconstruction – reconstruction of their ideologies, culture, administration, economy, social norms and education structure. The state as the chief political institution, actively engaged in the process of institution building – institutions like political parties, legislative bodies, bureaucracy and system of election based on universal adult franchise.[30] Political system, when understood as the state, is characterised by an ensemble of institutional patterns and political organisations. The state is distinguished from other organisations in society by its capacity to monopolise the legitimate use of violence within a given territory.

Others alike the postcolonial state in India, its nature and the role has been interpreted in different ways. In India's case the liberals consider the active intervention of the state as an agent for recovering from centuries of colonial exploitation and underdevelopment. Earlier during the nationalist movement the major policy initiatives stressed the need for the creation of an interventionist state. After independence the popular perception saw the state as an instrument of modernisation-socio-economic, political and cultural and the capitalists foresaw the state as an instrument to catalyze development. The Marxists criticised the national bourgeois, including a large section within the Congress party to support the capitalist path of development and reshape the economy and society with a view to expand national capitalism in India.[31] State capitalism in India performed dual functions immediately after independence – acquiring social legitimacy and accumulating capital without external dependency. According to C.P. Bhambhri, 'the modern Indian state, like capitalism in the country was established by the Britishers to safeguard the class interests of the metropolitan capitalism.[32] The active role of the state in development as explicated by the Nehruvian model of development, facilitated the mobilisation of economic resources for the interest of capitalist. Nehruvian socialism, in fact, strengthened the capitalist state. By controlling the state apparatus, the national bourgeoisie decisively influenced the developmental policies of the government.

Thus from the beginning of the two prevalent approaches – state – centric and society centric, in relation to the way in which society is organised and governed, India is clearly near the former. State- centrism is described as the perception that operators of the state system – politicians, bureaucrats, the military, industrialists and representatives play the most decisive roles in the determination of public policies. Such actors influence the structure and content of public policies introduced by the state, which embodies a system of law and government; a structure of offices with jurisdiction over a definite territory in which its citizens are located; and a centre of bureaucratic skills focused on information, calculation and implementation.[33] It also implies that the state is comprised of essentially of politicians and bureaucrats, since the making of public policy is the responsibility of the former while interpretation and implementation of public policy falls under the jurisdiction of bureaucrats. For many developing countries, the state centric approach becomes very useful when there are few sustained, well-organised social groups and when the population has limited international exposure. However its overdose may bring about discontent among the population and diminish the acceptability of state elites.

In contrast to the state–centric model which assumes the state to be an autonomous entity, the society–centric approach treats the state as an entity dependent on society and on social forces. Advocates of this approach argue that causes of decisions about public lie in understanding relationships of power and competition among individuals, groups or classes in society or in their international extensions. In this system the state becomes a representative structure that translates the expressed demands of members of society into policy outputs. According to Blondel a key function of government is to convert suggestions, values and ideas from inputs to outputs.[34] Society is assumed to be comprised of a large number of groups with varying interests and desires that they pursue. The dominant or allied classes eventually influence and shape the processes of the state.[35] In nutshell state – centric and society – centric approaches differ in their emphasis on the values, perceptions and preferences of the state versus those of societal classes and groups in the political decision-making process. However, both are used, in practice, depending on the type of activity sought; the prevailing social, political and economic circumstances; and the time available to accomplish the activity. Since the state arises out of society while society can not exist without some kind of administration or state, it is difficult to consider any of them as being independent of others in the decision-making process. The society – centric approach emphasises the centrality of social classes and interest groups in the initiation of public policies, while the state centric approach focuses on the operators of the state system or the government.

2.3 Party System

In a democratic set up party-system of the state is essential and has profound effects on the process of social, economic and political changes. Democracy seems to be the order of the day which is a widely accepted form of governance and still activities are on to democratise the institutions, the organisations and the society. In a state, writes Harold J. Laski in his book, *A Grammar of Politics,* 'Parties arrange the issues upon which people are to vote. It is obvious that in the confused welter of the modern state there must be some selection of problems as more urgent than others. It is necessary to select them as urgent and to present solutions of them which may be acceptable to the citizen body. It acts, in Lowell's phase as the broker of ideas. From the mass of opinion, sentiments, beliefs, by which the electorates move, it chooses out those it judges most likely to meet the general acceptance. It organises persons to advocate its own view of their meaning. It states that view as the issue upon which the voter has to make up his mind. Its power enables it to put forward for election candidates who are willing to identify themselves with its view.[36] Countries which have granted universal adult franchise expect their voters to exercise their franchise in a free and fair manner and also expect the political parties to extend their support to ensure on their part purity and transparency in the electoral process as held by Ivor Jennings, 'in a democracy political power rests in free elections'.

With the spread of democracy, the role of national as well as regional political parties has also assumed immense significance for participation in the elections, formation of the government and discharge their functions as responsible opposition parties for the success and smooth functioning of democracy and its institutions like parliament, state legislatures etc. The political parties serve as a link between the ruler and the ruled. The Party in power is entrusted with the task of running the government in accordance with the programmes and policies envisaged in its Manifesto and the opposition parties serve as a watchdog on the actions of the government to find out its shortfalls and make the people aware about them.[37] The opposition party is always in look out for an opportunity to dislodge the ruling Party from the seat of power through the electoral process, whereas the ruling party becomes conscious about its rivals' tactics and tries to rectify its policies to retain in power. In this manner political parties play significant role in strengthening the process of democracy and consolidating the foundations of democracy.

The Constitution of India gave citizens of the country the right to elect their own Government and the Parliamentary democracy needs parties which are eligible to be elected by the broadest possible strata of the population. This opportunity for co-determination of political actions would have been without any impact if every voter were obliged to express his opinion individually, for the interests and opinions of the people vary according to their social position or origin. In such a situation the necessity of parties becomes very much clear. The working of the Party system as well as the role of political leaders significantly influences the process of modernisation so crucial to developing societies like India. In fact the political parties evolve on the local dynamics, ideological past and socio-cultural as well as political expediency. The development of Indian Party system can be traced to the freedom movement days which resulted in the wide-ranging political recruitment, vast political socialisation and mobilisation of the masses. The Indian National Congress led the freedom struggle more as a mass movement for political emancipation than as political party. The ideological multiplicity and other contradictions within the Congress itself resulted in the development of parallel political parties/movements. Some of the Political parties have their origin from before India's independence, for example, Indian National Congress, Forward Bloc, Akali Dal, National Conference and some other parties. Some of these parties were either social or political organisation before India's independence and they became political parties after India's independence. However, many of the present parties were established after independence.

Since the inauguration of its republican constitution in 1950, India, like other developing countries, presented an exciting scenario of Party system. On account of the continental size of the country and due to the large scale diversities based on religions, language, region caste, history and physical features, the makers of Indian constitution opted for the Parliamentary form of government. The heterogeneous and pluralist character of Indian society impelled them to form a liberal and secular constitution. Along with parliamentary democracy they also decided to have a federal system instead of unitary system.[38] Federalism in India defines the power distribution between the federal government and the states. The government abides by constitutional checks and balances. But to maintain unity integrity and development of the Indian polity they also decided to have a strong centre in this federal system. It was seen as a basic requirement for accelerating the process of modernisation, economic growth and institutionalising political democracy.

Apart from this, keeping in view the vastness and diversity of the country and the enormity and variegated nature of the problems confronting the nation, Indian Republic envisaged the existence of multi-party system, which represents the multiethnic and culturally plural character of Indian society. They introduced the single ballot simple majority electoral system that is generally considered essential for the success of Parliamentary democracy. This type of system envisages majority government which, in turn, is based on the game of numbers. The Party which gets majority of seats in the lower house of the legislature is asked by the Head of State to form the government. This government does not have a fixed term but continues to exist so long it enjoys the confidence of the lower house of the parliament. The term of the Indian Parliament is, however, fixed for five years. But when no Party gets majority of seats in the legislature, it becomes difficult to form a government in such a situation. A coalition of parties is then thought upon to tide over the crisis created by a hung legislature. A number of parties in that situation come together and form a coalition to claim support in the legislature.

But the multi-party system obtaining in India is basically different from that prevalent in western countries like France and Italy. In a model multi-party system seldom any single party is able to obtain majority of seats in the legislature and such a system is more often than not results in the formation of a coalition government. In contrast, initially, India marked a departure from such a model. Scholars designated Indian Party system as "one dominant party system" and the concept was popularised in the 1960s by W.H. Morris Jones and Ranji Kothari. In a classic study they held the view that a dominant party system is a multi-party system, in which free competition among parties occured but in which the Indian National Congress enjoyed a dominant position, both in terms of the number of seats that it held in Parliament in New Delhi and the state legislative assemblies, and in terms of its immense organisational strength outside the legislature.[39] From 1952 to 1967, the peculiar party system generally described as the one-party dominant system as only the Congress was voted time and again with an overwhelming Parliamentary majority on plurality of votes in democratically contested elections. The Congress by virtue of being a pioneer in the freedom struggle, became an increasingly effective election winning machine. In 1952 the Congress had absolute majority in 18 out of 22 state assemblies. In the second and third general elections the Congress Party retained its hold on masses and occupied the seats in Lok Sabha more than required for making the government.

However, the Indian model of one Party dominance, in early years, was different from the one-dominant Party system of Ghana, Mexico, Alger and Egypt. The Indian Party system's dominance was democratic and constitutional. It was marked by in-built corrective and restraining force provided by factionalism within the Congress and occasional threats from without. The Congress maintained an "umbrella" character and tried to build "consensus" and in this process accommodated various shades of political ideas and interests. In view of Maurice Duverger a party is dominant, if it displays the following two characteristics in a two-party or multi-party system : (i) It clearly outdistances its rivals over an extended period of time; and (ii) it identifies itself with the nation as a whole. Its doctrines, ideas and even its style coincide with those of the times. The electoral success and the working of the Congress Party during the first twenty years after independence prompted Morris Jones and Rajni Kothari to characterise the Indian Party system as that of one Party dominance. The historic role of the Congress in the national movement, trauma of partition, the charisma of Nehru's leadership and the weaknesses of regional political parties led to the beginning of Parliamentary democracy in India with Congress at its centre. In the formative years, the founding class drew its legitimacy from its association with the freedom struggle, it renewed that legitimacy from the democratic promise, a promise that was at total and complete variance with the colonial state and feudal order.[40] Within a decade of Independence, the constitutional order was definitely fulfilling two primary conditions, of popular acceptability and political representativeness. Simultaneously, the new nation-state was trying to prove its competence by undertaking a welfare agenda. The political culture was remarkably commensurate with the state's self-assigned goals and objectives.

On the whole, the Congress occupied the broad centre of the political spectrum as well as most of the left and right. Throughout the 1950s, and 1960s, Indian National Congress was able to assimilate divergent interest, dividing the opposition by responding to the fragmentation on the lines of caste and ethnicity within Indian society and winning wide support. Indians gather around a leader either on the basis of caste, religion, economic interests or may be even birth. All that the leader has to do is to feed a hundred such people and push his caste or community or religion or even personality to assume leadership status of course, the importance of the leader is directly proportional to the number of people he can feed.[41] This was the phase of Nehru's undisputed supremacy in the country and the total dominance of the Congress party. K. Santhanam, a well-known Indian writer on federalism writes in succeeding year that the Indian republic started with a contradiction. While the constitution established a federal system of government, all the political parties existing at the time it came into force were unitary and highly centralised. This was particularly the case with the Congress.[42]

However, despite single party dominance and supremacy of Jawaharlal Nehru in the dominating party, opposition parties of the time never felt uneasiness. The Indian political parties are categorised into two main types – national level parties and state level or regional parties. The national parties are those political parties, which participate in different elections all over India, while state parties or regional parties are political parties, which take part in different elections but only within one or two states. In the first phase the national opposition consisted mainly of the Socialist Parties, the Communist Parties, the Bharatiya Jana Sangh and the Swatantra. The Praja Socialist Party (PSP) emerged as the largest opposition party in the parliament after the first general election in 1952. Split in the Party led to severe battering of the Socialist parties in the second and third general elections. The Communist Party of India was particularly strong in West Bengal, Kerala and Andhra Pradesh since the first general election. In Kerala a Communist Government was in power from April 1957 to July 1959. The Party had been weakened by personal and ideological differences of its leaders, which climaxed in a split in July 1964. The Swatantra Party formed in 1959 under the leadership in C. Rajgopalachari, was the "first democratically oriented conservative Party of any importance in India."[43] Some of the regional parties, which came into prominence during this period, were the DMK in Tamil Nadu, the Akali Dal in Punjab, the Muslim League in parts of Madras and Kerala, the Republican Party and Peasants' and Workers Party in Maharashtra, the Ganatantra Parishad in Orissa and the Jharkhand Party in Bihar and Orissa.

But in the formative years when Congress was dominant and on winning hatrik, the opposition parties of the time functioned on the margin and do not hold an alternative to the ruling party. Indian party system's experiences were of co-existing with competition but without a trace of alteration.[44] As a result the opposition parties confined themselves to a role quite distinctive, instead of providing an alternative to the Congress Party they functioned by influencing sections within Congress. They opposed by making Congressmen oppose. In other words, groups within the ruling Party assumed the role of opposition parties, often quite openly reflecting the ideologies and interests of other parties.[45] The Congress, in the period, occupied most of the space in the political system because 'there was plurality within the dominant Party which made it more representative, provided flexibility and estimated internal competition. At the same time it was prepared to absorb groups and movements from outside the Party and thus prevent other parties from strength.[46] But Congress, ever during the height of its power and influence, represented the democratic model allowing elements of opposition leading to the existence of a multi-party system. It was competitive in character in as much as it permited political struggle among a number of parties which functioned within the four corners of the Constitution.

In general, political parties are born of the natural contrast between those who cling to the old and those who embrace the new but on the other some accept that they arise from the pugnacious instinct of men. In any society there is a conflict of wills in society, and that conflict is decided by the decision of the intermediate mass which is not firmly convinced of the truth of any general cause. To attract its support it is necessary to advertise one's view. Parties are the natural method of effecting that end. Their form is largely dependent upon the conditions of any given time. They may group themselves about religious issues, economic issues or there will be a tendency for radical solution to attract the young.[47] Under the natural origin of political parties, they suffer from all the evils of group separatism. They distort the issues they create. They produce the divisions in electorate which very superficially represent the way in which opinion is in fact distributed. They secure, at best, an incomplete and compromising loyalty. They falsify the perspective of the issues they create. They build about persons, allegiance which should go to ideas. They build upon the unconscious and they force the judgement of men into the service of their prejudices.[48] But in case of Indian Party system the above complexities did not arise particularly in the years following country's independence. It all started in a happy and purposeful manner.

In addition, of the two types of parties: one broad-based and functional, and the other local in character and based on primary groups or centred around personalities. The co-existence of both the types of parties must be regarded as an important characteristic of the Indian Party system. Thereby the numerical representation of the parties or their territorial diffusion does not have any significance in categorising them in one way or the other.[49] The classification is entirely related to the degree of their social differentiation.

Although these parties are frequently built upon traditional loyalties and to a great extent, they are considered eligible by various social, linguistic and religious groups. They comprise very heterogeneous social currents and interests in the complex of which differences in political representation naturally exist. In the process of creating political consciousness these parties work as a media of integration and have the capacity to provide the public with a measure of national identification as distinct from parochial parties.[50] In fact, there is a strong underlying feeling among all the people and political parties of the basic need for one sovereign Indian identity, even from the point of view of regard for their individual regional interests or pride in their regional identities. It is this feeling, historical, emotional and also utilitarian – that makes them use their separate identities for pressuring the Indian polity to giving them regional concessions rather than for breaking up the country's single political identity.[51] Dr. Rajendra Prasad, also rightly pointed out on the occasion of his parting-speech, that if a constant compromise between the many heterogeneous social groups is not made, democracy in India is bound to collapse. At the same time he demanded of the Parties to strive for inter-party tolerance and political restraint'. In fact, political parties coordinate between various thoughts-ideologies, represent heterogeneous social interests and provide political training to citizen. While acting as a ruling party, they translate the dreams and aspirations of the country to reality. As opposition they aim at keeping the ruling Party on right track by adopting various methods.

In a republic like India political leaders are the torch bearers of the nation. They are the path breakers and path makers who become the hope, the dream, the friend, the philosopher and guide for the common man. Fortunately India witnessed at the dawn of independence the titanic leaders, who set the example of sacrifice, strength, support, sensitivity, sympathy simplicity and super will power. The independence struggle, in its earlier phases under the influence of the liberal philosophy and in its later period under the leadership of Gandhi, Nehru and others were fundamentally democratic in inspiration. The sovereign republic of India was proclaimed as a democratic one in the Preamble and Article providing for adult suffrage inserted in the Constitution along with a Election Commission to ensure free and fair elections for the successful working of the new democracy.[52] In an initial and experimental manner, we accepted and dealt with this great world-moving force of man-on-the-March, which is democracy. We are aware that such experiment in democracy is sure to bring about revolutionary changes in our individual and social life.

At independence the Indian National Congress was converted into not just a ruling party, but a dominant framework institutionalising the whole process of power. The party system that emerged from such a framework was somewhat distinctive and served Indian democracy well during this period of consolidation and consensus making. In particular, Jawaharlal Nehru's idea on democracy can best be attributed to his submission to the objective laws that led him to realise the direction of the historical process, to understand as an objective and progressive course of events proceeding from the higher to lower.[53] He played a very significant role in oder to strengthen political institutions under the framework of the Indian Constitution. Nehru was a democrat by instinct and temperament and contributed immensely towards inculcating the true parliamentary spirit and values in our people. Although he commanded absolute majority in the House, he never believed in streamrolling the Opposition and showed utmost respect to them, listened to their views and tried to accommodate them as far as possible. He recognised the due space of dissent in a true democracy favouring healthy and constructive criticism from all sections of the House. Some of his strongest critics in Parliament happened to be his greatest admirers, and perhaps there cannot be a better compliment to Nehru's democratic credentials than this fact.[54] And without any doubt it can be added that the opposition was not frowned upon; it was seen as a vital part of the arrangement. Within Parliament, the opposition was deemed to be entitled to have its say and the government was to have its way; rather effortlessly the Westminster model was accepted, imitated and practised. In the process, a few rules of the game were formulated and finessed: political rivals were not to be treated as enemies, nor were the state's coercive powers to be used to tame political opponents.[55] The democratic system so established certainly worked well for a number of years.

Nehru did not confine his opinion to the realm of politics alone but the arena of economic was not out of his reach. He considered that political democracy by itself is not enough except that it may be used to obtain a gradually increasing measure of economic democracy. In the period of freedom movement the Congress had evolved the idea of a planned economy to fight the poverty of the mass and, to this end, established a Planning Committee in 1938, in order to prepare a draft plan for the socio-economic development of India.[56] In the debates of the Constituent Assembly Nehru rejected all attempts to call India a 'Socialistic Republic, although after independence liberal economic ideas were popular in certain ranks of the Congress there was actually no discussion about whether at all a policy of economic planning should be followed or not. As a result, the economic policy of the Congress Government had led India into a paradoxical situation.

On the one hand since the beginning of economic planning the objective of a socialist pattern of society had been realised in so far as the public sector had constantly expanded but on the other the rate of economic growth as postulated had been partially fulfilled. In reality the rich became richer and poor became poorer.[57] Nehru believed in industrialisation and a strong industrial base. He was for a mixed economy and a good deal of progress was achieved but during his economic period he invested more in industry. More emphasis was laid on industry than agriculture.

However, the hold of Congress had begun to decline in the post – 1960 period on account of its failure on the economic front. People accused him of being a prisoner of the socialist maxims when in the beginning of the sixties the country faced an acute economic crisis. Mahatma Gandhi is also of the opinion, 'Economic equality is the master key to non-violent independence... A non-violent system of Government is clearly impossibility so long as the wide gulf between the rich and the hungry millions persists. The contrast between the palaces of New Delhi and the miserable hovels of the poor labouring classes cannot last one day in a free India in which the poor will enjoy the same political powers as the richest in the land. A violent and bloody revolution is a certainty one day unless there is a voluntary abdication of riches and the power that riches give and sharing them for the common good.'[58]

Till Jawaharlal Nehru was alive the Congress Party and the Government as well remained a one-man show and both realised no difficulty in sailing the boat of Indian republic. In the opinion of Lucian W. Pye, 'Under the unassailable leadership of Nehru, Congress leaders had little trouble in thinking of themselves as the administration and Government of India, and they apparently convinced themselves that the future unity and progress of India as a nation was absolutely dependent upon Congress remaining in power.[59] Professor W.H. Morris-Jones, a perceptive observer of the Indian scene in the mid-fifties noted that Indian Parliament at that time was Panditji's sounding board" or "echo room". Nehru put this to splendid use. Through his rambling but always thoughtful speeches he educated his countrymen in the imperative need to transform India's medieval society into a modern one and preached to the world at large the virtues of peace, disarmament and a ban on nuclear weapons. He added further that somehow the world listened to him with a respect, it has not bestowed on any other world leader with the possible exception of de Gaulle.[60] Even the impregnable position of the Congress was largely attributed to Nehru's immense popularity among the masses.

But all this was perhaps too good to last though it did last for well over a decade. Suddenly things began to change and the seeds of present owes were sown during the last three or four years of Nehru's era itself. The process of the decline of Congress got further accelerated after the 1962 Parliamentary and assembly elections on account of the national humiliation caused by the defeat at the hands of China in 1962. At the time and thereafter Nehru was criticised by opposition parties and several Congress members for country's security lapses. Already during Nehru's lifetime the Chief Ministers consolidated their own position and ignored central direction on policies that did not suit them. With the crumbling of a united central leadership, the States 'Satraps' have practically been forced to act more antonomously. The overall situation in the Party and government deteriorated markedly after the death of Nehru in 1963. The post-Nehru elections took on a different character because the great leader, who had lost public esteem, because of defeat in Sino-Indian war, was no longer at the helm. Lal Bahadur Shastri succeeded Nehru. The short-lived Shastri era was essentially a continuation of the tragic, twilight years of Nehru. In fact things became worsen because language became a highly explosive issue soon after Shastri became the Prime Minister. He was handicapped moreover by the general feeling that Nehru's shoes were too big for him. And just when, in the wake of the 1965 war between India and Pakistan, he looked like coming into his own, this most undramatic of men passed into history in highly dramatic circumstances.[61] After Shastri, Indira Gandhi became the Prime Minister of the country in January 1966. This period may be rightly termed as the advent of a political development with many non-Congress national political parties coming to the fore and the rise of regional political parties in most state of India. The hegemony of the Congress had to face a serious challenge from the national opposition parties as well as from the regional parties.

Despite all goodness of leaders and organisations in the first two decades following India's independence, the period also witnessed the starting of several social evils and a clear degradation in public morality. Although Nehru had a scientific temper for the country, he was a poor judge of men, and therefore, he could not distinguish between real friends and sycophants. In the later phase of his life he took the support of undesirable elements to remain in power. Though he was popular with the masses he did not take action against vested interest which exploited the masses. He did not mind taking funds from anti-social elements. The Congress Party started accepting black money for elections during his time. Though soft, he was not always straightforward in dealing with his colleagues. His 'soft pedaling' of corruption had a disastrous effect on public morals. Nehru admitted the facts of public life, then prevailing and said, 'Unhappily during the war and afterwards various types of corruption have grown. Controls have added to them and general standards fallen, both in government servant and in the public. Black marketing in India is not merely an individual offence, but a social evil. There can be no two opinions that adequate measures should be taken to check and end this degradation of our public life.[62] In post – Nehru years the rumblings of a system beginning to come under socio-economic stress were first clearly heard. Politically the most significant manifestation of this gathering crisis appeared in 1967 elections which saw the once unassailable Congress Party lose out to a motely assembly of opposition parties in a number of northern states. On the other Congress was faced with leadership problems during the period 1967-69. This period was, marked by India's transition from a dominant party system to a system of competitive sharing of power.

2.4 Indian Republic Around 1967

The outstanding result of 1967 election had been the 'collapse of the erstwhile pattern of one party dominance of the Congress and the expose of the artificial level of political stability, democratic maturity and Parliamentary sophistication at which the political system had so far appeared to be operating'.[63] The political change that took place in 1947 began to move with the existing social structure on the basis of give and take. The new institutions and the new leadership offered economic opportunity, administrative patronage, and positions of power which drew the articulate sections of society into the modernist network. Even at this stage the caste associations and federation had the less pressing role and the upper tiers of each of the rival chains were recruited into politics and carried the whole network with them. It increased the importance of individuals and leadership took on a more positive note. But this all was limited to the leading two or three castes – well to do, educated and generally upper caste. The democratic experience, with intensely contested local, state and national elections, have socialised the Indians across the traditional divides.[64] Likewise Nehru's concept of modernisation of Indian economy became sophisticated with highly vulnerable to disruption. The economic optimism which involved advances and hope now began to give way to serious doubts. In post-Nehru phase it was clear that the system which had seemed hitherto be sailing in tranquil waters, had entered a turbulent sea.[65] Thus the changed socio-economic position of India demanded a new type of leadership. Now, the social and economic cleavages that contained at lower level for so long, tended to gravitate upward towards the policy process.

The post-independent India presented itself as a new cultural bastion of several socio-cultural and political influences. The colonial experience also added to it a sudden sense of loss of self, the identity and transformation in language, culture, science and social and political thoughts. The long and arduous struggle to freedom provided a sense of responsibility to govern itself in future with a total reconciliation of its plural bases despite the setback caused by the trauma of partition.[66] However, the social identity and religious differences persisted. This was not a national divide but the prevalence of what is political. When India became independent in 1947, the society was organised into an active, but declining feudal class, a small class of industrialists, a slender intelligentsia, which had influenced the intellectual and political life in the freedom struggle and millions of farmers.[67] The broad masses followed their age-old traditions and were guided by their caste authorities, religious masters and elders of the villages. For these people institutions like, caste-less society, freedom of profession, democratic self-determination and individualism which were embodied in the Constitution remained totally unknown concept. Although many changes in style of life took place in the past and lead to an increased social interchange between groups which formally had retained a degree of separateness.[68] A hundred year ago of India's independence, in 1853, Karl Marx in his article *The British Rule in India*, argued that England has demolished the total structure of the Indian society. Yet we observe that the loosening of the caste system has in no way paralleled the process of modernisation of the country.[69] But after independence ancient ways of life were being changed, old customs are being replaced by new, and the individual gets a glimpse of the wider horizons of the modern world without having to tear up his, and his nation's past by the roots. The gains achieved by these gradual methods seemed modest.

Apart from this the Indian social order was not stagnant and passing through an evolutionary stage. As the villagers begin to improve their living conditions, they become eager to start saving through the rural credit system, and begin to have new wants which before they had either not experienced or had no hope of satisfying. Where once they could walk on foot in their villages, now they need bicycles to get around the community development area. The men want an extra shirt, the women an extra sari.[70] In the process of change from a static to a dynamic society differences between the generations, between sexes, and between urban and rural areas are considerable. Tensions and social conflicts are visible signs of a disturbed traditional balance. Development, as has been said often means discontent. It is only when relatively stable societies are sought to be changed rapidly and profoundly that they begin to undergo ferment. Since 1947, tremendous social forces with the most far reaching implications had been at work in cities and the countryside. As early as the midfifties when the agitation over the linguistic reorganisation of states made its appearance, these forces released largely as a result of state social and economic action had begun to run their powerful course.[71] Thus, on social side there has been considerable change in a progressive direction. Many members of the submerged and deprived sections of Indian society are now getting out of their traditional bondage and entering into the mainstream of society; and women now play a more prominent role in all activities, including the political and professional, than they do in practically most developing and even in some developed countries.[72] The economic and political opportunities, both legitimate and otherwise, now available to its citizens have brought into existence a large, growing, and dynamic middle class especially not only in urban but also in rural areas, that did not exist in pre-independence period. The process of social mobility gathered even greater speed since independence in view of economic development, the spread of education, adult franchise and so on.

India viewed economic progress as an unalienable ingredient of the political development. As leaders turned away from the task of liberation, and came face to face with the harsh realities of the country's economy, for whose future they were henceforth solely responsible. The new Indian pattern which it described as "the Socialist Pattern of Society", represented an attempt to create a mixed economy which combined private enterprise with government planning, overall direction, and control as well as government initiative in fields that private entrepreneurs might not find attractive, and to subject both the plans and their implementation to the scrutiny of a parliamentary democracy Jawaharlal Nehru had made this policy more and added that in India there is no private sector and no public sector, but only one national sector. The Indian National Congress under the leadership of Nehru, elaborated its idea in the Election Manifesto of the 1951, on the eve of first general election and declared that the Party favoured a planned approach to economic development in order to make it possible for the people to live a good life. It emphasised the need for an increase in agricultural productivity and improvement in cattle breeding; stated that small and cottage industries would be encouraged; declared that there would be state ownership or control of basic industries and defined its objective as a mixed economy consisting of a public and a private sector, both of which were to be fitted into an over-all national plan.[73] In first two five year plans the major goals had been to increase productivity throughout the country and to reduce social inequalities through improved living standards.

In post-independence phase India badly needed foreign capital to base and boost the ravaged economy. A developing country, wishing to move towards the goal of prosperity required economic aid from outside the country and from world economic organisations. But the organisations and the countries, who offer economic aid, also dictate their own terms and conditions which may hamper the fulfilment of needs and requirement of aid receiving countries. This trend ultimately leads to economic imperialism which in long term, widens the gap between developed and developing nations and between rich and poor people of the country which is trying to provide and distribute all the resources to its people equally.[74] A polity devises through painful experiences, and sometimes through joyful energy an operative work culture commensurate with the state's objective interests and designed to deepen its legitimacy. But the measures taken by the Government of India failed to reduce the dangerous unbalance in the ratio between food and population. A fourteen member team of US agricultural experts headed by Dr. Sherman E. Johnson, in a report published on April 20, 1959 declared that India is heading for a disaster. The team also called for an emergency programme of action to mobilise India's resources of soil, water and manpower. It required that India's economic planners should assign top priority to agriculture. At the juncture the government realised that it must rebuild not only the strength of its people but also the strength of the soil.

In the circumstances, unfortunately the Third Five Year Plan (1961-1966) has failed on many counts. The targets of economic growth remained unfulfilled; although 104 billion rupees were invested as planned.[75] Even earlier the Second Five Year Plan (1956-1961) had not yielded the expected results. In the agricultural sector the progress was negligible. Bottlenecks in the supply of food for the population had set in. In the industrial area the list of failures was even longer. Prices rose and unemployment increased. The idea of Third Plan that a big plan would automatically lead to the maximum rate of economic growth proved to be wrong. It appeared that the Planning Commission viewed the whole question of economic development mainly from the expenditure point of view, but ignored the capacity for production and the sociological constraints. The already acute economic crisis was also aggravated by two successive bad harvests and the military conflicts with Pakistan and China. The economic crisis affected mainly the poorer sections of the society, whereas they should have got a greater share in the economic growth. The economic status of the agricultural labourers and factory workers, of the small and middle class peasants and of the salaried class hardly improved during the Third Plan period. On the contrary the business community, the landlords, the professionals and skilled workers, in other words the upper middle class benefited. In a pre-poll survey conducted in Delhi, Calcutta, Bombay and Madras by the Indian Institute of Public Opinion (I.I.P.O.) showed that the share of firm Congress voters increased till February 1966 despite the fact that the serious economic crisis had already started in 1965.[76] But within the next three months it dropped by 19 per cent. It seemed that the economic crisis was perceived by the urban population only after few months had passed. As the election results clearly bring to light, this change in voters' behaviour prevailed in the States where the socio-economic conditions were worse.

When a republic comes to birth, it is the leaders who produce the institutions. Later, it is the institutions which produce the leaders. On account of socio-economic policy/initiatives of the government there appeared a general social mobility that had made the popular demand for performance. The social reality began to break surface in the fifties despite the Congress Party's monopoly of power and domination in it of a modernist and modernising leadership headed by Nehru. By the time of the second general election in 1957 it became clear that land-owning castes had become sufficiently influential at the state level to be in a position to block land reform. Although Nehru persuaded the Congress at Nagpur in 1959 to adopt a resolution favouring co-operative farming but he was not in a position to get it implemented. On political front too there were many icons like Sardar Pratap Singh Kairon of Punjab, Bakshi Ghulam Mohammad of Kashmir and Biju Patnaik of Orissa who were not particularly concerned with political norms as practised in those days. They subordinated the administration to their will; they were not averse to arbitrary use of power; they were not respectful of the independence of judiciary and the press and they were intolerant of criticism.[77] And this was not the end of story. Rapid politicisation had inevitably led to attempts to subordinate every other institution to political control.

The economic ladder generated by independence and government support had led to a spurt of money power among the upper and middle classes and given them a position in society and an influence that far exceeded that exercise done by the professional classes in the pre-independence period. However, the development of the upper and middle classes was a by-product of modernisation. The tiny upper class at independence expanded quickly and moved into the political, administrative and business space vacated in the higher reaches by the British. The expansion of the middle class had been slower as the annual growth of the economy.[78] It is made up of the middle and lower rungs of politicians and bureaucracy, small time entrepreneurs, most professionals, well-to-do farmers and unionised workers. The middle class are every influential in India as they are spread through all sectors-politics, bureaucracy, industry, services and agriculture.

With all the above, the infant Indian republic also faced sharp politicisation and a clear decline in the moral and intellectual quality of politicians. Labour unrest and indiscipline, frequently resulted in violence were a part of politicisation, ironically enough the agents of the process, political parties had also suffered as a consequence. Imported ideologies – liberal democracy with its accent on the rule of law, independence of the judiciary and the press, sovereignty of Parliament, accountability of the executive to the legislature and indispensability of rival political parties, and Marxism with its emphasise on equality and social welfare and all that they imply by way of state control over, and intervention in, the economy – have been not only essential but predominant constituents of the modern language of Indian politics. As lower and lower sections of our once rigidly hierarchical society have become active participants in the political process and as politics has become one of the principal avenues for upward social mobility, the liberal intelligentsia, which had imbibed the British as well as the Gandhian concepts of public morality, has given place to men who carry no such burdens on their conscience.[79] As it has very appropriately been said by an analyst, 'In the fifties, we had many eminent men in public life who were every inch a gentleman. In the sixties we had many public figures who were every alternate inch a gentleman. Unfortunately in the seventies we had an unacceptably large number of politicians who were no inch a gentleman.[80] Independence and elections brought a new class of politicians seeking power and money, while the expending power of government and controls increased the number of bureaucrats and gave them a money generating power they never had earlier.

It was in that kind of situation, India witnessed the fourth general election in 1967 which revealed something more basic – a combination of social conflicts within the traditional caste hierarchy and widespread public discontent with the Congress itself around issues of rising prices, the highhandedness of both Congress bosses and officialdom, corruption, growth of large pockets of poverty, and above all, a leadership that had failed to inspire confidence in the people. The outstanding results of this election had been the collapse of the till date pattern of one Party dominance of the Congress. The fourth general elections to the Lok Sabha and the state assemblies held in February 1967 had a radical impact on Indian politics. The Congress Party had exhausted its mandate and lost its character and motivation as a party of social and institutional change. In the party there was a large-scale disenchantment, especially with its top leaders because of corruption and the lavish lifestyle of many of them. Many of the regional and local Congress bosses were perceived by the people as being devoted to loaves and fishes of office, political wheeling dealing and factional infighting.[81] Although for rounding off the strategy of the electoral campaign the Congress put its political services into perspective and reminded the voter of the historical role the Party played for over eighty-two years and its consistent struggle to ensure for India an open, democratic and socialist society.[82] This strategy, however, did not come up to the level of performance of Nehru who was extremely capable of raising questions of broad national interest, thus overplaying over local affairs. At the time it was clear that the Congress itself lacked the drive and cohesion for providing the nation with a stable and strong government. The result was a continuous power-struggle at all levels of Congress leadership and the rapid erosion of such Party discipline, confidence and comradeship as Congress had built up during the independence movement, and without which it could not hope to remain united.

The results of the Fourth General Elections showed that the Congress Party was no more an impregnable fortress that it once was and as a consequence it lost heavily both at the Centre and in the States. As against 361 seats which the Congress had won in the Lok Sabha in 1962 with 44.73 per cent votes, it was able to secure only 284 seats with 40.82 per cent of the total votes polled. Among the opposition, the Swatantra Party got the leading position with 42 seats as against 18 in 1962 and 8.54 per cent votes. Next to it was the Jana Sangh with 35 seats and 9.29 per cent votes. As a whole all the opposition parties of the time including CPI, CPM, SSP and PSP had done much better than ever before. From 133 seats in 1962 their strength had gone up to 236 in 1967, a remarkable increase indeed. However, despite the rise of opposition Party's strength India's Parliament was still without an officially recognised opposition Party which required minimum of one-tenth of the total membership of the Lok Sabha while Swatantra Party which led the opposition had only 42 members – 10 short of the required numbers.[83] In this election the Congress Party retained comfortable majority at the Centre, it however, was in great loss in the majority of states, though it differed in its extent from region to region and it could be divided into four groups. In three States – Orissa, Bihar and West Bengal, the Congress lost more votes than the all-India average. The second group included Gujrat, Assam, Tamil Nadu and Maharashtra, where Congress performance was correspondingly to the all-India trend. In another group of three States – Andhra Pradesh, Mysore and Uttar Pradesh – the Congress losses were minimal. Rajasthan, Haryana, Kerala, Madhya Pradesh and Jammu and Kashmir formed the fourth group, where the Congress share of votes slightly went up. The results of the election underlined the social and economic strains lay at the heart of the political change. For example, the fall in the Congress share of votes had catastrophic proportions in Orissa and Bihar where hunger and famine had been of very serious dimensions before the election.

Earlier, in January 1966 Indira Gandhi succeeded Lal Bahadur Shastri as the next Prime Minister of the country and Congress fought the elections without Jawaharlal Nehru, who was the symbol of its unity, stability and progress. The new leader of the Party was Indira Gandhi and this was the first general election under her leadership which itself was yet to be firmly established. At the time Indira Gandhi took over the reigns of Administration, the economy was in recession and fast deteriorating. Industrial production and exports were declining. The rains failed for the second successive year in 1966, and the drought was more severe than in 1965, and led to galloping inflation and grave food shortages. Famine conditions prevailed in large parts of the country, especially in Bihar and eastern UP.[84] As a result the year was known for continuous popular turmoil of economic discontent and political agitations provoked by spiralling prices, food scarcity, growing unemployment, and, in general, deteriorating economic conditions. In addition, 1966 also witnessed the beginning of the downslide of the Parliament as an institution. There were constant disturbances and indiscipline in the Parliament with some members of the opposition showing complete disregard for Parliamentary decorum and niceties.

The overall deteriorating situations in the country and Congress Party itself provided a fertile ground for the rise of 'right' and 'left' extremism. The widespread discontent among the masses was favourable for their election strategy. Both at national and regional levels the opposition parties began to form the United Front or a cohesive political unit, which could serve as a new restraint upon the Congress Party and provide an alternative to it. The development, in fact, was not a polarisation of Indian Party system, but instead there was scores of parties making appeals to such primordial factors as caste, religion, race, region, and language at the expense of secular values.[85] For instance, the CPI(M), advised its State units to exploit and aggravate the prevalent discontent in order to mobilise the public in favour of the Party.[86] The demonstrations in the streets and the go-slow tactics in the factories which were organised by leftist forces demonstrated their desire to radicalise the masses. At the same time they repeatedly created violent scenes in the Lok Sabha, so to say, as a corollary to these actions. On the other the orthodox religious forces – the Rashtriya Swayam Sevak Sangh (RSS), the Hindu Mahasabha, the Sanatana Dharama Sabha and the Sadhu Samaj intensified their activities with the objective of pressing Government to concede their demand for a ban on cow-slaughter. Even Jana Sangh members cooperated with them and it appeared that secular democracy in India was on the brink of collapse.

In the elections of 1967 the ruling Congress Party and the opposition parties of the time had different objectives in view. The Congress aimed at winning the elections by an absolute majority in the Lok Sabha so that it would be legitimised to form the Government at the Centre. And by and large, the leadership appeared fully convinced to be able to reach this numerical power-level; however, it was not sure about the margin with which it would accomplish that task. On the other opposition parties were also knowing the fact that the Congress would not loose its hegemony at the Centre but its position in many States would be shaky. It is also to note here that the Congress had not formulated any official policy towards forming coalitions at the Centre or in any State, in case such an eventuality would occur. But the opposition parties had obviously reconciled that at the national level the position of the Congress could not be challenged seriously and therefore, they could not projected themselves before the electorate as a veritable alternative to the Congress. In the States the situation was different and some of the opposition parties offered themselves to the electorate as alternative parties to take over the reins of office. In the electoral strategy while Congress Party seemed to divert the voter from the critical socio-economic onslaught and remind him of the priority of political problems by expressing its doubt in the ability of the heterogeneous opposition parties to maintain law and order in the country, the opposition parties gave an all-out fight to the Congress but failed to prevent a split of possible anti-Congress votes in the country and also did not succeed in forming a viable alliance against the Congress at national or regional level. The striking fact was that the Congress popular vote dropped could not immediately be transformed into an alternative Government because the opposition was heavily fragmented. In this context the lack of organisational and ideological coherence and constitutional norms was a warning not to put too much faith in coalition Governments.

The election results revealed certain long-term trends with certain long-term consequence. Apart from general disenchantment with Congress because of the various factors, defection by the rich and middle peasants from the Congress camp played a major role in the Congress debacle in the northern states. They felt that their newly acquired economic position and social status, associated with control of land, was threatened by the projected foodgrains procurement policies, the land reforms, and other populist rhetoric of Congress. In contrast, in South India class and caste structure or configuration was different from that in the North and the large presence of Communists kept the rural landowners tied to Congress. In all fairness it can be said that problems of income inequality, regional disparity, urban and rural unemployment persisted as earlier. The level of social development was also considered slow. On the one hand, there was an acute inter-regional and inter-state disparity in socio-economic development. On the other, there is also a serious problem of intra-state disparity in economic and social development. In context of India's development policy and strategies, the role of the dominant social, political and economic forces in determining the process and nature of development cannot be undermined. The problem of inter and intra regional disparity is a problem that will affect not only the economc development but the social and political development of the country.[87] The changing bases of our political society has become a major concern of our polity.

This apart, the year 1967 was the beginning of the politics of defection. The elections broke Congress's monopoly of power in the states and was replaced not by a single party in any of the states but by a multiplicity of parties and groups and independents. Coalition governments were formed in all opposition-ruled states except in Tamil Nadu. Congress too formed coalition goverments in some of the states where it had been reduced to a minority, allying with independents and breakaway groups from the opposition parties. These governments were ideologically heterogeneous; and the left-right or secular-communal divides were almost completely bridged in them. As a result all the coalition governments suffered from constant tensions and internal strains because of the heterogeneity of the partners. Most often, except in West Bengal and Kerala, the continuous bargaining among the partners was not on policies but on ministerial berths, patronage, and interest groups. Many of the governmental changes in the northern states were result of defections or floor crossings by individual legislators both party members and independents. Corrupt legislators indulged in horse trading and freely changed sides, attracted mainly by lure of office or money. The problem of defections was to become long term and perpetual because defectors, who changed sides and toppled governments for purely personal and often corrupt reasons, were seldom punished by the voters and were elected again and again.

Political defections and consequently unstable majorities became a particularly malignant disease of the body politic.[88] Some of the governments do not exist any more, though their consequences do; it is an old and not altogether untrue saying that the good that men do dies with them, but the evil that they do lives after them. In this wave anti-Congressism gained ground with these elections both among the opposition parties and a large section of the intelligentsia. Anti-Congressism as a political phenomenon was, of course, to be distinguished from opposition to Congress, which was based on differences in ideology policies or programme. On the other hand, anti-Congressism represented 'a weariness with Congress and a hankering after almost anything else'.[89] The high priest of anti-Congressism was Rammanohar Lohia who, in the words of Rajni Kothari, devoted himself to the mission of destroying the Congress monopoly of power by uniting all anti-Congress forces in the country.[90] The anti-Congress intellectuals and the Socialists were willing to back any party from CPM to BKD to Jana Sangh in order to weaken Congress. The new change heralded the era of the greater importance of rich and middle peasants in Indian politics, their hegemony over the rural social, economic and political scene, and their dislike of Congress and Communists which persisted even later.

Many analysts viewed these elections as the consolidation of anti-Congressism in Indian politics but, in fact, this was not so. Congress was still not only the largest party in the country with a majority in the Parliament but also the only nation-wide party with a nation-wide organisation and following. In addition, there was no cohesive opposition, and the opposition parties had failed to keep power in the states where Congress had become a minority. The primary strategic objective of every party is to gain as much support as possible in the various arenas - electoral arena, Parliamentary arena and internal arena – and the three types of support relevant for all arenas are: opinion support, resource support and vote support.[91] A participant's behaviour in one coalition has a direct bearing on that participant's future influence and future access to new coalitions. But throughout this rise and fall of many state governments, the central government remained stable despite the small majority enjoyed by the ruling party, it however, changed the balance of power inside Congress.

References

1. Subhash C. Kashyap, 'President – Prime Minister Relationship, Dr. Rajendra Prasad's Presidential Years', *South Asia Politics*, Vol. 7, No. 5, September 2008 (New Delhi : 2008), pp. 3-4.

2. *Ibid.*, pp. 5-8.

3. Dipankar Gupta, 'Flagging India's Missing Freedom', *The Hindu*, 29 September 2012.

4. *President K.R. Narayanan's farewell speech* at the function hosted by the speaker of the Lok Sabha in the Central Hall of Parliament on 22 July 2002.
5. *Ibid.*
6. *Encyclopaedia Britannica – A New Survey of Universal Knowledge*, Vol. 19 (Chicago : Encyclopaedia Britannica, 1768), p. 201.
7. *Ibid.*, pp. 201-2.
8. As quoted in P.P. Rao, 'Working the Constitution', *South Asia Politics.*, Vol. 9, No. 6, October 2010 (New Delhi : 2010), p. 5.
9. Arvind N. Das, 'India Invented – Ostrich Approaches to National Unity', *The Hindustan Times*, 19 September 1991.
10. *Ibid.*
11. Somnath Chatterjee, 'Parliamentary Democracy and Some Challenges', *The Hindu*, 15 November 2007.
12. Harish Khare, 'At 60, the Political Culture Needs Renewal', *Ibid.*, 16 August 2007.
13. V.R. Krishna Iyer, 'Needed, a Renewed Socialist Concern', *Ibid.*, 5 February 2008.
14. Geeta Chaturvedi, 'Democracy in Global India', *The Indian Journal of Political Science*, Vol. LXIX, No. 4, October-December 2008 (Meerut : 2008), p. 843.
15. Vilfredo Pareto and G. Mosca, *The Rise and Fall of Elite* (Newyork : 1968) as quoted in Ibid.
16. J.A. Schumpeter, *Capitalism, Socialism and Democracy* (Newyork : Harper and Row, 1952).
17. Reena Nand, 'The Dynamics of Indian Political System', *IJPS*, Vol. LXXI, No. 2, April-June 2010 (Meerut :2010), pp. 413-14.
18. Jag Pal Singh, 'Divisive Versus Inclusive Democracy', *South Asia Politics*, Vol. 7, No. 3, July 2008 (New Delhi : 2008), p. 17.
19. *Ibid.*
20. Dr. Rajkumar Singh, 'State of Indian Democracy', *Third Concept*, Vol. 16, No. 189, November 2002 (New Delhi : 2002), p. 26.
21. Gopalkrishna Gandhi, 'Three Cheers to Parliament', *The Hindu*, 17 April 2012.
22. Inder Malhotra, 'The Changing Face of Parliament', *The Times of India*, 17 April 1980.
23. As quoted in Dr. Rajkumar Singh, 'State of Indian Democracy', p. 27.
24. Greene, Joseph N., 'Goal of Democracy', in Sardar Patel Institute of

Administration (ed.), *Administration and Politics in Modern Democracies* (Allahabad : 1976), p. 19.

25. G. Palanithurai, 'Indian Democracy – A Rethinking', *South Asia Politics*, Vol. 6, No. 5, September 2007 (New Delhi : 2007), pp. 22-23.

26. *Ibid.*

27. N.A. Palkhivala, *We the People : India the Largest Democracy* (Bombay : 1984), pp. 41-44 and 198.

28. M.V. Pylee, *India's Constitution* (Bombay : Asia Publishing House, 1962), p. 90.

29. V. Biju Kumar, 'Postcolonial State : An Overview', *IJPS* Vol. LXVI, No. 4, October-December 2005 (Meerut) pp. 935.

30. *Ibid.,* p. 936.

31. A.R. Desai, *India's Path of Development : A Marxist Approach* (Bombay : Popular Prakashan, 1984), p. 76.

32. C.P. Bhambhri, *The Indian State : Fifty Years* (New Delhi : Shipra, 1997), p. 36.

33. Leonard Tivery, 'State, Nations and Economies', in *The Nation State: The formation of Modern Politics* (Oxford : Martin Robertson,1981), p. 66.

34. Jean Blondel, *The Organisation of Government : A Comparative Analysis of Government Structure* (London : Sage Publications, 1982), p. 24.

35. J.W. Bjorkman, 'Changing State/Society Relations : Broad Brush Approaches and Analytic Models', *Administrative Change*, Vol. XXVIII No. 2 and Vol. XXIX, No. 1, January-December 2001 (Jaipur, 2001), p. 1.

36. Harold J. Laski, *A Grammar of Politics* (New Delhi : S. Chand & Com. 1979).

37. Ramesh Kumar, 'Political Parties in India and the United States : A Comparative Analysis, *IJPS* Vol. LXX, No.4, October – December 2009 (Meerut : 2009), pp. 1227-28.

38. Kushal Pal, 'Dynamics of Party System and Formation of Coalition Government in India, *IJPS*, Vol. LXIX, No. 2, April-June 2008 (Meerut : 2008), p. 329.

39. Atul Kohli (ed.), *India's Democracy : An Analysis of Changing State-Society Relationship* (Hyderabad : Orient Longman, 1991), pp. 63-64.

40. Harish Khare, 'At 60, the Political Culture Needs Renewal'.

41. Piloo Mody, 'We Have No Parties – Only Leaders', '*The Times of India*', 17 August 1980.

42. K. Santhanam, 'Political Parties in India', *The White Star*, Vol. 6 (Bombay : 1969) as quoted in Dr. Subhash C. Kashyap (ed.), *Union State Relations in*

India (New Delhi : The Institute of Constitutional and Parliamentary Studies, 1983), p. 58.

43. Pratap Chandra Swain, 'Dynamics of the Indian Party System : The Emergence of Competitive Multi Party Coalitions', *IJPS* Vol. LXIX, No. 1, January-March 2008 (Meerut : 2008), pp. 62-63.

44. Atul Kohli (ed.), *India's Democracy : An Analysis of Changing State – Society relationship*, p. 64.

45. Rajni Kothari, 'The Congress System in India', in *Party System and Election Studies* (New Delhi : Allied Publishers, 1967), as quoted in Pratap Chandra Swain, 'Dynamics of the Indian Party System : The Emergence of Competitive Multi Party Coalitions', p. 61.

46. *Ibid.*

47. Harold J. Laski, *A Grammar of Politics*, p. 813.

48. *Ibid.*

49. W.H. Morris Jones, *The Government and Politics in India* (London : 1964), p. 165.

50. Horst Hartmann, *Political Parties in India* (Meerut : Meenakshi Prakashan, 1971), p. 38.

51. V.K.R.V. Rao, *The Current Indian Crisis-Darkness Before Dawn* (Allahabad: Vohra Publishers, 1984), pp. 15-16.

52. V.K.N. Menon, *India Since Independence – From the Preamble to the Present* (New Delhi : S. Chand & Co., 1970), p. 40.

53. Rajkumar Singh, *Contemporary India with Controversial Neighbours* (New Delhi : Gyan Publishing House, 2011), p. 42.

54. Somnath Chatterjee, 'Parliamentary Democracy and Some Challenges'.

55. Harish Khare, 'At 60, the Political Culture Needs Renewal'.

56. J. Bandopadhyaya, *The Congress and Democratic Socialism* (New Delhi: 1968), as quoted in Horst Hartmann, *Political Parties in India*, p. 57.

57. George Rosen, 'Democracy and Economic Change in India' (Bombay : 1966), *The Statesman* (New Delhi), 29 January 1963.

58. Vera Micheles Dean, *New Patterns of Democracy in India* (Delhi : Motilal Banarsidass, 1961), pp. 141-42.

59. Lucian W. Pye, 'Party System and National Development in Asia', in Joseph La alombara and Myron Weiner (eds.), *Political Parties and Political Development* (Princeton : 1966), p. 384.

60. Inder Malhotra, 'The Changing Face of Parliament'.

61. *Ibid.*

62. Jawaharlal Nehru, *India's Independence and Social Revolution* (New Delhi : Vikas Publishing House, 1984), pp. 134-35.

63. S.C. Kashyap, *The Politics of Defection* (New Delhi : National Publishing House, 1969), p. 1.

64. Dr. Rajkumar Singh, *India and Pakistan-Social, Political and Military Perspectives* (New Delhi : Regal Publications, 2009), pp. 35-36.

65. *Ibid.,* pp. 62-63.

66. Dr. R. Balasubramanian, 'Indian Polity in Transition', Presidential Address, *53 Annual Conference of Indian Political Science Association,* 27-29th December 2006 (Jaipur : University of Rajasthan, 2006), p. 6.

67. Howard L. Erdman, *The Swatantra Party and Indian Conservatism* (Cambridge: 1967), as quoted in Horst Hartmann, *Political Parties in India,* p. 22.

68. Andre Beteille, *Castes: Old and New-Essays in Social Structure and Social Stratification* (Bombay : 1969), p. 200.

69. *The Newyork Tribune,* 25 June 1853.

70. Vera Micheles Dean, *New Patterns of Democracy in India,* p. 157.

71. A.S. Abraham, 'Decade of Turbulence: System Under Growing Stress', *The Times of India,* 21 December 1979.

72. V.K.R.V.Rao, *The Current Indian Crisis-Darkness before Dawn,* p. 20.

73. Vera Micheles Dean, *New Patterns of Democracy in India,* p. 105.

74. Geeta Chaturvedi, 'Democracy in Global India' p. 849.

75. Indian Institute of Public Opinion, *Quarterly Economic Report,* October 1966.

76. *The Statesman* (Delhi), 28 July 1966.

77. Girilal Jain, 'Language of Indian Politics-Borrowed Idiom Giving Way', *The Times of India,* 2 April 1980.

78. Dr. Rajkumar Singh, *India and Pakistan-Social, Political and Military Perspectives,* p. 37.

79. Girilal Jain, 'Effects of Politicisation-Need to Strength Institutions', *The Times of India,* 1 December 1980.

80. As quoted in Dr. Rajkumar Singh, 'State of Indian Democracy', p. 29.

81. Bipin Chandra, Mridula Mukherjee and Aditya Mukherjee, *India After Independence 1947-2000,* p. 225.

82. See *Election Manifesto of the Indian National Congress,* 1967.

83. M.V. Pylee, *India's Constitution,* pp. 401-402.

84. Bipin Chandra, Mridula Mukherjee and Aditya Mukherjee, *India After Independence 1947-2000*, p. 221.

85. Pratap Chandra Swain, 'Dynamics of Indian Party System: The Emergence of Competitive Coalitions', p. 63.

86. *The Statesman*, 25 June 1966.

87. Dr. R. Balasubramanian,' Indian Polity in Transition', pp. 7-8.

88. V.K.N. Menon, *India Since Independence-From the Preamble to the Present*, pp. 42-43.

89. W.H. Morris-Jones, *Politics Mainly Indian* (Madras : 1978), p. xii.

90. Rajni Kothari, *Politics in India* (New Delhi: 1986), p. 183.

91. Hanne Marthe Narud, Electoral Competition and Coalition Bargaining in Multiparty System', *Journal of Theoretical Politics*, 8(4), (1966), pp. 501-503.

3 Post-1967 Indian Republic with Present Status

3.1 Political Trends in Post – 1967

After the elections of 1967 the parties which had competed with each other in the opposition changed the mutual relationship and cooperated, though in a limited way, in forming coalition government. In the evolution of the post-Congress dominant Party system, political contradictions were minimised and attempts were made to reconcile different views. Even in coalition, there exists an ideal as Hermens has put it, 'rests on true political party, proportitional influence of the partners and common responsibility'.[1] In India, this ideal has been achieved partly because of the drawbacks of political heterogeneity prevalent in the country. It appeared that a unique dynamic movement based on anti-Congressism pushed the coalition partners ahead, for the time being, to form governments in different states. Very soon the coalition governments suffered from the same disruptive weaknesses which were true of the Congress rule. However, it heralded a change in the party and Government system. The immobilism in the political power-structure was broken up and in many States the opposition could realise its aim to come to power.[2] The realisation of a change in the power-constellation had a healthy impact on the public, as frustration and loss of faith in democracy found a legitimate outlet in the change of Government. In the situation when the one party dominant system has broken up the way of constitutional life changes considerably. The continuing and prevailing norms of political behaviour began to be challenged while new norms have to be evolved.

The decline of Indian National Congress considerably started with the death of Nehru in 1964. It was the beginning of the erosion of popular support for the party which continued in successive years. It was increasingly ridden with groupism and factional rivalries at every level, leading to the formation of dissident groups in almost every state. After the death of Shastri, Indira Gandhi took over the leadership of the Government without direct personal legitimation and she hoped that a convincing victory of the Congress in the elections would prepare the necessary ground for a plebiscitary consensus in her favour. On becoming the Prime Minister, initially she had not been able to form a cabinet of her own choice, having had to leave all important portfolios-Home, Defence, Finance, External Affairs and Food-undisturbed. Kamaraj, the Party President and the Syndicate consistently tried to reassert the party organisation's position vis-à-vis the Prime Minister and to restrict her freedom of action in framing and implementing policies. Indira Gandhi had to tolerate all this because of 1967 being an election year. But in order to attain her objective of retaining power as well as reasserting her authority within the Congress Party, Indira Gandhi used Machiavellian strategy and tactics. However, for both- Kamaraj and Indira Gandhi the result of 1967 election was a not so good experience. Kamaraj lost his State (Tamil Nadu) to the Dravida Munnetra Kazhagam (DMK) and suffered himself a humiliating defeat. With that he lost the legitimacy of claiming the Prime Ministership. On the other Indira Gandhi also lost prestige because of unfavourable election result for the Congress Party though she herself was elected with a convincing majority. But she could not prove herself to be an 'election locomotive,' as the Congress leadership expected of her.

In the larger interest of the Party a compromise formula was put forward by Kamaraj and was accepted by all including Indira Gandhi and Morarji Desai. Accordingly, Desai was inducted into the cabinet of Mrs. Gandhi as Deputy Prime Minister and Finance Minister. But the solution was short lived as they both – Mrs. Gandhi and Desai differed fundamentally in their character and approach. They both had always been ideological opponents. The leftist tendencies of Mrs. Gandhi were as well known as the conservative ideas of Desai. In between the deepening organisational crisis Mrs. Gandhi took several pro-left steps that strengthened her position in the party. She suddenly came out with the proposal of bank nationalisation and finally succeeded in carrying through her resolution at Bangalore Session and Morarji Desai also supported it. But finally on the issue of Presidential candidate and consent of Mrs. Gandhi in favour of a non-Congress candidate, V.V. Giri, the split in the party became imminent. The Congress got split up in 1969 into Congress (Ruling) led by Indira Gandhi and the Congress (Organisation) led by Kamaraj. This result was in reality a result of the power struggle for power within Congress between the parliamentary or ministerial wing headed by Indira Gandhi and the organisation wing led by then Congress President, Kamaraj. However, Indira Gandhi gave it an ideological cover by abolishing privy purses and by nationalising bank. Consequently, the party system got polarised into the so-callled progressive and reactionary forces.[3] The crucial point was made clear in the 'Unity

Resolution' where it was declared that the Prime Minister and the Congress President were not centres of power. The Prime Minister is the leader of the legislative party and the Congress President has no right to control her actions.[4] In this way the power game was dressed up in ideological terms. It was conceived as a fight between young socialism and old conservatism.

As a result of the split that took place in the Indian National Congress the Party which had so far enjoyed an absolute majority at the Centre for the first time since independence, lost that position in both the Houses of Parliament. The Congress Parliamentary Party of President, S. Nijalingappa group elected Morarji Desai as its Chairman and Dr. Ram Subhag Singh, former Minister of Railways, and S.N. Mishra as the leaders of the Party in the Lok Sabha and the Rajya Sabha respectively. The new group claimed a strength of 111 members in both the Houses of Parliament-65 in the Lok Sabha and 46 in the Rajya Sabha –who were later allotted regular seats on the opposition benches.[5] But as a result of Mrs. Gandhi's steps soon the Congress under her became what the undivided Congress was before the Bangalore session of AICC. The old brand of Congressism had shown remarkable resistance in reasserting itself and in this connection election of V.V. Giri as the President of India, was her first victory. Her pessimism soon gave way to hope and confidence when she nationalised the major Indian banks, abolished the princes' privileges and launched a radical–sounding if essentially populist, personist style "garibi hatao" programme. Further she continued her remarkable offensive, she called a mid-term poll in March 1971 and won it resoundingly, the ship of state which had been rocking on a sea of crises in the preceding six or seven years, seemed once more to have been put on an even keel.[6] The sense of returning security was reinforced a hundred fold at the end of 1971 with the Bangladesh war when India, politically dominant and militarily triumphant, emerged as the undisputed subcontinental power.

On the eve of 1971 election, apart from political groupings and power struggle among political party, economic priorities continued to remain on the top of agenda. In her announcement of the dissolution of the Lok Sabha, Mrs. Gandhi underlined the necessity to seek a fresh mandate from the people so that the Government could go ahead with its proclaimed social and economic programme. For that purpose it was understandable that all the national political parties brought economic issues to the fore. They revealed some very significant shifts in emphasis. The split and the subsequent development influenced the party line on the management of the public sector, the procedure of licensing and simplification of the tax structure. To quote Congress (R) manifesto, 'Where licensing is needed, it will be simplified, its regulations widely advertised and prompt decision assured. All licensing will be for promoting industrialisation and not for hampering growth'.[7] By 1971 a clear shift in both the social basis of Indian politics and its party and governmental apparatus began to take place. This shift was also due to the food crisis of 1965-67 which resulted in a series of other steps in the revision of other strategy. The Government of India's steps included a new irrigation policy with emphasis on minor irrigation, a concentration of inputs-improved seeds and fertilisers on highyielding areas as the principal way out of stagnation, a comprehensive soil survey, a reassessment of plan priorities and a re-allocation of scarce resources including foreign exchange. This meant that the people at large started reviewing the economic and administrative performance of the party in power in terms of how it affected their day-to-day life and related this to their own electoral decision-making.[8] As a result the popular demand then was for performance. The people wanted a government that works and an economic system that delivers in terms of production. The talk of social justice in the sense of distributive justice, as earlier defined has taken a back seat. In plain terms the country was ready to move forward on a realistic basis. In addition the emancipation of women, especially among the urban middle classes, the growing assertion of their rights by the scheduled castes and tribes, the increasing secularisation of thought and life and the declined of the joint family are some other important manifestations of this remorseless process. The result is the strangely contradictory situation which has arisen in India-the decline of democratic institutions amidst the growing democratisation of our society.

The election results of 1971 Lok Sabha showed that the Congress (R) secured 58 per cent of seats. It swept the polls, winning 352 of the 518 seats. The February election turned out to be an overwhelming personal triumph for Indira Gandhi and a rude shock to the Opposition. This gave the party a two-thirds majority required to amend the Constitution. The "grand alliance" of the Swatantra, the Jana Sangh, Congress (O) and the PSP performed very poorly in the parliamentary elections while most of the regional parties such as Bharatiya Kranti Dal in UP, the Bengal Congress in West Bengal, Shiv Sena in Maharashtra, the Akali Dal in Punjab and the Utkal Congress in Orissa were substantially weakened by the polls. The only opposition to fare well were CPM, CPI and DMK, the last two being the Congress allies. The fifth Lok Sabha was considered as the reminiscent of the Nehru era with packed treasury benches and a mere sprinkling of opposition members though Mrs. Gandhi had fallen short of performance of her father who won 74.4 per cent of all seats in 1952, 75.1 per cent in

1957 and 73.1 per cent in 1962. Likewise in the State Assembly elections of 1972 Mrs. Gandhi-led alliance returned with a landslide victory. This happened as coalition government based on anti-Congressism had failed to deliver. The charisma of Indira Gandhi revived the Congress. The dominance of Congress was conspicuous as it was voted to power in all the states in which the elections were held. This success story of Congress in the elections was the impact of war politics that resulted in the formation of Bangladesh, a separate nation. But Indira Gandhi's main political achievement was that she checked the mood of despair, frustration, and cynicism that had prevailed since 1962 and initiated a climate of hope and optimism. As a result of her radical and egalitarian programme and slogans, Mrs. Gandhi's popularity grew further; and she replenished the Congress party's social support base, especially among the rural and urban poor and to some extent, among the middle classes.[9] Her steps went a long way in projecting Indira Gandhi as a dynamic leader. It led to refurbishment of the image of the new Congress and emergence of Indira Gandhi as the saviour of the poor.

The 1971 elections restored the Congress party to its dominant position in Indian politics. By voting for Congress the people had simultaneously voted for change and stability. Now it was for the Congress (R) government to come to the expectations of the electorate. If the new government failed to be as effective as the Nehru-led Congress, its popularity would be a short-lived. But that would a failure of leadership and not of Parliamentary democracy as such. Indira Gandhi received the mandate she had sought and she now became the unchallenged leader of Congress and the dominant political figure in the country. The elections also represented further politicisation of the masses. People's votes had cut across religious, caste and regional barriers. Elections had also shown that once national issues were raised, vote banks and politics of patronage became relatively irrelevant and that increasingly people could longer be dictated to, bullied or bought. Indira Gandhi had demonstrated that building a coalition of the poor and the disadvantaged around a national programme could be a viable political option. In the circumstances, the faith of the voters, especially the poor, had reposed in her also represented a dangerous signal. She had raised high hopes among them; and she had now to deliver on her promises, for she had the parliamentary strength to pass any laws, to take any administrative measures, and there could be no excuses for failure.[10] For the next few years there was no substitute for performance. She must create the impression of a decisive forward movement, and she must produce results.

The succeeding years of Mrs. Gandhi's regime were meant to fulfil its electoral promises. There was political stability in the country; the government had a two thirds majority in the Lok Sabha; and Indians had acquired fresh and heightened self-confidence in their own capacities and capabilities as well as faith in the political leadership. In fact during 1971-74 the government undertook several measures to implement its left-of-agenda. In August 1972, general insurance was nationalised and five months later the coal industry in 1973. Ceilings were imposed on urban land ownership. Earlier in 1969 the Monopoly and Restrictive Trade Practices (MRTP) Act was passed to check the concentration of industrial enterprises in a few hands and in 1971 it appointed a MRTP Commission to implement the Act. The central government initiated a programme of cheap foodgrains distribution to the economically vulnerable sections of society and a crash scheme for creating employment in rural areas. It also made it compulsory for nationalised banks to open branches in underbanked areas such as small towns, rural clusters and the poorer parts of the cities and to make credit available to small industries, farmers, road transporters and self employed persons.[11] But despite all these and others, under the pressure of the CPI and leftists within the party Mrs. Gandhi refused to go any further in nationalising industry and she remained fully committed to a mixed economy.

However, with the Parliamentary elections, Mrs. Gandhi was able to assert her authority, encompassing many features of the pre-1967 era. A major difference in the new model was the collapse of the competitive mechanism within the dominant Party. The Congress split and the emergence of Indira Gandhi's leadership destroyed the balance of internal factional competition. Factional bosses were suppressed and crushed. Such a combination of the monopolistic dominance of the Congress led to steady erosion of the openness of the system and there emerged an authoritarian concentration of power.[12] In India it was the beginning of the politics of populism, opportunism and of naked power. The dominant party ruled through the mechanism of centralised command. Even the tendency to impose leadership on the states seemed to grow and in the process intra-party democracy was weakened. At a later stage, the social ills that posed a direct threat to the political system of the country were rated high, resulting in the worsening of the quality of political management. Indisputably the standards of public life have declined sharply. And it would be dishonest for anyone to think that standards had fallen only in public life. The same story began to be repeated in almost all other walks of life.

But soon in 1973 the tide changed for Indira Gandhi and it came sooner than expected. The economy, the polity and the credibility of her leadership and Congress government started going downhill. After the 1971 election victory, a series of further such measures increasing government control and intervention were introduced with the active support of left radical intellectuals like P.N. Haksar, D.P. Dhar and Mohan Kumaramangalam. As a result, the disenchantment followed rapidly. In 1972 came another drought and the underlying economic crisis, which had first manifested itself in the mid-sixties, resurfaced after the euphoria of the three preceding years. In May 1973 the UP provincial constabulary mutinied and had to be suppressed ruthlessly. It sent a shock-wave down the entire system for this was a major revolt by those whose duty it was to enforce law and order to keep the system itself going. In addition, the external factors-the five-fold oil price rise by OPEC countries at the end of 1973 and the energy crisis it precipitated was for the Indian economy the last straw on the camel's back.[13] By then the system was in deep crisis. Industry was in recession, the level of investment had fallen, successive droughts had lowered agricultural productivity, traders had begun to cash in on, even as they helped to worsen, shortages and the consequent black market in a wide range of commodities from steel and cement to edible oil and foodgrains. Hardpressed by this array of hostile economic forces, large sections of the population stepped up their demands on the system at the very moment when it was least able to meet.[14] The ideological short-sightedness of the Congress government on the economic front on the one hand and rise in corruption on the other led to great resentment against the Congress regime throughout the country.

In the situation the dominance of the Congress party began to decline by 1974 on account of the failure of the Congress government at the centre and in most of the states due to its failure in fulfilling the rising expectations of the masses. The party system adopted in India is described as multi-party system with one dominant party. The causes for the multiplicity are many and interesting. In this hybrid growth, one dominant factor has been the personal ambition of some leader. Such a person, when he feels that his avenues are blocked, he thinks of leaving the party and forming a new one or joining other and he tries his level best to cover his action with some ideological justification. On the other the changing bases of our political society has become a major concern of our polity. In India, the idea of the State as a protector of the rich as well as a liberator of the poor has survived for long. The State in India is a compromise between the two, without giving principle an exclusion dominance over the other. But in reality the divide between the poor and the rich has remained deep. Almost like the distinction between the electoral promise and political performance of our parties.

In the meantime, the Indian society has also been on rise and several international developments took place in decades, fifties and sixties. The political recognition of Indian middle class had begun in the seventies after the evaporation of political slogans-'garibi hatao'. The increasing pace of urbanisation especially of the cities and metropolitan centres, with slums, housing, transport, civil maintenance, and proletariat problems combined with the steady drift of the rural skilled and the rural poor to the urban areas is adding to the duality of Indian society. Further the increasing extension of duality in Indian society is conducive to discontent and discord and cannot promote the needed harmony. Thus the country was not happy with the inflation accompanying economic development, which had brought misery to the poor and the fixed income groups and increased inequality in income and consumption levels.[15] Inflation and black money diminish the people's faith in the efficiency of government and have reinforced the atmosphere of discontent, distress and anger in the country.

It was in this context that Jaya Prakash Narayan launched his movement for "Sampoorn Kranti" in 1974. Earlier in January 1974 a major upheaval occurred in Gujrat when popular anger over the rise in the prices of foodgrains, cooking oil and other essential commodities exploded in the cities and towns of the state in the form of student movement which was soon joined by the opposition parties. As a solution the central government was forced to ask the state government to resign, suspend the assembly and impose President's rule in the state, however, it proved a failure and due to continuing unrest and fast unto death by Morarji Desai, Mrs. Gandhi dissolved the assembly and announced fresh elections to it in June. On being inspired by its success, the similar agitation was started by students in Bihar and in line they commenced an agitation with the gherao of state assembly on 18 March, 1974. Jaya Prakash Narayan also decided to go beyond Bihar and organise a country-wide movement against widespread corruption and for the removal of Congress and Indira Gandhi who became a threat to democracy and portrayed as the fountain head of corruption. Although the movement against the Congress and Mrs. Gandhi began to decline by the end of 1974, the month June of 1975 proved fatal for the Congress, Mrs. Gandhi in particular.

A sudden twist to Indian politics was given by a judgement of Allahabad High Court on 12 June, 1975 which against an election petition by Raj Narain, convicted Mrs. Gandhi for having indulged in corrupt campaign practices and declared her election invalid. Against the judgement Mrs. Gandhi refused to resign and appealed to the Supeme Court. Justice V.R. Krishna Iyer, the vacation judge of the Supreme Court created further confusion when he decided on 24 June that, till the final disposal of her appeal by the full bench of the Supreme Court, Mrs. Gandhi could stay in office and speak in Parliament but could not vote in it. Both the Congress Party and Mrs. Gandhi suffered another political blow when the Gujrat assembly election results came on 13 June, 1975. The opposition Janata Front won 87 seats and the Congress 75 seats in a house of 182. The Janata Front succeeded in forming a government in alliance with Chimanbhai Patel. In the circumstances, without any wait Jaya Prakash Narayan and the coalition of opposition parties, decided to seize the opportunity and, accusing Mrs. Gandhi of clinging to an office corruptly gained. In a rally in Delhi on June 25, 1975 they announced that a nation-wide one-week campaign of mass mobilisation and civil disobedience to force Mrs. Gandhi to resign would be initiated on 29 June. Ultimately, she found herself placed in a situation where imposition of emergency was the only way to keep things under control. But what prompted Jaya Prakash Narayan to oppose Congress and Mrs. Gandhi was the naked tyranny of her rule. With a massive majority in Parliament, the Congress government acquired unprecedented power which it utilised for self-aggrandisement. It now had a halo which gave it a touch of permanence. It went about destroying merrily all democratic traditions, norms and values. Jaya Prakash clearly saw that a major surgical operation was urgently needed.[16] With his selfless devotion to the cause of the consolidation of independence, JP thought that, though a sick, old man with one foot in the grave, he could still save India from further disgrace and humiliation. His democratic conscience deeply hurt, he could not remain a passive spectator any longer.[17] Austerity is too well ingrained in Indian character not to seek political expression at some stage. But there were no obvious candidates for that role right now.

Mrs. Indira Gandhi, the then Prime Minister of India, retaliated by imposing internal emergency on 26 June, 1975, under Article 352 of the Constitution. She explained the situation later and claimed that faced with an extra-constitutional challenge she had no other option. Resignation, she said, would have strengthened the forces that were threatening the democratic process and bringing the country to the edge of anarchy and chaos. There was, moreover, no legal, political or moral reason why she should step down during the hearing of her appeal. But as indicated by several scholars and analysts, in reality she too had another democratic option. She could have declared that Lok Sabha would be dissolved and fresh elections to it would be held in October-November. Even simultaneously she could announce that the Emergency would be lifted as soon as the opposition gave up its demand for her resignation, agreed to adhere to the Supreme Court or

Parliament's judgement, and accepted the test of elections, exactly what General de Gaulle did when faced with the much more pervasive and radical upsurge of student and workers in May 1968 and the protestors accepted the challenge to face de Gaulle in elections. The political tragedy was that both the JP Movement and Indira Gandhi shunned the option of elections, and created a political atmosphere in which dialogue and accommodation between the two opposing forces was not possible. The declaration of emergency followed a major shake up in the government machine, as well as in the political atmosphere of the nation. In the early hours of 26 June, hundreds of the main leaders of the Opposition were arrested under the Maintenance of Internal Security Act (MISA). Among those arrested were Jaya prakash Narayan, Morarji Desai and Atal Bihari Vajpayee and Congress dissidents such as Chandra Shekhar. In addition several academics, newspapermen, trade unionists and student leaders were put behind bars. Nearly 200,000 political detainees who were in jail without trial remained there during the Emergency. The government had grown arrogant treating people as ignorant mass with the only duty and right to obey.

In a calculated move during the emergency the Parliament was made utterly ineffective. The state governments were rigidly controlled. The two non-Congress government of DMK in Tamil Nadu and Janata in Gujrat were dismissed in January and March 1976 despite being quite compliant. A series of decrees, laws and constitutional amendments reduced the powers of the judiciary to check the functioning of the executive. The Defence of India Act (DIA) and the MISA were amended in July 1975 to the detriment of the citizens' liberties. In November 1976, an effort was made to change the basic civil libertarian structure of the Constitution through its 42nd Amendment. The period of Emergency concentrated unlimited state and party power in the hands of the Prime Minister to be exercised through a small coterie of politicians and bureaucrats around her. The worst part of the emergency was the creation and promotion of a caucus which controlled not only the Party organisation but also the government. The caucus was described as an extra-constitutional centre of power. It was criticised for giving 'orders' to the government servants and directions to the governmental machineries both in the Centre and in the States. A sharp attack was also made on the role of Sanjay Gandhi who was being projected as a national leader and became in the phase a de facto ruler. In other words a few people took advantage of the emergency to destroy what little of democracy we had in the Congress.

The Emergency which Mrs. Gandhi imposed in the name of internal security was largely in response to a desperate coalition of dominant groups she represented to and a deep rooted, all pervasive structural crisis. The pre-emergency assumption was that it would give full and free play to demands by diverse groups for the fulfilment of their new found expectations.[18] Mrs. Gandhi obviously was alive to the dangers inherent in rapid politicisation. During the emergency she shout to devise a system which could insulate the executive from popular pressures via the press and appeared favouring a French – type Presidential system with the same end in view. But India's case was different and you cannot contain a flood by closing the gates. You have to let the waters pass. You can do so safely if you have had the wisdom to raise and strengthen the embankment in advance. Our embankments have got weakened and eroded with the rise in the intensity of the floods. Simply put, Mrs. Gandhi was to do all that she could to restore the prestige and autonomy of institutions like the judiciary and the civil service if she was to ensure that the pressure politicisation inevitably generates would not overwhelm the system and, indeed the country.[19] In contrast during the emergency social contention was artificially held in abeyance, aspirant groups were inhibited about voicing their claims and social conflict was sought to resolve not by accommodation through the free play of argument but with the iron hand. Not surprisingly, this approach brought rapidly diminishing returns in terms of discipline; 'order' and 'stability' though the experiment in constitutional dictatorship was short-lived.

On the other was the positive side or public response to the Emergency. The people, except intelligentsia, initially responded to the situation with passivity, acquiescence, acceptance or even, support. Apart from the arrest of opposition leaders, the repressive measures were almost entirely directed either against anti-social elements or against the extreme communal right or the miniscule far left who had enjoyed little popular support before the Emergency and who were in any case known to be averse to democracy. With the restoration of public order and discipline, many felt relieved that the country had been saved from disorder and chaos. There was less crime in the cities, gheraos and uncontrolled, often violent, demonstrations came to an end. Inder Malhotra, a perceptive journalist of the time wrote later, 'The return of normal and orderly life, after relentless disruption by strikes, protest marches, sit-ins and clashes with the police, was applauded by most people. In its initial months at least, the Emergency restored to India a kind of calm it had not known for years.[20] In addition, there was an immediate and general improvement in administration, with government servants coming to office on time and being more considerable to the public, quick, dramatic and well-publicised action was taken against smugglers, hoarders, blackmarketeers, illegal traders in foreign currency and tax evaders, with several thousand of them put behind bars under the MISA. A major factor in the people's acceptance of the Emergency was its constitutional, legal and temporary character. It was proclaimed under Article 352 of the Constitution. It was approved by parliament and legitimised by the courts.

However, throughout the Emergency Mrs. Gandhi asserted that she was fully committed to multi-party democracy and a free press, that the Emergency was an abnormal remedy for an abnormal situation, and that democratic conditions would be restored and elections held as soon as the situation returned to normal. But from mid-1976 popular discontent increased as relief to the people did not last long and economic growth of the first year of the Emergency was not sustained. Mrs. Gandhi and Congress failed to create any new agencies of social change or organs for popular mobilisation. For common people there were no avenues of protest or any other mechanism for the voicing and redressal of their grievances. Simultaneously the drastic press censorship and the silencing of protest led to the government being kept in complete ignorance of what was happening in the country. Further the denial of civil liberties began to be felt by the common people it began to impact their daily lives in the form of harassment and corruption by petty officials. Delay in lifting the Emergency began to generate the fear that the authoritarian structure of the rule might be made permanent or continue for a long time. The already exiting climate of fear and repression, corruption and abuse of authority was further worsened by the excesses committed under Sanjay Gandhi's direction. Suddenly on 18 January, 1977 Mrs. Gandhi announced that elections to Lok Sabha would be held in March. She also released political prisoners, removed press censorship and other restrictions on political activity such as holding public meetings. Political parties were allowed to campaign freely.

3.2 Political Experiences after Emergency

The sudden announcement of elections came as a surprise both to the Congress and the opposition parties. Earlier in 1974 a new process of consolidation of opposition forces by merger was evolved. The Bharatiya Lok Dal (BLD) was formed by merger of seven political parties and in this process the constituent units lost their identity in the BLD. Its chairman Charan Singh, invited the Congress (O) and the Jana Sangh to join, but these two could not choose to lose their existence. They were, however, willing to cooperate with the BLD and also to join a federal type of organisation where they could maintain their identity. But in the period of emergency which was imposed on 26 June, 1975, the ruling party treated alike all the non-CPI opposition and made no discrimination between a secular, religious, leftist or rightist parties. Such an action of the government proved a blessing and now they considered only one aspect, and that was whether they could challenge the Congress leadership at the polls in or at any other front. At the time the opposition parties of India also realised that the Congress was in power with a minority of popular votes, but because of division of opposition votes. Their detention during emergency provided them enough time for introspection – to review the political situation, forces which helped Congress to power, and to realise the friends and foes. The new situation arising out of emergency and excessive use of political powers combined had bound them understanding each other and of sorting out their differences, and chalking out a common programme.

The declaration of Parliamentary elections followed the release of leaders and workers of different political parties which created a situation congenial to the flowering of democratic institutions in a healthy atmosphere. Immediately after their release, the opposition leaders of four major non-communist parties – the Congress(O), the Jana Sangh, the Bharatiya Lok Dal and the Socialist Party announced their merger to form a new party at the instance of Jaya Prakash Narayan for giving a united fight to the Congress. Meanwhile the Congress was dealt a blow by the sudden defection from it on 2 February, 1977 of Jagjivan Ram, a noted scheduled castes leader along with H. N. Bahuguna and Nandini Satpathy who not only formed the Congress for Democracy (CFD) but joined hands with the newly formed Janata Party which also entered into alliance with some regional parties - the DMK, Akali Dal and CPM. The Congress leaders widely criticised the Janata Party as 'hotch potch' and its unity a façade. In the circumstances Jaya Prakash Narayan, the chief mentor of the time, explain the whole under which the party was formed. 'It is not born out of expediency but out of realisation of a political necessity. The opposition parties have realised that if the country has to be saved for democracy they must come together not merely as an alliance but as one single party.'[21] He also said on the occasion that the party was commited to Gandhian principles in evolving its socio-economic programme. After the merger of constituent units and formation of a front, the Janata Party decided to contest elections on a common programme and a common symbol. The opposition front made the Emergency and its excesses, especially forced sterlisations and the restrictions of civil liberties, the major issues of its election campaign.

The 1977 Parliamentary election resulted in the victory of the Janata Party and defeat of the Congress due to a strong anti-Congress wave. The people treated the elections as a referendum on the Emergency. With the popular upsurge in favour of them, the Janata Party and its allies became victorious with 330 out of 542 seats. Congress trailed far behind with only

154 seats, with CPI as its ally getting 7 and AIADMK 21 seats. The election results were variously described – "second liberation", "ballot revolution", "popular upsurge", "elections without parallel". For most observers it was the beginning of a new process of political consolidation. In fact, it was that excesses during the family planning drive and stories of harassment and coercion, particularly affecting the Muslims, the Harijans and the backward classes, and exaggerated figures of casualties in police firings. All alienated a large section of the Muslims and the Harijans from the Congress Party and that this was a decisive factor in its defeat.[22] In the elections the Congress Party had secured 34.54 per cent of the votes against 43.17 per cent of the Janata Party. A drop of 8.52 per cent from the 1971 poll had cost the Congress party as many as 197 seats.[23] In nutshell, the Congress defeat can be accounted to the 18-months of authoritarian rule, forced sterlization, resettlement, beautification of cities and the bulldozing programmes. These were in addition to the rampant corruption in the administration, nepotism, and operation fund collection by the party workers. Consequently, the Janata Party had not got positive support for its programmes; but it had got only negative support as an alternative to the Congress. In it, the people had shown their capacity to discipline an arrogant government; however, it turned out to be a referendum on certain aspects of the emergency and not an election on clear-cut socio-economic programmes. It was a case of personalised politics in which there is a strange relationship between an individual and the organisation. Firstly it is the party organisation which imposes a leader from above; he does not emerge from the grass roots. This leader later receives hero's treatment and develops arrogance. He creates a halo of sycophants and also a clique. Then after, he is not guided by the organisation but controls it.[24] In such a system an individual has the capacity to do immense harm to the party.

The post-emergency phase of Indian politics was marked by the assumption of power by the Janata Party by dislodging the Congress from the Centre consequent upon the sixth general election of 1977. The national politics underwent a fundamental change when a coalition government headed by Morarji Desai was formed on 24 March, 1977. The Janata Party emerged as an alternative to the Congress and led to speculations about the prospect of political polarisation in the country. It appeared that a two-party system had ultimately emerged in India because the Janata Party asserted as the ruling party and the Congress was the major opposition party. But the political support to the Janata regime soon began to decline and disillusionment with it set in, given its non-performance in administration, implementing developmental policies, and realising the social justice. It lost the political momentum by the end of 1977 and the uneasy coalition that was Janata Party began to disintegrate. The new regime was not able to deal with the rapidly growing social tensions in rural areas, of which the increasing extent of atrocities on the rural poor and the Scheduled Castes was one manifestation.[25] Janata Party's social base in North India consisted primarily of rich and middle peasants belonging mostly to intermediate castes and large landowners belonging to upper castes and the urban and rural shopkeepers, small businessmen and the petty bourgeoisie. The rural landowners felt that with the Janata governments at the Centre and the states, they had now unalloyed power in the country as a whole and in rural areas in particular. On the other hand, the rural poor, mostly landless labourers and belonging largely to the Scheduled Castes, too had become conscious of their rights and felt emboldened by the prolonged functioning of democracy and adult franchise.[26] In economic sphere the Janata regime explicitly repudiated the Nehruvian vision of rapid economic development but it also failed to evolve any alternative strategy or model of economic and political development to deal with the problems of economic underdevelopment.

The Janata experiment failed on two counts: Firstly, it adopted the manipulative politics of Congress Party by dismissing its governments in states, although it had declared in its manifesto that since there had been a high degree of centralistion, it would pursue the decentralisation of economic and political powers.[27] Secondly, the intra party rivalry and high political ambition of its leaders had already started by the end of 1977 but by 1978-79 the government was completely paralysed by the constant bickering and infighting in the party at the Centre and in the states. Each political component tried to occupy as much political and administrative space as possible. It remained a coalition of different parties and groups and was a victim of factionalism, manipulation and personal ambitions of its leaders. The different constituents were too disparate historically, ideologically and programmatically; bound only by an anti-Indira Gandhi sentiment and the desire for power.[28] Janata Party's character as a ruling party was quite different and it was more a contingent formation than result of a genuine political realignment representing a coalition of social interests.[29] Its awfully conglomerate character deprived it of a reasonably unified leadership and outlook. Infighting in the party at the state level had an adverse effect on its national leadership. Though the Party emerged as a result of a broad consensus among many parties and leaders, it failed to contain the conflicts, which jeopardised the moving and delicate equilibrium of consensus.

In fact the Janata Party was not a party in the true sense of the word but a hurriedly formed coalition of political parties having conflicting ideologies and clashing constituencies.[30] The political ambitions of all the leaders of various fractions – Morarji Desai of Congress(O), Charan Singh of BLD, Jagjivan Ram of CFD and Chandra Shekhar of the Socialist faction had resulted in a consistent and brazen stuggle for office. In addition, the party's task was greatly complicated by the personality factor. The Party had Morarji Desai as its Prime Minister who was temperamentally incapable of presiding over what was essentially an alliance. Not that he was intellectually and morally inferior to the front-rank politicians in the Congress or in terms of political experience and administrative ability he was second to anyone. His obstinacy, his one-track mind and his well-known fads singled him out as man and a colleague difficult to get along with. He had cultivated a doubtful virtue of never bending even when the alternative was breaking. This may be most precious, most sterling quality of a saint or a moral preceptor, but in a politician it was the most deadly trait. Whatever be the political, administrative system, compromises are the staple of politics.[31] The formation of the Janata Party could have been a net gain for the nation if the leadership, in fact, had the courage to take the merger decision of its constituents to its logical conclusion. It's two other most important figures – Charan Singh and Jagjivan Ram were hardly on speaking terms. They perhaps believed that the clash between them was an expression of the most fundamental conflict in the countryside, the conflict between the landed intermediate caste and the landless labour.

The factional struggle in the Janata government and the Party took an acute form in the middle of 1979. Earlier Charan Singh, the Home Minister, had been forced to resign from the cabinet on 30 June, 1978, and was then, brought back as Finance Minister in January 1979. This ultimately led to a split in the party and the formation of Janata Party (Secular) by BLD leader Charan Singh and the fall of Morarji Desai - led Janata Party government. In July 1979, the Janata Party had to leave the Government at the Centre. Morarji Desai's government resigned on 15 July and a week later Charan Singh formed the government but unfortunately he never got to face the parliament as, on 20 August, a day before the confidence vote, Indira Gandhi withdrew her support. On Charan Singh's advice, the President dissolved the Lok Sabha and announced mid-term elections to be held in January 1980. For the first time in India, a two party-system seemed to gain salience and it was in existence from 1977 to 1979 when only two parties—the Janata and the Congress accounted for over 80 per cent of votes and seats. Had this trend continued, the two-party system would have prevailed in India. But the developments of 1979 put a curb on it. The emergence of two-party system was merely an outcome of specific circumstances and a matter of mutual convenience.[32] The first coalition government at the Centre could not continue more than 28 months due to a tug-of-war among the different leaders of the Janata Party and the country was left to have fresh mandate. Clearly the formation of coalition government became a game of selfish, opportunist power hungry and unscrupulous politicians who had to look after nothing but their personal interests. This scenario gave rise to the notion that Parliamentary government and coalition arrangement could not go hand in hand.[33] Especially when Mrs. Gandhi staged a come-back the widely created impression was that coalition government can not work at the apex of the political and administrative arrangements. It can work only in the States under the aegis of the Union Government constituted by a single party and led by a powerful and charismatic leader.

The election results of the seventh Lok Sabha held in January 1980 showed that the people of India had repudiated the charges of authoritarianism, arbitrariness, abuse of power and personal corruption against Mrs. Indira Gandhi. The fall of Janata government paved the way for an astonishing victory for the Congress and after having been out of office for thirty four months, Indira Gandhi was once again the Prime Minister and Congress was restored to its old position as the dominant party. The elections of January 1980 were fought primarily between Congress (I), Congress (U), Lok Dal, the new party floated by Charan Singh and Socialists, and Janata Party. The Janata Party's main appeal during campaigning consisted of warnings against the threat to democracy and civil liberties while Indira Gandhi concentrated on Janata's non-governance, asked the people to vote for 'a government that works'. The people cutting across caste, religion and region gave a massive mandate to Congress (I), which secured 353 out of 529 seats. Lok Dal became victorious with 41, Janata with 31 and Congress (U) with 13 lagged far behind. By electing Mrs. Gandhi and her nominees in overwhelming majority the people of India had given themselves another chance to continue the task of building a viable nation-state. Once again the country gave office to a leader who was firmly in command of her party and whose appeal cut across all the great divides in the Indian community-religious, social, linguistic and regional. On the other the Janata Party had betrayed the trust of the people by its failure to hold together and to address itself to the urgent problems of the country. In the absence of a strong leader and a well-defined ideology the desire to keep Mrs. Gandhi out of office was not strong enough to keep them united. In voting Mrs. Gandhi to power the electorate had responded to her promise of stability, security and efficient administration. At the same time it had also punished Janata Party for its failure on a number of fronts including the economy and law and order.

The 1980 Parliamentary elections helped the Congress (I) led by Indira Gandhi in restoring one-party dominance on account of her promise to give a government that works and due to the disenchantment of the voters with the political instability created by the leaders of the Janata Party. Moreover, the projection of Mrs. Gandhi as being a champion of the minorities and the weaker sections also enabled her party to regain its lost support base.[34] However, on having assumed office she adopted the same old style-placing total reliance on small coterie, extensive use of media for personality projection and deferring of organisational elections in the party. After her coming she got the Janata governments in nine states and dismissed them through Article 356. Though Congress came to power in some of the states yet in Andhra Pradesh, Tamil Nadu, Jammu and Kashmir, Karnataka and West Bengal non-Congress governments were formed. The government in these states were basically regional party governments. They started clamouring for less intervention by the Centre and more participation by the states in the policy formation of the country. In this context Indira Gandhi appointed the first ever constitutional review commission on Centre-State relations in 1983 headed by Justice R.S Sarkaria of Supreme Court of India. At organisational level, like earlier, her major weakness was the continuing organisational weakness of Congress and her failure to rebuild it and strengthen its structure. This inevitability affected the performance of the government and its popularity, for a weak party structure meant the choking of channels through which popular feelings could be conveyed to the leadership and the nature and rationale of government policies explained to the people. Apart from this the second innings of Indira Gandhi also faced certain intractable problems arising out of communal, linguistic and caste conflicts; none of these was dealt with firmness and insight and all of them were to drag on for years.

In the circumstances the most unfortunate for Indian polity was the continuing split and extreme differences among political parties at national and state level. Earlier after the Lok Sabha elections of 1980 the Janata Party witnessed further division. This breakup was not on the basis of programme, principles or ideology but on account of personal conflicts. Charan Singh and Rajnarain broke up into Janata Party (Secular-Charan) and Janata Party (Secular-Rajnarain). The original Janata Party under the Presidentship of Chandrashekhar had to full back upon the name of the founder Jayaprakash Narayan, to keep itself going and became Janata Party (J.P.). In another split the old Jana Sangh leaders left it to form the Bharatiya Jana'a Party (BJP) at the end of 1980 and Atal Bihari Vajpayee became its chairman. Jagjivan Ram also joined Congress (U). Political parties, which are the kingpins of a democratic political structure, have gradually become the weakest link in India's political system. Political parties and party system have been decaying and suffer from several maladies. Among these are : inter and intra-party instability; intense fighting and factionalism within parties; weak and inefficient organisation in many of them, resulting in their fragmentation; the continuous proliferation of parties, leading to the formation of unstable coalitions; continuous shifting of loyalties of political leaders and workers from one party to another; lack of democracy and debate within most parties, failure to mobilise and provide support to developmental, welfare and social justice policies. In India political parties cannot easily build a strong and viable opposition, however, skilful, principled and determined they may be. Indian society is inherently incapable of sustaining the Westminster model of Parliamentary democracy if this implies the existence of two parties of nearly equal strength so that the one in opposition can easily take over the task of running the government if the ruling party fails to deliver the goods and forfeits popular support. It is a highly disturbing conclusion for all those who believe that Parliamentary democracy is best suited to meet India's needs.

After the assassination of Mrs. Indira Gandhi on 31 October, 1984 her eldest son Rajiv Gandhi became the new Prime Minister of India the same day. Even during her tenure from 1980-84 she pursued the politics of confrontation instead of consensus that aggravated the crisis in Punjab and Assam. Besides, deviation from the path of socialism led to the alienation of weaker sections and non-adherence to secularism began to alienate the minorities. Her mishandling of the demand of a separate Sikh state was accompanied by her refusal to understand the socio-political changes occurring across the country and manifesting themselves mainly in the form of regional assertion.[35] The brutal death of Mrs. Gandhi followed the Eighth General Election held from 24-27 December, 1984 and the Congress won by its largest ever majority. Including the polls held later in Punjab and Assam, the party garnered 415 out 543 Lok Sabha seats, The projection of the clean image of her successor, Rajiv Gandhi, by the media on the one hand, and the subtle use of Hindu card[36] by the Congress (I), on the other, enabled this party to receive a massive mandate in the 1984 Parliamentary elections. The sympathy wave caused by the assassination of Indira Gandhi was also a vital factor in his victory. It gave the Congress a three-fourth majority in the Lok Sabha and an assurance to millions of people that a stable government ensuring peace and effective governance elusive for a period of time, had returned. On the other the election held in the aftermath of Mrs. Gandhi's assassination, reinforced the one party dominance of Congress (I) under Rajiv Gandhi's leadership and virtually put the national opposition to political disarray and wilderness. There was only one important issue in the elections, namely, the unity and integrity of India. The euphoria generated by Rajiv's massive mandate subsided a number of scandals against the central government, the failure to solve the Punjab problem and the government's nonperformance on the social-economic fronts.

The political process in the period of Rajiv Gandhi was marked by a "crude combination of technologism for the elite and communalism for the masses. He set up a 'technology missions' to apply science and technology to six areas of underdevelopment in which a scientific approach would be useful in solving problems. But some parties like the BJP found in communal politics a new lease of life for themselves. Increasingly, Mullas, Sadhus and Jathedars assumed political roles that ought to have been played by the Party leaders. Rajiv Gandhi had earned considerable goodwill by initiating peace processes of political disputes through negotiations. He adopted the style of consensus and signed accords for ending militancy in Punjab and Assam. Although he was successful in Assam, he failed in Punjab owing to several reasons. In addition, it was Rajiv Gandhi and his government that took the initiative to deepen and strengthen Panchayati institutions by generating debates and bringing forward legislation to make Punchayati elections mandatory by giving them a constitutional sanction. He declared his intention at the centenary celebrations of the Congress in December 1985 to restore inner Party democracy and to free it from the power brokers.[37] He used the occasion to launch a frontal attack on what he described as the power-brokers who had reduced the great party to a shell of its former self, and promised to rejuvenate it by removing their strongehold. This was read as a signal to the old leaders to get their act together or else. Many partymen who were otherwise sympathetic to Rajiv's policies did not appreciate his disrespectful style. Rajiv Gandhi too was no more successful at holding elections within the Party and soon found that he needed to build links with Party Stalwarts and politics was different from running an efficient corporation. The elections of 1989 were held in an environment charged with emotion variously by the anti-corruption campaign in which Rajiv Gandhi was the main target. He had not only to face the charges of corruption in the purchase of Bofors Gun but the vocal opposition of V.P. Singh-led faction that contributed significantly to the end of the dominance of the Congress (I) in 1989 Parliamentary elections.

3.3 Configuration of Coalition Politics in India

With the election results of the Ninth General Election held in November 1989, once again, the phase of coalition politics commenced in India. The coalition era has definitely had its share in contributing to the deepening and strengthening of Indian democracy. The Indian experiences in 1977,

1989 and thereafter till date have suggested that it is not the cultural homogeneity which is a requisite for political stability and integration, the chances of stable democracy are enhanced to the extent that the group has a number of cross-cutting, politically relevant affiliations.[38] It simply meant that the larger the number of groups identities are included / involved in the democratic political process of a country, smaller are the chances of any one inter-group conflict to spill over from its limited orbit. This would considerably reduce the chances of it causing any grave concerns for the stability and survival of the political system. A coalition situation can be regarded as "the joint use of resources to determine the outcome of a mixed-motive situation involving more than two units.[39] It involves: (i) application of power (in the sense of joint use of resources to determine outcomes'); (ii) a 'mixed motive situation' means the existence of both conflict and cooperation; and (iii) this is a collective activity (which involves interaction of more than two units). In Indian context it can be safely argued that coalition politics has come to settle at the Indian federal level and that it cannot be viewed as a sudden and unexpected development but on a deeper analysis, it is reflective of a societal metamorphosis: wherein day by day larger number of hitherto latent groups of Indian society are getting mobilised and politicised. Most of scholars have termed it as a 'crisis of governability'; but it is a crisis of governability for those who have almost owned the state power as an inherited right. What is under challenge is the status-quoist and hence unequal and unjust division of rewards and benefits.[40] The coalitional model of politics offers a broadening of this realm of active politics where democracy is not only present but alive and kicking. Coalition politics at the federal level in India has also led to the regionalisation and decentralisation of power.

In the election of 1989 the Congress (I) had failed to retain majority but V.P. Singh - led National Front government was formed with the outside support from the Left Front on the one hand and the BJP on the other. Earlier in April 1987 V.P. Singh, the defence minister in Rajiv Gandhi's cabinet resigned from the government and started a single-minded crusade against corruption which had touched a sensitive chord. Apart from choosing an emotive issue he also fashioned a consummate political strategy for isolating Rajiv and Congress. Gradually, V.P. Singh courted and won the support of a wide range of forces, which included Sarvodaya workers, trade unionists, the farmers' movement and some sections of radical anti-Congress intellectuals. On 2 October, 1987 V.P. Singh along with other Congress dissidents-Arif Mohammad Khan, Arun Nehru, Ram Dhan, V.C. Shukla, Satpal Malik, formed the Jan Morcha or People's Front. He placated the left parties by calling them his natural allies and issuing statements against communalism, but made sure he had the BJP on his side by speaking from their platform and maintaining close links with Vajpayee and Advani. The strategy for opposition unity was conceived as a three-stage process. The first stage was the unity of centrist non-Congress secular national parties, second the formation of a National Front of all non-left secular parties, regional and national, and the third the seat adjustments with left parties and BJP. The National Front of seven parties being formed on 6 August, 1988. On 11 October,1988, the birthday of Jayaprakash Narayan, Janata Dal was formed with the merger of the Jan Morcha, Congress (S), Janata and Lok Dal.[41] However, in the whole process more than V.P. Singh's strategy it was the inherent anti-Congressism of the left and BJP that brought them to support V.P. Singh. The broad alliance formed in 1989 was definitely one of the factors responsible for the rise of BJP in coming years.[42]

However, the results of November 1989 elections to the Lok Sabha was a rejection of Rajiv Gandhi and his Congress, but no clear verdict in favour of any other leader or his party or the five parties' National Front. It was a blow to Congress even if it was still the single largest party with 197 seats and 39.5 per cent vote share. The National Front had won 146 seats and after declaring that Congress was not interested in trying to form a government, the second non-Congress government was supported by the BJP with 86 and left parties with 52 seats. The party which won such a massive mandate barely five years ago frittered away people's faith and confidence and the election held in 1989 threw up a hung parliament. Thus the year 1989 witnessed the formation of second non-Congress government at the Centre but it was not merely the change of government. It was, in fact, a culmination of the struggle waged by a section of India's political elite against what it perceived to be the force of authoritarianism which, under their dispensation had allegedly destroyed democratic institutions and severely undermined democratic rights of the people.[43] Internationally, it was the year of the triumph of the forces which had continued their campaign against what they perceived as anti-democratic, corrupt and oppressive regime of the Congress (I), coincided with the euphoric upsurge of democratic forces in the socialist world. There was Glasnost and Perestroika through which ideological distortions and socio-political and economic bureaucratisation of society and polity are sought to be put to an end to.[44] Amid these national and international developments a minority government of National Front took the reigns of administration on 1 December, 1989.

However, the beginnings were not smooth with Chandra Shekhar totally opposed to V.P. Singh as Prime Minister, and Devi Lal was to be made deputy prime minister. With elections over, all the differences caused by closing ambitions, oversized egos, ideological preferences, came to the fore and it was with some difficulty that the new prime minister took the oath of office. Though V.P. Singh started out with a high-profile ambitions, the main reason for the inability of the government to get its act together was the enormous amount of time and energy spent on trying to resolve internal differences. In addition a major of instability was inherent in the situation as the two supporting parties had crucial roles without the responsibility of running the administration. National Front government was not only an internal coalition within the National Front, but also and more importantly, an external alliance made between the National Front, the Left Front and the BJP. The one dominant Party system that generally characterised the Indian political scene for nearly three decades came under severe strain. But even this phenomenon did not pave the way for the clear emergence of the two party system.[45] The delicate triangular balance upon which the viability of the National Front government rested was finally upset by the BJP when it pressed its viewpoints on Ramjanmabhoomi Babri Masjid controversy beyond the tolerance limits of the National Front and the Left Front.

India in fortunate is the sense that its ethnic divides – linguistic, religious and caste - do not reinforce one another as they do in Sri Lanka, Malaysia, Israel and Sudan. But the salience of divides particularly of religion is present in our society. It is capable of creating fissures not only between the majority and minority religions but also within the majority. The divides within the Hindu faith, on account of castes and languages, are many. In Western democracies politics is followed by a decline of religious influence in public life, but in a county like India, in which a strong religious culture is dominant democratic politics would show the imprint of popular religious notions. Since our politicians had not direct access to the knowledge of Western Parliamentary styles of governance, they simply translate these unfamiliars to the rural India. All these alterations began to reflect in Indian politics in the form of style, language and modes of behaviour.[46] In post-Mandal phase which was announced by the National Front government the BJP got an opportunity to complete its own agenda. Seeing the strong popular reaction to Mandal BJP had started making noises about withdrawing support. Meanwhile on 25 September, 1990 L.K. Advani embarked on his 6000-mile-long rath yatra from Somnath in Gujrat to Ayodhya. It resulted in Advani's arrest but at the same time aroused communal passions in the country. The developments paved the way for the fall of V.P. Singh's government and a Janata Dal split which took place on 5 November, elected

Chandra Shekhar as their leader who headed a short-lived government with the support of the Congress.

All the major political parties of India had a direct or indirect political agenda which included the themes of cultural democracy. Earlier, the uneven and unjust distribution of the benefits of development had prepared the ground for two types of political dissent- an economic critique of class and an indigenist critique of modernist cultural privilege. And it was the second kind of resentment that has found expression through regionalist and communal politics, through the politics of Hindu, Hiduism and finally Hindutva. Excessive reliance on the state, its increasing less accountable bureaucracy and other factors created a situation in which forces of Hindu majoritarionism can claim the dignity of cultural self-assertion against a dispensation in which individuals are penalised for speaking their mother tongue of evincing interest in their own culture.[47] This cultural indigenism is a likely consequence of democracy, and the unwillingness of liberal and left politics in India to allow expression to these impulses has enabled Hindu communal and Hindi chauvinist politicians to appropriate the considerable power of such cultural democracy. The Bharatiya Janata Party is first to take advantage of the situation prevailing at that time. In the seventies when communal propaganda seemed to bring a few dividends and the destiny of the then Jana Sangh seemed irreversibly on the decline, some elements inside the party suggested that the party should subtly shift its appeal to the middle class. They also advised that instead of the traditional appeal to Hindu Chauvinism, it should try to project itself as a substitute for the Congress offering a cleaner, more efficient, less corrupt government.[48] The Indian National Congress too under the leadership of Indira Gandhi began to adopt a more Hindu-oriented strategy beginning 1982. The party got its biggest victory in 1984 general elections in the background of killing Mrs. Gandhi by her Sikh guards as it followed a communally surcharged atmosphere. From then on the Party had sought support of the Hindu communal in a manner it had not done earlier. Encountering implacable opposition from an array of regional forces the political centre gave Hindu majoritarian communalism its head.[49] In 1986 the Congress under its policy of appeasement allowed to open the doors of Babri Masjid and the Hindu shrine for worship which were kept locked since 22 December, 1949. It created the setting for a sustained mobilisation of the Hindus that led to the Shilanyas for a new temple in November 1989.

In fact, the Bharatiya Janata Party from seventies onwards sincerely executed its two-pronged policy. Especially after the dramatic success of the Rathyatras its own agenda was rewritten in a retrograde direction but it also adhered to its more secular constituency. From advertising tactics it continued to appeal to the constituency of modernist groups but on the other it persisted with its blatantly communal propaganda aimed at the more traditional Hindu groups. It, now within the context of democratic politics, seeks to turn numerical majority into political majoritarianism, thereby subverting democracy itself. While democracy is based on the majority-minority dichotomy, it is also given strength by the existence of pluralism. A person may think in one context that he belongs to a majority community but he may also be part of a minority in terms of caste, region, language or political persuasion. It is this which moderates majority rule within democracy.[50] The danger of Hindutva as the defining principle of Indian nationhood is that it seeks to create and perpetuate a permanent majority, one based on an artificial and homogenised Hinduism. On the other the apprehensions and reservations about democracy have also increased with the implementation of the Mandal Commission recommendations and the demolition of Babri Masjid in 1992 preceded by an intense communal chauvinist campaign proved landmarks in Indian political and social life.

For the last two decades, the Indian state had been facing momentous challenges. It went through a process of rapid centralisation of power ever since Indira Gandhi effected a split in the Congress Party in 1969 and met all such challenges increasingly with sharp authoritarian measures. It set in motion a process of realignment of sentiments and preferences, and the general outlook among the articulate sections of society the elite in its entirety, barring the critical intelligentsia in academia and the political activists. It paved the way for rapid and popular reversal of moods. Gradually, the electoral process and the outcomes of elections, as well as the structuring of political responses between them were breached. The same people who voted the governments in with huge mandates soon turned against their own government, and the Indian state was under constant popular assault.[51] The Janata government which followed the defeat of the Emergency regime and which restored democracy faced the same situation of popular agitation. The same was the case in 1980 and 1984. This was an important indicator of the unresponsive nature of the ruling class vis-à-vis the problems of the people and the lack of adequate accountability of the government of the day. These swings came to an end after the 1989 elections which ushered in the era of coalition or minority governments. This is inferred as the phase of politics devalued the leaders, political parties and certain institutions which lost their autonomy and were converted into mere instruments of powers - a condition imposed during Emergency.[52] It is therefore understandable that people have lost faith in them. People experienced government by the Congress and rebuffed it, the replacements led by Janata Party or Janata

Dal tried to rule with good intentions but could not sustain themselves for long.

The contemporary revival of Hinduism and implementation of Mandal Commission's recommendation cast a deep impact on the social equations that exist in Indian society. The disturbances in social equations do not just indicate the sharp changes in the relations between the upper castes, and the OBCs and Dalits. It also affected the equations of power and domination, which kept people subservient, were subject to drastic upheaval in the Indo-Gangetic belt; and in varied degrees in the rest of the country. Especially after 1977 with the formation of first non-Congress government, the Jana Sangh acquired a certain degree of respectability among the varied sections of society, having functioned as part of a larger platform fighting for democratic restoration. But in the wake of the anti-Mandal agitations and its aggressive campaign for the Ram Mandir, its position improved significantly. While the BJP remained an upper caste party drawing overwhelming support in the areas where its presence was strong before the anti-Mandal agitation, its support steadily increases in every caste. The increase is related to the income level of the various strata within these caste groups.[53] The 1990s have witnessed the phenomenal growth of the BJP. The figures cutting across had shown that the preference for the BJP is not limited to the upper castes. The relatively well-off sections among the oppressed castes have also expressed the preference for the BJP. These are the sections that are mobile, and aspire to success and privilege. They perceive in the BJP, the political force which is best positioned to further and protect their interests. Such a bloc has emerged in Indian society and politics for the first time since independence.

It was in this socio-political milieu that the general elections to the tenth Lok Sabha were held in May-June 1991 and the Congress (I) emerged as the single largest party getting 245 seats and formed the government under the premiership of P.V. Narasimha Rao. Again like 1984 the Congress (I) got sympathy vote to emerge as the single largest party as Rajiv Gandhi, the ex-Prime Minister and star campaigner of the party was assassinated after the first round of voting by a LTTE human bomb in Sriperumbudur, forty kilometers from Madras. On the other the failure of two successive coalition governments at the centre indirectly benefited BJP to emerge as an alternative to Congress. The splintered constituents of the National Front and the Left Front lagged far behind the Congress (I) and the BJP. As a matter of fact, a two-party plus multi-party system had come to the fore in these elections. In this election while the left parties maintained their position, the Janata Dal under V.P. Singh suffered a decline with around 55 seats but significantly, the BJP emerged with flying colours as the second largest party with 119 seats. It provided a stable and effective opposition to the party in power at the centre. At the juncture what bedeviled the opposition's efforts for unity was the want of a credible long-term strategy with clear cut policies and programmes. A patchwork of parties fighting their common political foe and one another cannot hope to make considerable headway. Distribution of opposition votes among several parties naturally gave Congress a clear advantage in getting seats. Although P.V. Narasimha Rao after forming the government was able to manipulate majority by engineering splits and purchasing supports, he could not revive the dominance of the Party. Instead, he weakened it further by his failure to prevent the demolition of Babri Masjid on 6 December, 1992. The backward classes and scheduled castes, which had drifted away from the Congress before these elections, too, could not be won over by him. In addition, the large number of scandals during his regime caused the alienation of a segment of the middle class. All these cleared the desks for the rise of the right wing political pragmatism of BJP and alliance in next coming elections.

Further between 1996 and 1999 the general elections for the 11th 12th and 13th Lok Sabha were held which marked a significant departure from the earlier trends of Indian politics and society. The 1996 elections brought back the situation that prevailed in 1977 and 1989. Between 1996 and 1998 three coalition governments were formed and one of them lasted only for thirteen days. The support promised by the Congress form outside to governments formed by Deve Gowda and I.K Gujral fell when the Congress pulled the carpet from under their feet.[54] The 1996 parliamentary elections witnessed the strengthening of the multi-party system. The electoral battle of 1996 occurred mostly among three politico-electoral formations: one was the Congress (I) and its Tamil Nadu ally All India Anna Dravida Munnetra Kazhagam (AIADMK) along with certain minor allies in a few states like Kerala. The second was the Bharatiya Janata Party, its ally Shiv Sena (SS) along with the emerged Samata Party and the Haryana Vikas Party (HVP). The third force was the United Front a combination of National Front, Left Front, Samajwadi Party (SP) and few other regional parties like Tamil Maanila Congress (TMC) etc.[55] Even at general level the changes were most visible in the distribution of votes between the national and regional parties. In 1971 the percentage of vote for the national parties was 78; even in 1967, which saw the first regional assertion, the vote for the national parties was quite high at 76 per cent. It had then steadily risen to 85 per cent for the national parties in 1980; and erratically moved between 78 and 81 per cent between 1984 and 1991. Interestingly there has been a sharp decline in the proportion of votes for the national parties, by 12 per cent in 1996, the percentage was down to 69. The crucial difference, unlike earlier, was that most of the manifold assertions of the regional identities have now become part of the very definition of the 'national'. The antagonism between the national and the regional, in a stroke, seemed to have evaporated. Even the nature of the government formed at the Centre, after the 1996 elections, could be defined as co-governance of the nation and the various regions. This was distinct from a conventional coalition. Political parties have talked of 'cooperative federalism', but what we are witnessing is a co-federal government'. The coalitions since 1996 are a manifestation of this phenomenon. This is the fusion of the nation and the regions, named as and expressed through political parties.

In the general elections of 1996 again no party got the absolute majority but the BJP emerged as the single largest party and the Congress (I) had been relegated to the second position. As a result a coalition government led by Atal Bihari Vajpayee was formed in the centre in which BJP was a major partner. Some regional parties like the Akali Dal and Shiv Sena but this government could not prove its majority in Lok Sabha as the post-elections coalition remained narrow and most of the regional parties decided to stay away from it. After its fall, in less than a fortnight, a United Front (UF) coalition government came to power under the leadership of H.D. Deve Gowda which included Janata Dal, CPI and some regional parties with Congress support. On 30 March, 1997 the Congress withdrew its support but having failed to form the government again supported a United Front government with I.K. Gujral as prime minister. The withdrawal of support by the Congress paved the way for general elections to the 12th Lok Sabha in February 1998 which led to the formation of BJP-led government with Atal Bihari Vajpayee as prime minister. The BJP got only 182 seats but managed to secure the support of secular parties like Telegu Desam Party (TDP), AIADMK and Trinamul Congress (TC), but a little later unfortunately Jayalalitha withdrew her AIADMK support from alliance leading to the government losing the vote of confidence in April 1999. The BJP government continued as a caretaker and a fresh elections to the 13th Lok Sabha was held in September and October 1999. Earlier again before the 1998 Parliamentary election a two-party plus multi-party system emerged. The BJP and the Congress (I) retained their position as the largest and the second largest parties but due to AIADMK's decision to withdraw support it lost majority in the Lok Sabha and had to quit. The BJP-led alliance under the leadership of Atal Bihari Vajpayee was able to secure a clear majority in the 13th Lok Sabha which was the third mid-term poll within a period of four years.

By the time the general elections in the year 1999 held many political analysts conceded that regional parties have become more important than the national parties in these elections because both the formation and survival depended on the support of the regional parties. Such type of political developments allowed chaos to prevail at the centre[56] and political observers considered coalition not a luxury but a necessity for India. It also proved the political opportunism, irresponsible behaviour and greed for power of the heterogeneous opposition parties on the one hand and the failure of the ruling alliance to effectively manage the floor as well as govern the nation on the other. But this time the BJP restored to socio-political engineering and alliance with 23 smaller/regional political parties of diversified character. It was a pre-electoral alliance led by BJP which crossed the magic number to form the government. The BJP-led National Democratic Alliance (NDA) captured 299 seats sharing 40.48 per cent of the popular votes. The NDA government proved to be more stable and successfully completed its term. A coalition of parties, factions and groups had formed the government and every constituent unit was bent upon drawing optimum political mileage by threatening to withdraw support but there was a national agenda, no doubt, which was followed more in breach than in observance. In the circumstances, there was no cohesiveness, not the faintest shadow of it, and each one was pulling in the designed to keep it in power and the coalition government on tenterhooks. Inspite of the fact that the coalition government remained in doldrums, Vajpayee government took some momentous decisions notably about the second Pokharan tests to make India a nuclear power state.

The continuing coalition phase of Indian politics has been considered by many analysts including Paul Wallace as the period of 'catch all' coalition. As a result of these elections the party system in India has entered an era whose important features are (i) The two political parties, the BJP and the Congress (I) competed for the leadership of the alliances; (ii) The third front lost relevance; (iii) Regional parties assumed great importance; (iv) Parties represent small segments of electorate became a feature of the party system; and (v) Leadership became more important than the institutions.

In the light of these developments in Indian party system the BJP-led coalition government headed by Atal Bihari Vajpayee proved to be a stable national level coalition and almost completed its five year term only because Vajpayee himself was a skilful manager for conflict resolution among the partners and practiced what is known as 'coalition Dharma.[57] In line, the other partners in the coalition were keen to retain power and were able to adjust even with those decisions which appeared to be ideologically opposed to the instance of their parties. In other words, power had become more important for them than the ideologies of their parties. However, a sense of uncertainty prevails and an impression was being extensively created that the government is not only inept, unskilful and largely dysfunctional but being so disparate and widely distanced from each other ideologically and politically that they cannot function as a team and give the country a semblance of good government.

Along with the frequent practice of coalition government in recent decade there is and should be a strong tradition of Common Minimum Programme (CMP) which not only outlines the minimum objectives of a coalition but also reflects the political give and take in such an arrangement. It is for the parties that are part of the arrangement to form the government and not for the entire political system. In India the history of coalition politics can be traced back to the year 1967 but much later George Fernandes, former Defence Minister in the NDA government, in an interview to the Rediff on January 13, 1998, said, 'In 1967, it was after the election that we went in for a common minimum programme. It was known as the Samyuktha Vidhayak Dal programme. In each state the parties concerned sat together and formulated a programme and formed a government. So it is my conviction that, when a party goes to the people, it should go with its programme because each party has an entity. Election is a time when the people are exposed to the various aspects of the policies, programmes and leadership of political parties. So a common minimum programme should emerge only when we reach a point when a coalition government is inevitable'.[58] The last time a single party got an absolute majority in Parliament was in 1984. The governments formed in 1989 and in 1991 were minority ones. From 1996 to 1999 four different prime ministers have led six different governments and all these have been coalition arrangements. All political parties prepare a manifesto before the elections to seek popular support for their respective agenda. In the case of the 11th, 12th, 13th, and even 14th held in 2004, the governments had to design a CMP, as the coalition partners were not able to share a common manifesto before going to the polls.[59] Although the Vajpayee government known as the National Democratic Alliance (NDA) coalition did not have a CMP, the alliance which consisted of some 23 parties, had a common election manifesto known as the Agenda for Development, Good Governance and Peace. The fractured mandates received in coalition carry with them an element of 'checks and balances' required for the sound functioning of any democracy. For this reason, coalition governments often have a common minimum programme of policies to be implemented while in office.

The general election of May 2004 was more or less the same as that of 1996, 1998 and 1999 elections which saw coalition politics and large scale defection in action. It also retained the party system that had emerged in earlier elections,the 'catch all'[60] coalition system or two party dominated multi-party system. Another distinctive feature of party system which has emerged as a result of the 2004 Parliamentary election was the strategic importance of the Leftist Front which had improved its earlier position. But the general election of 2004 saw a new set of power equations which had no clear precedent in our political history. The NDA which had brought the poll date forward fell far short of the required number and for the first time since 1996, the BJP slipped to the second slot in the House of the People. The Congress which secured just 145 seats in comparison to BJP's 138, was able to form the government followed by strong bloc Left, Rashtriya Janata Dal (RJD), Lok Jana Shakti Party (LJSP) and few other regional parties.[61] The election witnessed the battle between two major coalition of the political parties viz. BJP-led NDA and Congress-led United Progressive Alliance (UPA). The Congress-led UPA was pre-election alliance of 19 political parties which became victorious. This alliance secured victory in 220 seats and with the outside support of 63 members of left parties, formed the government with Dr, Manmohan Singh as prime minister of India. In addition, the UPA experiment in coalition politics carried certain new features; (i) Sonia Gandhi is the chairperson of United Progressive Alliance and has more power than Manmohan Singh; (ii) The Left Front has considerable power but no responsibilities as it has not joined the UPA government; and (iii) The UPA has a secular image. Although in later development the left parties with its 63 members withdrew the support to the UPA government on 23rd July, 2008 when serious differences arose on nuclear agreement with the United States of America, yet Dr, Manmohan Singh, playing as a seasoned politician, saved the government with the support of Samajwadi Party (SP) led by Mulayam Singh Yadav and other parties.[62] It again proved that coalition government could survive to its full term in India.

The general elections for the 15th Lok Sabha were held in May, 2009 in which the UPA secured 262, NDA 159, left 24 and others 98 seats. Once again the UPA-led coalition government was formed with Dr, Manmohan Singh as the Prime Minister of India on 22 May. 2009. The results of the election were an indication of the fact that Indian voters are definitely politically matured, it however, exihibited several new features of our party system. The voters appeared to have delivered a decisive verdict, one that heralded a new era in the country's politics. It provided greater stability to the national government and reduced the bargaining and blackmailing capacity of coalition allies vastly. The verdict eliminated the need for a Congress-Left coalition and was widely seen as a paving the way for greater economic liberalisation.[63] However, it showed two basic points. First, for all the excitement following its outcome, the election was a normal one. It was not woven around an emotive issue, it was not centered on a personality, and it was not a plebiscite on any one issue. Secondly, while there was a nationwide pattern in the outcome for the two big parties, the principal area of political contestation was very much located at the State level. The political choice available to the voters, the familiar social equation of who prefers who, and the major issues that determine voter choice were all State-specific.[64] No doubt, national issues played an important role this time, but these issues and factors manifested in different ways in different States. National politics reached the people through the prism of the State. Thus, as long as the States remain the principal arena of politics, State-specific parties will be relevant.

The general election of 16th Lok Sabha is due in 2014. Based on the dynamics of party system and other elements there are four possible outcomes of 2014 elections. (i) Re-election of the UPA under Rahul Gandhi; (ii) Victory of the NDA with the BJP in a strong but not commanding position within the alliance; (iii) Emergence of a Congress-supported centre left 'Third Front' (iv) A BJP-supported centre right 'Fourth Front' led by someone like Nitish Kumar.[65] But the anti-corruption movements of Baba Ramdev and Anna Hazare if overcome the organisational and leadership challenges can offer a possible breakthrough for creating an alternative politics.

In nutshell, the last decades and contemporary politico-electoral developments reveal that the way to power in a pluralist society like India lies in the creation of political, regional and social alliances. The vastness and diversity of the country and the enormity and variegated nature of the problems confronting the country will make it unlikely for the emergence of two well-organised parties even in foreseeable future. The Congress and the BJP are the two political parties which have advanced two contradictory but monolithic definitions of the Indian nationhood. They contend that India has existed as a nation since time immemorial. For the Congress, it is a nation on the model of nations in Western Europe, where, as a pattern, nationality and state are coterminous. The Congress conception is the secular version which emerged after the French Revolution, except for the aspect of immemorial existence. For the BJP India is quintessentially Hindu. For them, a nation is first and foremost the culture of its original continuation, in case of India, it is the Hindu religion. In their notion, the secular is both alien and fake.[66] However, the unity of India is not dependent on any one monolithic conception derived from the secular or the Hindutva models of the nation. Both these in different ways have been rejected by an overwhelming majority of Indians in varied regions of the country. Developments, following the 1996 Parliamentary elections, have drastically altered the nature of relations between the Indian nation and the various linguistic – cultural communities, many of which form the constituent states of India.

In the circumstances, it would not be wrong to say that it is natural for India's plural society to have a multi-party system and coalition government. The term 'coalition' is derived from the Latin word 'coalition' meaning to grow together. In the political system it implies that some political parties or groups will come together and form alliance or temporary union in order to exercise control over political power. In the *Encyclopaedia of Social Sciences* Professor A. Ogg defines coalition as a 'co-operative arrangement under which distinct political parties or at all events members of such parties unite to form a government or Ministry.[67] The formation of coalition government takes place as a sequal to the inability of a single party to command a majority in the legislature. A combination of some political groups or parties is essential to command the majority. These political parties or groups join together to form a government. They do not lose their separate identity. They agree to a common minimum political, economic and social programme and when differences arise, any group or party is free to withdraw from the coalition. The first UPA government of Dr. Manmohan Singh, after long negotiations released Common Minimum Programme (CMP) which spelt out the broad agenda agreed upon between the coalition partners.

In India the coalition system of government is the outcome of the failure of the Parliamentary system to satisfy the norms of getting absolute majority of seats in the Lower House to form the government. It is an alliance between two or more hitherto separate or even hostile groups or parties formed in order to carry on the government and share the principal affairs of the state. A coalition government is formed when more than one political party or group comes together on the basis of common understanding or agenda.[68] The immense social plurality in India will, obviously reflect itself in its polity. It is only natural that under these conditions various parties may garner the confidence of sections of this vast social diversity and thus no single party may acquire the requisite majority to form its own government.[69] But such fractured mandates carry with them an important element of 'checks and balances' required for the sound functioning of any democracy. For this reason, coalition governments of today should have a common minimum programme of policies to be implemented while in office.

Coalition governments all over Western Europe have worked very successfully because of broad-based consensus and the underlying willingness to function together for good governance. But in India's case the scenario is drastically different and there is no early prospect of durable and effective unity at the national level. The BJP has little or nothing in common with the other political parties, Right, Left or Centre. For good or ill the party is looked upon a fundamentalist organisation wedded to Hindu revivalist policy or Hindutva. In it the question of who is an Indian is determined by the person's religious denomination. The worth of human beings should be defined in terms of features, abstract and general, such as dignity, respect and concern. The use of specific criteria like religion, culture or prefixed history can result in inequality and cause serious trouble. For the BJP being a Hindu makes a person more of a human being. Humanness is determined by religious denomination.[70] Even the socio-economic programmes of the BJP are quite different from the programmes of other parties. The communists have been following improvised socio-economic programme designed to suit the circumstances more than to conform to Marxism. Other political parties including the Congress, have no distinct socio-economic programme.[71] As a result 'the process of bipolarisation will remain a far off thing so long as factionalism, rivalry are chronic in the major political parties; bases of political action lie in such irrational factors like caste, community, region, language, creed, personality and charisma; the fight for power is not imbued with some altruistic motive and does not reflect the social and economic urges of the masses.[72] The realignment of political parties remains an uncertain factor in Indian politics.

At present the sole objective of political parties is to stay afloat and capture or share power with other political parties wherever and whenever possible. They are not averse to entering into alliance or electoral understanding, or even shake hands with the devil himself if that gesture can help them capture power. There are casteist outfits, ethnic organisations, and regional parties, each operating within the given parameters and without any qualms of conscience ready to hitch their wagon to the rising star. The Congress, the Communists and Socialists have nothing to do for the time being, with the BJP. Others being not so obstinately opposed to the BJP, would get along with it merrily. In the situation horse trading has become the part of political system. A Prime Minister or Chief Minister heading a coalition government dare not drop a corrupt minister so long as he commands the support of a coalition partner, unless he is prepared to risk the fall of his government. Integrity and ability are no longer the main criteria for appointment of minister. But on the other the contemporary scenario of politics has also contributed to a definite change in the level of political socialisation, interest articulation, interest aggregation and political communication. In every polity there is a period of political stagnation, uncertainty and instability. India is a developing democracy where democratic traditions are evolving with the passage of time. Likewise it will take time for the political parties to mature and come to the level of general expectations.

3.4 Indian Polity and Globalisation

Indian democracy has moved a long way since the country became independent and adopted a republican constitution decades ago. It has created new political arrangements as it has faced new political challenges. It has shown considerable resilience, and in some ways strengthened itself even while setting aside old arrangements and established ways of thought and action. In comparison to the dawn of independence which began with great, in today's circumstances, it is unrealistic to expect that a new leader will soon emerge, a true statesman who will combine in himself all the virtues that we expected in our political leaders at the time when the new republic came into being. The new sovereign, democratic national state that came into existence was multi-class in nature and was open-ended in the sense that the class-balance among the constituent classes could be altered. Among the most significant features of India's political development has been the commitment of its leaders to democracy, national unity and economic development, accompanied by their ability to establish the necessary political institutions, both of the state and civil society, and to root them in Indian society to create and maintain the structure of a democratic state. These institutions have been sustained despite rapid social change, with new social groups regularly entering the political arena and asserting their rights.[73] In the actual working of the system, the central government gradually acquired greater influence over the states because of the pattern of economic development adopted, which was based on planning, public sector, central funding of anti-poverty programmes, and central financial disbursement to the states from its greater tax resources. From the very beginning the Nehru-Mahalanobis strategy of growth with equity had assumed that popular mobilisation from below would be necessary to effectively implement radical measures in favour of the poor initiated by the government. But while persisting poverty has been the most important failure in India's post-independence development, the survival of the democratic structure has been its greatest success. It led to the growing demands on the state by various classes and groups including the poor. To accommodate these demands all political formations, since the late seventies, began to indulge in competitive populism using state resources to distribute largesse to the various constituent classes of the Indian state including the poor.

Apart from this for several decades the political leadership had functioned without any strategic design or perspective ideology or well thought about tactics for managing the political system. It had relied instead on *adhocism* and gimmickry for meeting the challenges in the polity and on populism, personal appeal, and use of big and black money to maintain itself in power. The major culprit for the weakening of the political institutions has been the quality of political leadership. It is the quality of political leadership which plays a critical role in nation building and development of political institutions.[74] Gradually, political parties became the weakest link in India's political system. It has developed its own distinctive party system. It is neither a two-party system nor a multi-party system with three, four or even half-a-dozen parties of the kind commonly found in continental Europe. It is a system with a multiplicity of parties. This multiplicity is a reflection of the size and diversity of our social and political order.[75] At the close of 1980s, India's economy, polity and society were strained by grave structural imbalances and distortions. The problems were challenging and the correctives required were to be complexed and painful.

The concept of globalisation began to dominate the world since nineties and it has added new dimensions to pre-requisite of success of democracy in any country. It challenges the importance of the authority and welfare function of the state, the complex implications of which are far reaching to the developing countries.[76] It is a multidimensional phenomenon comprising numerous complex and interrelated processes that have a dynamism of their own. It involves a deepening and broadening of rapid trans-boundary exchanges due to developments in technology, communications, and media. Such exchanges and interactions occur at all levels of governance and among non-state actors, creating a more interdependent world.[77] Globalisation has also affected domestic politics and thereby the capacity of governments to manage the new forces. Economic liberalisation and integration has led to greater income inequality within countries without strong welfare states as the incomes in increasingly demanded skilled workers rise while those of unskilled labour drop. The change in the nature and role of the state evoked concerns among the people at large. The relative autonomy of the state weakened and the dominant class acquired supremacy over it. The popular perception of the State as an instrument of modernisation and empowerment has also witnessed changes. In the 1990s when the market reforms shrunk the role of the State, the expectations from it did not materialise. Whenever the state found it difficult to accommodate all their demands, the discontended social groups used their identities to larger share from the State resources.[78] The basic philosophy underlying the economic reform was that the state was no longer an active agent for development, but a facilitator for corporate business.

The process of economic reforms started in 1991 when the country was at the edge of default during the premiership of P.V. Narasimha Rao. It was the result of long-term structural weaknesses of three types. The first set of problems were related to the emergence of structural features that bred inefficiency. The excessive protection to indigenous industries for long through import restrictions had made Indian industry inefficient and technologically backward. This situation was further accentuated by the so-called 'licence quota' Raj-a whole plethora of rules, regulations and restrictions which stifled entrepreneurship and innovation. The second set of weaknesses that emerged in the Indian economy was related to the continuation of the inward-oriented developmental path followed by India since independence. Especially after mid-sixties India was unable to respond adequately to the new opportunities thrown up by the changing world situation. No advantage could be taken of the internationalisation of production and of the increased international flow of funds. In the period between 1965-1991 India failed to use the opportunities provided by the changed world scenario to rapidly industrialise and transform its economy, increase levels and drastically reduce poverty levels, as did many of the East Asian countries. Even China changed track in 1978, opening up its economy, participating in the globalisation process, welcoming foreign investment, pushing up its exports, and so on.

The third set of problems which overtook the Indian economy was primarily the result of certain political imperatives, and which was related to the manner in which the Indian state structure and democratic framework evolved. Over time more and more sections emerged which made strong, articulate demands on state resources and the governments in power were increasingly unable either to meet these demands fully or diffuse the clamour for them. In the process a situation arose when macroeconomic balance, which was maintained in India, unlike many other developing countries, with great caution for the first twenty five years or so after independence, was being slowly eroded. The deteriorating situation was aggravated further by the growing political instability and political competition. The erosion in Congress Party's sole hegemony led to competitive populism with each party trying to outdo the other in distributing largesse. In the race among political parties for prestige and influence the Congress was no longer able to stand above competing groups pressing for an immediate increase in their share of the national cake and reign them in with the promise of rapid growth and a just income distribution in future.

At organisational level too with the coming of Mrs. Indira Gandhi who increasingly centralised powers in her hands, democratic functioning within the Congress party declined. Consequently the party lost its organisational links with the grassroots and began political bargaining with sections of society through budgetary allocations. It paved the way for widening gap between public investment and public savings. The deteriorating fiscal and balance of payments situation had led to a mounting debt problem, both domestic and foreign, reaching crisis proportions by the end of the eighties. In earlier phase both Mrs. Gandhi after her return in 1980 and Rajiv Gandhi when he took over in 1984 attempted to make economic reforms through their policies. Mrs. Gandhi in 1980 tried to bring in liberalisation measures, mainly in the area of deregulation of industrial licensing and reduction of restrictions on large monopoly enterprises. Likewise Rajiv Gandhi in 1984 attempted reforms at a relatively quicker pace towards industrial deregulation, exchange rate flexibility and partial lifting of import controls. But the policy of liberalising the economy and opening it for foreign capital, private official and institutional, with wide-ranging implications for fiscal and investment priorities, income distribution and manpower management and even educational and cultural policy had been attempted to be given the shining label of modernisation to enter the twenty-first century.[79] Again the adopted policy of liberalising country's economy because of certain constraints and deficiencies succeeded in developing a dual society with a wide gap between the impoverished mass of people and a thin crust of affluence at the top. This can only result in unrest, violence and social tension and further diversion of resources away from development.

The economic reforms initiated in India in 1991 have direct impact in shaping the structural framework of our economy. A very important pillar of the new economic policies of the government, is the globalisation of the Indian economy. The government has given a firm commitment to the International Monetary Fund (IMF) to implement economic reforms and also to invite foreign capital for investment and to open many areas of the Indian market for foreign multinational corporations.[80] A developing country, wishing to move towards the goal of prosperity needs economic aid from outside the country and from world economic organisations. But the organisations and the countries, who offer economic aid, also dictate their own terms and conditions which may hamper the fulfilment of needs and requirement of aid receiving countries. This trend ultimately leads to economic imperialism which in long run, widens the gap between developed and developing nations and between rich and poor people of the country which is trying to provide and distribute all the resources to its people equally.[81] The beginning of the second stage and the new industrial policy declared, 'it involves a struggle for social and economic justice, to end poverty and unemployment and to build a modern, democratic, socialist and forward looking India. It also implies building a society wherein 'India grows as part of the world economy and not in isolation.[82] However, the economic impact and the reform programmes under the process of globalisation have also affected the social and cultural life of the people in several countries including India.

Evidently, the economic issues particularly, capital, has come to acquire centre stage in the process of globalisation. Earlier the attempt by conquerors to bring the world under one system of rule was primarily related to looting the wealth and politically subjugating the conquered people. But during those days, wealth could not be converted into capital in order to buy labour power, raw materials and instruments to turn out commodities in order to amass profits. Wealth could be converted into capital only when human society entered the stage of capitalism and wealth plundered from the conquered could be transformed into capital. It led to the further rise of capitalism from the 19th century onwards when it emerged as a world wide system and the whole world fell into its trap. Its further advancement resulted into the search for cheap labour, raw materials and also of markets which led to the establishment of colonial rule in poor developing countries of Asia, Africa and Latin America also known as the Third World.[83] Capitalism breeds capital but also provides them sufficient leverage and opportunity to extend their mantle over poor and developing countries. These rich and industrialised capitalist countries also control and direct the international financial institutions, because of being the big contributor to it, to provide aid/capital to the needy countries and, thus, dictate their terms over them so as to suit their own economy. Their big industrial empires in the form of multinational corporations, Multi National Companies (MNCs), trade all over the world carry huge profits to their parent countries. The huge profits earned by such capitalist production, later, caused to press for export of capital as their capital cannot be invested in their domestic markets because they were already saturated. This way the problem of surplus capital came to forefront in Western /advanced countries.

In the circumstances, the developed nations wish to maintain their political-economic hegemony over developing or underdeveloped nation. They dictate such political systems and their policies to suit their own interest rather than taking care of welfare of people's living in that country. Developing countries are particularly vulnerable to global event and action and have come to depend heavily on the international community for financial and technical assistance. As a result, national policies are interlocked with global issues. 'Because poor countries generally have fragile politics and weak systems of accountability, with few autonomous institutions and little power to offset that exercised by the central government, external agencies are potentially key political players, capable of exerting considerable influence'.[84] Harold Lasswell, while writing in 1968 also maintained, 'As the globe shrinks into interdependence, relying more fully on science and technology, the policy sciences gain significance. Interdependence implies that every participant and every item in the social process is affected by the context in which it occurs.[85] Empirical observations point out the fact that during 1960s, 1970s and 1980s, the average rate of profit and share of profit in national product of advanced capitalist had declined. The process of globalisation entered a new intensive phase in the 1980s with the gradual opening and breakdown of the communist bloc.

At the close of the eighties the intensive phase of globalisation started mainly due to the pressing needs of developed countries to outlet the growing volume of surplus capital in less developed or underdeveloped countries in spheres of manufacturing, real estates, raw material extraction, financial sector, advertising, media etc. Between 1980 and 1990, the amount of capital directly invested in foreign lands nearly tripled. Prior to this unexpected and contingent events the global capitalism had produced a whole new technology of communication which made possible a virtual leap in the level of communication and exchange. Information could now be transferred still faster in enormous quantities, and global flows of information, money and people intensified at unprecedented speed. Recent scientific revolutions, particularly in the field of information technology and economic liberalisation have contributed in accelerating the onward process of globalisation. As regards economic liberation the formation of World Trade Organisation (WTO) and MIGA are the landmark achievements towards integration of world economy which is supposed to boost productivity and elevate the living standards in all parts of the world. In addition, the electronic information technologies are part and parcel of the new financial instruments many of which have technical powers which are clearly ahead of the protocols for their regulation.[86] As a result of technological development, especially in the electronic, transport and communication sectors, there has been a proliferation of economic, scientific, technological and cultural innovations, which have greatly affected all areas of human life and particularly the development process in the third world.

India, in response to global milieu for Liberalisation, Privatisation and Globalisation (LPG), in 1990, initiated four important measures: fiscal policy reforms, monitory policy reforms, exchange rate adjustments and realistic wages and income policies. The second phase of economic reforms include: financial, social and public sector reforms, capital market, trade policy and investment reforms. These reform measures have brought about further globalisation of Indian economy with more free flow of foreign capital. Under the policy India is trying to attract foreign investment essentially from three sources. These are Foreign Direct Investment (FDI), Portfolio Investment and NRI Bonds. After the collapse of USSR, US emerged as the only super power in international order based on free trade, the free movement of capital and the construction of liberal states with representative political institutions. According to Achin Vanaik,' Neo-liberals when they talk of economic globalisation are basically claiming the following: A truly global economy is now emerging for the first time ever. It is dominance of the world market that is now the main issue. The most important economic agents are Multinational Corporations which no longer have serious national allegiance. They roam and operate worldwide.[87] Even in case of India no individual, MNC or any investing agency normally use to invest in this country for the good of the people. They do so only for their own financial benefits. This immediately keeps them aloof from certain important sectors of our national life, namely, the fields of education, health and infrastructure development. The foreign investors have confined their investment to the fields of power generation, communication, oil and gas exploration and all those fields where the returns are high and fast. In other words, the terms and conditions attached to the flow of foreign capital in India and the spheres in which it is being invested are not according to our national priorities, needs and goals, namely, the eradication of poverty, employment generation, improvement in social infrastructure relating to education, health, potable water and equitable distribution of the fruits of the development.

Thus, the process of globalisation has increased the vulnerability of the countries of the Third World which are in the process of being integrated into the world economy. As the recent financial crisis has illustrated, financial liberalisation including speculative and volatile financial flows over which the developing countries have little controls, in the absence of adequate institutional arrangements to manage the process has generated significant instability in the international economics with especially disasterous results for developing countries. It has become a new source of instability in both product and financial markets. This has already been observed by the economic crises in East Asian economies, few years ago. Scholar Robert Heilbroner comments rightly, 'The problem becomes still more complex insofar as the interconnectedness of the global economy widens the field of competition beyond national boundaries. The 350 corporations whose combined sales come to a third of the aggregate Gross National Product (GNP) of the industrial world are giant beams in the structure of world capitalism, and by that very fact, a new source of national economic instability within individual national economies. Even today there exist no effective means to protect production within a nation if the transnationals should begin to shake'.[88] As a result 80 countries containing a third of the world's population are being increasingly marginalised, and over the past 20 years developing countries' share of global trade fell from 0.8 to 0.4 per cent[89]. The fact is that 3 billion people live on less than $2 a day, and 1.2 billion live on less than $ 1 a day. This horrific level of poverty persists despite unprecedented increases in global wealth in the past century.

Indian society is drastically changing after globalisation. In this era different forms of difference have come to the foreground in relation to identity politics, gender, minorities rights, indigenous peoples, and ethnic and religious movement. The lower and weaker section of society has to be the worst sufferers as they will not get jobs. Consequently the income gap between lower and upper level of society is bound to rise and this, along with consumerism, and its demonstration over modern electronic means of communication, will lead to crimes, anarchy and destruction of social harmony and equilibrium. On the other the role of government is changing as we witness a fragmentation of policy responsibility in society in which the traditional mechanism of government control are no longer workable or even appropriate. It challenges the traditional relationship between economy and state. The globalised market system stretches beyond the political authority of any single government. Faced with a network of connections that escape their power of surveillance or regulation, national governments have become increasingly unequal to providing the legal, monetary, or protective functions that are their contribution to a well divided loyalties – on the one hand eager for its firms to maximize revenues, which are subject to national taxation, on the other hand, reluctant to see employment or research capabilities that it wants as part of its national economic strength located in a competitive national entity. Since the focus of development shifted from social goals to profit motives, the state was neither considered as a positive instrument for social transformation nor an agency for resource allocation.

The new capital flow that comes in has totally changed the class character of Indian people. Now the market products only the goods that cater the needs of those who have high purchasing power because the profits are likely to be higher in such spheres. For the time being it created the impression of growth and prosperity. But the needs of the bulk of the population are normally neglected or overlooked. C.T. Kurian mentions that globalisation usually benefits people who can play the game, but the chances are very less for those who are resourceless, uneducated and those who make livelihood through traditional production activities, will come under various kinds of pressures. So, on the one hand he talks about the marvelous technological innovations such as email and flights that convert this earth and its people into a 'global village' but at the same time he also accepts that this globe has been integrated by capital practices and ideological polarisation has largely been removed.[90] Thus, negative aspects of globalisation include the unnecessary interference of developed countries pressure to follow particular policies and programmes which are not very suitable to the people and society leading to imbalanced development and growth.

In the continuing marginalisation policy of the Government of India since independence the negative waves of globalisation added fuel to the fire. It altered the role of state as an agency for the empowerment of the socially deprived sections. Such a transition from state-oriented development to market-oriented one evoked mixed responses among the various social groups in India as different aspects of the reform processes, in one way or other threatened the very existence of these social classes and organisations. In the years following the independence the dominant classes and castes showed much enthusiasm to divert the public policies of the government for acquiring more resources from the government. Consequently the support base of the state, and its policies and programmes which were intended to empower the socially marginalised sections were tempered for attaining the ambitious target of high economic growth. The coming of globalisation and new economic reforms gave birth to a critical moment when there was an upsurge of the poor and Dalits to achieve increased shares in the allocation of economic resources and political power. It led to a change in the functioning of democracy in India in the late 1980s and early 1990s with the passage of the 73rd and 74th Amendments which gave constitutional status to two elected bodies, the Panchayats and the Nagarpalikas. As a result the political competition at the local government level witnessed crucial change of a positive nature. These constitutional reforms allowed democracy to locally democratise.[91] With democracy taking root any meaningful assessment of the structure, organisation and working of political parties in India would necessarily involve an in-depth evaluation of the dynamics of party politics at the grassroots level. But in the process of globalisation, the rural poor began tc experience the dislocation of their economy in its totality for the first time in the history of their existence.

However, the fiscal austerity measures, intended to bridge the fical deficit, exhausted the state capacity to meet the increasing demands on the state from various sections of the society especially the newly politicized social groups. While the fruits of the economic reform accrued to the urban elite and middle classes of the society, the traditionally backward social groups like the Dalits and the tribals were haunted by its adverse impact. Agrarian structure and Indian villages were affected negatively as seventy four per cent of India's population lives in rural areas and their livelihood mainly depends on agriculture and the related activities. The small and marginal farmers and agricultural labourers constitute the vast majority of rural society.[92] Globalisation resulted in the neglect of agriculture that adversely affected the vulnerable classes of rural society in their employment conditions, income and consumption pattern, their education and health status. Not only the village agriculture but the Indian women, Dalits, rural poor, economic organisations, media, public services, political leaders, political parties and government along with other aspects of human life registered a significant change. Under the unleashing of the market oriented economic reforms, the socially vulnerable sections became handicapped in responding to the market signals as they found their entry to the market very difficult, especially those who did not have assets or skill.[93] The benefits of the fast developing areas like information technology did not evoke much impact on the living conditions of the down-trodden sections of the people. The attack on the state by the market can be considered as a denial of the rights and livelihood to the socially marginalised sections. The measures for attaining fiscal discipline like cuts in government expenditure had a direct bearing on the welfare programmes of the SC and ST in the areas of rural water supply, poverty alleviation schemes, educational benefits, employment schemes, and other related destinations.

3.5 Post-globalisation: Problems and Challenges

As a result of the globalisation and its all pervasive adverse effects society has resulted in a growing discontent and disenchantment among the people and thereby their isolation from power centres. The new middle class emerged in the era of neo-liberal policies of the government has adopted an exclusive and parochial approach that affected negatively the living conditions of the other classes and groups. It generated anomie trends in society. On the other the exclusion can be seen with the emergence of identity politics based on caste, especially among the lower strata of the society who are demanding wider power sharing in the political system. According to Rajni Kothari, 'The yawning vacuum created by the alienation of people from the developmental exercise was filled by deeper pathologies like communalism and fundamentalism which found a fertile ground.[94] In contrast to the early middle class that emerged after independence, secular in outlook and sensitive to social coherence, the new middle class showed allegiance to the Hindu nationalist politics. The BJP succeeded in bringing on the loyalty of the middle class and filled the political vacuum by the decline of the Congress by providing a Hindu nationalist alternative to the Congress. The adoption of neo-liberal economic policies produced two new social groups- the loser and the winner. While the poor and the socially marginalised sections constituted the disadvantageous sections, the consumerist middle class constituted the advantageous sections. In course of time, the losers attracted to the caste-based parties, which had in fact no concrete policies and programmes for their genuine empowerment, and the gainers were mobilised towards the Hindu nationalist party like BJP. Initially, in post-independence era many promises and assets were provided by the government's of the day to different sections of the people, including the socially marginalised groups. People's expectations from the state were belied in the 1990s, when the market reforms shrunk the role of the state and hopes failed to materialise.

The waves of globalisation in India have accelerated the pace of political competition, changing structures of power and influence, and widening base of political consultation and persuasion. Although Indian policies have been subject to foreign or outside pressures since the days of the Cold War in the 1950s, yet until the mid-1980s, the decisions were accepted as being in the "long term national interest". There were accusations in the procurement of the Jaguar aircraft also but these did not create the furore that the Bofors scam did. Since the late 1980s, as in the case of Bofors or the new economic policies in 1991 or the Indo-US nuclear deal, sectional or individual interests have become dominant.[95] In India, by and large, politics is neither suppressed nor confined to a small elite. On the contrary, politics provides the larger setting within which decision making in regard to economic development and social change, and application of pressures for redirecting development and change takes place. The Indian model of development is thus characterised by the politicisation of a fragmented social structure, through a wide dispersal and permeation of political forms, values and ideologies. The process culminates by closing the gap that has traditionally divided village society from the polity.[96] In a democracy the contest for power is never free from uncertainty and anxiety, and Indian politics is now marked by increasing turmoil. Those who make politics their career became accustomed to its turbulence and some even take a peculiar pleasure in it. These have played havoc with national politics. Pressures and counter pressures are mounted through political parties and their leaders and big bosses.

In India there is a multitude of parties based on caste, religion, ethnicity, regional affiliations, linguistic differences, and political ideology. They are frantically preoccupied with aggrandizing their own narrow interests, apathetically disregarding the larger interests of the society and the nation. The democracy in India has caused fragmentation of the society into smaller, antagonistic, belligerent segments; had led to disintegration of the states into economically inviable units plagued with adversial relationships; and has created an ambience of incessant mistrust, discord, and internecine conflicts.[97] Because of the multiplicity of parties, the politicians, propelled by expediency and opportunism, spend their time, energy, and resources in forming often transient alliances, to capture power. Each constituent element has its own agenda; hence the alliances are usually ephemeral. At present the relations between government and opposition have become increasingly acrimonious. Even where there is broad agreement over, let us say, foreign policy or economic policy, each side maintains an adversial relationship with the other, fearing that there will be a loss of face if not a loss of support from its constituents if it appears conciliatory. The habitually confrontationist conduct of both government and opposition is complicated by the fact that neither the one nor the other speaks in a single voice. This may be a good thing where it serves to defuse tension but it is not conducive to deliberations on policy.[98] Therefore, the stability of the government is precarious, and the scourge of elections always haunts the Indian electorate. Despite the advent of information age and the commencement of global interaction, the world perspective of majority of the legislators are woefully limited; and their comprehension of international issues with national and local ramifications is virtually non-existent.

In the circumstances good governance is viewed as the exercise of economic, political, and administrative authority to manage a country's affairs to all levels and as the means by which states promote social cohesion and integration, and ensure the well-being of their population. The new turmoil among Indian masses and the new forms of protest and struggle waged by a new set of actors as part of the continuing commitment to democracy, indeed to its deepening and broadening. They need to be located in the larger context of transformaion. In this context the Indian democracy witnessed two changes; First, the resurgence of the people themselves, both in consciousness and in behaviour. They are asserting their democratic rights and challenging the established order, at local levels to begin with, but affecting the entire social and political order. Though they are by no means close to transforming it. Secondly, the emergence of a new social class of mediators in the political process and the activists. They are upper and middle class in their origin, but identify themselves with the lower orders of society - the poor, the oppressed and the segregated; social strata ranging from the untouchable and the destitude among the tribes and ethnic minorities, to the victims of sexual, ecological and generational descriminations, atrocities and violence.[99] Globalisation needs to be countered not just with decentralised and regional alternatives, or new initiatives with regard to natural resources and ecology, but also with political and ideological initiatives at the national, regional and global level.

India is currently passing through a period of many challenges in different spheres – economic, social cultural and political. Contextually, there has been a welcome shift from traditional concepts of government and politics to good governancc and its attributes. Governance refers to the quality of government and manner in which power is exercised by governments in managing country's social and economic resources. Governance means, 'The process of decision making and the process by which decisions are implemented or not implemented. It also focuses on the formal and informal actors involved in decision-making and implementing the decisions made and the formal and informal structures that have been set in place to arrive at and implement the decisions. There are so many actors in governance and the government is one of them. In urban areas, the other major actors constitute political parties, voluntary organisations, rescarch institutes, religious leaders, finance institutes, the military, media, lobbyists, international donors, multi-national corporations.While in rural areas, actors may include influential landlords, associations of peasant farmers, cooperatives and NGOs.[100] These actors,urban and rural, other than government and the military are grouped together as part of the civil society. All these may play a role in decision-making or in influencing the decision making process. The pre-requisites for quality governance are that the system should be good and suited to the need, aspirations background and ethos of the concerned people.

The term 'Good Governance' was highlighted by the World Bank in one of its documents in 1989 in context of third world countries. It is not only confined to political governance but would include all types of governance, such as international, national, state or provincial or local. Further in 1992 the World Bank's Document on governance and development said, 'Good governance is central to creating and sustaining an environment which fosters strong and equitable development and it is an essential complement to sound economic policies. It identified three aspects of governance: the form of political regime, the process by which authority is exercised in the management of country's economic and social resources: and the capacity of governments to design, formulate and implement policies and in general, to discharge government functions.[101] But besides the World Bank indicators of good governance encompassing democracy, transparency and accountability, it may be said that the whole idea of good governance is that of a participative democratic system in which those who are called upon to govern on behalf of the people are motivated with a will to giving their best, serving and doing good to the people and in particular, solving the problems of the poor and the underprivileged and making their lives more liveable, satisfying and enjoyable. However, at large, good governance is a dynamic and value-laden concept. The values it gives importance to are eight in number. Modern concept of good governance is participatory, consensus-oriented, accountable, transparent, responsive, effective and efficient, equitable and inclusive and follows the rule of law.

In India the democratic structure of governance, which is the largest democracy of the world, badly fails on the counts of good governance. Although people have got the right to participate in governance directly as well as indirectly but peculiar situation is that this characteristic of good governance is partially realised. Especially the reforms in economic governance were started in the country under the fiscal stabilisation in early 1990s, with the World Bank/IMF loan conditional ties to improve the balance of payments and fiscal discipline, and the reorganisation of economy, polity and society, as in several other third world countries. The agenda of reforms has been clearly stated in recent official documents and reports of the government. The Indian state has adopted a largely favourable stance towards the processes of globalisation, liberalisation and privatisation.

It has embarked on the path of reorienting and restructuring its governance system. A whole new set of policies and programmes has been put in place. The canvas of reforms covers both the centre and states. It encompasses reforms in economic, social, administrative and political spheres. At present the innumerable issues regarding political economy and political sociology are surfacing that highlight the relationship that exists between development paradigms and actual development, government and governance, common people and the state. But there is no denying the fact that governments continue to play a central role in the lives of its citizens, governance came to be equated with government. Development and reform also constituted the functions of governments. Now, when one talks of governance, one refers to participatory governance which works towards development of individuals as well as the society and nation.

Earlier and in very recent the Tenth Five Year Plan (2002-2007), Eleventh Five Year Plan (2007-2012) and the Twelfth Five Year Plan (2012-2017), have focused the themes of good governance and its implementation.

The Tenth Plan states, 'Governance relates to the management of all such process, that, in any society, define the environment which permits and enables individual to rise their capability levels, provide opportunities to realise their potential and enlarge the set of available choice. These processes, covering the political, social and economic aspects of life impact every level of human enterprise, be it the individual, the household, the village, the region or the national level. It covers the state, civil society and the market, each of which is critical for sustaining human development.[102] Chapter six of the tenth plan included governance issues and strategic identifies, such as people's participation, decentralisation, right to information, civil society involvement, civil service reforms, procedural reforms, judicial reforms, using information technology and empowerment of the marginalised. It was felt at the higher level that good governance is helpful in achieving human well-being and sustained development. Moreover, it is equally important to recognise that poor governance could well erode the individual capabilities as well as institutional and community capacities to meet even the basic needs of sustenance for large segments of the population. In line the new Right to Information (RTI) Act came into force on 12 October, 2005.

In fact governance has a critical role to play in the process of development and is required as an essential tool in striking a balance between the diminishing role of government and threat of an increasingly powerful private sector. This is of great importance in the developing world where many governments appeared to have failed in performing their duties, and major changes were considered necessary for arranging new patterns of interactions between government and citizens.[103] Under the camoulage of the slogans of one world and a global village, ordinary citizens instead of being the masters in democratic polity have been increasingly reduced to being mere consumers of goods and services. The result is tremendous erosion in democratic rights and freedoms of the individual vis-à-vis the organs of the State substantially reducing the space for the voice of the poor and the underprivileged. Once K.R. Narayanan, the President of Indian Republic, felt the pains and said, 'We find that justice-social, economic and political-remains an unrealised dream for millions of our fellow citizens. The benefits of our economic growth are yet to reach them. We have one of the world's largest reservoirs of technical personnel, but also the world's largest number of illiterates, the world's largest middle class, but also the largest number of people below the poverty line, and the largest number of children suffering from malnutrition. He added further that there is sullen resentment among the masses against their condition erupting often in violent forms in several parts of the country. Many a social upheaval can be traced to the neglect of the lowest of society, whose discontent moves towards the path of violence.[104]

Tragically the growth in our economy has been accompanied by great regional and social inequalities.

Decades passed since the globalisaion, liberalisation and privatisation have been commenced in India and now there has been a lot of debate about their impact and outcome. There are some who acclaim the results while there are others who oppose both the process of globalisation and its impact. Without doubt, globalisation has led to technological transformation which has resulted in international mobilisation. Exchange of information, technologies and methods have led to a decline in diseases, facilitated communication, made life more comfortable. But on the other the sovereign States of the time feel very uneasy, especially the developing and underdeveloped, in working within this vast array of international regimes and organisations. The rapid growth of transnational issues and problems has involved a spread of layers of political regulation both within and across political boundaries. It has been marked by the transformation of aspects of territorially based political decision-making the development of regional and global institutions and organisations and the emergence of regional and global law. It has paved the way for rapid emergence of new forms of multilateral and transnational politic involving Governments in Intergovernmental Organisations (IGOs) and a wide variety of transnational pressure groups and International Non-Governmental Organisations (INGOs). However in the whole process poor and the deprived are the worst sufferer and therefore some consider globalisation to be a threat to a nation or society in general and to the marginalised in particular.

In the needs and aspirations of the nation and international pressure / lobbying the actual position of India exists. On the one hand the country is blessed with significant natural resources and mineral wealth; there is a complete collapse of governance that needs to be rectified soon on the other. Even today it is felt at various levels that little has been done to bring the unprivileged to the level of the privileged, to provide equality of opportunity and a life of dignity to all. In this context a wake-up call was also given by President Pratibha Patil in her Republic Day-eve address to the nation, 'The disadvantaged too should find a place to enjoy the sunshine of the country's growth and development. Our efforts and our commitment, while pursuing the goal of high growth rates, should be to ensure that all people of our country benefit from it. Our pledge will remain unfulfilled until, as Gandhi had said, 'We have wiped every tear in every eye'.[105] In line in the 12th five year plan (2007-2012) and 13th five year plan (2012-2017) the planning commission has focused on "inclusive growth". The steps taken are expected to encourage the development of Indian agriculture, education, health and social welfare schemes through government spending.

Thus, the political vacuum created by the national and international factors paved the way for governance-related movements in India whose first target in the present is rampant corruption at all levels leading to a breakdown in the rule of law and lack of accountability all around. Although the anti-corruption movement led by Anna Hazare and Baba Ramdev's dramatic call for 'Congress-hatao' have confirmed that a movement for good governance is overdue. Earlier in the 1980s there emerged the people's movement sector-comprising farmer's movement, Dalit movements, women movements, environmental movements and the movements for information and deepening of democracy is one of the most vibrant spaces in the democratic arena. These movements are inherently political in that they seek to challenge the settled relations of power. They have quietly shifted the terms of political engagement and brought new issues to the foreground. Legislation and policies like the Right to Information, the Mahatma Gandhi Rural Employment Guarantee Act, the Forest Act and the new Land Acquisition and Rehabilitations Act are a tribute to the power and creativity of these movements.[106] Yet these movements have not succeeded in posing a direct challenge to mainstream politics, they involved some of the finest activists and thinkers of our time. There have been many creative organisational experiments and ideological innovations, however, they remained largely invisible. At large these movements failed to translate their support in electoral terms and in order to give effect to their political agenda, remained dependent on the very political establishment they critiqued and struggled against. In post -1989 period while the idea of third space has expanded, the third force has shrunk.[107] The energy of the third space is in search of a national political vehicle, especially because the mainstream politics of UPA & NDA have become more insulated from popular struggles and movements.

However, a breakthrough appeared in the field when an anti-corruption movement was started by the Team Anna in the year 2011-12. It is after more than three decades that a movement outside the organised party sector has registered a nationwide presence and visibility. What mattered in this is that the Anna Hazare-led movement spawned smaller protests in a large number of towns and even villages. A fairly large proportion of citizens who did not participate in any protest heard about it and sympathised with it. But its success depends not so much on whether it wins an election but on how much of positive energy it releases into the political system. Even Anna Hazare's fast-unto-death organised on occasions more than one and recently in July-August 2012, which attracted un-precedented attention and adulation for the enactment of an effective Lokpal Bill to curb corruption in the top echelons of the establishment, has raised several doubts about its success.

Taking important lessons from the earlier JP movement for the posterity of revolutionaries, and reformers wanting to bring macro-level change in the country, JP himself wrote for a revolution to succeed, it required a revolutionary leadership as well as a revolution organisation. In addition to JP's view, it also needs revolutionary programme of action. In this movement only one component was present: a revolutionary leadership. Apart from this there was no attempt to build a revolutionary organisation to assist the leadership and no revolutionary programme of action entailing a broad roadmap for change.[108] In addition, the movement shows that agitators are not trying to build a parallel mass base on the strength of a constructive programme as was done by Mahatma Gandhi. Team Anna lacks other tools of mass mobilisation or social reconstruction. Thus, the movement should be made holistic and there has to be a larger vision and roadmap for the country. The sooner this is understood the better it is for Team Anna and, perhaps, the country.

At present there is a widespread belief that the kind of democratic system in which we operate is failing us. Today 80 per cent of Indians are poor, and there is massive unemployment, lack of healthcare, housing and good education. In the recent period the rich have become richer, and the rich-poor divide has increased. Economic growth has benefited only a handful.[109] India is a representative democracy where people select their representatives once in five years to make laws and policies on their behalf. Limiting the participation of the people merely to voting once in five years has significantly reduced the responsiveness of the representatives to the people. One reason is that our democracy has become formalistic. Legislatures should check corruption but it would not be so if the elected are beholden to the corrupt or are themselves corrupt. The problem is political; it cannot be resolved through technical fixes or by having more laws - these are anyway being circumvented. A weak democracy presents a no-win situation; if a democracy is weak, the corrupt get elected and misuse their autonomy; if the legislator's, autonomy is curbed, democracy weakens.[110] The super – watchdog which should deliver all-round accountability, has become weak in India. The ruling class has played havoc with the watchdog institutions so as to control them for their narrow ends. That is why the demand for a strong Lokpal gained momentum.

The problem in India is not that there is too much democracy but too little. Whether the solution lies in direct democracy or devolution of powers to village councils deserves closer scrutiny. One innovative solution of direct democracy tried in numerous countries is the Referendum and Initiative. These are instruments whereby some decisions of policy and lawmaking are referred to a direct vote by the electorate, rather than solely being decided by their representatives. Countries that regularly practise some degree of direct democracy like Switzerland are small, homogeneous and renowned for their clockwork efficiency. Other countries that have had referendums, whether smaller ones like Sweden or larger ones like Brazil, have had them only rarely. The idea that village councils should contribute to State and national law-making is a radical one but closely related to referendums. Panchayats have existed in ancient times and have been reintroduced in modern times. But they are still struggling to find their feet, clamouring for devolution of more powers and big budgets.[111] It enjoys the same potential strengths and suffers from the same weaknesses. Unless electoral reforms can be introduced, reducing entry barriers in politics and levelling the playing field in political parties, it will be hard to keep arguing that elections are the lone remedy to unsettled issues of national importance. No such electoral reforms are on the horizon, but it is conceivable that sustained activism could put them on the agenda.

In the present scenario of Indian politics participatory democracy is being considered more and more as not merely desirable but necessary. Under conditions of globalisation, where national-level institutions of representation are being subordinated to hegemonic global power with the structure of political and economic decision – making more remote and alienated from people, the politics of participatory democracy has acquired a new relevance. Whatever be the challenges in introducing such democratic reforms the time has come to discuss such a change to ensure that our government truly represents the people.

References

1. Horst Hartmann, *Political Parties in India* (Meerut: Meenakshi Prakashan, 1971), pp. 181-82.
2. Iqbal Narain(ed.), *State Politics in India* (Meerut :1967), p. 643.
3. Kushal Pal, Dynamics of Party System and Formation of Coalition Government in India, *Indian Journal of Political Science*, Vol. LXIX, No. 2, April-June 2008 (Meerut: 2008), pp. 331-32.
4. *Congress Bulletin*, August-September 1969.
5. M.M. Rahman, *The Congress Crisis* (New Delhi: 1970).
6. A.S. Abraham, 'Decade of Turbulence-System Under Growing Stress', *The Times of India*, 21 December 1979.
7. See *Election Manifesto of Congress* (Ruling), 1971.
8. Dr. Rajkumar Singh, *India and Pakistan-Social, Political and Military Perspectives* (New Delhi : Regal Publications, 2009), p. 40.

9. Bipin Chandra, Mridula Mukherjee and Aditya Mukherjee, *India After Independence 1947-2000* (New Delhi: Penguin Books, 2002), p. 237.
10. *Ibid.*, p. 238.
11. *Ibid.*, pp. 243-244.
12. Ramesh Kumar, 'Political Parties in India and the United States : A Comparative Analysis, *IJPS*, Vol. LXX, No. 4,October-December 2009 (Meerut : 2009), p. 1230.
13. A.S. Abraham, 'Decade of Turbulence : System Under Growing Stress'.
14. *Ibid.*
15. V.K.R.V. Rao, *The Current Indian Crisis-Darkness Before Dawn* (Allahabad: Vohra Publications, 1984), pp. 26-27.
16. A.S. Raman, 'Revolution in India', *Contemporary Review*, Vol. 233, No. 1352, September 1978, pp. 152-53.
17. *Ibid.*
18. Girilal Jain, 'Effects of Politicisation- Need to Strengthen Institutions' *The Times of India*, 31 December 1980.
19. Rajkumar Singh, 'State of Indian Democracy', *Third Concept*, Vol. 16, No. 189, November 2002 (New Delhi : 2002), p. 26.
20. Inder Malhotra, *Indira Gandhi* (London : 1989), pp. 173 and 182.
21. *The Sunday Standard*, 13 March 1977.
22. N.L. Chowla, 'Indian Democracy in Perspective', *The Times of India*, 22 December 1980.
23. *Ibid.*
24. Horst Hartmann, *Political Parties in India*, p. 288.
25. Bipin Chandra, Mridula Mukherjee and Aditya Mukherjee, *India After Independence 1947-2000* p. 262.
26. *Ibid.*
27. Reena Nand, 'The Dynamics of Indian Political System', *IJPS*, Vol. LXXI, No. 2, April-June 2010 (Meerut: 2010), p. 421.
28. Bipin Chandra, Mridula Mukherjee and Aditya Mukherjee, *India After Independence 1947-2000*, pp. 263-64.
29. Rajni Kothari, *Politics and the People*, Vol. II (New Delhi: Ajanta, 1990), p. 329.
30. K.K. Katyal, 'Coalition Politics: The Latest Phase', *The Hindu* (Madras), 17 March 1997.
31. A.B. Mathur, 'The Indian Polity: A Mild Indictment,' *Administrative Change*

Vol. XXIX, No. 2 & Vol. XXX, No. 1, January-December 2002 (Jaipur: 2002), pp. 32-33.

32. Ramesh Kumar, 'Political Parties in India and the United States: A Comparative Analysis', pp. 1230-31.

33. Rajesh Paliwal, *Janata Experiment in Indian Politics* (New Delhi: Raj Publishers, 1985), pp. 150-56.

34. Kushal Pal, 'Dynamics of Party System and Formation of Coalition Government in India,' p. 333.

35. *Ibid.,* p. 334.

36. M.P. Singh, 'From Predominant to Polarisation: The Indian Party System as cited in A.S. Narang, *Indian Government and Politics* (New Delhi: Gitanjali Publishing House, 2004), p. 100.

37. Atul Kohli, *Democracy and Discontent: India's Growing Crisis of Governability* (Cambridge: Cambridge University Press, 1990), pp. 340-50.

38. Arend Lijphart, 'Cultural Diversity and Theories of Political Integration,' *Canadian Journal of Political Science,* IV (March, 1971).

39. William A. Gamson, 'Experimental Studies of Coalition,' in Leonard Berkowitz (ed.), *Advances in Experimental Social Psychology* (Newyork: Academic Publication, 1964).

40. Kavita Navlani, 'National Integration and the Dynamics of Coalition and Federalism in India', *IJPS* Vol. LXVII, No. 1, January–March 2006 (Meerut: 2006), pp. 125-27.

41. Bipin Chandra, Mridula Mukherjee and Aditya Mukherjee, *India After Independence 1947-2000,* pp. 285-57.

42. Seema Mustafa, *The Lonely Prophet: V.P. Singh, A Political Biography* (New Delhi: 1995), p. 129.

43. Rajkumar Singh, *Relation of NDA and UPA with Neighbours* (New Delhi: Gyan Publishing House, 2010), p. 18.

44. *Ibid.,* pp. 18-19.

45. Pratap Chandra Swain, 'Dynamics of Indian Party System: The Emergence of Competitive Multiparty Coalitions,' *IJPS,* Vol. LXIX, No. 1, January-March 2008 (Meerut: 2008), pp. 65-66.

46. Rajkumar Singh, *India and Pakistan-Social, Political and Military Perspectives,* p. 48.

47. Sudipta Kaviraj, 'Religion, Politics and Modernity', Upendra Baxi and Bhikhu Parekh (eds.), *Crisis and Change in Contemporary India* (New Delhi: 1995), pp. 313-14.

48. Rajkumar Singh, *India and Pakistan-Social, Political and Military Perspectives,* pp. 49-50.

49. Ayesha Jalal, *Democracy and Authoritarianism in South Asia: A Comparative and Historical Perspective* (Cambridge: 1995), p. 95.

50. Arvind N. Das, 'India Invented–Ostrich Approach to National Unity', *The Times of India*, 19 September 1991.

51. Javeed Alam, *Who Wants Democracy Tracks for the Times*, Second edition (New Delhi: Orient Black Swan, 2012), p. 16.

52. *Ibid.*, pp. 16-17.

53. *Ibid.*, pp. 101-6.

54. A.B. Mathur, 'The Indian Polity: A Mild Indictment,' p. 33.

55. Pratap Chandra Swain, 'Dynamics of the Indian Party System: The Emergence of Competitive Multi Party Coalition', pp. 66-67.

56. Sebastian Alappatukunnel (ed.), *Politics, Policy and Reconstruction: India Since Independence* (Jaipur: Aalekh Publishers, 2001), pp. 123-24.

57. *Economic and Political Weekly*, Vol. XXXIII, No. 12, March 21-27, 1998 (Mumbai: 1998), pp. 619-21.

58. D. Syamala Devi and G. Lakshmi, 'Need for a CMP in Coalition Governments, *South Asia Politics*, Vol. 6, No. 8, December 2007 (New Delhi: 2007), p. 32.

59. *Ibid.*, pp. 32-33.

60. Vandana Mishra, 'Analysing the BJP and Congress,' *Mainstream*, Vol. XLII, No. 19, May 2004 (New Delhi: 2004), pp. 21-23.

61. Jawahar Pandey, *State Politics in India* (New Delhi: Jawahar Publishing House, 1992), p. 30.

62. *The Times of India* (New Delhi), 23 July 2008.

63. *The Hindu*, 'How India Voted-Verdict 2009,' 26 May 2009, p. 2.

64. *Ibid.*

65. Siddharth Varadarajan, 'Politics After President Pranab', *Ibid.*, 19 June 2012.

66. Javeed Alam, *Who Wants Democracy-Tracts for the Times*, p. 92.

67. Rajni Kothari, *Politics in India* (New Delhi: Orient Longman, 1970), p. 201.

68. Ramesh Kumar, 'Political Parties in India and the United States: A Comparative Analysis', pp. 1233-34.

69. D. Syamala Devi and G. Lakshmi, 'Need for a CMP in Coalition Governments', p. 35.

70. Javeed Alam, *Who Wants Democracy-Tracts for the Times*, p. 97.

71. A.B. Mathur, 'The Indian Polity: A Mild Indictment', p. 34.

72. S.C. Hazary, 'Wither Indian Party System', *Political Scientist* (1980), pp. XIV-XVI.

73. Bipin Chandra, Mridula Mukherjee and Aditya Mukherjee, *India After Independence 1947-2000*, p. 471.
74. *Ibid.*, p. 472.
75. Andre Beteille, 'Politics Without Policy', *The Hindu*, 28 June 2012.
76. A.K. Ojha, 'Globalisation and Liberalisation–Propects of New World,' *Third Concept*, August 2002, p. 13.
77. V.N. Vishwanathan, 'Human Rights in a Globalised World-The Indian Experiences,' *IJPS*, LXIX, No. 1, January–March 2008 (Meerut: 2008), p. 51.
78. Suditpa Kaviraj, 'The Modern State in India', in Zoya Hasan (ed.), *Introduction: The Political Career of the State in Independent India* (2000), p. 56.
79. Balraj Mehta, 'India: Perspective and Prospectives; *Employment News*, 7-13 April 1990, p. 3.
80. Y. Gurappa Naidu, 'Globalisation and its Impact on Indian Society', *IJPS*, Vol. LXVII, No. 1, January-March 2006 (Meerut: 2006), p. 68.
81. Geeta Chaturvedi, 'Democracy in Global India', *Ibid.*, Vol. LXIX, No. 4, October-December 2008, p. 849.
82. K.S. Thakur, 'Indian Economy After Globalisation', *Third Concept*, June 1997, p. 51.
83. Sudhanshu Tripathi, 'Globalisation and its Consequences,' *South Asia Politics*, Vol. 9, Nos. 3 and 4, July-August 2010 (New Delhi: 2010), pp. 32-33.
84. Pierre–Landell–Mills and Ismail Serageldin, 'Governance and the External Factor,' *World Bank, Proceedings of the World Bank Annual Conference on Development Economics, 1991* (Washington: World Bank, 1992), p. 309.
85. H.D. Lasswell, 'The Policy Sciences', *Encyclopaedia of the Social Sciences*, Vol. 12, (Newyork: Macmillan, 1968), p. 184.
86. Sudhanshu Tripathi, 'Globalisation and Its Consequences, p. 33.
87. Achin Vanaik, *Economic Globalisation: Myth or Reality* (New Delhi: People's Publication House, 2001), pp. 2-3.
88. As quoted in Sudhanshu Tripathi,'Globalisation and Its Consequences,' p. 34.
89. R.K. Sapru, *Development Administration*, 2nd edition (New Delhi: Sterling Publications, 2002), p. 275.
90. Sakhi Athyal, 'Globalisation, Youth and Religion in India', p. 1.
91. Shastri Sandeep, 'Local Democracy and Political Parties in India in Ajay K. Mehra, D.D. Khanna and Gert W. Kueck (eds.), *political parties and party systems* (New Delhi: Sage Publications, 2003), p. 384.

92. A. Maria Alphousal and J. Belphine Prema Dhanaseeli, 'Strategy Against the Threat to Rural Poor, '*Eubious Journal of Asian and International Bio Ethics* (2003), p. 2.

93. V. Biju Kumar, 'Post–Colonial State: An Overview', *IJPS*, Vol. LXVI, No. 4, October–December 2005 (Meerut: 2005), p. 948.

94. Rajni Kothari, '*Growing Amnesia: An Essay on Poverty and Human Consciousness* (New Delhi: Penguin, 1993), pp. 121-22.

95. Arun Kumar, 'Why Fears of a Foreign Hand are Real', *The Hindu*, 22 June 2012.

96. Moumita Ghosh, 'Democracy in India–Background and Emerging Challenges, '*South Asia Politics*, Vol. 9, No. 8, December 2010 (New Delhi: 2010), pp. 25-26.

97. C.L. Sharma, 'State of Democracy in India,' *IJPS*, Vol. LXVII, No. 1, January–March 2006 (Meerut: 2006), pp. 11-13.

98. Andre Beteille, 'Politics Without Policy.'

99. Moumita Ghosh, 'Democracy in India–Background and Emerging Challenges', p. 27.

100. Subhash C. Kashyap, 'Democratic Governance–Space for the Underprivileged', *South Asia Politics*, Vol. 7, No. 8, December 2008 (New Delhi: 2008), p. 7.

101. Deepali Singh, Nafees A. Ansari and Shaifali Singh, 'Good Governance and Implementation in Era of Globalisation,' IJPS, Vol. LXX, No. 4, October–December 2009 (Meerut: 2009), pp. 1110-11.

102. *Ibid.*, pp. 1114-15.

103. Harish Chandra Behera, 'Political System and Governance in South Asia,' *South Asia Politics*, Vol. 8, No. 11, March 2010 (New Delhi: 2010), p. 23.

104. As quoted in Subhash C. Kashyap, 'Democratic Governance–Space for the Underprivileged,' p. 13.

105. V.R. Krishna Iyer, 'Needed, a Renewed Socialist Concern', *The Hindu*, 5 Feburary 2008.

106. Yogendra Yadav, 'Imagining a New National Politics,' *Ibid.*, 12 August 2012.

107. *Ibid.*

108. P.K. Siddharth, 'Revolution Without Idea,' *The Times of India* (Nagpur), 1 August 2012.

109. Markandey Katju, 'Four People's Principles', *The Hindu*, 11 January 2012.

110. Arun Kumar, 'The Corrupt Rule the Roost', *Ibid.*, 7 January 2012.

111. Baijayant 'jay' Panda,'Choosing between Reform and Referendum,' *Ibid.*, 11 January 2012.

4 Secularism: Concept, Context with Critical Reviews

4.1 Origin with Western Dimensions

Secularism is a concept born of civilized, rational discourse. It is gentle, humane and accommodative in its approach. In this age of shrill and spicy fare, it is also somewhat bland. It lacks the emotional splendour and missionary zeal of a resurgent ideology.[1] The origin of this concept may be traced from the Renaissance, a movement that influenced Europe from the fourteenth to the sixteenth century. This movement aimed at the revival of the Greek spirit of reason and sought to liberate the society from the dominance of religion.[2] But it gained real strength from the enlightenment, which had become a powerful force in Europe. From the 17th century onwards, discoveries in science challenged deeply held beliefs and faiths which were an integral part of the broad canvas of religion. The application of these technologies and the rise of industrial societies necessitated the change in the social equilibrium that was then prevalent, that laid stress on reason and rationality. This is what helped the growth of secularism through the promotion of the scientific temper and rejection of the superstitions and faith in religion.[3] However, even in Western political thought two divergent concept of secularism developed, the liberal concept of secularism and Marxian concept. According to the liberal concept of secularism, the state should neither be religious nor anti-religious. It should not only have no religion but also be neutral towards it. There should be complete separation of religion and politics. Religion should be regarded as a private matter of an individual and there should be no place for it in public affairs. On the other the Marxian concept regards secularism as an anti-thesis of religion.[4] The Marxists believe that the inducement of religion was developed by the capitalist class to establish its hegemony and for countering the class struggle by using religion as opium.

The term 'Secularism' was first coined by a British writer, George Jacob Holyoake (1817-1906) who used this word in 1846 to promote a social order separate from religion without actively dismissing or criticising religious belief. Originally it was used by Holyoake to refer the practice of the ethics of free thought. He did not believe that secularism and atheism were related and defining secularism he wrote in his 1896 *English Secularism*, 'Secularism is a code of duty pertaining to this life, founded on considerations purely human, and intented mainly for those who find theology indefinite or inadequate, unreliable or unbelievable. Its essential principles are three: (i) The improvement of this life by material means; (ii) That science is the available providence of man ; (iii) That it is good to do good. Whether there be other good or not, the good of the present life is good, and it is good to seek that good. The term had a primary ideological meaning towards the middle of the nineteenth century when it appeared to have used. It denoted the doctrine that morality should be based on rational considerations regarding human well-being in this world, to the exclusion of the considerations relating to God or the afterlife. Later it was more generally for the belief that public institutions, especially general education, should be secular not religious. But in ancient and later before the question of supremacy arose we must be conscious about the relationship of the religion and state. The institution of religion came in existence prior to state. It came into being to establish a social order in ancient times because at that time there was neither any law or any institution like state in existence. The main purpose of institution of religion was to regulate the activities of individual on the basis of religion and religion was the supreme law. The institutions of state came too much later.

As a doctrine, secularism is usually used in reference to any philosophy which forms its ethics without reference to religious dogmas and which promotes the development of human art and science. Perhaps the best definition of secularism was given by Virgilius Ferm in his *Encyclopaedia of Religion* where he wrote, 'Secularism is a variety of utilitarian social ethic which seeks human improvement without reference to religion and exclusively by means of human reason, science and social organisation. It has developed into a positive and widely adopted outlook which aims to direct all activities and institutions by a non-religious concern for the goods of the present life and for social well-being'. The term secularism has also been explained in *Wikipedia*, the free encyclopaedia it connotes, 'that certain practices or institutions should exist separately from religion or religious belief. It asserts the right to be free from religious rule and teachings, and freedom from government imposition of religion upon the people, within a state that is neutral on matters of belief, and gives no state privileges or subsidies to religion'. It refers to a belief that human activities and decisions, especially political ones, should be based on evidence and fact rather than religious influence'. In the political sphere, it came to mean that a temporal ruler was entitled to exercise power in his own right.[5] Although the word secular means "of this world" in Latin and is the opposite of religious, in broader sense, it was used not as opposed to religion but as divorced from all religion having nothing to do with the conduct of state affairs.

However, in the twentieth century the word secularism has acquired a somewhat wider range of meaning derived from the older and wider connotations. In particular it is frequently used, along with "separation" as an approximate equivalent of the French term *laicisme*, also used in other languages. In European *laicism*, it has been argued that secularism is a movement towards modernisation, and away from traditional religious values'. It is very much different from the traditional definition in which secularism is the neutrality of government and all public services in matters relating to one or more religions.[6] But in the *Princeton Wordnet*, it is defined as a doctrine that rejects religion and religious considerations. This is quite a difference, a move from neutrality to rejection. Similar to this is the law of laicite in France which prohibits the state from recognising or funding any religion which would seem to fall within the neutral definition of secularism. The doctrine of separation of church and state is one of the most essential elements in the fabric of true representative democracies. It is indispensable and fundamentally predicted upon protecting the religious freedom of all groups in society by preventing any one group from imposing itself upon the practices of another.

Thus, normally in the West and most European countries the majority of the people have very little attachment to religion or the role of God in their daily lives. Most people in the West have given up attachment to religion at least since World War II. In fact the basic ethos of the Western society has changed over to material pursuits, science and technology, belief in their own prowess, as opposed to the role of God in their lives. Natural calamities in the West are hardly ever described as "Acts of God." The faith of the common people in God or prayer is at very low level. The same is true about most countries in Europe. The state after all reflects the public opinion at large and those who operate the organs, and agencies of the state come from the common populace. In Western countries such as the United States of America, England, Germany and others it is easier to separate the state from the church in real practice. In United States, some argue that state secularism has served to a great extent to protect religion from government interference, while secularism on a social scale is less prevalent. In USA the word secular is not to be found in the Constitution but the doctrine is embodied in it. Section 3 of the Constitution drafted by the Philadelphia Convention was ratified in 1789 reads, 'The senators and representatives before mentioned and all executives and judicial officers, both of the US and of several states, shall be bound by oath or affirmation, to support this constitution, but no religious test shall ever be required as a qualification to any office or public trust under the United States.[7] The key words here are 'no religious tests' shall be required to hold an office.

But unlike the US in England there is a close alliance between the Church and State. The Church became independent of the Pope in the 16th century and is the official Church of England. The monarch is the head of the state and head of Church. Though there is religious freedom, the Church of England has a special status inasmuch as the monarch of England must join in communion with the Church of England. In Germany the word secular means that government and religion are two separate things and must be kept separate. The state has to deal with people irrespective of their faith or religion. All laws are same for every citizen, either minority citizen or majority one. There are no special laws for special interests of minorities/majority.[8] But even there every Christian pays income tax to the Church of up to 9 per cent. If one is not a Christian, he can disclose it and this amount will not be charged. Even a Christian can decide not to pay this amount but then he has small social problems like no priest of any Church will arrange his marriage in any church. Plus he will have trouble to get his children admitted into some Kinder Garden schools run by Church.

In Muslim world perhaps Turkey is the single secularised country which is essentially closer to the Western model. In 1920s Kamal Pasha encouraged the wearing of European dress. All monasteries and religious houses were confiscated by the state, Muslim religious schools were abolished and State non-religious schools were started, Shariat Law was replaced by Swiss Civil Code, the Italian Penal Code and German Commercial Code, polygamy was abolished. A society for defence of woman's rights was established, purdah was abolished and women were persuaded to enter various professions. Latin script replaced Arabian script and Turkish language was purged of Arabic and Persian words.[9] In nutshell, the ban on religious schools and replacement of the Shariat Law meant it separated state from politics. In contrast is the case of Arab world where the entire Middle East allows little or no freedom to religious other than Islam. But in Southeast Asia inspite of being Muslim majority countries, Malaysia and Indonesia, due to centuries old Indian influence respect diversity and allow freedom to followers of religions other than Islam. For instance, Diwali is a national holiday in Malaysia, an image of Lord Ganesha is imprinted on some of Indonesian notes and their national emblem is Garuda, the vehicle of Lord Vishnu.[10] When a concept as important as secularism is not defined it is subject to misinterpretation and abuse. In political terms, secularism is a movement towards the separation of religion and government. It also can be the social ideology in which religion and supernatural beliefs are not seen as the key to understanding the world and are instead segregated from matters of governance and reasoning and in this sense, secularism can be involved in the promotion of science, reason, and naturalistic thinking. Thus it is evident that the true meaning of the term secularism is more of philosophical and sociological nature rather than political.

However, very recently and especially after the event of the Al-Qaeda terrorist attacks in US on 11 September, 2001 the picture of the secular and religious tolerant has developed some cracks, following the further terrorist attacks in London, Madrid and elsewhere in Europe. As a result in their pursuit to make their countries safe from terrorist attacks many centres of power including the state apparatus in the Western countries are falling prey to the Islamophobia attitudes of the small number of zealots. The doctrine of separation of church and state is one of the most essential elements in the fabric of true representative democracies. It is indispensable and fundamentally predicated upon protecting the religious freedom of all groups in society by preventing any one group from imposing itself upon the practices of another. But in contrast, in France and Holland the law of *laicite* has been enacted which bans large crosses, Jewish skull caps, Sikh turbans as well as Muslim headscarves. On the one hand the laws refuse the right given by international law, the right to freedom of thought, conscience and religion in diverse documents, it forfeit the individual right to claim a belief in freedom of choice and freedom of religion on the other. Article 18 of the Universal Declaration of Human Rights, Article 18 of the International Covenant on Civil and Political Rights, Article 9 of the European Convention, Article 12 of the US Convention and Article 8 of the African Charter all echo the same sentiment.[11] Barring the last all other clauses specifically mention the right "to manifest his religion of belief in teaching, practice, worship and observance". Even some treaties, for example, the International Covenant makes this right non-derogable, that means that they cannot be suspended during a proclamation of emergency. The International Covenant permits such limitations only if imposed by law and if necessary to protect public safety, order, health or morals or the fundamental rights and freedoms of others.

Not only this but the French law asserting equality of treatment under a secular law has extended the law to all other visual forms of Sikh, Jewish or Christian attire. The interpretation of this law also covers to ban students from bearing conspicuous religious symbols in primary and secondary government schools. Accordingly, student may not wear prominent religious symbols such as large crosses yarmulkes, Sikh head coverings, or hijabs-the head coverings of female Muslims. One argument against the law suggests that its interpretation aims primarily to restrict Muslim girls, and that the similar restrictions on students of other faiths is of secondary or even incidental importance. Thus, it appeared that the French state wishes to protect a group in society by preventing everyone from freely practising their religion remains absurd. It seemed that the French state has inadvertently recognised religion, even if only for the purpose of limiting it.[12] Likewise, in Holland the Dutch cabinet has recently supported a proposal by the Dutch immigration minister to ban Muslim women from bearing the burqa in public places. The justification has been given that the burquas disturb public order, citizens and safety and that integration and tolerance will be promoted by removing this barrier.[13] Once again preventing a group in society from freely practising their religion in the name of religious harmony is not only difficult, it creates an insurmountable paradox. In the context the positive Indian concept of 'Sarva Dharma Sama Bhava' is replaced by a more antiseptic and negative view of secularism as practised in some western developed economies. The approach is almost anti-religious in the sense it equally limits manifestations of all religions under so-called secular law. In this sense, secularism itself becomes a state-sponsored religion.[14] Any person is well within their rights to personally reject religion but to expect the state to practice the rejection of religion leads to laws that infringe on others. If the state is neutral, then it cannot prevent people from wearing hijabs or burqas. In accordance with the true definition of secularism, the state should not be able to pass laws restricting the religious freedom of individual citizens. No group in an established democracy would seriously advocate a move to theocracy, the installment of state sponsored religion or the mandatory state sponsored exercise of religious practices contrary to other's beliefs.

4.2 Indian Secularism

In contrast to the West, the term 'Secularism is commonly used in present day India to describe the relationship that exists, or which ought to exist, between the state and religion.[15] Technically, the secular state is a state which guarantees individual and corporate freedom of religion, deals with individual as a citizen irrespective of his religion is not constitutionally connected to a particular religion nor does it seek either to promote or interfere with religion. In India the concept has been used not as state's indifference meaning towards religions but as treatment of all religions in an equal fashion and ruling out discrimination of any Indian on the ground of his religion. In its political terminology 'secularism' governing the term 'state,' that is the expression

'Secular state', implies a contradiction to 'theocratic state' or a 'state with an established church', or to imply a polity that has no any 'state religion' or which is not a 'religio-ideological state'. With the independence of India in 1947 the secular group held that the system of the country's governance should be run along purely secular lines, independently of religion, whereas the thinking of the religious group was quite the contrary. They insisted that the political system of the country should be governed in accordance with the dictates of religion. The analysis and debates of the Constituent Assembly reveals a rejection of the Western concept of secularism, that is, absolute separation of state and religion, and acceptance of the Indian concept of 'Sarva Dharma Sambhava' or equal regard for all religions.[16] At the time although secularism failed to become one of the fundamental tenets of the Constitution, yet the declaration of India as a secular state came only with the enactment of the 42nd Amendment to the Constitution (1976) and now the Preamble proclaims India as a secular state. However, the peculiar nature of secularism in India is responsible for many unhealthy trends and practices in Indian politics. In the name of religious tolerance we have allowed religion to pervade every sphere – social, economic and political life. This has blurred the boundary which should essentially exist between religious and secular activity. In other words, the state in India while claiming to be secular overlooks the basic universal ingredients of secularism like separation of state from religion, religion from politics, administration, economic, and education, and adherence to nationalism, humanism and scientific temper.[17] Secularism in India, although embodied in the constitution, is as yet only an aspiration. It has not yet permeated our social life.

4.3 Tradition of Secularism in India

The Indian concept of secularism has always been different from its western counterparts. It grew out of its past history of a wide and general movement in thoughts and feelings, which emerges gradually from the intermingling of different groups and communities in consequence of the impetus given to it by changes in social economic and political life. Religions of India are known to have co-existed and evolved together for many centuries. India is a country where religion is very central to the life of many people. India's age-old philosophy as expounded in Hindu scriptures called Upanishads is Sarva Dharma Sambhava, which means respect for all belief system. This basic trait of Sanatan Dharma is what keeps India together despite the fact that India has not been a mono-religious country for over two millennium. In its whole history the ancient Indian polity never needed confrontational experience with the philosophies of secularism and liberty for fostering religious freedom. But in the context opposite was the experience of the west where the bitter atmosphere divided loyalties between the Caesar and God. It made clear distinction between spirituals and temporals, a theory quite in accord with the teachings of Saint Augustine was of the essence of the Christian point of view, and for this reason the relation between religious and political institutions presented to the Christian a new problem - the problem of Church and State. The concern for separation between Church and State in Europe was mainly voiced by the clergy to first maintain the superiority of the ecclesiastical order and subsequently to contain the advance of the lay monarchy.[18] Thus, for the Western thinkers, 'religion' signified 'sect' rather than universal philosophy or universal science of God. Even the divinity of King in the divine origin of State theory was essentially his conformity to Christianity. The whole Western approach towards religion-secularism interrelationship was fight oriented and basically antagonistic.

In ancient India Dharma was the true sovereign of the State; the Rule of the Law. The King was the executive called the Danda to uphold and enforce the decrees of the dharma as the spiritual sovereign. Dharma in wider sense comprised rules and principles of conduct relating to men and extended to entire range of Hindu society, all classes and castes within its fold. It conceived rules for celestial to civil subjects. Of this sacred law the sources were, tells Manu, four fold; Veda, tradition, customs and happiness.[19] Further the theocratic foundation of the State did not pose the problem the West experienced, because, for one, there was no duality of religion for a long stretch of centuries; Secondly, even after the advent of Buddhism and Jainism these sects were never pitted in confrontation with the ancient religion, and thirdly, the king was duty bound under Rajdharma to treat equally all his citizens and patronise their sects and religions and apply equal laws to all.[20] Originally Buddhism, Jainism and Sikhism were reformist movements which had absolutely no quarrel with the general principles of the 'Sanatan Religion' nor any ambition to establish a separate religion. They were partly protestant reactions against thoughtless overplay of self-importance by the Brahmanical order and partly genuine efforts to simplify and reform the overdone ritualism.[21] The perfect harmony between the three schools of ecclesiastical thoughts was symbolic of the liberal outlook in matters academic entertained by the leading thinkers of the time. In subsequent periods the rules of Kanishkas, Guptas, Harshavardhana and several other kings accorded equal treatment to Hindus, Buddhists and Jains - the only three religions co-existing at that time in India.[22] People were exhorted to lead religious, pious and moral life without any compulsion about faith, belief or worship.[23] At least up to the invasions by Mughals, difference on account of religion, race and language never posed any problem before the governments.

Freedom of religion of the individual which is one of the basic features of a secular state had for centuries been rooted in the Asian countries. It has made Indian culture a "composite" one, which, means blending of separate elements into a single whole. However, the Muslim invasions shook the Hindu and for the first time drew him out of the deep inner sanctrum of his temple. The Muslim theocracy in India under the Sultanate was based on distinction between the Hindu and the Muslim subjects. But in the period the Sufi and Bhakti movements gave a tremendous impetus to bring the people of various communities closer. The leading lights of the movement were Khawaja Moinuddin Chisti, Baba Farid, Kabir, Guru Nanak, Dadu, Tukaram and Mira Bai who contributed to the development of composite culture in such measures that was not really possible only through a political or administrative system. In the context Guru Nanak remarked, 'There is no Hindu, no Mussalman" as he saw no distinction between man and man. The spirit to tolerance has been hallmark of secular attitude and outlook[24]. In the Mughal dynasty Akbar was the single liberal ruler who was alive to the dangers of religious strife and tried to promote national solidarity by his catholic eclecticism and secular policies. His propagation of 'Din – e – Illahi (Divine Faith) Sulh – I – Kul (peace with all) were all imbued with the spirit of secularism. The mediaeval period was radically different from the modern Indian understanding of the concept of secularism.

The British Raj in India witnessed main contradiction not between religious and secular but it was between secular and communal. In the Western world main struggle was between Church and state and Church and civil society but in India neither Hinduism nor Islam had any church – like structure and hence there never was any such struggle between secular and religious power structure. Although the British period in India was not a theocracy; nevertheless one characteristic, viz., state involvement in religious institutions was conspicuously present and new dimension were given to the use of religion in politics. It was a blessing in disguise as its nature helped the Indians in abandoning the ostritch pose it had stuck to during the Mughal period. With the coming of the new ruler came the realisation of modern type of liberty, meaning thereby an artificial condition achieved and maintained by the process of fight with the state of opposed to the natural condition of society in the ancient India. Unlike the rough Moslem invaders of Yore and some begotted sultans, the British were sophisticated, liberalist rulers in matters of social, cultural and religious. Persuasion, impartiality and benevolence were the rudiments of the governmental policy in dealings with other religions. They kept nostalgically falling back on their home – land for cultural inspiration; neutrality towards heathen way of life and worship was, therefore, more akin to their nature. The British never denied freedom of conscience or worship; nor disturbed it.[25] As the patrons and indeed throughout their stay as benevolent despots' the British were concerned with many things in the Indian way of life quite closely, never excluding religion.

In India the British practised a double policy towards religion. In the spiritual, personal and ritual aspect of religion of the natives they refrained from interference and so also in the social aspect to a large extent. They were aware that religious faith continuously provide the passion to preserve in the way of life and if it declines, obedience degenerates into habit and habit slowly withersaway. The laws, customs, conventions and fashions are not the only means of social control but the religion and morality also formulate and shape the human behaviour. Religion and morality are the most influential forces of social control as well as the most effective guides of the human behaviour. The social life of a man in addition of its economic, political, philosophical, scientific and other aspects, has also religious aspects. However, on the other hand they sagaciously cultivated a new facet of religion-the political. In this role the policy of equanimity and neutrality was discarded after the 1857 Revolt in favour of the policy of counterpoise. This policy was followed by the British despite the fact that Queen Victoria had put in the Charter that her government would be neutral in matters of religion.

Earlier with the grant of Diwani in Bengal in 1765 the British rooted themselves as India's new administrators and in this capacity assumed the role of patrons of religions. In line they abolished certain cruder customs like Sati and other forms of corporal punishments sanctioned by distorted versions of scriptural rules. In addition, as a shrewed merchant the East India Company was aware of the fact that for a prosperous trade with the natives it was wise not to disturb the religious sentiments of the local inhabitants and therefore, in the whole process the method employed was of persuasion with no compulsory conversion and no interference. Emboldened by their hold over the situation and sway over native powers and helped by native reformers the British undertook a few reforms in such native practices as were repellant to the humanitarian values cherished by them. They took benefit of the favourable situation and in a special treatment, the Christianity was officially acknowledged, the British government had directed the company to meet the expenses for managing the affairs of the Church of England from the Company's Indian revenues. In this period religion was always an expressly enumerated item of powers of the Central/ State governments under the Indian Council Act and the Government of India Acts from 1858 to 1935. Such favours apart, other religions also received varying attention by way of grants for temples, expences on festivals, affording of civic facilities to religious places and fairs, encourage to study of scriptures and their translations, efforts to understand and implement the ancient laws, are the details of the Company's relations with religion.[26] Thus, the British, in their own way, continued religious involvement and all along patronised the counterpoise policy initiated especially in post - 1857 period.

The British policy of counterpoise was founded on the political use of religion in the wake of the traumatic experience they had of the great Revolt of 1857. In the context communal disharmony was the remedy suggested by Governor – General Lord Lawrence (1864-69) to thwart the recurrence of 1857 type revolt against the British, 'Among the defects of the premutiny army… was the brotherhood and the homogeneity of the Bengal army, and for this purpose, the remedy is counterpoise; first the great counterpoise of the Europeans, and secondly the native races'.[27] Such subtle of communalism was never known to India before; so far it was either swords or songs, never was religion a disguised medium of power politics. Brick by brick the British built a wall of separation between the religious communities of India, particularly the two numerically largest, most vocal and influential ones – Hindus and Muslims. The new policy of counterpoise became a tool and exihibited carefully by the Morley – Minto Reforms of 1909 and nurtured into a giant by the subsequent Government of India Acts. Starting with the Muslims in 1909, the separate electorate was extended further to the Sikhs in 1919 and Indian Christians, Anglo – Indians, Europeans, Harijans, Marathas and non-Brahmins in 1935. The misuse of religion as a counterpoise was further confirmed when Lord Dufferin in his farewell address at Calcutta said on 23 March, 1888, 'God forbid that the British government should ever seek to maintain its rule by fomenting race hatred among its subjects'.[28] Thus, from Morley – Minto Reforms (1909) to the Cabinet Mission Plan (1946) the British kept on harping the strain. 'The Indian Mohommadans are much more than a religious body. They form in fact an absolutely separate community'.[29] The persistent British hints created the sense of insecurity in Muslim mind that they had to work hard only to succeed, to salvage 'their territory, Muslim majority areas from Hindu usurpation'. It led to the partition of the country in August 1947.

4.4 Secularism Around Independence

On the eve of independence we decided to establish a secular state with its own characteristics of religious tolerance, liberty and equality. Religious tolerance is a key element in the concept of Indian secularism because it has been a significant element of our historical tradition.[30] Sociologically too, secularism in India is a way of life. In a country where there are at least 12 religions, over 300 castes, nearly 4,000 sub castes, over 20 languages, over 300 dialects, mixed traditions, the only way to reduce internal tension is to inculcate tolerance and co-existence.[31] The idea of secularism in a country like India with its pluralist tradition lasting over thousands of years cannot succeed without respecting pluralist ethos. The West has discovered pluralism recently – after the Second World War and hence calls it post – modernist phenomenon. But India has known it even during mediaeval ages. Modernisation brought new problems and we began to imitate the West without understanding our own social realities. These problems are getting intractable as our society is not changing especially when it comes to the mass of people.[32] In modern political sense the Hindu who in the past performed religious worship as his religious duty, now began demanding a right to freedom of worship; and the fellow citizen Muslim, who had till only a recent past enjoyed the reassuring privilege of state protection and promotion of his religious interests, began realising the necessity of a 'secular' state that would grant him, and not withhold, his right to religious freedom. Religion had always exercised a great influence on the people in their social ways and habits. The epochs in which religion stood for deeper philosophies in quest of the Absolute, were the epochs when society represented vitality, and tolerance, vigour and elasticity.[33] Religion is part of society. It is a universal, permanent, pervasive and perennial institution and it has a vital function in maintaining the social system as a whole.

Around the period when India was to be freed from the British rule there were many great men who have come and left their imprint on the sand of time as men of thought and action, vision and dynamism, conviction and commitment. They passed the test of being called a very great man. About the test, to quote Isaiah Berlin, 'To call someone a great man is to claim that he has intentionally taken a large step, one far beyond the normal capacities of men, in satisfying or materially affecting central human interests. Similarly, in the realm of action, the great man seems able almost alone and single handed to transform one form of his life into another... permanently and radically alters the outlook and values of a significant body of human beings.[34] In pre and post – independence periods the concepts of secularism and religious freedom remained significant in the minds of public as well as leaders. Among leaders there are many who belonged to the Indian National Congress (INC), such as Mahatma Gandhi, Jawaharlal Nehru, Maulana Abul Kalam Azad, B.R. Ambedkar, staunch supporters of "Hindu Rashtra"- M.S. Golwalkar, Veer Savarkar and a host of others. Earlier in the Nehru Report of 1928 the right to freedom of conscience, profession and practice of religion was included explicitly to prevent one community domineering over another. In its original conception secularism meant anti – theism, but not atheism; it was philosophically a movement intentionally ethical, negatively religious.[35] It introduces science, technology and rationalism in the society and forms the basis of a modern secular state. In the process it has to oppose and struggle against the clergy and vested forces in the society. And as such, the fundamentalist communal onslaughts are the 'other' of secularism and secularization. The Indian leaders during the freedom struggle and thereafter made secularism the mantra of the Indian nation, though each expressed their concerned views in different manners, representing the aspirations of the different sections of society. Especially Gandhi and Nehru with others preferred to keep India secular in the sense that Indian state will have no religion though people of India will be free both in individual and corporate sense to follow any religion of their birth or adoption. Secularism in India meant equal respect for all religions and cultures and non-interference of religion in government affairs. Thus, India remained politically secular but otherwise its people continued to be deeply religious. It is perhaps due to the influence of ancient Vedic doctrine that truth is one but is manifested in different forms. The real spirit of secularism in India is all inclusiveness, religious pluralism and peaceful co-existence.

Both Gandhi and Nehru had varied concept on secularism due to their difference in approach towards religion. Right from the beginning towards the end of his life Gandhi was a staunch follower of religion. It was religion which has played a central role in making of the Mahatma. To him religion is the basis of life which teaches right conduct, right faith right knowledge and finally shows the way in acquiring deliverance. Gandhi believes that it is religion which makes man a man in the real sense. On the contrary Nehru was not so overwhelmed by religion. His ideas were the product of deep introspection. He thinks of religion as a means not an end. He was rational and utilitarian thinker to whom political freedom and material development was more important than the spiritual and moral side of things.[36] Basically Gandhi was by nature a religious man whereas Nehru had a scientific and western bent of mind. Gandhi openly praised Hindu religion, while Nehru rarely indulged in such advocacy of religion. Gandhi repeatedly stressed the virtues of religion but practically overlooked its vices, while Nehru did the exact opposite.[37] However, a close examination also reveals that they appeared to have common views regarding the basic elements of religion. Gandhi and Nehru were not fundamentalists in their conception of religion, secular in their religious approach and believed that religion was instrumental in holding people together. They did not believe in state religion even though the whole community had one religion. They were against the state aid to religious bodies. They regarded religion as a private matter but the teachings of ethics were certainly regarding as a major concern of the state.

Especially in context of Gandhi secularism has come to be defined in four ways:

(I) Separation of religion from politics, economy, education, large areas of social relations, culture, and treatment of religion as a private or personal affair.

(II) Neutrality of the State towards all faiths or, as many religious persons would put it, equal regard for all faiths, including atheism.

(III) Treatment of all citizens as equal and absence of discrimination in favour of or against citizens on grounds of their religion.

(IV) A clear – cut opposition to communalism.[38]

However, before taking up the Gandhian view of secularism it is necessary to know that Gandhi often used the word religion in two different senses: one, in its denominational sense that is, in terms of Hinduism, Islam, Christianity, etc. And the other in the traditional sense of dharma or the divine moral order or ethics or the moral code which guided a person's life and the social order. In asserting that politics would be based on religion, he clearly meant that it should have a moral foundation in dharma and not in religion in the denominal form, or the sectarian form, in terms of sectional or sectarian beliefs. It was in this sense that Gandhi believed Hiduism and other religion being tolerant and secular could not make state un-secular. Therefore, there was no need for separation between state and religion. He was of the view that state while giving fair treatment to all religions, could still maintain equal distance from all religions as well as religious communities.[39] Gandhi, a deeply religious man saw merit and truth in all religions and he felt that any form of political association based exclusively on adherence to a particular religion was worse than undemocratic.

Undoubtedly, for decades Gandhi emphasised the close connection between religion and politics. In his case, his patriotism, his deep social commitment and strong sense of the moral were based on deeply held religious beliefs. There was, he said, no politics without religion as "religion is the basis on which all life structure has to be erected if life is to be real". For instance, during 1920-21, he repeatedly referred to the Non-Cooperation Movement as "a religious, purifying movement and as religious effort". But for Gandhi, this close connection between religion and politics was because politics had to be moral, it had to be based on morality. And religion to him was the source of morality, it was, in fact, morality in the

Indian sense of dharma.[40] No secular person would disagree with the view that politics should be moral and that this sense of the moral can be imbibed in various ways and forms and from diverse sources, religious as well as non-religious.

However, more important is the fact that during the 1940s Gandhi began to change his linguistic formulation regarding the relationship between religion and politics when he saw that the communalists were using religion in its organised, denominational or doctrinal form, or religion not as dharma or a code of morality, but in the form of Hinduism, Islam and Sikhim, to promote communal divide, to demand religion-based States and to raise the cry of religion in danger. He now began to assert that religion and politics should be kept separate and that religion should be treated as a private concern of the individual. Continuously in 1942, 1946, and 1947 through his speeches and writings, Gandhi was emphatic in asserting that religion is a personal matter which should have no place in politics. He told a missionary in September 1946: If I were a dictator, religion and State would be separate. I swear by my religion. I will die for it. But it is my personal affair. The State has nothing to do with it. Likewise in 1947 he laid emphasis on the fact that the State is bound to be wholly secular and even opposed religious instruction as part of school curriculum as approved by the state even if the whole community had one religion.[41]

While Nehru, explaining his view on religion argued, 'Probably it consists of the inner development of the individual' the evolution of his consciousness in a certain direction which is considered good. Religion lays stress on this inner change and considers outward change as the projection of this inner development. There can be no doubt that this inner development powerfully influences that outer environment. But it is equally obvious that the outer development powerfully influences the inner development.[42] Unlike Gandhi, Nehru held that whatever the characteristics of the various religions may have been, it did not matter because economic development and scientific culture would provide a sufficient basis for secular tolerance. He was an agnostic and his views was that of neutrality of the State in matters of religion - the State would have nothing to do with religion.[43] He has been a leading champion of the concept of the secular state and creation of India as a secular state may be accepted in the words of Chester Bowels as 'one of his greatest achievements'. Nehru was especially concerned with transforming India from a "caste – ridden society" in which communalism constitutes a major threat to all the values that he cherished to a nation state which included people of all religions and shades of opinion and was essentially secular as a state.[44] In case of India he insisted that it should be a non-communal, secular state. The government of a country like India, Nehru declared, 'With many religions that have secured great and develop followings for generations can never function satisfactorily in the modern age except on a secular basis.[45] Later the religious views of Gandhi and Nehru laid the firm foundation of secular state in India. Like Gandhi and Nehru Maulana Abul Kalam Azad also expressed his view in favour of making India a fully secular state.

In addition the Indian views and expressions on secularism were influenced by Dr. B.R. Ambedkar, Dr. S. Radhakrishnan and Vivekananda. Explaining the concept of secularism Ambedkar said during a debate, 'It (secular state) does not mean that we shall not take into consideration the religious sentiments of the people. All that a secular state means is that this parliament shall not be competent to impose any particular religion upon the rest of the people. That is the only limitation that the constitution recognises'.[46] In India no one can deny the importance of religion in personal and social life. Religion is the major concern of man. Man is always having religious quest which makes him able to become a restless creature even beyond the satisfaction of his physical needs. Religion revolves around man's faith in the supernatural forces. In the context President Radhakrishnan quotes the significance of secularism in the following words, 'When India is said to be a secular state, it does not mean that we reject the reality of an unseen spirit or the relevance of religion to life or that we exalt irreligion. It does not mean that secularism itself becomes a position religion or that the state assumes divine prerogatives. Though faith in the supreme is the basic principle of the Indian tradition the Indian state will not identify itself with or be controlled by any particular religion'.[47] India has adopted the concept of positive secularism and composite Indian culture that permit differences but eliminate divisiveness and bring about a harmony of unity in diversity. When positive secularism accompanies the practice of multiple religions, it is bound to be helpful in promoting national integration and communal harmony.[48] The essence of Vivekananda's teaching on religion was the universality of God and his accessibility both in form and without form, the divinity of man, respect and understanding of all religions.

However, in a multi – religious society if politics is not based on issues but on identities, it can prove highly divisive. The mediaeval society in India had religious tolerant as it was non – competitive. The modern Indian society has proved to be more divisive as it is based on competition. It is being a mixture of religion, is always prove to dominance and conflict. Around the independence and even before the supporters of Hinduism and Hindutva the RSS/VHP/BJP sought the formation of a "Hindu Rashtra" whose initial exponents include V.D. Savarkar, M.S. Golwalkar, Deen Dayal

Upadhyaya and others who followed the principle and line of action. They wanted to construct independent India on the basis of the religious denomination of its people. This vision had a twin expression. One was the demand for a "Hindu Rashtra advanced by the RSS and other for the creation of an Islamic state advanced by the Muslim League. While the latter achieved its objective through the cruel partition of our country, the former vision was rejected by a majority of Indians. Savarkar, in his Presidential address to the Hindu Mahasabha in 1938 said; India can not be assumed today to be unitarian and homogeneous nation, but on the contrary there are two nations in the main, the Hindus and the Muslims.[49] Thus in pre – independence period the three visions of what should constitute independent India were voiced by Hindu Mahasabha, Muslim League and the Indian National Congress in which the last favoured India to be a democratic secular Republic. In the freedom struggle while the Hindu Mahasabha and Muslim League remained poles apart, the INC continued adhere its secular image and spirit.

Thus in opposition to Mahatma Gandhi's tolerant Hindusim was Savarkar's violent Hinduism and they both represented alternative concepts of Hinduism and the Indian nation. Both Veer Savarkar and M.S. Golwalker wanted India to be a sovereign Hindu State. Perhaps for the first time in 1923 Savarkar propounded the two nation theory in his essay *Hindutva*, We Hindus are bound together – by the tie of the common homage we pay to our great civilisation - our Hindu culture ——We are one because we are a nation, a race and own a common sanskriti or civilization. Further he reiterated his view in 1937 and 1938 where he decrised that we Hindus are a nation by ourselves because religious, racial cultural and historical affinities bind us intimately into a homogeneous nation.[50] The same sentiment was expressed by Golwalkar in his *Bunch of Thoughts*. It is the concept of cultural nationalism as opposed to territorial nationalism. He, in his treatise, *We or Our Nationhood Defined* pleaded that non – Hindus in Hindustan must either adopt the Hindu culture and language, must learn to respect and hold in reverence Hindu religion, must entertain no idea but those of the glorification of the Hindu race and culture, that is, of the Hindu nation and must lose their separate existence to merge in the Hindu nation, claiming nothing, deserving no privileges, far less any preferential treatment not even citizen's rights.[51] However, the views and visions made public by Savarkar, Golwalkar and others did not find much appreciation at the time, but it proved an asset for future politicians of the country whosoever may be. In fact we need religious value in politics as Gandhi said but certainly not politicisation of religion. A state should never priorities one religion over the other, particularly in a secular country like India. India is a secular country as per the declaration in the Preamble to the Indian Constitution made at the time of independence and implemented on 26 January, 1950.

4.5 Secularism and Indian Constitution

India has been declared a secular state by its written constitution but a number of efforts to secure the inclusion of the word 'secular' in the fundamental law of the land did not find favour with the framers of the Constitution.[52] The coming of the partition emphasised the great importance of secularism. Notwithstanding the partition a large Muslim minority, constituting a tenth of the population of India, continued to be citizens of India. Secularism became the mantra of the Indian nation, a nation exhausted by partition and sectarian riots and above all the assassination of Gandhi did not want any more divisive talk. In the circumstances, a secular constitution of independent India, under which all religions could enjoy equal freedom and all citizens equal rights, and which could well together into one nation the different religious communities became inevitable. Our Constitution did not erect any 'wall of separation' between religion and the State. While prohibiting religion- based discrimination between the citizens, it did not prevent the state from participating in the people's religious affairs. It enabled the State to generally "regulate or restrict secular activity associated with religion".[53] First under Jawaharlal Nehru and later under his successors in the Congress Party, the concept of a secular nation state was officially adopted as India's path to political modernity and national integration. Unlike in the West, where secularism came mainly out of the conflict between the Church and the State secularism in India was conceived as a system that sustained religious and cultural pluralism.

The word 'secular' is not written in the Constitution, but it does not mean that the founding fathers of the Constitution had any doubt about the nature of the Indian state being secular. The framers of our constitution properly debated the issue of secularism and individual's religious rights with other members and after due considerations they decided to make India a secular state. While our constitution has been based on secularism or Dharma Nirapekshita, our society is stepped in religion. Religious feelings govern our mode of thinking and we observe religious festivals and rituals as part of our day-to-day life. In comparison to other countries of the world secularism has a very different meaning in India. In the context, wrote Jawaharlal in his autobiography 'no word perhaps in any language is more likely to be interpreted in different ways by different people as the word religion. That being the case, secularism which is a concept evolved in relation to religion can also not have the same connotation for all.'[54] Even during the course of the discussion in the Constituent Assembly on the fundamental rights relating to religion, the idea of secularism was extensively pressed into service by the members as the most handy tool to substantiate various view-points, often diametrically opposed. The members of the Constituent Assembly were in no doubt that the phase 'secular state' and the terms secular and secularism should help us in understanding that the principle is meant the constitutional concept of equality and freedom for all religions, infused every provision of the fundamental rights with this spirit and therefore very wisely avoided institutionalising it in words interminably capable of connoting varying and conflicting meanings.

Several members of Constituent Assembly including K.T. Shah, H.V. Kamath, Tajamul Hussain, Lakshmi Kanta Maitra and Loknath Mishra presented their views/modifications in the fruitful discussion on secularism and religious rights of Indian citizens. In course of the discussion K.T. Shah proposed a new Article 18-A to be inserted under the heading 'rights relating to religion' which would emphasise, 'The State in India being secular shall have no concern with any religion, creed or profession of faith; and shall observe an attitude of absolute neutrality in all matters relating to the religion of any class of its citizens or other persons in the Union. He also added, 'All I wish to say is that with the actual profession of faith or belief, the state should have no concern.[55] India being the secular state with having nothing to do with religion, Tajamul Hussain wanted that caste names, signs and dress be done away with. 'We should not being a secular state, be recognised by our dress'.[56] While H.V. Kamath warned the Assembly not to adopt any religion as it would split the country he made it clear that by this he does not mean to say that a State should be anti – religious or irreligious. According to him a secular state is neither a Godless state nor irreligious nor an anti – religious state. He even advocated imparting spiritual training in educational institutions.[57] In the debate discussing the right to propagate religion Lakshmi Kanta Maitra laid stress on the fact that there should be no discrimination whatsoever on the ground of religion -means in essence that no particular religion in the State will receive any State patronage but he accepted the fact that even in a secular state there is necessity for religion.[58] However, there was a school of opinion in favour of India being made a Hindu state.

In the Constituent Assembly Loknath Mishra represented Hindu point of view and opposing right to propagate religion said, 'We have declared the State to be a secular State. For obvious and for good reasons we have also declared. Does it not mean that we have nothing to do with any religion? Why do you make it a secular state? The reason may be that religion is not necessary, but as India has many religions, Hinduism, Christianity, Islam and Sikhism, we cannot decide which one to accept. Therefore, let us have no religions. No. That cannot be. If you accept religion you must accept Hinduism as it is practised by an overwhelming majority of the people of India.[59] He continued on saying, 'gradually it seems to me that our secular state is a slippery phrase, a device to by-pass the ancient culture of the land'. He said he failed to understand the 'exact meaning of secularism'. So he wanted that the Constitution should say nothing about right to religion, 'or at least drop the word propagate' from the right.[60] Particularly, the Hindu members in the Assembly totally disagreed with the view that the propagation of religion should be considered a legitimate aspect of religious freedom. But the overwhelming majority of members did not agree with the view. Explaining the word propagate K.M. Munshi remarked, 'Even if the word were not there, he assured under the Freedom of Speech which the Constitution guarantees it will be open to any religious community to persuade other people to join their faith'.

The individual right of freedom of religion as given in the Indian Constitution is of far greater importance, particularly for the religious minorities and for their smooth development. Apart from this, most of the constitutions of the world that provide freedom of religion, such as Switzerland, former USSR, the Peoples Republic of China and Japan do not explicitly guarantee right to propagate religion as a justifiable fundamental right. The word 'propagate' does not find a place in any other constitution where it deals with religious freedom. Despite vehemently opposition to the inclusion of this term by the members as they thought that it might be perilous to guarantee it and might freely be used for the purpose of wholesale conversion. However, it did not find favour of the majority and one member pointed out, 'After all propagation is merely freedom of expression. I would like to point out that the word 'convert' is not there. Those who drafted this constitution have taken care to see that no unlimited right of conversion has been given. People have freedom of conscience, and if any man is converted voluntarily owing to freedom of conscience then well and good. No restriction can be placed against it.[61] Further, it is perhaps in consonance with the provisions of United Nations Declaration of Human Rights, which say, 'Everyone has the right to freedom of thought, conscience and religion: this right includes freedom to change his religion or belief, and freedom, either alone or in community with others and in public or private, to manifest his religion or belief in teaching, practice, worship and observance'.[62] Thus, without doubt, the scope of the freedom of religion in India is considerably wide and broad.

However, as a result of debates and discussions the term 'secularism' was first defined by the Constituent Assembly on April 3, 1948 , 'Whereas it is essential for the proper functioning of democracy and the growth of national unity and solidarity that communalism should be eliminated from Indian life, this assembly is of the view that no communal organisation, which by its constitution or by the exercise of discretionary power vested in any of officers and organs, admits to, or excludes from, its membership persons on grounds of religion, race and caste or any of them, should be permitted to engage in any activities other than those essential for the bonafide religious, cultural, social and educational needs of the community and that all steps, legislative and administrative, necessary to prevent such activities should be taken'.[63] On the basis of Constituent Assembly's resolution, the provisions of Indian constitution made clear the nature of secularism in India which broadly means four things: (i) the rejection of a theocratic or semi – theocratic state, (ii) the proclamation that religion is of private or group concern, (iii) equality of all citizens irrespective of his caste or creed, and (iv) the right of the state interfere in the religious practices of various communities in the interest of their peaceful co-existence and cultural development.[64] In addition, the freedom of religion guaranteed under Indian constitution is not confined to its citizens but extends to all persons including 'aliens'. This point was underlined by the Supreme Court in Ratilal Panchand vs. State of Bombay as it is very important because substantial number of foreign Christian missionaries in India were engaged at that time in propagating their faith among the adherents of other religions.

January 26, 1950, marked a great event in the long and chequered history as on that day, was brought into force, the present Constitution of India. A constitution is a set of laws and rules setting up the machinery of the government of a State and which defines and determines the relations between the different institutions and areas of government; the executive, the legislative and the judiciary, the central, the regional and the local governments. The Indian constitution is a blend of idealism and realism. In hammering it out, the framers traversed all the processes of "democratic manufactory" and ranged through the whole gamut of democratic factors. There have been careful thought, close analysis, argument and counter – argument. As a result, the Constitution emerged as a basis for all the people of India to work in cooperation and collaboration in a mighty endeavour to build a new, free India. Pandit Nehru contended that a Constitution was not only a legal document but also a social and political document and as such, it must reflect not only the aspirations and wishes of the people, but also serve as an effective instrument for carrying out a socio-economic revolution.[65] The objective of Socialism and Secularism, which they had tried to implement in the past, and would be more and more implemented in the future would have to be more accurately and correctly reflected in it.

In particular, the Constituent Assembly was satisfied with other provisions of right and in its bid to infuse complete confidence in the religious minorities, it adopted a separate group of articles dealing solely with the right to freedom of religion.

The Constitution of India provides the freedom of religion in Articles 25 to 30 but in first four articles (25,26,27,28) the rights are conceived in most generous terms to the complete satisfaction of religious minorities. They were in fact the result of an agreement with the minorities, almost unanimously arrived at in the Minorities Committee constituted by the Constituent Assembly. Accordingly part (1) of Article 25 secures to all persons freedom of conscience: and the right to (i) profess religion; (ii) practice religion; and (iii) propagate religion. The Constitution declares that every person has a fundamental right not only to hold whatever religious belief commend themselves to his judgement, but also to express his belief in such overt acts as are prescribed by his religion and propagate its tenets among others. The scope of this article is very wide and meaningful. Apart from so many other things it declares, 'The state or the Government cannot aid one religion, or give preference to one religion as against another. It means that in India no particular religion will receive state patronage.[66] But Article 25 (2) provides broad sweeping over interference to the state in religious matters. It imposes drastic limitations on the rights guaranteed under Article 25 (1) and reflects the peculiar needs of Indian society. The framers of constitution made Article 25 (2) a part of Article 25 (1) by placing three restrictions to the freedom of religion, namely, public order, morality and health. The Supreme Court of India in the case of Commissioner of Hindu Religious Endowment vs. L.T. Swamiar held, 'Article 25 guarantees to every person, subject to public order, health and morality a freedom not only to entertain such religious belief as may be approved of by his judgement and conscience, but also to exhibit his belief in such outward acts as he thinks proper and to propagate or disseminate his ideas for the edification of others. The expression 'practice of religion' denotes that the constitution not only protects the freedom of religious opinion but also acts done in pursuance of a religion'.[67] In other words the article protects the acts done in pursuance of religious belief as part of religion.

Likewise Article 26 is, in fact, a corollary to Article 25 and guarantees the freedom to manage religious affairs. Under this every religious denomination is given the right (i) to establish and maintain institutions for religious and charitable purposes; (ii) to manage its affairs in matters of religion; (iii) to own and acquire movable and immovable property, and (iv) to administer such property in accordance with law. In this context, the term 'religious denomination' has not been defined in the Constitution but the Supreme Court of India has accepted the definition as given in Oxford Dictionary, that defines it as 'a collection of individuals classed together under the same name a religious sect of body having a common faith and organisation and designated by a distinctive name'. The Supreme Court in number of cases held that Arya Samaj, Anandmarga, Vaishanave, the followers of Madhawacharya and other religious teachers, though not separate religions yet these are separate religious denomination and enjoys the protection under Article 26 of the Constitution. But the right of a religious denomination to manage its own affairs in matters of religion is subject to any law protected by Article 25 (2) (b) throwing open a Hindu Public temple to all classes and sections of Hindus. The object of this provision is to remove a potent cause of disunion and inequality among the various castes of the Hindu. It is indeed a corollary to the abolition of untouchability.

Undoubtedly Articles 25 and 26 provide every person vast rights pertaining to religious freedom, it however, is not absolute and subject to certain limitations. The text of these articles is concerned with provisions of the constitution and are subject to public order, morality and health. In addition regarding Article 25 there are two more exception. First this freedom is subject to the other provisions of Part III of the Constitution and secondly, under clause 2 (3): Nothing in this Article shall affect the operation of any existing law or prevent the state from making any law (i) regulating or restricting any economic, financial, political or other secular activity which may be associated with religious practice; (ii) providing for social welfare and reform or the throwing open of Hindu religious institutions of a public character to all classes and sections of Hindus. Judiciary in India has also on various occasions, upheld the view that freedom of religion is not an absolute one. In the case of Masud Alam vs. Commission of Police, it was decided that banning of electrical loudspeakers calling for prayer may be valid. No doubt every religion has a right to have propaganda. But when such propaganda is made through loudspeakers in a crowded and noisy locality to the detriment of public moral, health or order, it is prohibited by Article 25. A loudspeaker may take one to hell instead of Heaven by the very volume of its sound.[68] Similarly Chapter xv, Section 295 to 298 of the Indian Panel Code (IPC) deals with the offences relating to religions that is, injuring or defiling place of worship with intent to insult the religion of any class, disturbing religious assembly trespassing on burial places, etc. Even though these actions might be sanctioned by the offender's own religion, these are offences under the law.

Article 27 of the Indian Constitution provides an additional protection to religious activity by exempting funds appropriated towards the promotion or maintenance of any particular religion from the payment of taxes, while Article 28 lawfully permits to propagate religion by means of religious instructions in educational institutions.[69] Further it also provided that (i) No religious instruction shall be provided in any educational institution wholly maintained out of State funds. (ii) Nothing in clause I shall apply to an educational institution which is administered by the State but has been established under any endowment or trust which requires that religious instruction shall be imparted in such a situation. (iii) No person attending any educational institution recognised by the State or receiving aid out of State funds shall be required to take part in any religious instruction that may be imparted in such institution or to attend any religious worship that may be conducted in such institutions or in any premises attacked thereto unless such person or, if such person is a minor, his guardian has given his consent thereto.[70] In line, Article 29 and 30 guarantee cultural and educational rights to (i) every linguistic, scriptorial or cultural section of the citizens of India; (ii) every citizen of any religion, race, caste or language; (iii) every religious or linguistic minority, and (iv) every religious or linguistic minority educational institution.[71] The object behind Article 29 and 30 is the recognition and preservation of the different types of people, with diverse languages and different beliefs, which constitute the essence of secularism in India. This aspect is based on the idea that the individual, not the group is the basic unit. The undivided is confronted by the state which imposes duties and responsibilities upon him; in return the state guarantees rights and grants privileges to the individual. The sum of these individual state relationship constitutes the meaning of citizenship. There are numbers of provisions dealing with citizen's relations with state in social spheres. The provisions based on non-discrimination in political functions have also been dealt with under the Constitution.

However, the whole edifice of secularism in India took a large step. By the Forty-second Constitutional Amendment Act 1976 the Preamble was amended for the words 'sovereign democratic Republic' by the words 'Sovereign, Socialist, Secular, Democratic Republic'. For the first time the word 'secularism' was introduced in the Constitution and speaking on the motion for consideration of the Bill in the Lok Sabha on 25 October, 1976, H.R. Gokhale, the Minister of Law, Justice and Company Affairs, justified the inclusion of the words 'Socialism and Secularism' by citing the Congress Resolution passed in 1931 at Karachi in which Pandit Nehru remarked after getting political freedom their further objective was to bring about a socio-economic revolution in the country, 'The objective which we had always in view, namely socialism and secularism, which we had tried to implement, will be more and more implemented and will be more accurately and correctly reflected in a basic part of our Constitution, namely, the Preamble. Sardar Swaran Singh, justifying the addition of the concept in the Preamble observed, '......But secular now is a word which I think has become part of our Indian languages. People of India in their different languages use the word secular because it has assumed a definite meaning and the meaning is that there will be equality before the eye of the law in our Constitution with regard to the people professing different religions.[72] The Lok Sabha, after discussing the Bill for seven days, passed it on November 2, 1976. Two days later, on November 4, 1976, the Rajya Sabha took up the 42nd Amendment as passed by the Lok Sabha, after discussing it for six days, passed it on November 11, 1976.[73] By and large members from both the Houses welcomed the addition of the word 'secularism' in the Preamble. The declaration by the 42nd Amendment, inserting the word 'secular' in the Preamble, amounts to this effect: 'We the people of India, in the Constituent Assembly, on 26th November, 1949, constitute India into a Socialist Secular State as we declare so on 18th December, 1976. It was explained that insertion of the term meant equality, non-discrimination and equal respect for all religions.

The Indian polity having rejected theocracy or state church and adopted equality of all religions as the state policy in the post-Independence constitutional era the term secular had no relevance for the purposes of the interpretation of the Constitution and laws. Actually while, the word, 'secularism' is rather vague and was introduced by 42nd Amendment, Articles 25 to 30 of the constitution relating to the freedom of religion and freedom to manage religious affairs are more specific. The ideals of secular state have clearly been embodied under the Indian constitution and the provisions are being implemented in substantial measure. But the circumstances after independence have posed a challenge before secularism of India for a number of times. India being still a traditional society that contains not one, but many traditions owing their origin in part to the different religions that exist here. While India carries with it many traditions it has managed to retain the secular character of its polity.

However the overall environment around us do not certify the theme of secularism and when we examine the working of various non – government institutions, the various political parties, especially national parties, which are supposed to have thrown their membership open to all communities, we find that the spirit of secularism is being flouted day after day. We are not completely secular in our approach and attitudes. The universalisation of secular principles should enable secularism not to degenerate into an institutionalised policy of appeasement or domination of religious groups based on the needs of the day. A consensual framework that is based on mutual respect and common principles, not separate beliefs protected by law, needs to develop. The evolution of and adherence to such predetermined but definable principles of state and individual value based behaviour is essential if secularism is to become a universalist social and community ideology and not remain a purely political instrument of societal regulation within the contemporary Indian scenario.

4.6 Use and Misuse of Secularism in Indian Politics

Without doubt secularism has been one of the essential elements in the basic structure of our constitution which lays down that (i) the state has no religion; (ii) all citizens however have the fundamental right to follow and propagate their own religion; and (iii) it is the duty of the state to protect life, liberty and property of all citizens, provide security to them and enable them to exercise their fundamental rights. The state will not discriminate between the citizens on the grounds of religion and language. But while our constitution has been based on secularism or dharma nirapekshita, our society is steeped in religion. Observance of religious festivals and rituals is part of our day-to-day life. Religious feelings govern our mode of thinking. Thus there is a clear contradiction between the basic tenets of the Constitution and the character of our society. These get reflected in our politics and public administration, which often work in a manner contrary to what is envisaged in the Constitution. The caste and communal character of our politics inevitably enters in the conduct of public administration. While the constitution envisages secularism in the sense of dharma nirapekshita, our politicians have conveniently interpreted it as sarva dharma samabhava. This has given free licence to our politicians holding high positions to freely participate in all religious functions with the official paraphernalia in attendance. Going a step further all political parties use religion to gather votes. This starts from the selection of the candidates taking into account the communal character of the constituency. Vote banks are systematically built on the basis of caste and religion and the very leaders who take advantage of these vote banks do so in the name of secularism. This has been the hypocrisy of our secular democracy.

Although it is true that for centuries in India the people of different religious ideas and cultural values have lived together. During this period attitudes of tolerance for each other's religious faith did developed and a process of symbiosis and cultural pluralism resulted. But this was primarily due to two factors. First, sultans and rajas realised the need for accommodation, and along with military and aristocratic forces evolved ways of living together and common style of life. The Rajput-Mughal symbiosis is one example of this, second, at the mass level there were innumerable Sufis and saints who fought, against Mullah Islam and priestly Brahmanism pioneering equalitarian and universalistic values and practices, which established ties among communities rather than dividing them along caste and sectarian lines as part of a critique of existing religious political powers.[74] In the Post Independence scenario the social dynamics was very complex. The process of secularization/ industrialisation was going on at a slow pace. Even at this stage, though constitution was secular, the state apparatus: the bureaucracy, the judiciary, the army and the police were infiltrated by communal elements. The Congress government, though predominantly secular, had many leaders in important positions who were influenced by a Hindu communal ideology. This resulted in a social development that was mixed; on the one hand secularism thrived and on the other though communalism remained dormant, was never dead. The political use of Hindu religion begins under the impulse of colonial modernity in which proposals were advanced for a 'semiticised unitary Hinduism.[75] Originally it was first proposed by nationalists who thought that Hinduism suffered in comparison with Christianity because of its lack of effective ecclesiastical organisation. The idea of Hinduism itself is quasi-political in origin, in the sense that people did not wish to be Hindus in this abstract sense until they felt political need to do so. It is therefore easy to exploit it for overtly political purposes.[76] The reality in India is much more complex than western societies, which have been totally secularised.

Use of religion for political purposes or for gaining victory in elections was almost unknown for political parties at the time of independence. It is curious to note that communal politics gained strength after about forty years of national government. If it was entirely due to the forces of traditionalism it should have appeared at the time when forces of modernity had gained enormously in Indian society and economy. Since the sixties Indian politics has been a massive alteration in style, language, modes of behaviour, reflecting far more the actual cultural understanding of rural Indian society rather than the Westernist cultivation of the elite which inherited power in the Nehru years. It was more compounded by the forgetfulness and negligence of Nehruvian state who not merely failed to create conditions for a common sense in Indian politics, through which liberal secular political ideas could be communicated dialogically to them, rather, its neglect of cultural institutions like primary education which contributed to a further division in society. As a result the benefits of development were so unequally and unjustly distributed that it prepared ground for two types of political dissent – an economic critique of class and an indigenist critique of modernist cultural privilege. The second kind of resentment, naturally, has predominantly found cultural expression through regionalist and communal politics, through the politics of Hindu and Hinduism.

There are two consequences of this mixing up of religion, politics and public administration. First, it has given prominence in public life to religious leaders like 'Sants' and 'Mahants', 'Imams' and 'Priests'. They have started playing an active role in government's decision–making. The interference of religious leaders in administrative matters can prove dangerous to our secular democracy. Secondly, practices and festivals have started making serious inroads into the safety and convenience of our public life.[77] As a result a sea change of tremendous significance occurred both in Hindu religious community and in its relations to others. In the changed circumstances the Hindu community was now called into action, not as one of the various Indian communities, but as the Indian community. It was not only the religious revivalist, but the modernising reformists as well who identified the Hindu community with Indianism and patriotism. Steps were taken deliberately to create a Sanskrit – based, Hindu language, Hindi, as against the earlier composite language. Further there are two variants of this expression of Indianness. One is the overt religious concept of Hindutva; and the other is the 'secular' expression of Indianness as based on ancient Indian culture. The first is a religious, the second is cultural concept; but both together relate Indanness to the tradition of what is now identified as Hindu civilization.[78] On the lines drawn above the political parties of India may be grouped as religion – leaned and secularism – leaned.

India, despite partition on the basis of religion, resolved to be secular state and promulgated its constitution in 1950 accepting equal rights for all citizens irrespective of their caste, creed or race. It was undoubtedly a great step forward. But it was not easy to translate the constitutional ideals into practice in a society as complex as India. Indian state was characterized as 'Soft state' by Gunner Myrdal in his *Asian Drama*. The Indian state remained not only soft towards communalism but it also encouraged it, if it paid political dividends. 1970 onwards Central and different State Governments have started the practice of giving 'Iftar' parties to our Muslim brethren during 'Ramzan'. Now political leaders vie with each other to throw such lavish parties at national and state capitals and the practice continued even in the regime of a BJP Prime Minister. Wide publicity is given in the media as to who attended these parties and what was served. It is forgotten that such politicization of 'Iftar' is a sacrilege to sacred religious practice much to the disgust of truly religious people. Even the representation of the people act provides that appeals made on the grounds of religion to gather votes would be deemed to be a corrupt practice and would disqualify a candidate but this happen as a rule in all our elections.

Louis Dumont, one of the most influential writer on Indian religion and society viewed sadhus as the agent of the development in Indian religion and speculation, 'the creator of values' responsible for 'founding of sects and their maintenance', and for the major ideas and social innovations.[79] In the changed circumstance, this consensus on the role of religious figures began to change during the time of Mrs. Indira Gandhi who relied on populist measures and appeal to specific categories of voters. She drew Hindu religious figures into the lime light through her patronage of religious institution and played the 'Hindu Card' against the minorities.[80] The case of Sikh religious leader Bhindarwala is burning example of her creation. She was systematically encroaching on the traditional vote bank of Jana Sangh. Mrs. Gandhi also co-opted Muslim religious figure in her attempt to hold on to the Muslim vote, pursuing her strategy of what was then called Fatwa Politics. It was seen on certain occasions that persons holding purely religious office play a decisive role to the job of political recruitment. Religious saints and sages are in great demand on the eve of and during election for influencing the voters in favour of or against a particular candidate or party. Political leaders run from one religious leader to another to seek their blessings for their success in elections. The net result is not the secularisation of the socio-economic and political processes but the communalisation of these processes.[81] Thus, the ideology and practice of secularism in actual fact, however, is confronted with multi faceted and multi-dimensional challenges.

However, Indian secularism began to face a rough weather with the revival and strengthening of religion – leaned political parties in the country. The pro – Hindu strategies of the ruling Congress reminded the BJP, RSS and VHP its actual role for which they had been struggling in previous decades. Earlier in seventies several proposals were made for a judicious deradicalisation of the BJP's slogans from groups inside the party itself. The decade also witnessed communal propaganda seemed to bring in few dividends and the destiny of the Jana Sangh irreversibly on the decline. At the juncture it was felt inside the Party that it should subtly shift its appeal to the middle class. Instead of the traditional appeal to Hindu Chauvinism, it should try to project itself as a substitute for the Congress, asking for support not because of its ideological differences with the Congress, but its similarity – offering a cleaner, more efficient, less corrupt government. After the dramatic success of the rathyatras, its own agenda was rewritten in a retrograde direction, but it is remarkable how clearly the party has not rejected its other, more secular constituency. From the early eighties, Hindu communal organisations increased the scale, range aggressiveness and violence of their operations under the general direction of the militant Hindu right-wing party Rashtriya Swayam Sevak Sangh (RSS) and its mass fronts: the Vishwa Hindu Parishad (VHP), which coordinates religious bodies, and the Bharatiya Janata Party (BJP), its electoral wing.[82] Again in mid – 1980s (1984) elections were held to Lok Sabha in 1984 after Mrs. Gandhi's assassination the BJP under the presidentship of Atal Bihari Vajpayee got only two seats. Now Vajpayee resigned and L.K. Advani, considered a hawk in the party, took over and gave BJP a new hope and a decision was taken by the leadership of BJP to promote Hindu militancy to snatch away the Hindu vote bank from the Congress.

Now, there was a mad race among the national political parties to use religion for strengthening and expanding their political base. This had led to the growth of fundamentalism in India. The growth of strong communalism has made government more and more susceptible to communal pressures exerted by them, thereby finally accommodating and conceding the demands of these organisations. The decision of the Rajiv Gandhi Government to undo the impact of the judgement of Supreme Court in Shah Bano case and the withdrawal of Presidential ordinance (1990) acquiring the disputed land at Ayodhya on the pressure of Babri Masjid Action Committee can be quoted in the context. In the famous Shah Bano case the power elite among Muslims used Indian Secularism for their own power game and resolutely opposed any change or progressive measures in the name of right to practice their own religion and whenever it politically suited them they aroused Muslim sentiment. The Muslim leaders mounted pressure on the then Prime Minister Rajiv Gandhi to change the law in favour of Muslims. The ruling party could hardly resist such pressure and buckled under and changed the law and passed the Muslim Women's (Protection of Rights on Divorce) Bill 1986. This had very adverse effect on an average Hindu mind. It convinced them that Muslim leaders are a fanatic lot and secondly, that the Congress indulges in appeasement of Muslim and treats them as its vote bank. In addition, it adversely affected our secular polity in two ways: (i) The politicisation of religious entity, and (ii) The legitimisation of communal organisation as the bonafide representatives of the interest of different religious groups.[83] It is true for most of the Indian political parties.

As the political role of Congress in early eighties was nothing but exploitation of religious sentiments to win over certain sections of Indian society, the BJP which is not only a rightist but also a Hindu communal party chose to use the religious controversial issues to capture power at the Centre and some states mainly in Hindi heart land. In its view, the way the secular state has functioned in India has paved way for the growth of fanaticism and fundamentalism, emergence of the anti-national forces posing threat to our unity and integrity and a strong opposition to progressive social legislation. The Bharatiya Janata Party maintains that our present secularism is pseudo secularism as it amounts to "appeasement of the minorities, particularly Muslims. According to their understanding, Muslims constitute the biggest vote banks as they generally vote as a community while the Hindu consciousness at political level gets fragmented along caste, linguistic and regional lines. In turn, BJP and its groups has come out with a concept of positive secularism of true secularism meaning that the minority should not enjoy any special protection and all such provisions in the Constitution should be done away with. It usually puts it as "justice for all appeasement of none".[84] The RSS and organisations of Parivar have been constantly criticizing the Congress rulers for their appeasement of the minority, especially the Muslim. They are saying that though Hindus are in majority they are being discriminated. They want the creation of "Hindu Rashtra". They argue that their definition of Hindu is very wide. Whoever, irrespective of the religion to which he belongs, considers India as his janmbhumi, karmbhumi and pitrubhoomi is a Hindu.

In nutshell, the political parties of today, especially the national, are exploiting religious /communal sentiments for electoral gains. Cynical building up of Sant Bhindranwala to marginalise the Akalis or Akalidal, for instance, proved catastrophic not only for the Congress Party but also for the entire country.[85] It is a sorry state of affairs that the polity too has fallen prey to the lobbying of communal organisations and groups as illustrated by the enactment of the Muslim Women's (Protection of Rights on Divorce) Act 1986, banning of *Satanic Verses*, and opening of the locks on the Babri Masjid. Similarly, the wooing of Shahi Imam by the Janata Dal – led National Front resulted into fall of its government at the centre as the after effect of secularism.[86] If mullahs and sadhus, and mahants come to wield political clout, as it happens today, communal forces are bound to get string themed. It is amusing to note that we never hear them speaking against old traditions such as 'pardah' or the 'caste – system,' polygamy or extravagant feasting etc., but they talk of religious identity. In the context if the BJP is blamed to have been practicing majority communalism, the Congress and non – Congress parties should equally be held responsible for pampering minority communalism in our polity for their political gains, forgetting the fact that the indefinite variety of the land can only be preserved and enriched through a policy or substantive decentralisation and that a genuine federal set up is the only solution of our problems.

In fact with social changes of the late 1970s and the early 1980s communalism got a strong boost and it started attacking secularism in a big way. Among political parties, the BJP was quick to take up the mantle of 'the' communal party, riding on the wave of the post – mandal upper class/caste backlash. Supporting the BJP was the Vishwa Hindu Parishad, a relatively new outfit with branches all over the world and drawing on support, both moral and financial, from the Hindu diaspora in the West. This took an aggressive form when the Babri Masjid/Ramjanambhoomi controversy erupted. This period also saw the rise of other militant Hindu organisaions such as the Bajrang Dal and the Shivsena. These groups quickly mushroomed and poisoned the social space with communal rhetoric and the agenda of Hindu Rashtra; and launched an ideological, social and political onslaught on secular ethos, syncretic culture and composite nationalism. The attack on the Mosque at Ayodhya led to a rash of violence across the country. The events leading to the demolition of Babri Masjid and their aftermath of communal carnage marked a watershed in the history of free India. The calculated rise of the BJP took place on a fundamentalist Hindu platform to gain dividends in states in principally North India and Maharashtra as well as at national level. India was portrayed as a Hindu India. The BJP and the Sangh Parivar use Ayodhya and other Hindu images continually. The BJP which had got only two seats and 7 per cent votes in 1984 got 88 seats 11.4 per cent vote in 1989 in alliance with Janata Dal. And in 1991 election BJP won 120 seats with 20 per cent votes. Something never had happened in the electoral history of the right wing Hindu party. The party in its manifesto for the 1996 elections had proposed that Article 30 of the Constitution giving the right to the minorities to establish their own cultural and educational institutions, be removed. In the same election the number of seats went up to 161 though the vote share remaining stagnant. Finally it formed government in 1999 with the help of some so called secular parties on mixed bag of promises.

About the time decades 1980s and 1990s have witnessed violent secessionist movements in Punjab and Kashmir and an upsurge in the use of religious symbols and terminology in politics.[87] There onwards secularism has been challenged by the ascendance of the forces of communalism, fundamentalism and religious revivalism, accompanied by violence. Communal riots continue unabated. Meerut, Bombay, Bhiwandi, Ahmedabad, Surat and Hyderabad and most recently, Gujrat, are just a few cases in point. The ostensible reason for this fury was the burning of a train coach that was carrying Hindu pilgrims returning from Ayodhya. Fifty nine people including women and children died in the fire. But the post-Godhra incidents in 2002 communal riots accompanied by events of arson, loot, and murder in urban as well as rural Gujrat and rural areas of Haryana and Maharashtra have tarnished the image of Indian secularism and the reputation of Hinduism as a tolerant faith. The social climate is thoroughly vitiated and the atmosphere is surcharged with suspicion and hatred reminding of the pre-partition days. This marked the first time when the state has emerged as a major player and actor in violence by mobs, a qualitative change from previous such situations in India. As a climax in May 2002, conference at Bangalore the RSS passed a resolution that the security of the minority community depends on the goodwill of the majority.[88] The resolution was seen as an open threat to the minority, though the spokesman of the RSS tried to explain that it was not meant to be so.

For all this, common but heavyweight cause is that still the political culture of India is unstable and underdeveloped. Political culture depends on the people's attitudes, emotions and beliefs towards the political system of the country, whether it is homogeneous or heterogeneous. Besides, political culture is not static, it is dynamic and therefore, it envisages essentials or needs of the political system within or outside. A pragmatic orientation in this direction is known as the secularisation of political culture. The secularisation of political culture is the process whereby men become increasingly rational, analytical and empirical in their political actions. It is the process of increasing the political awareness of the masses enabling them to have growing information about their political system and their role as political actors in it.[89] The secularisation of political culture has two attributes, first, the pragmatic and empirical orientation, and second, movement from diffuseness to specificity. Times change and change the beliefs and values of the people. Political socialisation through its agencies like family, schools and educational institutes, peer groups, working and informal relations, mass media, government and political parties and leaderships play very major and significant role in the strengthening of secularisation of political culture. In the political systems of the different states of the world, developed or developing, political culture promotes political stability and social change.

The political culture of India, like other developing countries, is in the formative stage and continues to evolve. It is an admixture of historical, geographical, socio-economic structures, the contemporary and ancient social structures, old and new political ideologies and more importantly the practice and tradition of political apathy and non-violence. In Indian political culture, commitment to religious values remained strong. The political and socio-economic changes produced a response along caste lines. The Constitution outlawed caste, but the political institutions continued the same, dividing the country into many castes and sub-castes. As a result the Indian political system has become the hub of irrational politicians who manipulate the state machinery to advance their personal power and economic gain by disseminating the seeds of social conflict. The secessionist movements, caste assertions, Hindus nationalism and majority – minority schism on cultural identities has been entrenched often inspired by political parties and leaders for electoral gain. The politics of Hindus-Muslims – Dalits vote bank and more importantly the blame-game become the part and parcel of the Indian political culture.[90] Political system in India is facing plenty of problems such as corruption, extensive centralisation, political criminalisation, declining secularism, rise of national chauvinism based on religion, and growing divide between the included and excluded. In the circumstances, Indian political culture has failed to prevent communal violence, ethnic conflicts and political insurgency. Secularisation does not mean that religious institutions will cease to exist. It only means that they will cease to encompass or regulate all the other institutions of society.

Unlike West where the philosophy of secularism came into existence only as a result of the struggle for powers between the religions and the state, secularism in the Indian context should imply respect for pluralism and a non-coercive and a voluntary recourse to change. Respect for diversity not only embodies the democratic spirit, it is the real guarantee for unity. No democratic society can downgrade diversity and pluralism in the name of unity. In the background, India, shortly after independence adopted a new constitution providing a charter for a secular state and a secular concept of citizenship. Secular ethics can be strengthened only when the acts of vandalism are sternly dealt with and the guilty are made to pay for it. With secularism that insists on the inalienable rights of the citizens and a due process of law, it will be easier to mount public pressure against sectarian killers and those who promote hatred. Secularism begins in the heart of every individual if we have no feeling of "otherness" as we all share a common history that has so far retained the secular character of its polity. It is not only the basic tenet of India's ancient civilization but also the hallmark of the modern age of globalisation. The new age demands that we should not waste our time in religious discords but rather move ahead with the use of science and technology to make our lives better, richer and fuller.

References

1. S.S. Gill, 'Team Secularism', *The Hindustan Times*, 3 March 2003.
2. Groethuysen, B., 'Secularism' in Edwin R.A. Seligman (ed.), *Social Sciences* (New Delhi: MacMillan Company, 1959), pp. 631-34.

3. *Ibid.,* p. 635.
4. Ranbir Singh, 'Nehru and Secularism', in Baltej Singh Man (ed.), *National Integration and Communal Harmony* (Patiala: Publication Bureau, Punjab University, 2004), pp. 20-21.
5. *Encyclopaedia of the Social Science*, Vol. XIII (Newyork: Macmillan, 1954), p. 631.
6. Marco Mavromaras, 'The Definition of Secularism', *Social Commentary*, Vol. 3, Issue, 5, February 2007.
7. Sanjeev Nayyar, 'Definition of Secularism–A Global Perspective', October 2003; Also visit for detail esameskriti @ suryaconsulting.net.
8. *Ibid.*
9. *Ibid.*
10. *Ibid.*
11. Abhishek Singhvi, 'Secularism Unwrapped', *The Hindustan Times*, 22 September 2004.
12. Marco Mavromaras, 'The Definition of Secularism'.
13. *Ibid.*
14. Abhishek Singhvi, 'Secularism Unwrapped'.
15. Dipankar Gupta, 'Communalism and Fundamentalism: Some Notes on the Nature of Ethnic Politics in India', *Economic and Political Weekly*, Vol. XXXVI, No. 11&12, March 1991 (Mumbai: 1991), p. 573.
16. Donald Engine Smith, *India as a Secular State* (Princeton: Princeton University Press, 1963), as quoted in R. Rajarajan, 'Secularism in Indian Politics: Theory and Practice,' *The Indian Journal of Political Science*, Vol. LXXIII, No. 2, April-June 2007 (Meerut: 2007), p. 405.
17. Prashant Amrutkar, 'Indian Secularism: Is It a Way Out to Communalism?,' *Ibid.,* Vol. LXXI, No. 3, July-September 2010 (Meerut: 2010), p. 747.
18. V.P. Bharatiya, *Religion- State Relationship and Constitutional Rights in India* (New Delhi: Deep and Deep Publications, 1987), pp. 10-11.
19. B.A Saltore, *Ancient Indian Political Thought and Institutions* (New Delhi: Asia, 1963), p. 22.
20. A.S. Altekar, *State and Government in Ancient India* (1958), p. 62.
21. James Hasting, *Encyclopaedia of Religion and Ethics*, Vol. VII (1959), p. 192.
22. B.G. Gokhale, *Indian Thought Through the Ages* (New Delhi: Asia, 1961), p. 103.
23. V.P. Bharatiya, *Religion- State Relationship and Constitutional Rights in India*, p. 16.

24. Md. Mahtab Alam Rizvi, 'Secularism in India: Retrospect and Prospect', *IJPS*, Vol. LXVI, No. 4, October–December 2005 (Meerut: 2005), p. 903.
25. M.P. Jain, *Outlines of Indian Legal History* (3rd edition), p. 582.
26. J. Duncan M. Derrett, *Religion, Law and the State in India* (Newyork: Free Press, 1968), as quoted in V.P. Bharatiya, *Religion–State Relationship and Constitutional Rights in India*, pp. 52-53.
27. K.M. Munshi, *Pilgrimage to Freedom* (Bombay: Bharatiya Vidya Bhavan, 1967), p. 66.
28. Maurice Gwyer and A. Appadorai, *Speeches and Documents on Indian Constitution* (Bombay : Oxford University Press, 1967), pp. 548-49.
29. B. Shiva Rao, *The Framing of India's Constitution–A Study* (New Delhi: The Indian Institute of Public Administration, 1968), p. 745.
30. Manju Subhash, *Rights of Religious Minorities in India* (New Delhi : National Book Organisation, 1988), p. 141.
31. Das Gupta, S., 'Regaining the Faith,' *India Today*, 8 April 2002 (New Delhi: 2002), p. 32.
32. Dr. Asghar Ali Engineer, 'Who is for a Common Civil Code ?,' *The Hindustan Times*, 3 August 2003.
33. Rajkumar Singh, *Past, Present and Future of Kashmir* (New Delhi: Gyan Publishing House, 2008), p. 65.
34. K. Natwar Singh, 'Truth's Messenger,' *The Hindustan Times*, 30 January 2003.
35. James Hastings, *Encyclopaedia of Religion and Ethics*, p. 347.
36. Suneera Kapoor and Shrawan Singh, 'Gandhi and Nehru on Religion', *IJPS*, Vol. LXVI, No. 3, July–September 2005 (Meerut: 2005), p. 503.
37. Urmila Sharma and S.K. Sharma, *Indian Political Thought* (New Delhi: Atlantic Publication and Distributor, 1966), p. 305
38. Bipin Chandra, 'Truth is God', *The Hindustan Times*, 15 April 2002.
39. Islami Marhaz, *What Gandhi Has Done for India–Collection of Articles on Gandhi's Life and Work* (Lahore : YMCA, 1946), p. 121.
40. Bipin Chandra, 'Truth is God'.
41. *Ibid.*
42. Jawaharlal Nehru, *An Autobiography* (New Delhi: Jawaharlal Nehru Memorial Fund, 2001), p. 379.
43. *The Hindu*, 21 January 2003.
44. Donald E. Smith, *Nehru and Democracy* (Calcutta: 1958), p. 147.
45. *The Hindu*, 13 September 1950.

46. M.V. Pylee, *India's Constitution* (New Delhi: Asia Publishing House, 1947), p. 127.
47. *Ibid.*
48. V.K.R.V. Rao, *The Current Indian Crisis–Darkness Before Dawn* (Allahabad: Vohra Publishers and Distributors, 1984), pp. 61-63.
49. Sitaram Yechury, 'Fundamentally Flawed', *The Hindustan Times*, 25 September 2003.
50. A.G. Noorani, 'Every Picture Tells a Story,' *Ibid.*, 4 March 2003.
51. As quoted in Sitaram Yechury, 'Fundamentally Flawed'.
52. *Constituent Assembly Debates*, Vol. VII, p. 400.
53. *The Hindustan Times*, 23 August 2003.
54. Jawaharlal Nehru, *An Autobiography* (Bombay: Allied Publishers, 1962), p. 378.
55. *Constituent Assembly Debates*, Vol. VII, pp. 815-16.
56. *Ibid.*, pp. 818-19.
57. *Ibid.*, pp. 831-33.
58. *Ibid.*, p. 834.
59. *Ibid.*, p. 822.
60. *Ibid.*, Vol. I, p. 59.
61. *Ibid.*, Vol. VII, p. 835.
62. R. Rajarajan, 'Secularism in Indian Politics', p. 407.
63. *Constituent Assembly Debates*, Vol. VIII, p. 316.
64. Gani, H.A., *Muslim Political Issues and National Integration* (New Delhi : Sterling, 1978), p. 178.
65. K.C. Markandan, *The Preamble–Key to the Minds of the Makers of the Indian Constitution* (New Delhi: National Publishing House, 1984), p. 63.
66. *Constituent Assembly Debates*, Vol. VII, p. 837.
67. *M.V. Pylee, India's Constitution*, p. 131.
68. *Article 18 of the Indian Constitution.*
69. *Constituent Assembly Debates*, Vol. VII, p. 823.
70. *Ibid.*
71. V.P. Bharatiya, *Religion–State Relationship and Constitutional Rights in India*, p. 360.
72. K.C. Markandan, *The Preamble–Key to the Minds of the Makers of the Indian Constitution*, p. 67.

73. *Ibid.,* pp. 62-63.

74. Md. Mahtab Alam Rizvi, 'Secularism in India: Retrospect and Prospects', p. 908.

75. Rajkumar Singh, *Past, Present and Future of Kashmir,* p. 72.

76. Sudipta Kaviraj, 'Religion, Politics and Modernity', in Upendra Baxi and Bhikhu Parekh (eds.), *Crisis and Change in Contemporary India* (New Delhi: Sage Publications, 1995), pp. 312-15.

77. P.R. Dubhashi, 'Meaning of Secularism', *The Hindu,* 11 June 2002.

78. Dev Nathan, 'India: From Civilization to Nations', in Kumar Rupesinghe and Khawar Mumtaz (ed.), *Internal Conflicts in South Asia* (Oslo:1996), p. 24.

79. Louis Dumont, 'World Renunciation in Indian Religions', pp. 46-47.

80. Virginia Van Dyke, 'Religious Mobilisation and Sadhus in Politics: The Idealized Versus Real politik', in Paul R. Brass and Achin Vanaik (eds.), *Competing Nationalism in South Asia* (New Delhi: Orient Longman, 2002), p. 144.

81. A.K. Singh, *The Concept and Practice of Secularism in Indian Concept* (1999) p. 24.

82. Rajkumar Singh, *Past, Present and Future of Kashmir,* pp. 74-75.

83. Prashant Amrutkar, 'Indian Secularism: Is It a Way Out to Communalism?' p. 748.

84. Partha Ghosh, *BJP and the Evolution of Hindu Nationalism: From Periphery to Center* (New Delhi: Manohar Publications, 1999), pp. 108-13.

85. P.S. Ghosh, 'Hindu Nationalism: The Politics of Nation Building and Implications for the Legitimacy of the State' in S.K. Mitra and D. Rothermud(eds.), *Legitimacy and Conflicts in South Asia* (New Delhi: Manohar Publications, 1997), pp. 68-76.

86. *Ibid.*

87. Manoranjan Mohanty, 'Secularism: Hegemonic and Democratic', *Economic and Political Weekly,* Vol. XXIV, No. 22, June 3, 1989 (Mumbai: 1989), p. 1219.

88. Naidu Ashok, 'Secularism Re-examined', *IJPS,* Vol. LXVIII, No. 3, July – September 2007 (Meerut: 2007), p. 607.

89. Vinod F. Khobragade, 'The Secularization of Political Culture', *South Asia Politics,* Vol. 6, No. 6, October 2007 (New Delhi: 2007), p. 38.

90. *Ibid.,* pp. 38-39.

PART-II
INS AND OUT OF INDIAN REPUBLIC

5 Indian Federalism: Concept, Working and Challenges

5.1 Theoretical Connotations: Classical and Modern

Federalism is basically only an integrative device intended to keep different communities or divergent religious, linguistic, racial, tribal or other group identities together united under one nation state. The enactment and adoption of federalism since the World War II had shown how it has been taken to as a means to political unity among the new nations in Europe, South America, Asia and Africa. Of the many changes taking place in the Indian federalism, it is necessary to address the deep-rooted sources of conflicts. We need a new federalism which would build a united nation of a large number of autonomies considered not as subordinates or subsidiaries but as federal partners at various levels, rooted in our culture, ethos and genius, and taking into account our weaknesses and needs of making the federal union an ever-developing and lasting reality.

Literally and historically federalism is the result of an agreement. It is when two or more sovereign States resolve to surrender a part of their sovereignty and join hands to constitute a new nation, a federal polity is born. It is a union without the constituting units losing their own identities.[1] Irrespective of any variant of federal polity, federalism is relevant only in a situation where the pluralism is territorially based, where particular groups are concentrated in separate territorial units or where the societal diversities are territorially identifiable, definable and separable. It is an arrangement between separate territorial entities to come together or to avoid break-up and stay united by sharing power through free democratic will. In fact, in large nations with multiplicity of diversities, federalism is the only way to democracy. It is also generally understood that the actual functioning of the federal system in any country does not depend on the nature of the constitution or the general legal framework but on the various factors that influence the political processes in the country. The growing popularity of federalism in recent years as a model of political organisation, the survival of the older federation through the challenges posed by changing circumstances like economic crisis and global wars, globalisation and international terrorism and the launching of functional federalism provide a strong justification for a re-examination of the various approaches and theories of federal political system.

Conceptually, there are three categories of theories of federalism, namely-classical theory of federalism, origin theory of federalism and functional theory of federalism. In the modern period, the Constitution of the United States, of 1787, is treated as the first experiment in establishing a federal system of government. Hereafter federalism as a mode of political organisation was embodied in the constitution of the Switzerland, the Dominion of Canada and the Commonwealth of Australia and India. However, K.C. Wheare, a leading exponent of federalism conceded in 1945 that under the pressure of war and economic crises the trend in existing federations was towards a concentration of central powers sufficient in some cases to threaten the federal principle. But in 1953, Max Beloff noticed that federalism was enjoying 'a widespread popularity such as it had never known before'.[2] The traditional practice of upholding the American federalism as the ideal one had become absolete.

The classical theory of federalism tries to explain first what federalism is. In line, Lord Bryee, K.C. Wheare gave a traditional concept of federalism. In order to assess whether a constitution is federal or not he applied the test as follows: 'The test which I apply for Federal Government is then simply this. Does a system of Government embody prominently a division of power between general and regional authorities, each of which, in its own sphere, is coordinate with the other's and independent of them? If so, that government is federal.[3] The other outstanding exponents of the classical theory were Dicey, Harrison Moore, Jethrow Brown, Robert Garran. An eminent Australian scholar Robert Garran, while defined federalism as 'a form of government in which sovereignty or political power is divided between the Central and local Governments, so that each of them within its own sphere is independent of the other.'[4] Lord Bryce added further, 'the system was like a great factory where in two sets of machinery are at work, their revolving wheels apparently intermixed, their bands crossing one another, yet each set doing its own work without touching or hampering the other'.[5] In order to make the independence of each government real and secure, the classical theorists enunciate the following conditions for a federal system: (i) A written constitution, (ii) The constitution is to be rigid, (iii) There is to be an independent judiciary, (iv) Both levels of government directly operate on the life of the citizens; and (v) There should be allocation of adequate sources of revenue for the government at each level, general and regional.

Traditionally the study of federal systems has been focused upon the constitutional and legislative framework within which the two sets of government, one central and the other of component units operate together. It attempts to explain federalism in juristic terms. Further it enables us to distinguish a federal polity from a unitary state where the constituent governments exercise their powers in subordination to the will and discretion of the general or central government of the whole country. The theory of classical federalism is a static notion which takes the relationship between the national government and the states as something fixed for all times.[6] The critics of classical theory also raise objection about the use of the term 'independent' to represent the relationship between the general government and the regional governments in a federal political system. 'Independence', they apprehend, means isolation. But if a federal polity is to be a working system, neither the general government nor the regional government can operate in isolation from the other. For a more appropriate expression of the relationship between the general government and regional governments in a federation, some modern federalists have preferred the words like 'potentiality and indivisuality,' 'coordinate' and 'autonomy' to 'independence'. To avoid the particular term Professor Livingston had redefined the federal government as a 'form of political and constitutional organisation that unites into a single polity a number of diversified groups or component politics so that the personality and individuality of component parts are largely preserved while creating in the new totality a separate and distinct political and constitutional unit'.[7]

The origin theory of federalism explains the circumstances favourable to the establishment of a federal system and which thereby seeks to define the federalism in terms of the circumstantial factors and forces. As such it includes three categories of definitions: (i) the sociological theory, (ii) the multiple-factor theory, and (iii) the political theory. William S. Livingston is recognised to be the first exponent of the sociological theory. The central thesis of the sociological theory is that it is the federal nature of society that gives birth to the federal political system. According to him a federal society is one which contains within its fold elements of diversity. Usually, diversity is caused by differences of economic interests, religion, race, nationality, language, separation by great distances, differences in historical background, previous existence as independent states or separate colonies and dissimilarity in social and political institutions. Another sociological approach was applied by Wildavsky who distinguish 'social federalism from structural federalism. He cites the Common Wealth of Australia as an example of structural federalism, a framework devised and adopted to retain the unity of the Australian people as a nation. To him the United States serves as a good example of 'social federalism'[8] adopted because of the social make-up of territorial, religious and other diversities located in distinct geographical areas, corresponding roughly to boundaries of the states which united under the constitution of 1787 to form the federation of the United States.

However, the sociological view of Livingston and Wildavsky and others has not been spared of critical scrutiny. The critics have pointed out that it has merely narrated various kinds of diversity but he has not explained the factors which generate the desire among the diversities for establishing a general government within a federal framework. The chief drawback of the sociological theory is the absence of definite indices and criteria by which a federal society can be distinguished from a non-federal society. On account of its paradoxical claims Venkatragaiya therefore, considers the theory as unsatisfactory and concludes that 'the idea of federal society on which the sociological theory rests is vague and full of ambiguities, each scholar interpreting it and its bearing on federalism in his own way'.[9]

The multiple-factor theory was mainly enunciated by K.C. Wheare and Karl Deutsch in order to explain the origin of modern federations. It takes into account the necessary as well as the sufficient conditions of the birth of federal systems. For this type of federalism, Wheare lays stress on (i) the desire for union and the desire for establishing independent general governments, and (ii) the capacity to give reality to the desire. Among the factors that together produce the desire for union the most noteworthy are a sense of military insecurity and the need for common defence, a desire to be independent of a foreign regime, a hope for economic advantage, geographical neighbourhood, similarity of political institutions, and previous political associations in a loose treaty system or confederal union. The desire for union must be coupled with a similar desire for independence of regional governments. The desire for regional government is also motivated by several factors namely, previous existence as separate and distinct states or colonies, a divergence of economic interests, geographical factors favouring regional consciousness, dissimilarity of social institutions and so forth.[10] However given both the desires, the desire for union as well as the desire for regional independence and identity, a right kind of leadership with the foresight and vision of statesmen would be necessary, as Wheare maintained, to devise a federal system for accommodating both the tendencies.

But in the multiple-factor theory Wheare lays down no criteria to determine capacity and perhaps it meant the capacity of the regional governments to raise the financial resources needed to maintain their autonomy. Although the theory lays emphasis on a combination of several factors that give birth to federalism but it does not adequately explain the creation of federal systems by the process of devolution or disaggregation. In the situation it is necessary to turn to the political theory of federalism which seeks to explain the origin of federal systems formed by aggregation and those established by disaggregation.

The political theory of federalism recognised that political motives play a dominant role in the origin of federal systems. The principal thesis of the political theory is that federalism is a solution to what is essentially and primarily a political problem. The solution is political because it centres around power and stands for the division of political power. The theory finds a forceful exposition in William H. Riker's book, '*Federalism: Origin, Operation and Significance*. In the book Riker puts forward the thesis that federalism is one way of solving the problem of government in expanding societies. According to him federalism provides for an enlarged political community without the use of coercive and aggressive methods of imperialism. As a political solution, federalism is the result of a political bargain in the situation which follows either the collapse of an empire, or which seeks to strengthen the enlarged political community while respecting and protecting the autonomy of the constituent units. It reflects a bargain between those political leaders who desire to expand this territorial control over the whole area of the empire that collapses in order to meet military or diplomatic threat and are unable to extend their control by conquest, and those who stand for the independence of the constituent provinces to whom concessions are offered.[11] This, according to him, constitutes the essence of the federal bargain.

The political theory of federalism is very useful as it represents federalism as essentially a political solution to different situations that involve the potency of a political bargain. It successfully explains the origin of older federations like that of the United States, Switzerland, Canada and Australia as well as the formation of the new federations since 1945, such as, India, Pakistan, Malaysia, Nigeria, West Indies etc. The significance of the theory lies in the fact that it explains the origin of federations formed either by aggregation or by disaggregation. It, however, tries to explain the causes responsible for the creation and sustenance of a federal system of government, but it fails to point out how federalism, despite its extinction, tries to persist in the face of new challenges that have raised their heads in the present century.

In line, the functional theory of federalism took its substance from the classical definition of federalism. It is based on the concept of 'dual federalism' and acknowledges the existence of two coordinate and independent levels of government. The advocates of 'dual federalism' claim that in a truly federal system the central and regional governments must have their respective demarcated spheres of activity in which each can operate independently of the other, and that the functional division between the two levels of government is the key to the maintenance of a genuine federal system. However, against the theory of 'dual federalism', it is argued that in spite of constitutionally guaranteed demarcation of the spheres of functions and powers between them the two levels of government in a federal system are no longer substantially independent of each other. In fact, the emphasis has gradually shifted to their partnership, interaction, and interdependence in the performance of functions allocated to each of them. Even in context of American federal system the theory of 'dual federalism' has been rejected by M. J .C Vile and D. J. Elazar[12] who suggested that the traditional conception of federalism as involving a sharp demarcation of responsibilities between two independent sets of sovereignties has never worked in practice in the United States.

Since the First World War the alterations in the working of the federalism in the old federations like the United States, Canada and Australia have been profound. The older constitutions of these federations have been adopted to fit the needs of the present time by the development of extra-constitutional devices such as administrative cooperation between governments, the coordination of state policies by conditional grants from the federal government, and the purchase of federal monopoly of the taxation of incomes and profits.[13] The new constitutions, in general, included provisions for these practices, and also for other means of securing flexibility. Thus, the reality has moved far away from what is called 'classic federalism' and has given birth to the new phase of federalism in which the coordinate governments no longer work in isolation from one another. This view was also held by R.L. Watts who considered interdependence and cooperation between the two levels of government as a characteristic features.[14] An empirical study made by Watts of six new federal constitutions of India, Pakistan, Malaysia, Rhodesia and Nyasaland, Nigeria and West Indies shows that 'co-operative federalism' became the inevitable trend in their systems. However, in 'cooperative federalism' financial dependence of the regional governments partially depends upon the general government and the administrative dependence of the latter is based upon the former.

Today the idea of co-operative federalism is as old as the modern federal movements itself. Elements of cooperative federalism are found in the federation of the United States which is chronologically the first of modern federations. Using the broadest sense of the concept Professor M.P. Jain has observed that it is the promotion of co-operation and minimisation of friction between the various constituent governments of the federal union whether it is Centre versus State or State versus State.[15] The realisation that the promotion of the general public welfare is the common goal of governments at the centre and in the States and they should work in concert and not in complete isolation in their efforts to reach the goal is the essence of 'co-operative federalism'.[16] 'Co-operative federalism' visualises the national and state governments as partners in the common function of serving the people. It rejects the concept of two governments as antagonistic sovereigns jealously competing with each other for power. Further in the opinion of Elazar, 'federalism is not to be located on the centralisation decentralisation continuum' but on a different continuum altogether, one that is predicated on non-centralisation, or the effective combination of unity and diversity.[17] He has very correctly observed, 'When discussing federalism, it is a mistake to present unity and diversity as opposites. Unity should be contrasted with disunity and diversity with homogeneity, emphasising the political dimensions and implications of each.[18] Thus, it is the search for a middle ground between the either or attitude typified by discussion of national government versus the state governments or the advantages of centralisation versus decentralisation.

The elements of cooperative federalism were further elaborated in the constitutions of federations subsequently formed - the federations of Switzerland, Canada, Australia, the German Republic and Republic of India. In fact it is a continuous process of evolution of federalism as a system of government during the last two hundred years and to point out that the basic feature of this process is the incorporation of a larger and larger number of co-operative techniques and devices into federal constitutions. With the new developments in the older federations and the new characteristics of the post- war federations, the federalism has entered a new phase in which state and national governments supplement each other in their day-to-day working and jointly perform a variety of functions.

In the current phase of global political economy or globalisation the federal systems of the developing countries has become market-oriented. Earlier, writers like Milton Friedman Keith Joseph in 1970s and Hayek in 1940s, criticised the Keynesian State as a paranoia to the market forces as it causes slow growth and recession consequent upon deficit budgeting and inflationary policies. Further factors like oil price fluctuations and the Multi National Corporations (MNCs) also began to assert in the direction of market–preserving federalism. This new phase of economic practices was entirely aimed at rolling back the State from its interventionist role in the economy. In coming years the move had revitalised the concept of limited government.[19] Initial background for this was prepared by the concept of liberal democracy in the late mediaeval period which promised liberation from feudalism. On the other the modern democratic states also face their own crises of legitimacy due to a fulsome transition from the welfare state to *laissez faire*. The protagonists of globalisation rightly understood the situation and therefore tried to justify the transition by citing economic exigencies resulting from the 'inefficiency' of the welfare state vis-a-vis the emergent new international political economy. Their argument is, indeed, that the Nation State has become too big for small problems and too small for big problems given the complex demands of the populace and multiple compulsions from the ever enlarging international political economy.[20] Hence, the State restructuring programme of globalisation, right from the beginning, has been portrayed to be pro-people and pro-development.

On the other a critical reading of the inherent view of globalisation has also been made which falcify both the justification for globalisation and the supposed benefits it promises for the entire humanity. At the very outset it should be noted that globalisation is a natural outcome of the structural contradictions of the capitalist mode of production and is, therefore, part of its survival strategy. Globalisation today is also a by- product of the structural contradictions of western capitalism.[21] The only difference is that unlike the earlier epoch, the new agenda of imperialism now gets support from the ruling class of the third world countries. It seems to be a 'natural process' as far as its inner dynamics – adoption of privatization of national wealth and liberalisation of trade and capital flows is concerned. However the real fact is that it is deliberately planned at the initial phase with utmost political calculation, economic management and ideological masquerading. The basic impetus to such a programme in the developing countries is from external sources- the MNCs, Multilateral Agencies for Aid and Development viz., World Bank and IMF and the developed capitalist states which have a comparative advantage in the open economic competition at the international level.

As a result of the asserted demand for opening the national economies, both the federal and unitary States have to ensure meaningful structural changes. Compared to other forms of State organisations and their governing institutions, the influence of globalisation on a federal State and its institutions is unique. The permeation of free market mechanism into a federation has to tackle the multiple level governmental institutions and State structures, which requires a special strategy. In the circumstances, each level of the government has to be accommodative to the permeation process. Pursuing the new strategy the centre undergoes a change in character to become market friendly and, thereafter, it devolves its powers to the units for following the same. It ultimately forces the centre to intervene arbitrarily in the affairs of the states. In addition, the concept of globalisation also redefines the relationship between market and State at each level of the federal structure in favour of the former. A primary analysis shows that the centre devolves to the units only that power which is essential for the purpose of market facilitation. Thus federal systems, due to their unique institutional features and theoretical lenience towards the liberal view of the State, provide much scope for globalisation on many counts.

In the process of initiating a market facilitating and later for sustaining it, each institution and policy having specific statutory role in deciding inter-governmental relations need overhauling.[22] Initiatives in this regard usually begin with changing the macro-economic policies in which the central government has a commanding power. The new macro-economic policies appear multiple compulsions upon the federating units and in turn cause problems to them as the units are responsible for maintaining the micro-economy. Under it, the structural adjustment means a re-modification of policy and readjustment of the institutional framework. Surely this alters the institutional frame of federal governance. The policy change is more telling on those institutions which act as intermediaries between the centre and state governments- for instance agencies which allot central grants, apportion tax revenue and grant loans-as they have to reflect the term and conditions of the macro economic policies. These new criteria together with a drastic reduction in the federal grants in the name of promoting symmetry in developmental and/or consequent upon the general macro economic policies, cause practical difficulties for the federating units in micro economic management. All these trends further weaken regional political structures against the market. Since the market manages micro-economic affairs in accordance with the free play of demand/supply mechanism, the marginalised humanity find no solace in the States' social security schemes. The emphasis is always to provide concessions to the ruling class at the cost of the poor rather than the other way round, bringing in its wake severe resource crunch.

The initiation and further strengthening of globalisation, one of the fundamentals of the federal idea-autonomy of the units-also collapses in this era. At a time when national sovereignty itself is at a discount, the territorial authority and jurisdiction of the units would be conspicuous by their absence. Instead their authority is progressively eroded by the intervention of the omnipotent and constitutionally unfettered international market and the market facilitating national government. In the situation the market preserving federalism reflects a unique power relation of the political economy. Theoretically, the emerging federal structure takes the form of an omnipotent, politically uncontrolled and, therefore, undemocratic international market at the top level; Nation States as market facilitators at the intermediary level; and federating units as obedient followers of the market facilitation policies at the bottom.

Thus, the emerging federal set up is full of theoretical contradictions. It poses certain practical constraints to pursue developmental policies due to the deprivation of a democratic role for the State in accordance with the majoritarian will. Besides these political and economic dimensions, cultural and linguistic differences have also contributed to the emergence of a new kind of environment which had its impact on the general nature of federalism. In particular the emergence of coalition politics has brought forward a new power equation in which smaller states have found important position in the federal governance.

5.2 Indian Federalism in Initial Years

India is a nation having very old, rather ancient civilization. It is also a large country, as large as Europe excluding Russia. At the same time it has been a melting pot of races and religions, languages and cultures. History and geography have altogether conspired to create all possible kinds of differences and inculcate and foster the growth of sectional loyalties based on caste and creed, language and religion. Various Reports and Studies in pre and post independence era witnessed that India lacked nationality and patriotism which according to Professor J.H. Hayes constitute the bed-rock of modern nationalism.[23] Realising the hard realities of the Indian situation as well as in deference to its own enlightened self-interest that the British Government reversed its earlier policy of centralisation and provided, in the Government of India Act 1935, for the establishment of federal system of government in India. Experiments with a common government of India started with the enactment of the Regulating Act, 1773 and this government was strengthened step by step with consequent loss of power by the provinces. Between 1773 and 1921, the British Parliament experimented with two divergent principles of centralism and decentralisation in determining the relationship between the government of India and the provinces and at last the Government of India Act, 1919 introduced what has been described by K.C. Wheare as federal government in the context of a unitary state.[24]

India under the Government of India Act, 1919, was a unitary state with federal government and the provinces enjoyed delegated powers given to them by the Central Government. Some improvements were made in regard to federalism in the Government of India Act, 1935, which provided federal structure in part II. Under it, the Provincial Government did not derive powers from the Central Government and powers were distributed in three lists; (i) Central list, (ii) Provincial list, and (iii) Concurrent list. Although part II of the Act of 1935 also provided for a responsible federal government at the Centre but due to the outbreak of the Second World War, on 3rd September 1939, the federal scheme was abandoned. However, the provinces were made autonomous from 15th August 1947, when India emerged as a sovereign, independent nation. The federal idea and structure of 1935 caught on the Constituent Assembly who opted for adoption of a federal framework for the new Sovereign Democratic Republic because the federal principle provides an ideal compromise between centrifugal and centripetal forces.[25] The Indian leadership, it seems, was less concerned with the adverse impact of adopting an alien system. Evidently, they were so overwhelmed by the unsettled circumstances at the time of independence, that they failed to conceive of normal circumstances. They were so deeply immersed in the unhealthy present that they lacked the vision to construct healthy future.

Before independence on January 22, 1947, the Constituent Assembly adopted the 'Objective Resolution', 'that under the proposed constitution the territories constituting the Union of India-shall possess and exercise all powers and retain the status of autonomous units, together with residuary powers and functions of government and administration, save and except such powers and functions as are vested in or assigned to the Union or as are inherent or implied in the Union or resulting therefrom'. It establishes, said Dr. Ambedkar, introducing the Draft Constitution in Constituent Assembly on November 4, 1948, 'a dual polity with the Union at the Centre and the States at the periphery, each endowed with sovereign power to be exercised in the field assigned to them respectively by the Constitution. The Union is not a League of States, united in a loose relationship, nor are the States, the agencies of the Union, deriving powers from it. Both the Union and States are created by the constitution; both derive their respective authority from the Constitution. The one is not subordinated to the other in its own field; the authority of the one is coordinate with that of the other'.[26] Nevertheless Ambedkar went on to stress that the constitution was structured to be effective unitary or practically federal in contingent circumstances. In normal times it is framed to work as a federal system. But in times of war and other national emergencies it is so designed to make it work as though it was a unitary system.

The decision of the Constituent Assembly to have a federal constitution with a strong Centre was occasioned also by the circumstances in which it was taken. A strong central government was necessary for handling the situation arising out of the communal riots that preceded and accompanied Partition, for meeting the food crisis, for settling the refugees, for maintaining national unity and for promoting social and economic development, which had been thwarted under colonial rule.[27] The members of the Constituent Assembly themselves refused to adhere any dogma or theory about federalism. India had unique problems they believed, problems that had not 'confronted other federations in history'.[28] These could not be solved by recourse to theory because federalism was 'not a definite concept' and lacked a stable meaning.'[29] In fact, by the time the British left in 1947, provincial leaders, who had already tested provincial autonomy wanted to make it more real and substantial without loosing national independence to a new foreign power. While the threat of foreign aggression generated in them the desire to build up a common system of defence and protection, they were not prepared to abandon provincial autonomy.[30] The centralists like Nehru, Patel and others wanted expansion for enlarged governments, unity and security and were prepared to achieve this through negotiation and concession. The outcome of this bargain was the federal system of the constitution giving the whole country a strong central government and regional governments of the former provinces and acceded princely states a large measure of autonomy.

The views of Indian leaders including Nehru, Patel, Ambedkar and others were supported by his colleagues on the Drafting Committee whose opinion carried weight and authority in the deliberations of the Assembly. Yet the controversy continued and a large number of members still thought that the Centre was vested with excessive power and, in the process the federal principle which was to form the very foundation of States' system under the constitution was almost destroyed. From the floor of Assembly the controversy migrated to a wider arena, among political scientists and constitutional lawyers both within and outside the country. According to some the constitution is 'quasi-federal; it establishes a unitary State with subsidiary federal features rather than a federal State with subsidiary unitary features.[31] Others are of opinion that the unitary features are so strong that the federal framework of the Constitution is nothing but a facade without the substance of federalism in it. Professor K.C. Wheare takes the view that 'the constitution is quasi-federal'.[32] K.M. Munshi, a distinguished jurist, calls our constitution 'a quasi-federal union invested with certain features of unitary government'.[33] According to Ivor Jennings, 'India has a federation with a strong centralising tendencies.'[34] On the other hand, Appleby, an experienced administrator thinks that the Indian constitution is extremely federal.[35] Thus, federalism has now become one of those good echo words which evoke a positive response, but mean all things to all men, like democracy, socialism, progress, constitution, justice or peace. We see the term applied to almost any successful combination, of unity with diversity, to almost any form of pluralism and cooperation within and among nations.

Federalism in the modern age is a principle of reconciliation between two divergent tendencies, the widening range of common interests and the need for local autonomy. A look into the constitutional arrangement of federalism will show that the framers of the Indian Constitution preferred the term 'Union of States' to the term 'Federalism'. The makers had their own explanations. Considering the vastness of the country as well as variety in different fields, the primary task of the makers was to ensure cohesion and not division. Of course they did not ignore the issues like pluralism in social structure, openness in the political process and imperatives for economic development. They also provided enough scope for a multi-party system to operate. This was a clear departure from the Anglo-American model, Moreover, the creation of a federal system with a bias towards the central authority was a deliberate act.

India's Constitution has been variously described as quasi-federal, federal with a strong unitary or pro centre bias, federal in structure but unity in spirit, federal in normal times but with possibilities of being converted into a purely unitary one during Emergency, etc. The fact is that it is difficult to put our Constitution in any strict mould of a federal or unitary type; it has features of both. It cannot be considered unitary because it provides, for example, for distribution of executive and legislative powers between the Union and the States and provisions affecting the powers of the States or Union - State relations cannot be amended without ratification by the States. It cannot be strictly considered federal either because the residuary powers vest in the Union and territorial identities of the States can be varied by Union Parliament by ordinary legislation.[36] Reasons for this unique unitary federal mix are to be found in the constitutional history of India, the sheer size of the country and nature of her complex diversities based on religion, language, region, culture etc. However, at large the Indian Constitution cannot be accused of violating the federal principle; because there is no strict, true or pure federal principle. 'If there is such a thing as a strict, pure or unqualified federal principle, then the hard fact is that there are no federations and no federal constitutions.'[37] A close examination of the world federal constitutions would further reveal how much do they differ in numerous features and how difficult is it to find in them a common thread which can be described as a basic feature of the federalism.

The real value of federalism lies in the implications of contractual government and in their account of social, economic, political and institutional conditions which make federal government possible. The writers of federalism were right in emphasising the juristic equality of the federating units and the clear demarcation of jurisdiction between federal government and the States with the division of powers being 'policed' by the supreme court acting as the guardian and interpreter of the constitution. Even initially federalism was presented as one principle underlying the political and legal framework possible for the governance of large societies with social, economic, and religious diversities. The so-called co-operative federalism' does not replace the legal framework of federalism. The fact that a federal constitution, once established, functions in a changing social and political environment is now well understood. The constitution and political process function in close and continuous interaction and the framework of the constitution gets modified in the political process. And if federalism is a process it is bound to be linked up with political parties which inevitably seize the political and economic realities of the federal society in their efforts to come to power.

In the early stages of Indian federalism it laid emphasis on the structural considerations as these were deemed to be essential for federal arrangement. The underlying assumption behind this approach was that the introduction of a proper federal structure could create 'a functional federal system.' But gradually the limits of such an approach became clear as many polities with federal structures were not federal in practice, 'the structures marked a centralised concentration of power that stood in direct contradiction to the federal principle'.[38] In this context, a look into the nature of stresses and tensions may help understand the general course of federal process. The tensions which had their impact on the functioning of the federal system may be broadly classified into two i. Political tensions both within the ruling party and with the ruling party and other opposition party and ii. Economic tensions arising out of economic power bases and the attitude of the political parties towards them. It is accepted that so far as economic dimension of the tension is concerned, it is mostly due to the conditions of unevenness, leading to instability of the social base.[39]

According to a well-known Indian writer Indian federalism started with a contradiction. While the Constitution established a federal system of government, all the political parties existing at the time it came into force were unitary and highly centralised. It is a fact that federal systems function within a framework of politics and political parties which are concerned with the social, political and economic policies of the State may provide us with newer approaches to the dynamics of Centre - State relations. Particularly in case of the Indian National Congress the Constituent

Assembly presumed, despite the manifestation of political pluralism in the form of offshoots of the Congress and the relatively influential position of the Communist Party, that it (Congress) possessed political consensus and represented what may be called 'Great Nationalism'. At the juncture, Congress itself was considered the vehicle of national consciousness while the strong centre instituted by the Constitution would be the agency for translating into practice national goals on economic development and social change. But there was a general absence of sensitivity towards the 'Little Nationalism' representing the primary or primordial identities of diverse cultural, linguistic and tribal groups, and other developed or embryonic ethnicities, which had manifested itself in different forms in the course of the national movement. Consequently the federating process at the State level often resulted in friction between State and Union leadership. The currents of conflict ran on subterranean beds, occasionally rising to the surface.[40] The single most important source of conflicts in federal societies is the tendency of the Union to dominate the units, to make them dependent and to treat them subordinates and not as equal partners in government, and to work for centralisation of authority under a top down model.

Jawaharlal Nehru in pre and post independence era struggled hard and long, and on the whole successfully to lay the foundations of a strong nation. But for a variety of reasons, even he could not get much beyond the plinth.[41] Before independence, there was no certainty that different regional units or cultural and religious communities would be able to live and work in harmony. Good intentions on the part of different groups were clearly not enough. It was necessary to resort to a degree of compulsion to mould them together. It was therefore, necessary that the Centre should possess ample power to counteract divisive tendencies.[42] This is why the framers of the Constitution had clearly envisaged the evolution of a federal society through a process of bargaining and the possibility of a decline in the paramount position of the Congress Party was a matter of time. In 1953 Paul Appleby foresaw a time when different political parties would function at the different levels of the system. Federal government cannot function without the party system getting federalised but in India the Congress, itself unitary in its working, was confronted not by a well-ogranised party in opposition but by multiple parties enjoying, at best, the possibility of command in one or two States in the future.

From the beginning the structure of power in federal system has been largely affected by the nature of ruling party at Central level. So far as the Congress party is concerned it had been generally in favour of a strong centre with sufficient powers to control the policies in regard to matters assigned to the states. The economic and social reconstruction for the purpose of creating a socialist society had been on the agenda of the Congress party and for that reason it favoured a centralised federalism. The greatest weakness of this period of India's political development was the failure to evolve sound conventions and the creation of an impartial image of federal authority. The Nehru period left few guidelines for the federal system because conflicts between the Union and the States were dealt with at the party level rather than through formally established agencies. The 'Setalvad Report' expressed this aspect of Indian federal system and noted, 'Where a single party has control over affairs at the Centre as well as in the States, an alternative and extra-constitutional channel becomes available for the operation of Centre-State relations. In practice this channel has been very active during Congress Party rule and has governed the tenor of Centre-State relations. The political network connecting centre and state leadership was used amply to resolve conflict and ease tension or even to postpone consideration of inconvenient issues. In the process the Constitution was not violated, at least not deliberately or demonstrably, but was often by passed.[43]

Under Nehru's stewardship, no serious debate arose over the question of centralisation. This was largely due to the development of what is known in academic parlance as the Congress system which provided both the organisational pull and rallying symbols and metaphors that legitimised the national enterprise in the eyes of diverse population; it at the same time kept its doors open and provided a variety of entry points for both existing and emergent groups and interests and in a way also potential groups and interests because of its clear message of being the harbinger of an open society.[44] The Congress system worked successfully first, because of an extreme faith Indians had in the constitutional legal system, and secondly, the fact that the ruling party which fought for independence was held in high esteem, therefore, what was decided by the Congress Party and its leadership was accepted by the masses at large.

In addition the socio-economic agenda of the Congress Party also set the prospect of Indian federalism. As a result of Party's attitude towards these issues the so-called Congress system developed which, according to Frankel aimed at exploiting the potentiality inherent in the democratic process for converting the superior members of the poor into a powerful political resource, while continuing to recruit from among leading members of the dominant landowning castes-notables who had power and influence in local factional groupings and to organise popular participation in the wider political process through a complex pyramiding of vertical factional alliances, a technique which permitted the Congress to build winning coalitions, provide stable government and enhance national integration by concentrating power at the Centre under a one-party dominant political system. However, in this arrangement there was a contradiction in which the poor were expected to provide political strength to a party dominated by their exploiters, was highlighted by the actual outcome of land distribution programmes, which augmented the political and economic strength of the landowning classes and sharpened their contradictions with the small and landless peasantry.

The federal structure in our country has undoubtedly an important role in economic development. The founders of the federation have found it impossible to divide the functions of general and regional governments into two isolated compartments and have been forced to recognise the independence of governments. Generally, as a result of the placing of major fiscal instruments for economic policy in central hands, the regional governments have become heavily dependent upon the former for their financial resources. In this context it is also to note that States differ greatly in area, population, density, per capita incomes, net savings and contribution to the national economy through income tax and productivity. These aggravate other elements of regional disparity in literacy and education, administrative efficiency and urbanisation.[45] The larger States are able to exercise a greater influence on the Union Government. But the smaller States present the real problem for the Units are in competition with each other, the smaller and relatively more backward States seeking to emulate the more advanced ones. It provide a powerful factor in the dynamics of inequality which is one aspect of the structure of power in the Indian Federal system.[46] Under the Indian system, the States have been left with all the rigid and unproductive sources of taxation, rendering them financially dependent on the Centre.

At the same time, the central government tended to be heavily dependent for the implementation of national economic and social programmes upon autonomous regional ministers and legislatures directly responsible to their electorates. This situation of mutual dependence of each level of government upon the other has characteristically produced 'a proliferation of institutions and arrangements for consultation and cooperation in a wide variety of economic fields.'[47] The actual pattern of Union-State relations in India is one of 'Coalition administration' or a high degree of Collaborative Partnership both in political decision making and in implementing the operation of plan projects.[48] Meanwhile, the industrial capitalist component operated through the power structure of the Centre and the rich farmer component through the power structures of the States.

In the context of the dependence of both on State investment in infrastructure, State subsidies and the powers of the State to determine the terms of trade between the industrial and agricultural sectors, the scarcity of resources arising from the slow expansion of capital brought in main conflicts between the two segments and between each of them and the state elite. However, with the Congress system in control at the Centre and the States both, the sharpness of the conflict was blurred though with an increasing sense of alienation of the agrarian classes with the Congress, which provided one element of the growing decline of Congress influence in many States in the 1960s.

Apart from this there were other factors that played an importarrt role in weakening the Congress hold on the States in this period. One of these was related to the dispositions of other classes and groups having their own contradictions and conflicts with the elements of the dominant coalition, which had a growing feeling of being marginalised in respect of their claims on the attention and patronage of the State, or found the political system inadequate or unwilling to preserve what they regarded as special interests or to protect their material and cultural rights and concerns. The increasing disillusionment and despair of these classes and groups with the system and with the stagnation of State's drive for economic development and the removal of regional and sectoral imbalances, found expression in the form of intense movements or emergent mobilisations of diverse regional, ethnic and communal entities.

Under Nehru there was a successful operation of federalism in the country but through the Congress party system and not with the help of constitutional provisions. The party had been the chief instrument and vehicle of the freedom struggle. It held unchallenged sway in the political field after independence for more than a decade and for some years after independence, the old guards led the party in its crusade for socio-economic revolution. The most of the key positions of power were occupied by them. For them the base of legitimacy was their participation in the freedom struggle. They were men of ability, courage and integrity of high standards of public morality. Stalwarts at the Union and those in the States acted with a sense of mutual respect and accommodation. The dominance of the Party under the charismatic leadership of Nehru facilitated the successful operation of federalism, the central initiatives of planning were being successfully implemented; the improvement of agriculture and the transformation of rural society were being done by the community development, the reorganisation of the units of the country into linguistic states (1956) was being achieved; the political and parliamentary practices and conventions were being established. Nehru's position within the party was supreme and all basic policies of Congress were his intellectual offsprings. Undoubtedly, the monolithic character of Congress provided ample scope for a Unitarian approach to the working of Indian federation.

But the dominant position of the Congress Party and Nehru began to change gradually and it manifested during the last years of Nehru era. During his period with the process of cultural secularisation a multipolarisation started which led to the growth of parties of different political ideologies. The dominance of the Congress in some states was also challenged by the rise of parties committed to states' rights. The emergence of new regional forces calls for wider decentralisation of power and resources and better scope for the states to play in the federal governance. In a word the new power configuration that has emerged with the rise of coalition politics has altered the balance of power between the centre and the states with a definite tilt towards the state power so far as partnership pattern of federal relations is concerned in contemporary India. Meanwhile the death of Nehru in 1964 marked the end of an era in Indian society and politics.

5.3 Indian Federalism in Post- 1967 Period

In earlier phase Nehru's insistence on planning paved the path for the growth of a highly centralised elaborate planning mechanism with serious consequences for Centre-State relations in India. There were occasional murmurs from the States resenting the vital decisions of the centrally dominated Planning Commission impinging on State autonomy. All such resentments vanished before assuming any serious form, in the face of the dominant role of the Congress High Command, particularly of Prime Minister Nehru. During this phase in the operation of the political system, a clear tendency was visible that Congress Party would remain at the central stage and other parties will revolve around the Congress Party. But the scheme did not last long. With the rapid changes, both qualitative and quantitative, in the social and political structure newer and newer support bases began to appear. Interestingly these support bases began to act as the breeding grounds for further demands. The local political parties could realise that these local support bases needed to be exploited so as to derive popular support for action and agenda, Congress being the national party failed to address these local power bases and as a result it could not reach the people at the local level.

In course of time it was felt that whereas things like education, urbanisation and industrialisation were taking inroads into traditional sectarian loyalties, electoral politics have resuscitated them and re-established their legitimacy, and that this has given rise to disintegrative tendencies that will disrupt the democratic and secular framework of the Indian polity.[49] By mid-1960s the places of the 'old guards' were taken by a new breed of politicians, the younger generation, the regional bosses, the rural faction leaders; the ideology-oriented intellectuals were replaced by vote bank-based political leaders in the power structure. In most of them the high standard of public morality was wanting. They found it essential to combine money and muscle power. They were easy prey to nepotism, favouritism, casteism, communalism and parochialism and corruption was rampant. Further the developmental plans had brought about a heightened political awareness in the Indian masses. The exposure to modernisation created the revolution of rising expectations.[50] Its dilemma was, that political aspirations and expectations rose much faster than the system could develop the capability to meet them. The resulting discontent made for a political instability often encouraged by the extravagant hopes built by political leaders. In this process a new kind of tension and conflict developed between the rich and the middle peasants on the one hand and the poor peasants and landless labourers on the other hand.

Thus the gap created due to the changed socio-economic and political conditions also provided the scope for local or regional parties to play important role in the governing process. It is to be mentioned that these trends or patterns were not uniform all over the country. Once again the differences in manifestation were the results of wide variations in people's aspirations, awareness level and expressions. One may try to justify this development with the help of the theories of 'relative deprivation' or 'theories of dissatisfaction'. But it should be noted that not all the assertions can be explained with the help of these well accepted theoretical positions. One should go beyond the outward manifestations and look into the nature of socio-economic and political matrix in order to get at the truth. It is also admitted that the forces and factors engaged in this process are not only complex but also overlapping in character.[51] Under a federation which is relatively young and therefore, has not been able to develop necessary conventions in the short period of its existence, the relationship between the Centre and the States becomes all the more delicate and more prone to conflicts.

On the other hand Nehru's demise in 1964, the breakdown of the Congress system led to the rise of various other structures, both political and non-political, which became formidable in the era of mass politics. Despite Nehru's limitation as a statesman, the Congress Party under his tutelage both absorbed new demands and strove to provide avenues for their fulfilment. With the collapse of the Party as an institution and the 'unwillingness of the system to create a new institutional modes for dealing with the politics of demand on the part of the masses',[52] the chasm that was created between the party and the people became unbridgeable. The result was the politicisation of the masses outside the defined and confined structure laid out by the Congress.[53] Earlier the Congress derived its support from the people as promoter and guarantor of national independence and unity. In its election manifestos it claimed credit for winning freedom for the country, which was threatened by divisive movements or external dangers.

The deinstitutionalisation of the Congress Party contributed immensely to the India's federal system, 'by dismantling the Party's federal structure.[54] Not only did the process of deinstitutionalisation lead to massive concentration of power in the central leadership it also deprived the party of seasoned national and state party officials'. What was worse was a process of 'substituting loyalists and favourites at state and constituency level for party officials and candidates with local knowledge and support'.[55] The breaking down process in the Congress system became evident when Indira Gandhi afforded to ignore the Party as an instrument for creating a constituency of her own, because she succeeded in establishing 'a direct and unmediated line with the people who had transposed enormous faith in her charisma and her image as a deliverer and secular messiah'.[56] In her period, centralisation which was once appreciated as 'an instrument of purposive interventions by a cohesive and disciplined elite soon turned out to be suicidal to the prevalent party system and the federal structure and of wider affiliations that were built through them. Although even before she assumed charge as Prime Minister she hinted that her first task would be to restore law and order and the second to get the economy moving.

In between the years of Congress Party's deterioration, the results of Fourth General Election 1967 came which marked a watershed in the post-independence history and politics of India. By 1967 the euphrasia of independence had evaporated, the roseate dream of a prosperous country at peace with itself had come to nought, and for the new generation, angry, hungry and in a hurry, the Congress was no different from any other political organisation, and Gandhi and Nehru were mere names. The failure of Congress to provide economic and social benefits as per the public expectations was becoming more and more glarring. The early 1967 and 1968 were years in which most people experienced a decline in industrial production, unprecedented inflation, food scarcity and an unusually high level of violence over various issues.

The outcome of elections of 1967 gave a staggering blow to Congress dominance and generally considered as an important turning point in India's politics by putting an end to the era of one-Party dominance. In this election although Congress retained a bare majority in the Parliament-284 in a house of 520 but it was unseated in eight out of sixteen state Assemblies including the populous heartland States of Uttar Pradesh and Bihar. The Party lost its dominance in other six States- West Bengal, Orissa, Madras, Kerala, Rajasthan and Punjab. Latent social forces were coming to the fore in the states. It was significant that new tendencies were appearing not at the national but at the regional level. This shift of centre of gravity of public life from the centre to the periphery marked a qualitative change in politics.[57] Integrative politics of the kind that was needed for nation building in the past at the all-India level is now needed in the states. In other words, they required political leadership of a high order in terms of vision and skills.

In this new environment the issue of federalism came to be affected more by the ideological position, political strategy and support base of the new governments. It was found that many of the coalitions, in the face of urge for power of their partners, were marriages of convenience parties joined hands only in opposition to Mrs. Gandhi's government, but were sharply divided on the vital issue of Centre- State relations. In regards two schools of thought were identified; one stands for a thorough re-examination and introduction of amendments of far-reaching importance in the Constitution so that Centre-State relations could be rearranged to suit the needs of the changed political context and its unitary bias could be shed. The other school, however, does not consider all this necessary, and was content with a general reappraisal of the Constitution which may admit of a broad review of Centre-State relations within the existing Constitutional framework.[58] A descriptive hypothesis which perhaps best summed up the then situation was that cooperative federalism in India having lost support base in the Congress system was in search of a new anchorage amidst pressures of democracy, national development, regional growth and State autonomy.

But above all the emergence of coalition politics had brought forward a new power equation in which smaller states have found important position in the federal governance. Without going into the theoretical position of 'greater nationalism', 'lesser nationalism', 'little nationalism', and the like one can draw the conclusion that in the newly created political arrangement, smaller states with greater political capability in the field of power manipulation can play a very decisive role in the federal process. The experiences that the Indian state has gained over the years show that all types of regional or local issues create situations for the emergence of new types of demands-sometimes demand for autonomy and sometimes the creation of the state.[59] Among the points of growing tension in India federalism is the feeling in some communities that their cultural message for the world at large is not being promoted. Some others have grievances in economic matters. In the changed situation the Centre must learn to play an effective mediatory role even as it continues to safeguard the country's integrity and independence. But since regional movements struggling for greater expression also wish to uphold the national identity, the country is now in a position to move forward constructively in re-ordering Centre–State relations. It can also play a more creative role in furthering the emergence of new global institutions and values.

From the functional point of view it may be noted that there have been sharp changes in the relationship between the Congress Party and other non-Congress regional political parties. It is true that in most of the cases, before the emergence of coalition politics and because of the dominant position of the Congress Party, the local or the regional parties did not enjoy any influential authority in the total political process. But there have been significant changes since 1967 and a climate of bargaining politics had taken its roots and in this process local or regional parties have been able to come forward with their agenda of action.[60] It was for the first time that the hegemonic position of the Congress witnessed opposition from regional or local political parties. It may not be an exaggeration to say that the seeds of regionalisation of Indian politics had been sown during the 4th General Elections. Looking from the point of view of socio-economic configuration, it may be seen that a new social and economic class, mostly in the middle order, emerged and began to exercise their influence in the policy making process. No longer the issue of relative autonomy of states found favour with the national political parties and in its place the politics of bargaining came to the surface in which states began to assert themselves in the federal governing process.

The new environment encouraged political parties of the time to speak in favour and against of the nature of Indian Constitution. Among the parties the erstwhile Jana Sangh and present Bharatiya Janata Party (BJP) has stood for a centralised federalism. By its theory of Hindu revivalism it favoured a strong national government. It was of the view that only a powerful national government was the solution for checking the fissiparous tendencies threatening national integration and encouraging foreign invasion. Therefore, the BJP propagated the idea that in the interest of nation and preserving national unity it stood for some kind of a decentralised unitary system in place of federal set up. The Left Parties wanted a system of governance which would ensure substantial autonomy to the states. The Socialists, despite their awareness of the need for substantial regional autonomy, were in favour of a strong national government both for the maintenance of national unity and the accomplishment of concrete, time-bound socialist programme.[61] Of all the regional political parties, DMK and AIADMK, the Akali Dal and later on AGP in Assam demanded more devolution of authority for the regions. The changes brought about since 1967 had created a situation where there have been radical changes in the party positions all over the country. With the emergence of the Non-Congress government in several states and reduction in the Congress strength in Parliament after the 1967 General Elections the position of the states vis-a-vis the Union was strengthened. In 1968, the Communist Party of India stood for changes in the federal constitution of the country so as to divest the union government of its overriding powers to interfere in the affairs of the states and in order to widen the autonomy of states especially in the matter of finance and state economy.[62] In line the CPI (M) favoured widest autonomy for the various states comprising the Indian federation.

The loss of Congress Party's pre-eminent position on political scene led to the split of the Party in 1969. After 1967 it could not find a creditable alternative platform except demagogic promises such as garibi hatao. The Party, however, was not geared to achieve any but its nationalistic goals. And due to the lack of appropriate national objectives, the forces of the Party were being largely frittered away in petty personal quarrels or corrupt practices. Mrs. Indira Gandhi had little time to demonstrate her abilities. The absence of a consensus among some major political figures regarding the leadership of Mrs. Gandhi made her appear to be more of a partisan symbol than a national one. Party discipline was at its lowest ebb and the Central organisation found itself unable to control the State units. As a result, 'the general disillusionment and the Central intra Party conflict produced an organisational disaster'.[63] The split in the Party at national level had profound impact on the state level politics. Following it the state level Congress Parties also encountered similar splits in their respective state unit. Moreover, with a view to strengthening the party positions in the state by frequent changes in the leadership pattern, the party sought to regain political supremacy in the state. These changes had great bearing on the relations between the centre and the states. Thus the new political environment injected a good deal of strength to the theory of State rights and a new dimension was added to it by the national split of the Congress.

In post-split phase Congress under the leadership of Mrs. Indira Gandhi took some progressive steps towards radical, social and economic transformation. A series of constitutional amendments passed during this period clearly showed that the Congress had been trying to fulfil the pledges it made in its election manifesto during the midterm poll in 1971. In this election the Congress under Indira Gandhi emerged victorious and captured power in most of the states. The periods onward was characterized by one-Party dominance provided sufficient scope for the strong Central government successfully utilising the impetus provided by the Bangladesh liberation struggle to forge a new spirit of unity throughout India. The several attempts made during this period to augment the power of the Indian States were suppressed. The central government was able to tighten its hold over the Congress states which tended to become the feudatories of the central power. In many cases the chief ministers were mere nominees of the Prime Minister and obviously they looked to guidance from the prime minister in the matter of formation of their ministers. The trend was towards centralisation of power in the hands of the Prime Minister and state governments were mere shadows of the Prime Minister. In the period 1971-76, Mrs. Gandhi emerged as 'the chief spokesman of the superior claims of unitarism over federalism in the development of India'.[64] Her contention was endorsed ideologically by the fact that a strong Centre was the need of the hour in the interest of both, the balanced development and the unity and integrity of the country.

Once again the question of Centre-State relations came to the fore with the proclamation of national emergency in June 1975 which is considered to be a significant event from political perspective. It was the seeds of discontent among the constituent units of the Indian federation and agitations on national scale-the manifestation of such a trend. The declaration brought to the surface a number of issues which, otherwise, were not visible on the social and political front. During such a period there was much talk about the imposition of dictatorial rule upon the units of federation reducing those to mere municipalities. These forces, it was alleged, imparted a death-blow to the functioning of federalism. However, on the other, the emergency provided an opportunity to the opposition parties to chart-out joint programmes against the authority of the Congress at the Centre. The debate which was suppressed for sometime again cropped up during Parliamentary elections in March 1977. National leaders like Jaya Prakash Narayan[65] and Jagjivan Ram[66] appealed to the conscience of the people, time and again to eradicate the strong Unitarian attempts undermining the federal spirit of India. The result of the elections led to the establishment of the first non-Congress Government, the Janata Government at the centre. It was seen as a major turning point in the history of political process in India.

The results of 1977 elections brought about two important changes.

In the first place it proved that anti Congressism can be an alternative strategy for gaining political power. Secondly, it could establish that with the breakdown of the 'Congress system' the period of coalition politics had begun at the national level along with the state level. Now the regional political parties began to assert themselves in such a way as to become the controlling factors in the process of national mainstream politics. As 'More Powers to States' and Restoration of the Spirit of Federation were the major points in the election campaign of the Janata Party, with the advent of its regime, it was natural for the people to hope that there would be a greater decentralisation of authority. But when the suitable time for promises to keep approached, it started evaporating with the utterances of the Prime Minister. The Janata Government at the Centre favoured the case of strong Centre and supported the theory that a strong Centre is a binding force for the country. Morarji Desai, the then Prime Minister, making his intentions clear said, 'The Centre cannot be strong if the States are not strong, because he believed that a strong Centre with weak States could lead to dictatorship'.[67] However, from 1977 onwards a chorus of different political voices rose throughout India which argued for different degrees and levels of autonomy for the States and a variety of spheres in which the Centre should either drastically modify its powers or altogether cease to exercise them. Some political observers have viewed the victory of the regional parties as nothing but the victory of federalism in India.

With the break up of the Janata Party and its electoral defeat in January 1980 the Congress was back to power once again at the Centre but had lost more states than ever before in the past. Kerala, West Bengal, Tripura and Jammu and Kashmir, Tamil Nadu, Karnataka that is the whole of south and strategic states in the east and west were lost to it. It could be seen as a new dimension in Indian politics. In the period there had been instances where conflicts appeared among different segments of the society over the issue of managing the economic system. This was explained as a case for direct suppression of the conflictual situations by the state machinery. So there was attempt at searching for stability on the social and political fronts which had their profound impact on the centre-state relations in India. The developments that took place in Indian society and politics visibly indicated that the era of one-Party rule at the Centre and in the States had ended. The political scenario had undergone a transformation with different political parties holding the reins of administration in a number of States. Now it was imperative to evolve new codes of behaviour in dealing with centre – state relations.

In June 1983, the Union Government appointed a Commission under the Chairmanship of Justice R.S. Sarkaria to re-examine Centre–State relations in view of the growing demand for more autonomy to the States. The Commission's terms of reference included examination and review of the working of the existing arrangement between Union and the States with regard to powers, functions and responsibilities in all spheres.[68] Earlier in March 1983, the Chief Ministers of the four southern States of India, viz; Rama Krishna Hedge of Karnataka, M.G. Ramachandran of Tamil Nadu, N.T. Rama Rao of Andhra Pradesh and D. Ramachandran of Pondichery, resolved to form a Council for the Southern Region to restructure Centre-State relations in financial resources.[69] In addition, there were clear evidences as to Congress-1 Chief Ministers joining hands with the non-Congress-1 Chief Ministers on the issue of greater autonomy for States. A short while after the Karnataka and Andhra polls, Sripat Mishra, the Chief Minister of Uttar Pradesh, became a vehement critic of the Congress for being a hindrance to the State's development. Another Madhavsinh Solanki, the Chief Minister of Gujrat, in a memorandum to the Eighth Finance Commission, asked for the share of the corporate taxes one of the demands by the southern Chief Minister also.[70] In the face of such incidents the need for a Commission was no longer a matter of political gimmickry-it was a dire necessity. Justice Sarkaria had also stated that he has an open mind on the subject and that anything that emerges after full deliberation with all parties and wise persons will be given due consideration.

Among other things, the Commission was of the view that the Centre should remain strong and hence rejected any demand for curtailing the powers of the Centre, and transfer of more subjects from the Centre to the States as raised in the Anandpur Sahib Resolution, and referred to the Commission by the Government. The Commission opined that the transfer of some subjects like preventive detention, education, labour and electricity to the States would disturb the basic scheme of Constitution. Its emphasis upon 'unity and integrity' as a counterpoise to States' autonomy in the terms of reference of the Sarkaria Commission had given rise to a lot of controversies in the opposition circle. At large the Commission was appointed by taking due note of the changing political realities, strains within the federation and the validity of the demands consequent upon such a change.[71] However, in the context, it is true that being persuaded by several internal and international factors our constitutional fathers envisaged a strong Centre. It is common knowledge that a weak and ineffective Centre would produce anarchy and not viable and strong States. And by the same logic a strong Centre need not necessarily mean weak States. The case for strong Centre is a strong as the case for strong States.

5.4 Recent Perspective and Prospect of Indian Federalism

In the present day phenomenon we have the multi-party polity, with Congress ruling at the Centre and many a state under non-Congress governments, the financial and economic relations are being slowly but steadily readjusted in favour of the states, they asserting themselves effectively in the National Development Council, in the finance commission, in other forums to win for themselves greater benefit and authority within the constitution. It is this type and pattern of federalism-cooperative and bargaining federalism which seems to have stabilised in the present day situation of multi-party polity. This is not a denial of the central domination but concedes to the states their legitimate rights and privileges within the constitutional framework while ensuring the unity and integrity of the country. Within this there is much scope for flexibility and the powers of the centre and the powers of the states will continue to be determined by a number of variables.

The demand for restructuring Centre-State relations is as old as the adoption of the Constitution of India in 1950. The Founding Fathers of the Indian constitution took note of the emerging trend of cooperative federalism in the traditional federations. They were not committed to any principle of federalism rather their sole aim was to hammer out a constitution which was capable of solving the problems that the country was subjected to on the eve of independence and would also be confronted with in the future. Its makers were enamoured with the idea that it should work for the progress, peace and prosperity of the people. The framers evolved, developed and improvised a substructure in the constitution, to promote cooperation and minimize tensions between the centre and states. They provided a framework in which the federal governments was vested with wider powers than were granted to the governments of the states. The religious, linguistic and ethnic diversities of India, the outbreak of communal riots, the trauma of partition and its ghastly aftermath, Gandhi's assassination, the Communist upsurge in Telangana, problems of India's external security and complex international order, and squalor of the teeming millions affected the mood and thinking of the framers of the Indian constitution. They believed that only a strong centre can act as a foil to India's propensity to decentralise to the point of dismemberment, that the goal of the nation-the welfare of the people would be achieved only with a centralised cooperative federation.

The history of federalism and Centre – State relations in India is marked by political mobilisation and intermittent struggle to fashion a more federal set-up. In the first phase lasting until the last 1960s, the task of nation building and development was the main concern of the nation's rulers. This period was not solely dominated by the trend of centralisation. Whatever conflicts arose and there were many major ones-were all sought to be resolved under the Constitution. Geographic boundaries of the States have often been reorganised. In 1956, they were organised on linguistic basis. This laid the basis for the later assertion by the States for greater powers. Later more States were formed – Haryana, Himachal Pradesh, Nagaland, Manipur, Mizoram, Arunachal Pradesh and Goa. Even in 2003, three large States were bifurcated to create three new States of Jharkand, Uttarakhand and Chhatisgarh to respect and encourage the local aspirations of the people.[72]

In this regard installation of non-Congress governments at the state level after 1967 is considered as the beginning of the process of erosion of Congress hegemony. But in fact this was the starting point for the emergence of coalition politics in India. The decline of the 'Congress System' as advocated by Austin, brought a number of issues to the surface. One of these issues was to make room for other political parties to play their roles in the national as well as local politics. The 1977 development is the process of culmination which started way back in 1967. In post 1967 phase the Dravida Munnetra Kazhagam decided to carry on a campaign on Centre – State relations in a systematic and scientific manner. In February 1970, in the DMK Conference in Tiruchy, a popular slogan, 'Autonomy for the States; Federalism at the Centre', was given. In its 1971 Election Manifesto, the DMK announced: 'Though the Constitution of India is described as a Federal one, the balance is more tilted towards the Centre and hence the States are not able to function freely in the administrative and financial spheres. Only such powers as are necessary for the Centre to preserve the strength of India should be assigned to the Centre and all the other powers should be left to the States without impairing the ideal of a strong India'.[73] The DMK is of the view that for proper and ideal Centre–State relations, there should be more powers for the States.

In the reign of Rajiv Gandhi, the strategies adopted to meet the crises originating from the states under non-Congress government became counter-productive on many issues. Initially, the Congress tried to penetrate into the Hindi heartland states in order to regain their electoral superiority. But the results in the Assembly elections in as many as ten states did not register a steady growth. In Maharashtra and Punjab almost the same picture could be seen. In a bid to settle these issues, mainly in Punjab a peace accord was concluded between Rajiv Gandhi and the religious leader Harchand Singh Longowal which failed to satisfy either the people of Punjab or the government at the centre. The demand for state autonomy in the matter of finance, was also made by Biju Patnaik of Orissa towards the end of 1973 and in 1990 when he became the Chief Minister of Orissa. In an interview to *The Indian Express* in September 1991, Patnaik reiterated his demand and suggested radical restructuring of Centre–State relations.[74] In fact the framers of the Constitution adopted a federal form of governance in the hope that the Union and the States would work within the limits of the constitution by mutual willingness and cooperation. States should not become over ambitious and the Union should also not be too coercive. Federalism can operate only if the Union tolerates the States and vice-versa. 'Federalism is primarily a device with considerable potential for integrating the political assertion of diverse regional interests and providing a framework for reconciling demands for increased representation and participation in national development. Thus viewed, the issue is more than merely devolution of powers from the Centre to the States.'[75] In other words, the constitution avoids the tight mould of federalism and it can be both unitary and federal according to the requirements of time and circumstances.

For the first time in 1989, a National Front coalition government headed by V.P. Singh, which included major regional parties like the DMK, took office at the Centre. Though short – lived, this government took certain steps to strengthen the federal principle. The Inter – State Council was constituted in 1990. The entry of regional parties in coalition government at the centre became a regular feature in 1996 with the formation of the United Front government and in all subsequent ones – and presently in the United Progressive Alliance government. The left parties, which supported both the National Front government in 1989 and the United Front government in 1996-1998 and the present UPA government, are strong supporters of the federal principle.[76] An analysis of the nature and dimension of federal government in India will show that there has been qualitative changes in the inner dynamics of political parties in India, both at the national and regional levels.

In the beginning of 1990s the implementation of dual policies of liberalisation and decentralisation were significant as the local bodies in their functioning reduced the role of the bureaucracy while increasing grass-root level participation with State's support. A historic development took place in 1992, both in the Constitutional and federal history of India, by virtue of the 73rd and 74th Amendment Acts to the Constitution. The 73rd Amendment Act and the 74th Amendment Act made the rural local bodies and the urban local bodies respectively a compulsory and statutory provision. It was also entrusted with powers and responsibilities 'to enable them to function as institutions of self – government and such law may contain provisions for the devolution of powers and responsibilities.' Their main responsibilities is 'the preparation of plans for economic development and social justice in the matters listed in Eleventh and Twelfth Schedules for the rural and urban local bodies respectively. Both these Schedules are broadly derivatives of the State list and these are meant in further refining the developmental and welfare functions of the State and in the process, federalism too. In this regard the fact remains that decentralisation has often come to be regarded as a way of reducing the strength of governments and as synonymous with privatisation.[77] In these Amendments total of 29 responsibilities have been given to rural local bodies and 18 to urban local bodies respectively.

However, the controversy of the nature of Indian Constitution–federal or unitary is continuing till date. Ashok Chanda in his book, *Federalism in India*, has expressed the view, 'India is not a federal State. In the final analysis, it is a unitary State in concept and operation.[78] These and similar other comments were consequent due to the fact that the Union government is heavily loaded with powers and functions than the States. In the present times, emphasis being laid on development administration, the Union assumes greater responsibility and plays a substantial role than the States. Many State subjects and areas of functions, like education, health, rural and urban development, social security, etc. are more determined by Union policies and funding. The approach paper of the Second Administrative Reforms Commission 2006, states, 'paucity of resources at State level, need for standardisation of services, compulsions of reducing regional disparities, and the imperatives of meeting challenges of a growing economy in the modern world have necessarily enlarged the Union's role in these sectors'. It illustrates the significance of the Union and the growing dependence of the States on the Union, inspite of having a gradual maturing of federal democracy in India. In a statement B.R. Ambedkar clarified the greater role of the Union, 'though the country and the people may be divided into different States for convenience of administration, the country is one integrated whole, its people a single people living in a single imperium derived from a single source. The division of power among the units is, according to Ambedkar more an arrangement of division of labour than distribution of power.[79]

India for the last one decade and more is experiencing coalition politics and both the Centre and many States are being governed by coalition of different political parties. The earlier phenomenon of 'one – party system' or rather 'one-party dominant system' has been eroding to coalition system. Political parties or alliance of political parties are playing divergent roles in the Union-State governance. A Party, which is ruling the State, is in the opposition at Centre and vice-versa. 'This has made the spectacle of monolithic party organisations a thing of the past. Different segments of the same party are both cooperating and opposing the government of the day and this has thrown such a challenge to traditional thinking in regard to federalism that the President, the Prime Minister and the Chief Ministers are vying with each other in their expressions of mutual co-operation and smooth running of Union – State relations'.[80] The time is ripe now with almost every major political party realising by sheer experience and because of objective conditions - the need to establish a true federal system that would strengthen the bonds of mutual cooperation, unity, and cordiality between the Centre and the States.

The honest and the practical way ahead is for the Union to lose its extra weight and shed its tendency to be the centre with monopoly of power to dominate over the units and the people. In short, the only way to preserve 'India, that is Bharat' as a 'Union of States' is to work for building it as a 'federal Union' with multiple tiers of government and sharing of powers from the lowest grassroot levels of Panchayats to the Parliament and the Government of the Union.[81] When the basic units of the federal Union at the grassroots become small and autonomous, most of the conflicts related to ethnicity and quest for freedom may get resolved and it may be possible to involve various groups in governance more closely and this may make the Union stronger and the nation more integrated, emotionally and culturally.

Above all, it needs to be remembered that only the spirit of 'cooperative federalism' and not an attitude of dominance or superiority – can preserve the balance between the Union and the States and promote the good of the people. Under our constitutional system, no single entity can claim superiority. Sovereignty does not lie in any one institution or in any one wing of the government. The power of governance is distributed in several organs and institutions for good governance. Thus the element of cooperation, of seeking friendly counsel with each other and of ever keeping the larger end in view, is of paramount importance.

References

1. Subhash C. Kashyap, 'Innovative Federal Structures and Conflict Resolution in India', *South Asia Politics*, Vol. 11, No. 3, July 2012 (New Delhi: 2012), p. 11.

2. M. Beloff, 'The Federal Solution in its Application to Europe, Asia and Africa', *Political Studies*, 1953, p. 114, as quoted in S.A. Palekar, 'Federalism: A Conceptual Analysis', *The Indian Journal of Political Science*, Vol. LXVII, No. 2, April-June 2006 (Meerut: 2006), p. 303.

3. K.C. Wheare, *Federal Government*, Fourth Edition (Oxford University Press, 1963), p. 33.

4. Sir Robert Garran, *Report of the Royal Commission on the Australian Constitution* (1929), p. 230.

5. Morton Grodzins, 'The Federal System,' in Aaron Wildavsky (ed.), *American Federalism in Perspective* (Boston : Little Brown and Company: 1967), p. 261.

6. Dr. Chandra Pal, *Centre-State Relations and Cooperative Federalism* (New Delhi :Deep and Deep Publications, 1983), p. 27.

7. William S. Livingston, *Federalism and Constitutional Change* (1956), p. 9.

8. Aaron Wildavsky (ed.), *American Federalism in Perspective*, p. 178.

9. M. Venkatrangaiya, *Some Theories of Federalism* (1971), p. 41.

10. S.A. Palekar, 'Federalism: A Conceptual Analysis,' p. 306.

11. *Ibid.*, p. 307.

12. *Ibid.*, p. 308.

13. A.H. Birch, *Federalism, Finance and Social Legislation in Canada, Australia and the United States* (London: Oxford University Press, 1955), p. 304.

14. R.L. Watts, *New Federations: Experiments in The Common Wealth*, p. 12.

15. M.P. Jain, 'Federalism in India', *Journal of Indian Law Institute*, Vol. 6 (1964), p. 365.

16. Dr. Chandra Pal, *Centre-State Relations and Cooperative Federalism*, p. 20.

17. Daniel J, Elazar, *American Federalism: A View from the States*, 3rd Edition (Newyork: Harper and Row, 1984), p. 2.

18. Daniel J. Elazar, 'Federalism and Consociational Regimes', *Publius*, Vol. 15, No. 2, Spring 1985 (Temple University, 1985), p. 23.

19. John McGarry, 'Federalism (Federation) as a Method of Ethnic Conflict Regulation,' *Working Paper, Conference on From Power-sharing to Democracy : Post Conflict Institutions in Ethnically Divided Society*, 9-10 November 2002 (London: 2002).

20. B.L. Biju, 'Market Preserving Federalism: A Theoretical Hybrid of Liberal Democracy and Global Capitalism,' *IJPS*, Vol. LXVIII, No. 2, April-June 2007 (Meerut: 2007), p. 226.

21. *Ibid.*

22. Ralph Miliband, *Marxism and Politics* (London: Oxford University Press, 1979).

23. Carlton J.H. Hayes, *The Historical Evolution of Nationalism* (1931).

24. Shreeram Chandra Dash, 'Political Irrelevance in Constitutionalism', in Satya

Prakash Dash (ed.), *Constitutional and Political Dynamics of India* (New Delhi: Sarup & Sons, 2004), p. 48.

25. S.A.H. Haqqi, 'The Indian Federal Structure and National Unity', in Subhash C. Kashyap (ed.), *Union – State Relations in India* (New Delhi: The Institute of Constitutional and Parliamentary Studies, 1983), pp. 194-95.
26. *Constituent Assembly Debates*, Vol. VII, p. 33.
27. Bipin Chandra, Mridula Mukherjee and Aditya Mukherjee, *India After Independence 1947-2000* (New Delhi: Penguin Books, 2002), p. 50.
28. Dr. Chandra Pal, *Centre –State Relations and Cooperative Federalism*, p. 74.
29. *Ibid.*
30. S.A. Paleker, 'Federalism: A Conceptual Analysis', p. 307.
31. M.V. Pylee, *India's Constitution* (Bombay:Asia Publishing House, 1962), p. 304.
32. K.C. Wheare, *Federal Government*, p. 27.
33. K.M. Munshi, *The President Under the Indian Constitution* (Bombay: Bharatiya Vidya Bhavan, 1967), p. 1.
34. Ivor Jennings, *Some Characteristics of the Indian Constitution* (London: Oxford University Press, 1953), p. 1.
35. Paul H. Appleby, *Public Administration in India, Report of a Survey* (1953), p. 51.
36. Subhash C. Kashyap, 'Innovative Federal Structure and Conflict Resolution in India', pp. 11-12.
37. K.H. Bailey, *Summary Report of Proceedings – International Legal Conference* (New Delhi : 1953-54), p. 29.
38. Daniel J. Elazar, *Federalism and Consociational Regimes*, p. 22.
39. A.K. Bagchi, *Private Investment in India: 1900-1937* (Cambridge: Cambridge University Press, 1972).
40. S.P. Aiyar, 'The Structure of Power in the Indian Federal System', in Subhash C. Kashyap (ed.), *Union – State Relations in India*, pp. 58-59.
41. K.C. Khanna, 'Strong Centre , Weak States – New Problems in Perspective', *The Times of India,* January 1980.
42. Surindar Suri, 'Evolution of Federal Polity – Resolving New Problems', *Ibid.,* 11 December 1980.
43. *Report of the Study Team on Centre –State Relations* (Administrative Reforms Commission, Delhi: Manager of Publication, 1968), pp. 2-3.
44. Rajni Kothari, 'Integration Exclusion in Indian Politics', *Economic and Political Weekly*, Vol. XXIII, No. 43 (1988), p. 2224.

45. S.P. Aiyar, 'The Structure of Power in the Indian Federal System', pp. 63-64.
46. R.J. May, *Federalism and Fiscal Adjustment* (Oxford: The Clarendon Press, 1969), p. 44.
47. R.L. Watts, 'Recent Trends in Federal Economic Policy and Finance in the Commonwealth, *Sixth World Congress of the International Political Science Association* (Geneva: 1964), p. 22.
48. Ashok Chanda, *Federalism in India* (London: George Allen and Unwin, 1965), p. 289.
49. Dr. Rajkumar Singh, *India and Pakistan – Social, Political and Military Perspectives* (New Delhi: Regal Publictions, 2009), pp. 38-39.
50. M.P. Dube, 'Changing Pattern of Centre – State Relations in India in Hari Hara Das and Sanjukta Mohapatra (ed.), *Centre –State Relations* (New Delhi: Ashish Publishing House, 1986), p. 109.
51. Papia Deb, P.K. Sengupta, 'Coalition Politics and the Changing Perspective of India's Federal Governance', *IJPS*, Vol. LXX, No. 2, April-June 2009 (Meerut: 2009), p. 398.
52. Rajni Kothari, 'Integration and Exclusion in Indian Politics', p. 2225.
53. *Ibid.*
54. L.I. and S. Rudolph, *In Pursuit of Lakshmi: The Political Economy of the Indian State* (Delhi: 1987), p. 99.
55. *Ibid.,* p. 138.
56. Rajni Kothari, 'Integration and Exclusion in Indian Politics', p. 2226.
57. Surindar Suri, 'Evolution of Federal Polity – Resolving New Problems.'
58. Iqbal Narain, Arvind K. Sharma, 'The Emerging Issues and Ideas in Indian Federalism – A Post – Fourth General Election Review', in Subhash C. Kashyap (ed.), *Centre- State Relations in India,* p. 184.
59. Papia Deb, P.K. Sengupta, 'Coalition Politics and the Changing Perspectives of India's Federal Governance', p. 392.
60. *Ibid.*
61. Hari Hara Das, Sanjukta Mohapatra, *Centre–State Relations in India,* pp. 176-77.
62. *Communist Party of India: Six Point Programme, 8th Party Congress,* 1968.
63. K.L. Kamal and Ralph C. Meyer, *Democratic Politics in India* (New Delhi : Vikas Publishing House, 1977), p. 113.
64. T.V. Satyamurty, 'Centre – State Relations', *Economic and Political Weekly,* April 9, 1983, p. 577.
65. *The Times of India,* 16 March 1978.

66. *The Indian Express*, 2 March 1977.

67. *The Statesman* (Delhi), 1 August 1977.

68. Satya Prakash Dash, 'Indian Federalism and Distribution of Responsibilities', *IJPS*, Vol. LXVIII, No. 4, October – December 2007 (Meerut: 2007), p. 707.

69. *Ibid.*

70. *The Telegraph*, 25 March 1983.

71. Hari Hara Das, Sanjukta Mohapatra, *Centre–State Relations in India*, p. 199.

72. Subhash C. Kashyap, 'Innovative Federal Structure and Conflict Resolution in India', pp. 12-13.

73. Kalaignar M. Karunanidhi, 'Autonomy for the States, Federalism at the Centre,' *The Hindu*, 15 August 2007.

74. Satya Prakash Dash, 'Indian Federalism and Distribution of Responsibilities', p. 708.

75. Balveer Arora and Nirmal Mukarji, *Federalism in India* (New Delhi: Vikas Publishing House, 1992), p. 14.

76. Kalaignar M. Karunanidhi, 'Autonomy for the States, Federalism at the Centre.'

77. Pranab Bardhan, 'Decentralisation of Governance and Development, *Journal of Economic Perspectives*, No. 4 (2002), p. 186.

78. Ashok Chanda, *Federalism in India*, p. 124.

79. S.L. Verma, *Federal Authority in Indian Political System* (Jaipur: RBSA Publishers, 1987), p. 160.

80. Shreeram Chandra Dash, *The Constitution of India: A Comparative Study* (Allahabad: Chaitanya Publishers, 1968), p. 202.

81. Subhash C. Kashyap, 'Innovative Federal Structures and Conflict Resolution in India', pp. 14-15.

6 Experienced Challenges of Indian Republic

6.1 Genesis of Political Corruption in India

In India and abroad the issue of corruption drew the attention of analysts and public as well from the time of the emergence of civil societies in ancient times to the complex politics of the present day. Corruption is a fact of life. It is as old as the human society itself. It exists in one form or another in every society as said by Ralph Braibaniti, 'Governmental corruption is found in all bureaucracy and in all periods of political development. But its degree is not uniform at all times or under all conditions. It is also obviously more common in some societies than in others and more common at some times in the evolution of a society than at other times.[1] In recent times corruption has assumed the shape of a "hot issue" and its tentacles have become not only widespread but also far more serious. The phenomenon has become very serious both in developed and developing countries. Even the international organisations are busy in arranging scholarly debates on the causes and consequences of corruption because corruption is not only a human issue but developmental as well as social and economic issue.

Corruption Defined and Analysed

Rampant corruption is something which does not need any emphasis. Everyone of us knows it, everyone of us sees it, every moment of our life, wherever we go, it is present in some form or the other. The challenge begins with how to define it. Most people know corruption when they see it. The problem is that different people see it differently.[2] The word is often used loosely in a very narrow sense and often used with a wide connotation, but somewhat confined to morals or public offences. The etymology of the word can be traced back to a Latin word meaning "to break", which means that something is broken, such as, moral or social code of conduct and more importantly the violation of any law or administrative rule. Apart from outright graft or bribery, the use, abuse and non use of power, legal or political, for personal or private gain to oneself or others not rightfully entitled to it, does cover the various hues and nuances of corruption.[3] Thus the term includes all improper or selfish exercise of power and influence attached to a public office or to a special position one occupies in public life.

At large there is no internationally accepted definition of corruption. It depends upon the state of awareness, education, customs and contention, ethics, culture, state of economic development and legal framework over the interest of the society. High level of corruption is the result of wide divergence between the attitudes, aims and the methods of the government of a country and those of the society in which they operate, in particular, of the procedures and aims of the government which put particular groups of the population at a special disadvantage. In political context the word corruption has two aspects – social and political. Social aspect includes social behaviour, moral and religious while political aspect implies political and administrative or politico-administrative. Social corruption includes breach of social customs, habits, creeds affecting people; sexual harassment, creation of social evils etc. The politico-administrative corruption generally defiles the entire structure of society much more than social aspect.[4] The path of corruption has become clear and smooth when democratically elected people have come to constitute the administrative machinery and overtly or covertly indulge in corrupt practices.

India is rated as one of the most corrupt countries in the world. The global corruption perception Index of India is 87th out of 178 countries, slipping from 84th in 2009.[5] As a social phenomenon corruption has become so widespread that it has started eating into the vitals of our economy, our polity and our society. From top to bottom, prime minister to a peon, cutting across every office or organisation of all Governments, Central State or local, the vast majority of public officials in this country have become corrupt. From the practical viewpoint, corruption as defined by the 19th Conference of European Ministers of Justice, held in Malta in 1994, seems to serve the overall purpose, 'Bribery and other behaviour in relation to persons entrusted with responsibilities in public or private sector which violates their duties that follow from their status as a public official, private employee, independent agent or other relationship of that kind and is aimed at obtaining undue advantages of any kind for themselves or others.[6] However the overall composition of phenomenon of corruption in case of India and other developing countries may be summarised as follow :

Driving force	: Individual need and greed
Supportive environment	: Political interference
Restrictive environment	: Transparency and accountability
Opportunity	: Secrecy and complex regulation
Corrective measures	: Certainty of punishment

There is also an attempt by some to explain corruption as a process by which members of society can manipulate a political system which is unable to cope with the demands made upon it. They explain corruption within the framework of the 'leading' and lagging classes existing within any society undergoing rapid social change, and very much divided its values and allegiances.[7] In the situation who gets what from corruption depends in large part on the nature of both the political system and the political elite. Corruption takes place where there is a meeting of opportunity and inclination. Three forms of corruption – parochial, market and systematic are dominant in government organisations. Parochial corruption represents a situation where only ties of kinship, affection, caste and so forth determines access to the favour of power holders while the market corruption signifies a virtually impersonal process in which influence is accorded to those who can pay the most regardless of who they are. But systematic corruption is primarily a political phenomenon and those in power use the government to transfer illicit benefits to themselves or to the clients ... that the governing elite will seek to expand the flow of illicit benefits through official channels.[8] The presence of corruption is an important hindrance to economic growth and progressive social change.

Antecedents of Corruption

The problem is all the more important in developing countries because high political corruption would impede the establishment of a political order and the stability of political institutions and the legitimacy of the political class. In pre-democratic societies, where power rested on lineage and birth, corruption was not a salient issue because the actions of the rulers are perceived to be legitimate. But when politics emanate from the collective activity of the public and where the power of the politicians is based on public consent, corruption takes a newer dimension. Corruption, as agreed by all, is pervasive in all societies, though in different degrees and forms. Corruption inheres in all social systems, feudalism, capitalism, socialism, and communism. It affects all classes of society; all state organisations, monarchies and Republics; all situations in war and peace; in all age groups; both sexes and all times; ancient, medieval and modern.[9] To say that all was pure and idyllic in the early period of history will be travesty of truth.

Political issues – related corruption remained prevalent during the ancient and mediaeval period in Egyptian, Babylonian and Hebrew societies where judges did not hesitate to receive bribes. In Greece the growth of corruption was attributed to the increase of economic activity and political apathy.[10] In ancient Rome corrupt practices prevailed and bribery was a regular source of income for those who were in charge of issuing contracts of public works, however, the prevalence of wide-scale corruption seems to have been the consequence of an unwieldy electoral system which derived form history.[11] During the mediaeval times corruption manifested itself in Rome in the form of extortion of revenue by the local and central officials and the perversion of justice. Those who were in the service of the kings and feudal barons became instrumental in the collection of illegal money.[12] Even in the period of exploration and colonisation, corruption took the same form as under the Roman Republic.

Other countries alike, the period of ancient and mediaeval India was not free from corruption but the extent of evil was certainly far less than what is at present. A.L. Basham, the famous historian, while writing on the administration of justice in India observed, 'Though judicial corruption is often referred to, the standard set for judges and magistrates is very high, they are to be learned, religious, devoid of anger, and as impartial as is humanly possible to prevent bribery. Kautilya in his Arthasastra has written a chapter entitled 'Detection of what is embezzled by government servants out of state revenue.[13] and mentioned about forty types of embezzlement.[14] In the medieval period under the Khilji Rule, Tughlaq Dynasty and in the Mughal Empire, the problem of corruption was rampant at various levels of administration. Wrote Sir Thomas Roe at the end of the sixteenth century, 'the people of India live as fishes do in the sea and the great ones eat up the little. For first, the farmer robs the peasants, the gentleman robs the farmer, the greater robs the lesser, and the king robs all.'[15]

However, in the colonial days of British rule in India there was a systematic corruption which involved almost all officials starting from the Governor down to the lowest revenue official. From the days of Lord Clive and Warren Hastings down to a comparatively recent period bribery and corruption were prevalent even among the highest and were literally winked at by the Government.[16] Further under the British rule in the nineteenth and twentieth centuries, corruption and nepotism wove a strange pattern. About the British period it is commonly said that from the Governor down to the meanest factor people came to India not for the "good but for the "goods" of the country."

6.2 Political Corruption after Independence

A certain degree of dishonesty and corruption had existed althrough human history, in Independent India the issue has become rampant and all pervasive. Unlike earlier, today whosoever is indulged in immoral and corrupt practices is not socially discarded but are considered talented due to faulty implementation of systems, the political in particular. As a result, many well-meaning people, both in the rural areas and cities, seem to have become reconciled to the evil of corruption and even compromised by referring to their experience and inventing ways and means as to how to circumvent them. Politicians' cupboards are overflowing with skeletons and what is more, they appear to be out of the reach of the rule of law. The country is here because the political system is self-perpetrating and no party is accountable to anyone except a coterie of people that dominates all decisions. More worrisome than individual corruption is the widespread dishonesty at party levels. The aim of present day anti-corruption movements is also to strike at the root cause which is responsible for the omnipresence of corruption in all walks of life.

Birth of Real Danger

In the sphere of political corruption real danger started with the dawn of India's independence in August 1947. The situation has completely changed as in the past the scope for corruption as well as temptation was limited. The British evolved an impersonal law and enforce it by and large impersonally. Indian on the other hand have traditionally, accepted corruption and nepotism with a certain amount of tolerance. Resentment is felt and expressed only. When there is high-handedness or corruption is excessive in the Indian set of common values, it is generally assumed that those who exercise authority or happen to be close to those who do so must be entitled to privileged position and that, up to a point, their indiscretion must be overlooked.[17] Under British the economy was primitive, and only a segment of the population came in contact with public authorities. Official corruption therefore, touched their lives but rarely and briefly. In the period even the Indian National Congress which was almost the only effective political organisation, at the time of India's independence, had been something much more and much less than a political party. It was called by some writers an 'umbrella organisation, with men and women of diverse belief, outlook and background. Being in politics before independence also meant being in national mainstream and people in those days joined politics or supported the Party for reasons of high idealism, prestige and spirit of service in the cause of the country. They were not motivated by lust for public office or lure for political power or for getting rich quick through easy money.[18] However, everything changed with the assumption of power by the mainstream party. It ceased to be the all-embracing and unifying national movement but became a political party and the government of the country.

The broad fact of independent India is that it inherited two legacies from its past. The Raj gave to independent India, by and large, a clean public administration. The other with which India started its career as an independent country, was the heritage of clean politics led by Mahatma Gandhi. Gandhiji spiritualised politics, and for him the purity of means was of paramount importance. A politician was thus expected to observe always and without exception a high standard of purity, simplicity, nobility and selflessness. Clean politics and a strong and dedicated public administration were India's most valuable in 1947.

India following its independence made a constitution which came into force in 1950 and with its coming the mode of recruitment became election. Hitherto, anyone could join politics provided he had an urge as well as the willingness to defy the colonial rule and all that it signified and, if necessary, to go to jail at the call of national leadership. What politics promised was a self-chosen career of sacrifice and suffering.[19] Election, the new method of choosing of political leaders is expensive and costs money. Elections began to be bought at a very high pitch, costing many times more than the legally prescribed ceiling. As a result, politicians of the Gandhian era steadily bowed out of the electoral arena and the space so vacated was filled by the new politician, who had little resemblance to the first generation of politicians. The new politician was the product of electoral processes. He was one who had spent a lot of money in contesting the election and who necessarily had to collect funds to be ready for the next election.

In post-independence India, the laws and rules which are seemingly for the benefit of the people, are mostly theoretical exercises. These are not, actually, operational with respect to a citizen's problems. In reality, a different way of functioning prevails, to the advantage of those who wield power, namely, people in politics and in the Government and people outside who are their friends and associates. They run what has been called a parallel government, treating the people and the nation's resources as their private property. The politicians in power and the bureaucrats can act in disregard not only of laws and rules but of national interests and of rationality and morality. The decisive factor in each case is the advantage, monetary, political or other, to the politicians or bureaucrats in question or their friends and associates.[20] With the assumption of power by the dominant organisation at the Union and State levels, personal ambitions, fight for loves and fishes, in group rivalry, caste, communal, regional, and linguistic pulls within the Party began to grow much faster than any actual differences of ideology.

Wider Scope in Indian Context

In addition, with the advent of independence and the beginning of economic planning, the corruption front opened up for large-scale escalation. Because of its very nature, we have no systematic information of the shape or size of the monster of corruption and graft, but by all accounts they are truly formidable. The Central and State governments publish, from time to time, reports of the number of officers of various ranks arrested, prosecuted, convicted, fined, the figures published are themselves substantial.[21] Concern for political corruption was occasionally voiced in as early as the mid-forties; the responsible ministers coming to power were dogged by the talk of corruption and groupism.[22] In this background, in the years following independence of the country there emerged a general feeling that corruption in India spread to every part of the governmental machinery, and had a more rapid growth among politicians of many political parties.

In the whole atmosphere of political corruption, the Second Five Year Plan (1957-1962) with its industry orientation, acted as a catalyst. As a result, the businessman, either potential or actual, the politician, and the civil servant were drawn closer to each other, the new link being in exchange of money or favour. The businessman wanted a license; the minister was the granting authority; and the civil servant had to process the papers and make out a case in favour of the former. These developments speeded up the already existed political corruption and in the late 1960s or so, it has assumed an alarming proportion in public mind. The situation changed radically in the second and third decades of our Independence. Politics emerged as a well-entrenched profession. Politicians in power or close to power and authority realised that politics could prove the gateway to pelf and power.[23] A feeling began to grow that those in political power or with proximity to it could get away, although corruption may be legally a crime as well as social evil. And gradually even social or moral disapprobation ceased to have any value or effect.

In nutshell, the corruption of leaders tends to affect the trust, loyalty and personal integrity of their followers. The famous political thinker Machiavelli put it, 'Corruption of leaders is dangerous because leaders are the paradigms of the body politic. The leaders are usually those individuals charged with rooting out corruption.[24] And the Latin proverb goes 'Corruption of the best is worst.' Many Western writers, while taking the problem of corruption in developing countries like India, have two different stands. One group thinks that corruption is intrinsic and unavoidable in developing countries due to traditional values, social practices and community connections, extended family relationships, etc. This means the lack of modernisation and its people are bound to live with corruption and, at best, some efforts at containing the evil can be hopefully made.

The other school of thought opines that in a slow-moving, insensitive, inefficient developing country, corruption acts as a lubricant to make the wheels of governmental machinery move, ensuring economic growth and hence need not be looked as an unmitigated nuisance.[25] In case of India's corruption and the frequency of scandals bear testimony to both the facts of life. Foreign observers like Dr. Gunnar Myrdal and Myron Weiner commented on political corruption in India in late sixties and held the view that, 'Corruption was not only rampant but that it was growing particularly among higher officials and politicians, including legislators and ministers and they further argue that known offenders can continue their corrupt practices with little risk of punishment, are apt to re-inforce the conviction that this type of cynical asocial behaviour is widely practised in the Indian context.[26] In the 1960s, the atmosphere was thick with rumours about corruption and the government was forced to appoint the K. Santhanam Committee for Prevention of Corruption (1962) and S.R. Das Inquiry Commission (1963). The reports of both the committee confirmed the existence of widespread corruption in India.

From the mid-1960s onwards the whole structure and the political party system in India ushered in a new era in which members, legislatures were openly bought and sold like cattle and the prevailing prices were freely quoted. A trend began in which politics ceased to be for any purpose of public service. It became more and more an exclusive and lucrative profession and a specialised craft in the perennial pursuit of power for its own sake, with all those in the business of politics trying to get to power and once there to somehow retain it and augment it. Politics began to appeal to many as a gateway to better career, high status in public eye and not unoften considerable material gain.[27] The pressure of vested interests on the politicians grew stronger, and with it, corruption became profitable. Politics became a gainful calling with high social status and opportunities to wield power and avenue to privileges and patronage.

There was a contextual statement on corruption in the late 1960s that, 'It was a worldwide phenomenon', heralded the dawn of the first stage of indulgence. It coincided with the enormous growth of black money and the emergence of money politics as a major factor in public life. Since 1970s the anti-social elements began to openly enter in the political arena, first at lower levels. All political parties of the land began more or less mobilising such anti-social elements to win the election. Such elements have their own motivations to cover them with legitimacy and gain immunity from police action under the law.[28] The nexus between crime and politics, thus, began to develop which had the effect of impaling public agencies responsible for law enforcement. Many of the elected members are directly involved in cases of extortion and murder. The countryside is brimming with gun carrying criminals, trotting as politicians. Crime is their sources of livelihood but politics provides them the necessary cover of protection from law.[29] Vohra Committee's report revealed the nefarious nexus among the criminals, officials of law enforcing authorities and politicians.

In coming years there was a clear degradation and erosion of the democratic process. Earlier, the criminals preferred acting as the back-room boys; they themselves remained in the background and were content to support the politicians. This support was part of the larger protection deal, which they needed and in practice even got. The muscleman is made to carry out multiple tasks in Indian politics. The muscle power is used to intimidate the voter, to capture pooling booths and eventually to win the election. In several States, fighting elections is said to have become impracticable without the candidates having their own private armies or goonda gangs. In large cities, slums are big business both for the politicians and the criminals. The new business of kidnappings and abductions is known to be prospering with the active connivance of the politicians and even the Ministers and Chief Ministers involved in settling the deals. In this context the Shah Commission (1977-79) and Vohra Committee report have certified that there is a growing nexus between the politicians, criminals, bureaucrats, and politics.[30] They are virtually running a parallel government, pushing the state apparatus into irrelevance.

Clearly Supportive Environment

The forms and manifestations of corruption are continually changing. Although the incidence of corruption in public life is a worldwide phenomenon, in recent years it has assumed frightening proportions. It has not only spread to every part of the government machinery, but also has had a more rapid growth among professional politicians, party men at all levels and even in the highest echelons of political leadership both at the State and Central levels. The record of no political party in India is better than that of another on that score. The people's acceptance of corruption in public life and the feeling that those indicted with political corruption invariably go scot-free and in the process amass more power, status and wealth have led to a situation, where even the most determined efforts to fight the evil have failed miserably.[31] The government seems to be aware of the existence of the evil all around, and is also aware of the possible ways to check its monstrous growth, but seems to be lacking in will to enforce such measures effectively.

Further a number of scams took place such as the recently 2G scam and allocation of coal blocks etc. In fact, since independence India has lost many of its noble values and goals. Political corruption has been increasing enormously in India. Politicians' cupboards are overflowing with skeletons and what is more, they appear to be out of the reach of the rule of law. Now the people have become greedy with huge amounts of unaccounted black money indulge in extravagance and vulgar display of wealth. These filthy rich by their spending spree have been influencing the decision making authorities and subverting and corrupting the social and political system. The democratic system that has emerged is not strong enough in fighting the sinister interest, which accumulate and multiply the ill-gotten money surreptitiously.[32] The major cause for the perpetuation of such sordid practices is due to the general apathy, passivity and totally indifferent attitude towards the corrupt and corruption.

Over the years as one study concludes that, 'it is likely that elective institutions have amplified the pressure towards corruption and made it more systematic, because spiraling cost of fighting elections and nursing a constituency between elections[33] and also pointed out that the essential business of a State Minister is not to make policy. It is to modify the application of rules and regulations on a particularistic basis in return for money and loyalty. According to newspaper editorial corruption in India has passed through three different stages: "gaining legitimacy widespread indulgence and shameless defence".[34] Decades ago scholars, Dwivedy and Bhargava observed, 'It is not uncommon for a political branded corrupt to continue to be a national leader.[35] Hence, a fairly large section of society seems to have lost faith in the fairness and impartiality of the entire system of governance.

In this context two things have to be borne in mind. One, it is essential to devalue the importance of politicians in nation's daily life. While there are some very good men and women in our public life, the general run politicians today are social parasites and enemies of nation-building. The political parties are no better than politician-criminal combines sharing power and loot. They have no relationship with democracy and no concern for political good. Two, the people have lost faith in the ability of the system as a whole to provide protection, security, growth or conflict resolution. Only political party or electoral reforms alone would not succeed in stemming the rot. What is needed is a full-scale review of our politico-constitutional edifice and fundamental structural-functional changes. Mere patch work or piecemeal tinkering here and there will serve no purpose.

One of the best anti-dote to minimize corruption is to change the perception of corruption as low-risk high profit to high risk low profit understanding, since corruption is usually not a simple matter of enforcement, for the casualties often include the integrity system itself. As such, the national integrity system is to be designed to prevent corruption from occurring in the first place. In addition, the phenomenon of corruption can be combated by increasing judicial activism, restricting our supportive environment, increasing our destructive environment, minimizing the opportunities and controlling our needs with the help of existing control mechanism as well as by adopting new methodology in this era of Liberalisation, Privatisation and Globalisation.

6.3 Naxalism: Origin, Orientation and Overview

Naxalism, like communalism, fundamentalism and sectarianism has become one of the severe threats and internal security challenge ever faced by our country. Started from a village named 'Naxalbari' in West Bengal in May 1967 soon it became a revolutionary peasant uprising with the motto to free the oppressed classes living in the countryside from the clutches of the landlords and feudal elements. Its founder leaders–Charu Mazumdar, Kanu Sanyal and Jangal Santhal organised peasants' conference and gave a call for ending landlords' monopoly on land and land distribution. Although the initial armed struggle of naxalism was crushed within months, the ideology gained rapid momentum in many parts of India. Naxalism, in decades of its journey, witnessed several ups and downs, but its ideological underpinnings have not changed and in a major breakthrough the two prominent naxalite outfits–Peoples War Group (PWG) and the Maoist Communist Centre of India (MCCI) merged in October 2004. The formation of new entity has given the ongoing movement a sharpened tooth and impelled the Central and State governments to address the problem of growing left extremism with sound policy and greater attention.

Ideological Motivation

Naxalism, which is the most powerful armed struggle in the history of independent India, is heavily based on Marxism–Leninism and strategic alliance of Maoism as practised by him in Chinese context. The two basic philosophers–George Hegel (1770-1831) and Karl Marx enunciated that 'idea' and 'matter' are the essence of the universe and were the force behind all historical development. Although they both depended on the old Greek concept of dialectics in order to substantiate their philosophies, they remained essentially differ about the absolute truth. In contrast to Hegal, Marx proclaimed that the philosophy of Dialectical Materialism formed the empirical basis and held the view that social, political, and intellectual relations prevailing at any epoch of historical development is directly proportional to the economic conditions in that period. The integral part of historical materialism is class conflict or class struggle: the constant struggle between the dominant and the dependent classes. Marx and Engels had full faith in the Proletariat. They believed that it would topple capitalism and establish an egalitarian communist society. At the same time they also made a distinction between base and super structure. The base is the economic foundation of the society whereas the superstructure comprises of the institutions, organisations, literature, art etc. The political ideas of Mao Zedong in China did not grow from vacuum and he picked up from the point where Karl Marx had left.

Mao Zedong who practised and experienced Marxism in China stated that the class struggle does not vanish with the establishment of a communist state, rather takes on new forms. His understanding of the socio–political and economic condition of the Chinese peasantry was so supreme that it aided him to devise pragmatic strategies keeping in mind the Chinese scenario. He proclaimed the famous slogan, 'Political power grows out of the barrel of a gun', and he was successful, both in his judgement as well as in his implementation with the establishment of a communist regime in China in October 1949. The success of Chinese revolution created a wave of joy amongst the oppressed countries in South Asia. It served as the required fuel to ignite the hidden passions of freedom for many a third world countries.[36] In a primarily agrarian society like India, Maoism finds strong grounds, quite similar to the Chinese scenario. And in line in the period 1948-51 the undivided Communist Party of India characterised the newly independent Nehru government as a legacy of Anglo–American imperialism and that independence that India has got was a sham. It believed that masses of India were prepared to support an armed revolution to overthrow the Nehru government and in pursuit of that formulation prepared the party for armed rebellion after the second Congress of the Communist Party in Calcutta when B. T. Rana Dive was elected the new Secretary of the Party. As a result the Communists in Bengal, Kerala and Andhra and Telengana took to arms and mounted attacks on police stations. The communists armed actions or battles, were most extensive and intense in the Telengana region of Andhra Pradesh. The well–armed communist waged war, just like the Maoists of today against the government.[37] Sardar Patel, the then Home Minister and the Government of India saw this war in its true colour, that is, a communist armed rebellion against the state of India. The Government of India used the armed forces to engage and destroy and decimate the communist armed gangs. As a step further the Naxalism of 1960s gathered fresh strength in India basing on the epicentre of Marxism and in afterwards they both agreed to work in unison. In order to bring change one needs to fight in whatever form one wishes to. It can be a non–violent non–cooperation Satyagraha on the lines of Gandhi or it can be an armed struggle to the finish like the Chinese or the Vietnamese or the Cubian revolutions.

The term 'Naxalism' typify a particular kind of militant and violent armed struggle by the peasants, tribals, and dalits led by leadership drawing doctrinal support from Marxism–Leninism and strategic inspiration from Mao Zedong. It began with the 'land to tiller' slogan and inspired similar revolts in other parts of the India.[38] A section of the Communist Party of India (Marxist) particularly consisting of cadres who opposed the participation of the party in the election and government formation under Charu Mazumdar, organised the peasant resistance to landlords over land to the tiller issue in Naxalbari–a small village in the then Siliguri Subdivision of Darjeeling district in West Bengal. It started on March 2, 1967, when a tribal youth, who had a judicial order to plough his land, was attacked by goons of local landlords. Tribal peasants started retaliating by attacking the local landlords and started forcefully capturing back their lands. The incident echoed throughout India and Naxalism was born. The ideology of naxalism soon assumed larger dimension and various sections of the state units of Communist Party of India (Marxist) throughout the country joined the struggle. The birth and growth of naxalism is closely linked to the Sino–Soviet split in the Communist movement in India. In the context of structural realities of India the Communists were divided in pro–Chinese and anti-Soviet Union postures. The Naxalbari uprising was fully supported and praised by the organ of the Communist Party of China (CPC) as the movement advanced the revolutionary line adopted by Chinese leader Mao Zedong.[39] In succeeding years naxalism unleashed a flow of events that brought about far – reaching changes in India's socio–culture scene.

However, solid grounds were prepared for the Naxalbari uprising of May 25, 1967, from the early fifties following the Communist success in China in the year 1949. In Naxalbari area of Darjeeling district in North Bengal, Communists had been organising sharecroppers and tea state labour, mostly belonging to the Santhal, Oraon and Rajbanshi tribal communities. The sharecroppers worked for Jotedars or landlords under the 'adhiar' system in which the jotedars provided the ploughs, bullocks and seeds and got a share of the crops. Dispute over shares followed with the coming of the United Front (UF) government because of the fear that sharecroppers would be given the land. Charu Mazumdar, a prominent leader of the area was working on the issue and it became clear since 1965, that his ideas about agrarian revolution and armed struggle, apparently based on Mao Zedong's thoughts.[40] After coming of the UF government, Charu, alongwith other leaders organised around 15,000 to 20,000 peasants and formed peasants' Committee in villages who became the nuclei of armed guards, who occupied land, burnt land records, declared debts cancelled, delivered death sentences on hated landowners, and set up a parallel administration. They denied any agreement and, anticipating repression, the leaders began to incite the peasants against the police and the things took their predictable and inexorable course with a vicious circle of attacks on police, police reprisals and further clashes as we face today even after four decades of Naxalbari event.

Expansion and Support Base

Within months the Naxalbari uprising was crushed by the police forcefully, it however, expanded soon in other parts of the country with the same ideology and methods. The writings of Charu Mazumdar – the most famous being the 'Historic Eight Documents' formed the basis of Naxalite ideology. In the same year (1967) the Naxalites organised the All India Coordination Committee of Communist Revolutionaries (AICCCR) and it followed the birth of the most notable Naxalite organisation, the Communist Party of India (Marxist–Leninist) in 1969 which defined the objective of the party as, 'seizure of power through an agrarian revolution'. The strategy was the elimination of feudal order in the Indian countryside to free the poor from the clutches of the oppressive landlords and replace the world order with an alternative one that would implement land reforms. The tactics to achieve it was through guerilla warfare by the peasants. Gradually, they would set up a "liberated zone" in different parts of the country that would eventually coalesce into a territorial unit under Naxalite hegemony.[41] By the early 1970s, the Naxalite movement had spread from farflung areas like Andhra Pradesh and Kerala in the south, to Bihar in the east, and Uttar Pradesh and Punjab in the north. But in Andhra Pradesh and in West Bengal, the Naxalites found their main support among the aboriginal tribal communities, who had been the most oppressed and marginalised in Indian society- the Girijans in Andhra Pradesh and the Santhals in West Bengal.[42] Its continuity can be explained by the persistence and exacerbation of the basic causes that gave it birth – feudal exploitation and oppression over the rural poor.

The Maoists draw their sustenance from existing inequalities. Due to the existence of problems relating to land, in the absence of land reforms the small farmers, landless labourers and the tribals continue to suffer. The Naxalism, its ideology and means to achieve the object expanded rapidly in all parts of the country only because the fundamental factors behind the alienation persist: poverty, inequality, illiteracy, economic exploitation, uncertainty of the farm sector, unresolved issues of land relations and land acquisition, a large army of unorganised labour in the farm sector,' exclusion and exploitation of Dalits and Adivasis, failure to rehabilitate those displayed by development and so on. Although the Naxal movement underwent much churning in the succeeding decades, organisationally and politically, yet the emphasis on agrarian revolution remained at the core.

In post – 1967, Naxalbari movement the works and objectives of Naxalism were fulfilled by its two groups - the Maoist Communist Centre of India (MCCI), originally formed in the early 1970s and CPI (ML) People's War Group founded in 1980. Both groups are referred to as Naxalites, and prior to their consolidation in 2004 the MCCI ran a virtual parallel government in remote areas, where it collected a 'tax' from the villages and, in turn, provided infrastructure improvements such as building hospitals, schools, and irrigation projects. It ran a parallel court system wherein allegedly corrupt block development officials and landlords–frequent MCCI targets–had been punished by amputation and even death.[43] While People's War Group conducted a low–intensity insurgency that included attempted political assassination, theft of weapons from police stations, kidnapping police officers, assaulting civilians extorting money from construction firms, and vandalising the property of multinational corporations.

In addition, the newly formed Marxist group–The Communist Party of India (Maoist) is conducting people's war', a strategic line developed by Mao Zedong aims to establish a Compact Revolutionary Zone from which to advance the people's 'New Democracy Revolution'. Like the CPI (ML) People's War, it rejected Parliamentary democracy and capturing political power through protracted armed struggle based on guerilla warfare. It believed to be enlarging the scope of its influence and operates in the Indian states of Andhra Pradesh, Orissa, Jharkhand, Bihar, Chhattisgarh, and parts of West Bengal. It has also a presence in Bihar–Nepal border. The Maoist outfit has also been making attempts to establish and expand its presence in several other states such as Gujarat, Haryana, Punjab, Rajasthan and Himachal Pradesh. While the MCC's areas of influence extend over Bihar and Jharkhand, with some sway in Uttar Pradesh, the PWG's areas of dominance include Andhra Pradesh, Orissa, Chhattisgarh, Karnataka, Maharashtra and Tamil Nadu. Thus the various groups of Maoists, be they called Naxalite or People's War Groups or otherwise adjectived, all have declared very clearly that they have no faith in the constitution of India, in the multi–party democracy and elections.

For the expansion of support base of Naxalism and other forms of Maoists the process of globalisation is heavily responsible as it has polarised the world today than even before. Following the adoption of globalisation the society, at large, stood divided in two classes or categories–a small section that has enjoyed the benefits of globalisation and the second – a major category that is poor and devoid of facilities.[44] For instance, between 1970 and 2000 the level of poverty rose from 20 per cent to 70-85 per cent. Six out of eight children died before their first birthday, while eight die before 8th birthday. In year 2000, 2.8 billion people all over the world over, earned less than 2 $ per day while 1-2 billion earned less than 1 $. It appeared that globalisation does not about human development, which is restricted to small elite only. This inequality, not only creates disintegration, but also causes the emergence of social and national divisive forces. Globalisation also goes against the process of nation–building so far as the case of developing country, like India, is concerned and the concept itself has become irrelevant.[45] Violence, intoxication, terrorism, civil war, ecological degradation, economic disparity and terrorism have been globalised. Neither democracy nor civil society is meaningful for globalisation. Peasants, instead of producers are being turned into consumers. This kind of development is creating the feeling of loneliness in which the individual is getting cut off from his society and non material sources of his life.[46] It has paved the way for the rise of cultural colonisation. Drug, violence, sex and artists of Rock–enrole have become the ideals of youths and there is no left for traditional, social and ethical values.

Recent Trends and Response

In an important development the Maoist Communist Centre of India (MCCI) and the Communist Party of India (Marxist – Leninist) People's War, also known as People's War Group or PWG merged to form a new entity, the Communist Party of India – Maoist (CPI – Maoist) on September 21, 2004. Officially, the merger was announced on October 14, 2004, by the PWG on the eve of peace talks between the PWG and the State Government. It has given new teeth to the Maoists' movement in India and compelled the Central and State government to address the issue more urgently. It has also cast a dark shadow in all States already facing the Left extremism for decades. From there onwards both these groups of Naxalism agreed to work in unison–a pathbreaking step indeed. Now, as it became stronger the CPI (Maoist) altered its stance regarding revolution in India and were now ready to bring in mass – agitation, supplementing the already existing armed struggle. As a result the total number of people killed by the Naxalite violence rose by 30 per cent between 2003 and 2005 while the number of policeman killed jumped to 53 per cent between 2004 and 2005. Naxalite strength has grown over 50 per cent since 2001.[47] Till 2001, 60 per cent of the weaponary was country made. Today they have AK series, grenade launchers, mortars, carbine etc.

The 'objective of the new movement' was 'seizure of power' through an agrarian revolution. The strategy was the elimination of the feudal order in the countryside to free the poor from clutches of the oppressive landlords and replace the old order with an alternative one that would implement land reforms. The annual report of the Ministry of Home Affairs 2005-06 has also admitted that Naxalism is not merely a law and order problem but has deep socio–economic dimensions.[48] The Naxals, in India, has accordingly modelled themselves on the Indian Army lines from training manuals to undercover training. The fighting forces of Naxals are divided into three categories. The primary force is of extremely well trained personnel who spearhead any attack with superior weapons. The secondary force forms the bulk of a large group with less sophisticated weapons. Finally, the people's militia comprises farmers, labourers and others.

Gradually, Maoist violence gained momentum since the early 1990s and in succeeding years the Maoist–extremists launched such major attacks as killing Madhya Pradesh Transport Minister Likhiram Kavre in 1999, blasting the house of Telugu Desam Party leader G. Sudhakar Reddy in Andhra Pradesh in 2000, and attacking TDP leader N. Chandrababu Naidu in 2001.[49] Apart from this Naxal violence has claimed the lives of over 10,000 civilian and security personnel in the last five years with significant rise in the number of killings in Left–wing extremism hit States. Out of a total of 10,268 casualties' between 2005 and 2010, 2372 deaths have been reported in 2009 as against 1,769 in 2008 and 1,737 in 2007 according to an RTI reply by the Home Ministry. A total of 1,999 civilians and security men had lost their lives in 2006 and 1,952 others in 2005.[50] As of 2009, Naxalites were active across approximately 220 districts in twenty states of India accounting for about 40 per cent of India's geographical area. Naxal–related violence occurs in those areas where the administration has low reach. The people in those areas are living at the mercy of insurgents. The effects of the Maoist insurgency have already taken its toll on business. Rebels sided with farmers during violent protests by farmers, which forced the scrapping of the Tata Motor's Nano car plant and a chemical hub complex in West Bengal. In Orissa, bauxite production at the state – run National Aluminum Co. Ltd. has fallen following attack by Maoists in one of their mines in April 2009.[51] In a major deadliest attack the Maoist rebels killed 74 members of CRPF and destroyed an Armoured Personnel Carrier (APC) on 6th April 2010.

The first State response to Naxals in India was made by the United Front Government of West Bengal in 1967 to handle the first phase of the Naxalite movement, which *The People's Daily* characterised as 'spring thunder'. Hare Krishna Konar, the then Revenue Minister of UF government was of the view that so long there was dissatisfaction among the peasantry, militants could operate freely. He proposed the policy to wean away the angry peasantry from militancy by a massive programme of vesting of ceiling–surplus land of the big Zamindars and landowners. This programme resulted in good results and when the peasantry found that the large areas of land would be distributed amongst them, their loyalty shifted from the Naxalite militants to the normal political process. By its effects the Naxalite movement disappeared in the state in early 1970s.

The recent ferocity and the extent of attacks have reached such proportions as to invite the serious concern and involvement of the Central as well as the State governments. It compelled the Government of India to decide on 22 June 2009 to include 'CPI (Maoist)' in the Scheduled of organisation banned under the Unlawful Activities (Prevention) Act, keeping in mind the growing unlawful activities by the group. The party is regarded by some as a left wing extremist entity and a terrorist outfit and several of their members have been arrested by the Indian government under the Prevention of Terrorism Act (POTA). The group is officially banned by the State Governments of Orissa, Chhattisgarh and Andhra Pradesh, among others. In addition funds are given to the States under the Police Modernisation Scheme to modernise their police forces in terms of modern weaponary, latest communication equipment, mobility and other infrastructure. The Naxal affected States have also been asked to identify vulnerable police stations and outposts in the Naxal areas and take up their fortification under the Scheme.[52] Several new developmental schemes have been launched during the 11th Plan period in the naxal – affected states.

The Government of India has realised the fact that unlike other extremist movement, Naxal activities find it easy to garner mass support as they ideologically seek to render justice to socially backward classes. Blantant use of force and banning the outfit in past has evidently proved to be ineffective in tackling the spread of Naxal menace. If Naxals are to be dissociated from the rural support base, the Government must come up with plans to bolster socio–economic activity in Naxal–infested areas which, in turn can act as a means to upgrade standard of living of the poor population. The Indian administration can not escape its due share in the failure of tackling the Naxalite violence. On the other for the Maoists' creating terror and untaking violence is easy but to have a place in the heart and soul of the citizenry is difficult one to achieve. What Maoists are doing is just anarchism against democracy.

6.4 Gender Equality: Postmodern Prospects and Challenges

Gender equality holds the key–position in the world–wide development. In every society people as male and as female are expected to make some exclusive role performance. This role internalisation is done through the process of gender socialisation. Irrespective of gender, people have equal access to the resources and services necessary to achieve their individual potential and fulfil their obligations to household, community and more broadly, society. Traditionally, the expected role performance of the female places them in a secondary position in the social structure and in the minds of men and women alike. All institutions–social, economic, political, religious and ideological have been dominated by men. Despite legislative steps prejudices, traditional attitudes and practices continue to perpetrate discrimination against women and actually no country in the world can claim to have fully achieved gender equality. Significantly enough national efforts and international movement got momentum in previous decades and agencies have started adopting measures for integrating women into the development process. The present position is a step forward but far from satisfactory or set goals in this sphere.

Fact–File of the Problem

The term 'Gender' arose as an analytical tool for analysing the inequalities between the sexes due to the patriarchal institutional structures. It started with assessing gender role and gender analysis, gender needs, gender interests and perspectives. At present the entire world community and the developing nations like India in particular, is focussing its attention as matters relating to gender discrimination which led to societal imbalances. The realisation of the necessity of bringing to the limelight the issues of gender, gender equality, gender inequality has been primarily due to the fact that women constitute one of the crucial segments of the human population and it is widely accepted that without the active participation of women all developmental programmes remain fruitless. Women's special status and women's debilitated status stem from a common ideology, from a belief in an essentialist, biological and psychological incapacity which spans not only assessment of physical capability but also mental capacity.[53] Be they philosophers, religious preachers, political leaders, social reformers or scientists, they all justified inferior status of women in society. The natural differentiation between man and woman does not imply inequalities. Yet, natural and social differentiations have been manipulated through creation of systems of stratification and pattern of inequality.

The notion of society in this regard needs to be understood in terms of social conditions which specified the women to particular types of works and assigns that provided them lower status than that of men. Her lower status in comparison to men is generally irrationally legitimatised on the basis of her child–bearing capacity, distinct physical attributes and a built which is shorter in height than man and in certain sense her vulnerability. In fact the social structure was itself so arranged and patterned that its consequences led to inequality between genders. In a patriarchal society, the institutional patterns of residence, inheritance and lineage, patrilocal, patrilineal and patriarchal family structure, all represent and justify inequality between genders.[54] There is a direct relationship between marital residence and male dominance. Researches reveal that non – male based residence gives women more freedom of choice in mate selection, more protection from a potentially abusive husband and more freedom to end an unsatisfactory marriage. Altogether economic, legal, social and cultural beliefs generated a social definition and self image of women in a society.

Apart from these, religion as an institution, has been one of the most pervasive and persistent factor in defining women's role and her status. Ruether identifies religion as 'Undoubtedly, the single most important shaper and enforcer of the image and role of women in society. The transcendental source–which is omnipotent and sacred–acquires extremely powerful instrumentality of legitimacy for various pronouncements affecting the status of women directly and indirectly. In behavioural and institutional forms, it governs the entire life cycle and every day life of women in most of the societies.'[55] Likewise, in monotheistic religions, a woman can never have her full sexual identity affirmed as being in the image and likeness of God, whereas this experience is freely available to every man in the existing culture. The overall milieu of values creates conditions in which women work, behave and live in a particular way and it also creates a psyche and self–image which leads to development of self–perceived as inferior to men. Further it leads to formation of belief systems regarding women and also assigns them specific roles and defines the code of their behaviour pattern both within family and outside.

Basically, the gender inequality itself existed in the structure of division of work into public and private domains which leads to: I. Non–recognition of the work related to women in family–child–rearing and other domestic functioning. II. Certain economic activities undertaken by her in fields, economic activities related to handicraft etc; are not recognised as her economic contribution both by the society and for a long time by planners and officials. III. Creation of such values and institutions which make her work within family and deprive her of all such activities which are outside home and socially recognised. Commonly there are two distinct features of gender role of women. First, her role as a woman and second her status as a woman and unfortunately women suffer from dual deprivations: one that of being a woman and the other, of being a woman of a lower caste or class. Thus, women are never viewed as persons on their own rights. Moreover women don't view themselves as autonomous being due to their cultural socialisation. Because of their marginalisation in society women hardly exist as a public phenomenon.

The issue of gender equality is closely related to law, equality and justice and its denial has led discrimination of women in almost all fields of human activity. Social equality and social justice is one of the most prized ideals of contemporary society but social inequality and injustice has been a feature of every known society – past and present. Different forms of atrocities are linked to one another and are manifestations of gender ideology. 'The world which has always belonged to the men is still in their hands, the institutions and the values of the patriarchal civilization still survive in larger part.[56] In the circumstances the status and role of women and related issues, have attracted the attention of the academicians, political thinkers and social scientists both in developing as well as developed countries, because of the widely accepted truth that a society built on the inequality of men and women involves wastage of human resources which no country can afford. It is unanimously accepted fact that gender equality could be realised only by making women economically, socially and politically empowered. Women's empowerment has become the goal or ultimate objective of many development policies and programmes which also demanded for indicators of empowerment, both to reveal the extent to which women are already empowered and to evaluate if such policies and programmes have been effective towards their stated aims.

Global Response

The process of the first phase of development in relation to the human societies commenced in post–World War II period and the goal was rapid economic growth through rapid industrialisation in order to foster fast economic growth which would eventually hoped to benefit the entire population. After de-colonialisation during the 1950s and 1960s only the economic role of women in reproduction as home makers, bearers and rearers of children and house–wives was perceived by the development organisations, which was reflected in the inclusion of family planning, population, mother and child care policies in development planning in several developing countries like India. The initial development plans and their implementation were based on the separation of the public and the private spaces. The public space was designed on the model of the worker without any caring responsibilities and was the sphere of the breadwinner who was obviously the male. It placed women in the private space which gave her the care giving and domestic role. The concept of development in a broader sense is related to improvement in quality of life based on equality and social justice through such programme and activities which consequently could alter the structure and culture and create self–generating continuous processes.[57] However, gradually new openings came which were instrumental in breaking the traditional shackles not only for women but some other deprived sections also.

Meanwhile, the old role–models and concepts began to change globally. In the 1950s and 1960s the women activists who took active part in freedom movements of the newly independent states took keen interest in raising the development questions in the UN and challenged the legalistic perspective of the Commission on the Status of Women (CSW) which was formed by the world body in 1947 to monitor UN activities on behalf of women. The said commission observed, 'Women who contribute half of the world's population by virtue of an accident of birth, perform two–thirds of the world's work, receive one–tenth of its income and own less than one hundredth of its property.[58] Soon it was realised at world level that because women comprise more than half of the human resources and are central to the economic as well as the social well–being of societies, development goals cannot be fully reached without their participation. The changing dimension of development and the international movement for the development of women have created a policy perspective for gender equality which recognises both women's and men's needs and, most importantly, their healthy interactions. Against this backdrop of situation, Dreze and Sen viewed that gender equality and social justice are the urgent need not merely because of the fact that it is an 'issue' of the day. Rather, 'the emancipation of women is an integral part of social progress, not just a women's issue'.[59] The movement started earlier has called upon worldwide countries and international development agencies to adopt measures for integrating women into the development process which received a major breakthrough in 1970s.

The new policy perspective was promoted further by the publication of Easter Boserup's book, *Women's Role in Economic Development* in 1970 which demonstrated that development processes have been strongly male–biased and bypassed women led the international aid community to attempt to integrate women into the production system so that the economy could grow more vigorously. The book not only ignited a worldwide discussion on the need of women's participation but also seriously challenged the argument that benefits from development projects would automatically 'trickle down' to women and other disadvantaged groups in Third World nations. By the time, perhaps, being influenced from the new concept a new approach 'Women in Development' (WID) was coined which was based on the philosophy that women are lagging behind in society and the gap between men and women can be bridged by remedial measures within the existing structure.[60] In 1975 the First World Conference on Women held in Mexico brought about the issue in the forefront. As a result, the United Nations declared in the mid–seventies the 'United Nations Decade for Women (1976-85). It followed in 1977 the introduction of its first guidelines on WID. In 1986, the Women in Development issue became one of the four priority issues of UNDP and thereby, the Division of Women in Development (DWID) had been created in the next year (1987).[61] In 1992, the DWID has been renamed as the 'Gender in Development Programme' (GIDP). In the 1990s, the UNDP's new development discourse and its focus on 'equity' and empowerment created a new dimension in terms of women's development approach.

Gradually the world opinion and institutions as well responded in favour of gender equality and, in line in the late 1980s the concept of Women in Development was shifted to Gender and Development Approach (GAD). The new approach is based on two perspectives: Firstly it argues that women's status in society is deeply affected by their material conditions of life and by their position in the national, regional, and global economies; Secondly, it recognises the fact that women are deeply affected by the nature of patriarchal power in their societies at the national, community and household levels. It advocates for basic intervention with the analysis of men's and women's roles and needs, in an effort to empower women, to improve their position in relative to men in ways which will benefit and transform society as a whole. In the GAD two policy approaches - the Practical Gender Needs (PGN) and the Strategic Gender Needs (SGN). Practical gender needs relate to women's daily needs in caring for themselves and their children, whereas strategic gender interests relate to the task of changing gender relations and challenging women's subordinate position.[62] This new approach, GAD focuses on the interconnection of gender, class and race and the social construction of their defining characteristics. It recognises the differential impact of development policies and practices on women and men and sees women as agents, not simply as recipient, of development.

Within this context, meaning and perspective, the UNDP in the decade 1990s, introduced agenda for fruitfully incorporating the various development approaches. Its new development discourse and focus on 'equity' and 'empowerment' created a fresh dimension in terms of women's development approach. The earlier paper prepared by the GIDP named 'Gender and Sustainable Human Development: Policy Perspectives (1995); now 'gender equality and equity' is put forward as the essence of the programme and the operation of UNDP.[63] The contents of the paper also justifies women in terms of the goals of equality and empowerment. Women's empowerment is central to human development. Human development, as a process of enlarging people's choices, cannot occur when the choices of half of humanity are restricted. Targeted actions aimed at empowering women and righting gender inequalities in the social and economic sphere, as well as in terms of civil and political rights, must be taken alongside efforts to engender the development process.

Thus the perspectives of global policy have enabled the developing countries to identify the underlying causes of gender inequality. And, these have helped to develop a more desirable strategic approach, which has made it clear that 'Gender Equality' and 'Sustainable Human Development' are intertwined. Also, it has recovered a new sense of reality that girls and women should have opportunities for personal growth, security, realisation of rights, control of fertility and health, literacy and opportunities to participate in political and economic system.[64] In tune with this international movement, there has been a profound change in the status of women. The gender gap is narrowing down and women are entering in the production system, thus breaking the barriers of social moulds.

Other developing countries alike, India, perhaps the most complex democracies in the world, has a history of commitment, since the beginning of 1970s, to women's welfare and empowerment through constitutional provisions, legislations, policy and plans even while at deep levels structural gender biases persist within families, communities, economies and politics. Women still don't occupy a space as equal members and citizens in India and in other liberal democratic countries. The Government of India's II and III periodic Report on the Convention on the Elimination of All Forms of Discriminations against Women (CEDAW) 1997-2005 stated that the underlying causes of gender inequality are related to social and economic structures that are based on the social norms and practices. In India, where patriarchy from time immemorial has maintained a strong grip, the realisation of gender equality would not be a fruitful one unless some sort of positive discriminations for women like special social protection is not given.

Present Status

Gender discrimination acts as slow poison for the society and it is a growing recognition that countries cannot reach their full potential as long as women's potential to participate fully in their society is denied. Women's participation has become a key factor for success of all developmental programmes. In third world countries the concept of development has come to identified with government programmes to be managed by government with or without involvement of community. Institutions like panchayat have been associated and involved in execution of these plans. The social structure and cultural values determine consciousness. Consciousness raising shall help in greater participation in the women empowerment programmes. The term women empowerment has come to connote the processes by which the efforts of the women themselves are united with those of governmental authorities to improve the economic, social and cultural conditions of women and to integrate these women into the life of the nation and to enable them to contribute fully to national progress. Thus, women with respect to development–have to be viewed as both the participants and beneficiaries.

In general we see two contrasting trends: first, the growing poverty and misery of women accompanied by multifarious efforts of deprivation and secondly, despite the long wait for the change of women's position in society, the present global scenario gives some evidences to reaffirm that 'gender equality for the millions of people is not attainable'. Rather, today women are getting to the top more than ever before and their knowledge and insights are being treated significant, and the misconceptions about women are being dispelled.[65] Further, there is a need for development for women as a specific category and their full integration in the total development process. N. Yavari–d' Hellencourt, the coordinator for the United Nations Development Fund for Women (UNDFW) viewed in this regard, 'If we do not empower women, there will be no peace and no way out of poverty'[66] because, women have more potentiality than men and they can play the role of silent developer in a family. Because, 'a women gives first priority to her children; her second priority is the household. A man has different priorities; he does not give family the top position.[67] Thus women, at large, hold key position in all round development of a nation–both developed and developing.

It is a time to rethink, regroup and move forward on the issue of gender equality. An essential step forward has been made in general discussion of the role of women in society. Machanism for change such as women's forums, citizens' forums and issue–specific organisations and other supportive groups should mobilise establish goals and develop a plan of action. In fact, it is evident that the gender development policies are formulated without understanding the ground realities of the situation faced by the women.

The value–base of the society restricts women's role and status and the government programmes regulates women's rights to access and control self and resources. Any sensitive issue occurring in the society affects women since they have limited control, power and choices over resources. It is not enough to have right laws and the institution of justice, but also a change in values is necessary for the right implementation of justice to women out of patriarchal biases. It would be a significant contribution on women empowerment and justice in all societies in order to address the gender gaps and find a gender equality with sustainable human development.

6.5 Human Rights of Women and Globalisation

In larger context human rights refer to those inalienable rights that a person is entitled to enjoy irrespective of his/her nationality, caste, creed, sex, colour, religion, income or any other socioeconomic divisive category. Human rights are those entitlements which an individual own just because of his/her existence as a human being. The theoretical roots of human rights can be traced back to the histories of ancient and medieval times in India as well as in the Western liberal and humanitarian philosophy. Both these roots have a considerable appeal of promoting human dignity. Human life is given a distinctive weight over other animals in most societies precisely because we are capable of cultivating the quality of our lives. Several strong arguments have been given in favour of protecting and promoting human dignity. They are not requisites for health but to those things needed for a life of dignity – a life that can not be enjoyed without these rights.

The present status of women in society is a challenge for human rights. Women form nearly half of the human capital in the country but in terms of gender equality and gender equity, they remain the most deprived and long neglected segment of society, despite the constitutional guarantee for equal rights and privileges for men and women. In modern times all are given liberties and rights, freedom of expression as well as right to get education. Despite this women are fighting for crisis such as dowry, female infanticide, sex selective abortion, health, poverty, education, sexual harassment, domestic violence, etc.

In this era of Globalisation the growing attention is considered as a strategy for survival, competition and growth. As a result of this a new economic environment has been created wherein only self-reliant and self-regulated economic enterprises, including women enterprises will survive. In the situation in many developing countries structural adjustment programmes have been poorly designed and implemented and they are unable to meet negative effects of globalisation. Empowerment of women is the theme of the time and the general trend is towards improvement, however the achievements have still fallen short of expectations, particularly in developing countries like India.

Theoretical Proposition and Conception

Today human rights are universally accepted as those conditions of social life which allow the full development of human personality. They refer to a wide continuum of values that are universal in character and in some sense equally claimed for all human beings. We claim for these rights all over the world simply by being human. The term 'human' is itself a vague since the life cycle of a human being ranges from conception to death and decay. Even before conception, sperm and eggs exist that contain human genetic material but decision is made easily on the issue because they are human cells and not human beings. In between the discussions and controversies various groups hold the view that there is some special quality of human life that provides a basis for possessing rights; when that quality is acquired, so are rights.[68] This approach is favoured by many since it allows for the distinction between humans and other animals. Human rights are rights particularly to human beings, thus the basis of the claim to rights should be something that differentiates humans from other animals.

The modern concept and interpretations human rights have its bases in ancient Indian times as well as in Western countries of early history when well-known human rights movements started with ancient religions and societies and showed the evolution of concepts and institutions of human rights across civilizations. In developing the basic notion of human right we cannot deny the role played by the influence of ancient Indian Dharma with its universalistic and humanistic approach. In general ancient Indian society was peaceful within the moral codes of conduct of the society provided by religion which in due course of time hegemonised all sections of the society within its rule of the game.[69] Ancient thinkers like Manu and Kautilya all have tried to protect the rights and dignity of individuals from the whims and tyranny of the rulers. This was done primarily by imposing some moral restrictions upon the activities of the rulers and thereby providing some kind of shield to the rights of the individuals.

Addition and enhancement of human rights aspects continued in mediaeval and British period. In medieval period the three basic elements of the ancient Indian tradition; universalism and humanism in its philosophical thought, the struggle against caste discrimination and religious tolerance received a fresh relevance and impetus from Islam. King Akbar's great regard for rights, justice and secularism could be cited as an example.

Religious movements like Bhakti and Sufi made remarkable contributions towards eliminating the irreligious practices of the contemporary society. These movements tried to revive the ancient humanist tradition and preached the sacred principles of humanism and universalism.[70] With the coming of Britishers, English was introduced in education and some Indian leaders including Raja Ram Mohan Roy, being influenced, started a movement for Renaissance and Reformation. They demanded the abolition of Sati system, female infanticide, caste system and also initiated a movement for widow remarriage and female education. It resulted in the enactment of several humanitarian legislations in subsequent years.

Likewise the Western philosophical tradition manifests, from the ancient times, the stories of an inevitable conflict between the concept of individual rights and state authority. In the writings of great Greek individual's right to resistance against sponsored terror was highly glorified. In the later periods the theme of humanity was carried out in the classical philosophy of Plato and Aristotle who attempted to protect the citizens and non-citizens under a scheme of justice. Another Roman thinker Cicero first gave a philosophical foundation to the concept of rights and its association with the idea of natural law. The concept of natural right as a precondition for human development had received further staunch support in the works of Hobbes, Locke and Rousseau, who believed that the state as an institution is the most effective instrument for protecting the rights of the individual against the oppression of the rulers.[71] The concept of human rights found its further elaboration and promotion in the writings of Immanuel Kant (1724-1804), Thomas Paine (1737-1809), Jeremy Bentham (1748-1832) and Karl Mark (1818-1883), the revolutionary thinkers of the 20th century.

However, in the evolution of modern human rights the ideas of liberal humanism and universalism played a significant role. For instance John Rawls (1921-2002), who although did not assign the label of universalism to the concept of human rights, but attached a special status to it. 'These rights do not depend on any particular comprehensive moral doctrine or philosophical conception of human nature ...but basic human rights express a minimum standard of well- ordered political institutions for all peoples who belong, as members of good standing, to just political society of peoples.[72] He also made the human rights distinct from the constitutional rights, or the rights of democratic citizenship, or from other kinds of rights that belong to certain kinds of political institutions, both individual and associations. Jurgen Habermas, another important contributor, called it a part of the post-modern agenda and believed that human rights and the principle of popular sovereignty constitute the sole idea that can justify modern laws.[73] In today's society, human rights have become the necessary condition of a regime's legitimacy and of the decency of its legal order.

In the phase of globalisation, privatisation and liberalisation, the concept of human rights has been defined and analysed by Amartya Sen, the philosopher-economist and Tony Evans, the noted theorist of international politics. Dr. Sen has viewed rights usually in terms of political power and according to him the invoking of human rights tends to come mostly from those who are concerned with changing the world, rather than interpreting it. In the final analysis he concludes that human rights may or may not be reflected in a legal framework through specific human rights legislation, but there are also other ways of implementing human rights that includes, public recognition, agitation and monitoring.[74] While Tony Evans linked the concept of human rights and its universalisation aspect with the issue of power and hegemony.[75] For him, it is an instrument for empowering people in their fight against persecution and injustice. Evan's understanding of hegemony provides a new insight into the post-war politics of rights, particularly in the context of the emerging role of US as the leader of human rights.

The theoretical discussions held so far on the human rights, predominantly reflect that it is not citizens rights, but often a thinking about an abstract universal community and imposing political structures, conceptions of individual and peculiar relationships between individual and community that are not generally shared.[76] In the present there are three categorisation of right based on three major generations of the concept. The first generation of rights refers to the traditional or classical notion of rights denoting different political and civil rights. The second generation of rights mainly includes different types of socioeconomic rights, while the third generation of rights emerges in course of the worldwide anti-imperial movement in different parts of the world and includes cultural rights, environmental rights, right to development, minority rights, etc. All these rights are essential not only because of our existence, as human being but these are needed also to make each one of us an ideal human being.

Context of Indian Women

The development of a society is measured not only in terms of its material resources, economic growth and wealth creation but also in terms of the opportunities and capabilities of its people to explore the material resources and to contribute equally in the growth of their society. Such a process becomes unjust and discriminatory if most women are excluded from its benefits.[77] Respect for women is a necessary trait of a rising nation. It equally applies to the women in ancient India when they were not a meek, shy and weak creature but were bold, free and strong. In the pre-Aryan period, an average Indian women continued to lead a happy and contended life. In later years Aryans changed from a pastoral people to agriculturists and they became conscious of preserving the purity of their race which made them a victim of growing social evils.[78] The position of women in Indian society deteriorated further by the laws of Manu but improved a little as a result of the advent of Islam because it granted much stronger legal position. Europeans in general and Christians Missionaries in particular ushered India in an entirely new phase of women emancipation and gave birth to a powerful reforming movement.

The position of Indian women also deteriorated beyond imagination due to inequality inherent in gender. Gender is a basic organising principle of society that shapes how people have to think about ourselves. While gender concerns differ, it also involves hierarchy, because it affects the opportunities and constraints we face throughout our lives.[79] Females and males do differ biologically of course, but the physical activities of men and women are alike than we may think. In the social structure we can notice that men dominate in most of the categories of job and distribution of wealth. In any field, the greater the income and prestige associated with a job, more likely it is held by a man. But researches held so far show no overall differences in intelligence between male and females as Mahatma Gandhi once declared, 'Woman is the champion of man, gifted with equal mental capacities. She has a right to participate in every minute detail of the activities of man and she has an equal right of freedom and liberty as him. She is entitled to a supreme place in her own sphere of activity as man is in his.[80] There has been a dramatic change regarding the status of women in society and the earlier position has been totally transformed in the twentieth century where the female sex is in no way inferior to man.

The Constitution of independent India laid equal emphasis on human development and development of women, in particular. Generally there are three approaches used to measure the well being of the people as far as human development is concerned. The first one is, physical quality of life index which contains three indicators – adult literacy rate, infant mortality and life expectancy. The second approach is basic needs approach which argues that the basic needs of adequate nutrition, primary education, health, sanitation, water supply and housing available to the poorest to a reasonable extent. The third approach is human development index-most widely used index.[81] With a view to enshrine gender equality several provisions of the constitution of India guaranteed equality before law and equal protection of law through Article 14. Articles 23, 42, 51A, 29 and 30 establish provisions for the development of women. On the other the Government of India has made concerted efforts towards removing various gender biases to ensure that women enjoy equal status with men in real sense. The major enactments passed by the Government in this respect are Dowry Prohibition Act (1961), Medical Termination of Pregnancy Act (1971), Child Marriage Restraint Act (1976), Equal Remuneration Act (1976), and the 73rd and 74th amendments of the Constitution passed in 1992 and ratified in 1993.[82] The enactment which provided for 33 per cent reservation for women in local self-governing bodies is an important achievement in empowering women.

Thus in the post-Independence period, the Indian women were given equal status with men by the Indian Constitution and various provisions have been made to protect the interests of the female population. Right from the days of First Five Year Plan (1951-56), adequate services were included to promote the welfare schemes of women so that they can play their legitimate role in the family and the community. The Second, Third, Fourth and Fifth plans continued the same approach for the welfare of women. In 1976 a Women's Welfare and Development Bureau was set up under the Ministry of Social Welfare to initiate necessary policies, programmes and measures for women. Indian Development Planning has always aimed at improving inequalities in the process of development recognising the fact that women lag behind due to several socio-economic-cultural-political impediments. But the Sixth Plan (1980-85), for the first time, recognised women as participants of development and not merely an object of welfare. In 1982 a Women's Employment Programme was introduced with assistance from Norwegian Development Agency (NORDA). In this plan period two new schemes-Support to Training and Employment (STEP) and Awareness Generation Programme for rural and poor women (AGP) were introduced.[83] In early 1992 (31 January) the National Commission for Women was constituted which works as a friend, a counsellor and educator for the Indian women who are now considered as agents for change in the era of globalisation liberalisation and privatisation.

Trends in Globalisation

Trends of globalisation reflected in India and abroad in the early years of 1990s which is defined as a process of stretching, deepening and speeding up of global interconnectedness, i.e., the multiplicity of networks, flows, transactions and relations which transcend the states and societies which constitute the contemporary global system.[84] In the present pattern of globalisation, politics of rights is no longer a prerogative of the state authorities, diplomats and theorists. It involves plurality of agencies;

governmental, non-governmental and inter-governmental together. In the new world order dominated by the neo-liberals following the collapse of socialism and the emergence of cyber age not only the idea of human rights but the position of women worldwide faces certain paradoxes with positive and negative effects in sphere of women's development at large. Earlier, the United Nations Decade for Women (1976-85) was a global effort to examine the status and rights of women and to bring women into decision-making at all levels.

As a result the Government of India in the early nineties decided to bring a policy about the advancement, development and empowerment of women. Recognising the role and contribution of women in development, the Eighth Plan (1990-95) adopted the strategy to ensure that benefits of development from different sectors do not bypass women and special programmes are implemented to complement the general development plans. In continuation the Ninth Plan (1997-2002) made two significant changes in conceptual strategy for women. First 'Empowerment of Women became one of the nine primary objectives of the plan and secondly, it attempted the convergence of existing services, resource, infrastructure and man power available both in women-specific and women-related sectors. Likewise, the Tenth Five Year Plan (2002-2007) constituted three working groups: (i) Working Group on Empowerment of Women, (ii) Working Group on Child Development and (iii) Working Group of Improving Nutritional Status of Population with Special Focus on Vulnerable Groups.[85] Thus, the Five Year Plans have been paying special attention to women's welfare emphasising female education, access to resources and their political empowerment.

However, working of globalisation has not only widened the gap between the developing and developed countries but has also increased the difficulty of poor/developing nations and they are unable to cope with the challenges of this new trend. It has generated social crises arising from the increasing fear of marginalisation of some sections of society caused by the indiscriminate spread of capitalism and the free economy. Despair caused by social marginalisation, economic deprivation, and political defeat is another consequence of this modern phenomenon.[86] As a positive effect globalisation has enabled additional and various opportunities for women because employers within global, export-oriented sectors employ women and thus provide women opportunities to acquire new skills and knowledge. But on the other hand, due to gender discriminatory forces within the labour market and women's care responsibilities, women tend to earn lower wages and work fewer days than men.[87]

Today Indian women are emerging as equal partners of men in all fields of human endeavour. But the feminist revolution is far from being won, and the exploitation of women continues in many ways. In the situation, women themselves should be seen as agents to transform the existing power relations in society. External agents can only help them with material support and information but they can not bestow empowerment on them. Empowerment should lead to a situation where each one can become a whole being regardless of gender, and use their fullest potential to construct a more humane society for all.

References

1. Alatas, Syed Hussein, *Corruption : Its Nature, Causes and Consequences* (Aldershot : Avebury, 1990), pp. 3-4.
2. Elliot, Kimberly Ann (ed.), 'Corruption and the Global Economy', *Institute for International Economics*, June 1997 (Washington D.C., 1997) as quoted in Vishnu Bhagwan, 'Corruption and Good Governance', *The Indian Journal of Political Science*, Vol. LXVIII, No. 4, October-December 2007 (Meerut : 2007), p. 728.
3. T.N. Chaturvedi, 'Corruption in India : An Overview' in Subhash C. Kashyap (ed.), *Eradication of Corruption and Restoration of Values* (New Delhi : Sterling Publishers, 2000), p. 41.
4. Dr. Dibakar Ch. Das, 'Corruption and Society in India', *Third Concept*, Vol. 20, No. 235, September 2006 (New Delhi : 2006), pp. 26-27.
5. Rajindar Sachar, 'Lokpal Bill 2010 – A Farce on Public', *South Asia Politics*, Vol. 9, No. 10, February 2011 (New Delhi : 2011), p. 7.
6. T.N. Chaturvedi, 'Corruption in India : An Overview', p. 41.
7. Sympson, Antony, E., *The Literature of Police Corruption* (Newyork : John Jay Press, 1977), p. 20.
8. K. Balachandrudu, 'Understanding Political Corruption, *IJPS* : Vol. LXVII, No. 4, October–December 2006 (Meerut : 2006), p. 811.
9. *Ibid.*, p. 809.
10. M. Halaya, *Emergency : A War on Corruption* (New Delhi : S. Chand & Co., 1975), p. 6.
11. Arun Kumar Agrawal, 'Corruption in Historical Perspective : A Case of India' *IJPS*, Vol. LXVIII, No. 2, April–June 2007 (Meerut : 2007), p. 327.
12. M. Halaya, *Emergency : A War on Corruption*, p. 6.
13. Arun Kumar Agrawal, 'Corruption in Historical Prespective : A Case of India', p. 328.
14. *Ibid.*

15. As quoted in *Ibid.,* p. 330.
16. H. Harvey, *Cameos of Indian Crime,* as quoted in J.R.B. Jeejebhoy (Bombay: Sant Vartaman Press, 1952), p. 179.
17. Krishna Bhatia, 'The Ordeal of Nationhood', *Imprint,* November 1971 (Bombay : 1971), p. 43.
18. Subhash C. Kashyap, 'Corruption and Criminalisation of Politics', *South Asia Politics,* Vol. 7, No. 9, January 2009 (New Delhi : 2009), p. 21.
19. S.R. Maheshwari, 'Political Corruption : Its Magnitude and Cure', in Subhash C. Kashyap (ed.), *Eradication of Corruption and Restoration of Values,* pp. 85-86.
20. C.B. Muthamma, 'Corruption : Causes and Cures – Need for Systemic Change', in *Ibid.,* p. 49.
21. Arun Kumar Agrawal, 'Corruption in Historical Perspective : A Case of India', *IJPS,* p. 332.
22. S.R. Maheshwari, *Administrative Thinkers* (New Delhi : Macmillan, 1998), pp. 27-28.
23. T.N. Chaturvedi, 'Corruption in India : An Overview', pp. 41-42.
24. K. Balachandrudu, 'Understanding Political Corruption', *IJPS,* p. 814.
25. T.N. Chaturvedi, 'Corruption in India : An Overview', p. 43.
26. Myrdal, Gunnar, *Asian Drama,* Vol. 2 (Newyork : Pantheon, 1968), p. 940.
27. Subhash C. Kashyap, 'Corruption and Criminalisation of Politics', p. 23.
28. S.R. Maheshwari, 'Political Reforms for Good Governance', *The Indian Journal of Public Administration,* Vol. XLIV, No. 3, July–September 1998, pp. 309-10.
29. *Ibid.*
30. R.B. Jain, 'The Art of Political Corruption : An Analysis of Some Major Scams Since Independence', in Subhash C. Kashyap (ed.), *Eradication of Corruption and Restoration of Values,* p. 109.
31. *Ibid.,* p. 96.
32. Arun Kumar Agrawal, 'Corruption in Historical Perspective : A Case of India', p. 333.
33. *The Indian Express* (Bombay), 17 November 1993.
34. *Ibid.*
35. Dwivedy, Surendranath and G.S. Bhargava, *Political Corruption in India* (New Delhi : Popular, 1967), p. 121.
36. Uddipan Mukherjee, 'Maoism and its Future in India,' *South Asia Politics,* Vol. 7, No. 3, July 2008 (New Delhi: 2008), pp. 24-26.

37. T.H. Chowdary, 'Ending the Maoist Menace', in *Ibid.*, Vol. 8, No. 7, November 2009 (New Delhi: 2009), pp. 35-37.
38. Sohail Jawaid, *The Naxalite Movement in India: Origin and Failure of the Maoist Revolutionary Strategy in West Bengal–1967-1971* (New Delhi: Associated Publication, 1979).
39. *People's Daily* (editorial), 5 July 1967.
40. Bipin Chandra, Mridula Mukherjee and Aditya Mukherjee, *India After Independence 1947-2000* (New Delhi: Penguin Books India, 2002), pp. 426-27.
41. Madhumita, 'Naxalism–Development or Discontent–A Study of Jharkhand', *South Asia Politics*, Vol. 9, No. 6, October 2010 (New Delhi: 2010), pp. 27-28.
42. Kartick Das, 'Naxalbari to Today's Maoist: Uprisings and Implications', *IJPS*, Vol. LXXI, No. 2, April–June 2010 (Meerut : 2010), pp. 89-90.
43. *Ibid.*, pp. 429-93.
44. Report of the 1997 international IDEA Democracy Forum, Stockholm, as quoted in Shri Prakash Mani Tripathi and Santosh Kumar Tiwari, 'Socio – Economic Challenges of Globalisation,' *IJPS*, Vol. LXIX, No. 4, October–December 2008 (Meerut : 2008), p. 721.
45. Jean Dreze and Amartya Sen, *India: Economic Development and Social Opportunity* (New Delhi: Oxford University Press, 1995), see also in *Ibid.*
46. Barber R. Benjamine, *Jehad vs. Mc World* (Newyork: Ballentine Books, 1996), p. 17.
47. Madhumita, 'Naxalism–Development or Discontent–A Study of Jharkhand', pp. 28-29.
48. *Ibid.*
49. *Frontline* (Chennai), 17 July 2009.
50. Biswaranajn Mohanty, 'Tackling the Naxal Insurgency', *South Asia Politics*, Vol. 9, No. 12, April 2011 (New Delhi: 2011), p. 27.
51. Kartick Das, 'Naxalbari to Today's Maoist: Uprisings and Implications', pp. 494-95.
52. Biswaranjn Mohanty, 'Tackling the Naxal Insurgency', pp. 29-32.
53. Susan Edwards (ed.), *Gender, Sex and the Law* (New Hampshire, USA: Croom Helm, 1985), p. 1.
54. Mridula Bhatnagar, 'Gender Politics: In the Context of Social Structure and Development', *IJPS*, Vol. LXX, No. 4, October–December 2009 (Meerut: 2009), pp. 1035-38.
55. Ruether R. (ed.), *Religion and Sexism–Images of Women in the Sewdish and Christian Traditions* (Simon and Schuster, 1974), p. 9.

56. Antrobuo Peggy and Bizot Judith, 'Women's Perspective: Towards an Ethical, Equitable, Just and Sustainable Development', *Women and Development, ISIS*, International Issue 4/92 & 1/93, p. 30.

57. Mridula Bhatnagar, 'Gender Politics: In the Context of Social Structure and Development', p. 1039.

58. As quoted in K.G. Karmakar, *Rural Credit and Self–Help Groups–Micro - Finance Needs and Concepts in India* (New Delhi: Sage Publications, 1999), p. 168.

59. Jean Dreze and Amartya Sen, *India–Economic Development and Social Opportunity*, pp. 140, 167, 178.

60. Dolly Phukon, 'Gender Development Approach and Social Protection: Understanding the Case of Assam', *IJPS*, Vol. LXIX, No. 4, October–December 2008 (Meerut : 2008), pp. 771-74.

61. Khaiber Ali Mia, Mohammad Yasin and Yasmin, 'Gender Equality–Rhetoric or a Panacea ? : A Review of the Present Concerns', Ibid., Vol. LXVIII, No. 4, October–December 2007 (Meerut: 2007), p. 742.

62. Dolly Phukon, 'Gender Development Approach and Social Protection: Understanding the Case of Assam', pp. 775-76.

63. Shahra Razavi and Carol Miller, *Gender Mainstreaming–A Study of Efforts by the UNDP, the World Bank and the ILO to Internationalise Gender Issues*, Occasional Paper 4, August 1995, UNRISD (Geneva: 1995), pp. 22-23.

64. *UNDP Human Development Report*, June 1997, p. 9.

65. Khaiber Ali Mia, Mohammad Yasin and Yasmin, 'Gender Equality–Rhetoric or a Panacea ? : A Review of the Present Concerns', p. 744.

66. Clive Shirley, 'The Banker From Jamaat Karasu's in Choices, *The Human Development Magazine*, March 2002, p. 17.

67. Yunus Muhhammad, 'The Grameen Bank Story: Rural Credit in Bangladesh' in Anirudh Krishna, Norman Uphoff and Milton Esman (eds.), *Reasons for Hope – Instructive Experience in Rural Development* (New Delhi: Vistaar Publications, 1997), p. 16.

68. Prakash Talwar, *Human Rights* (Delhi : Isha Books, 2006), pp. 1-2.

69. Suresh Kumar, 'Human Rights Protection in India – An Institutional Framework', *South Asia Politics*, Vol. 7, No. 3, August 2008 (New Delhi : 2008), pp. 36-37.

70. *Ibid.*

71. Sarbani Guha Ghosal, 'Human Rights : Concept and Contestation', *IJPS*, Vol. LXXI, No. 4, October-December 2010 (Meerut : 2010), pp. 1103-7.

72. John Rawls, 'The Law of People', in Belgrade Circle (ed.) and Obrad Savic introduced, *The Politics of Human Rights* (London and Newyork : Verso, 2002), pp. 31-33.

73. Jurgen Habermas, 'Private and Public Autonomy', in *Ibid.,* pp. 60-64.

74. Amartya Sen, 'Elements of a Theory of Human Rights', *Philosophy and Public Affairs,* Vol. 32 (4), October 2004.

75. Tony Evans, 'Introduction : Power, Hegemony and the Universalisation of Human Rights', in Evans (ed.), *Human Rights Fifty Years On – A Reappraisal* (UK : Manchester University Press, 1998), pp. 1-7.

76. Michael Freeden, *Rights* (New Delhi : World View, 1998), p. 40.

77. *Human Development Report,* Government of Punjab (2004), p. 112.

78. Rajkumar Singh, *Contemporary India with Controversial Neighbours* (New Delhi : Gyan Publishing House, 2011), p. 61.

79. Myra Marx Ferrie and Elaine J. Hall, 'Rethinking Stratification from a Feminist Perspective : Gender, Race and Class in Mainstream Textbooks', *American Sociological Review,* Vol. 61, No. 6, December 1996, pp. 929-50.

80. Reddy Narayan, Kumar Vijay, Nalani S., *Women and Development Challenges and Achievements* (Delhi : Serial Publications, 2005), p. 1.

81. K. Muthalagu and Dr. K. Vijayarani, 'Perspectives on Human Development in India', *Third Concept,* Vol. 20, No. 235, September 2006 (New Delhi : 2006), p. 38.

82. S.S. Sree Kumar, 'Representation of Women in Legislature : A Sociological Perspective in the Indian Context', *IJPS,* Vol. IXVII, No. 3, July-September 2006 (Meerut : 2006), p. 620.

83. Dr. Priyanka Tomar, *Indian Women* (New Delhi : Shree Publishers, 2006), pp. 216-18.

84. Anthony G. McGrew, 'Human Rights in a Global Age : Coming in Terms with Globalisation', in Tony Evans (ed.), *Human Rights Fifty Years On – A Reappraisal,* p. 189.

85. Dr. Priyanka Tomar, *Indian Women,* pp. 219-22.

86. Sheikh Saleem Ahmed, 'Dimensions of Terrorism and Religious Extremism : Two Sides of the Same Coin', in Mahavir Singh (ed.), *International Terrorism and Religious Extremism – Challenges to Central and South Asia* (New Delhi: Anamika Publishers, 2004), p. 38.

87. C. Sheela Reddy, 'Globalisation – A Human Rights Perspective', *South Asia Politics,* Vol. 5, No. 11, March 2007 (New Delhi : 2007), p. 39.

7 Indian Republic: Today and Tomorrow in World Politics

7.1 Basics of India's Foreign Policy

Foreign policy is an instrument to serve the goals and national interest of a country. Managing relations with other states is a necessary activity of every state. This activity may very generally be called the framing of foreign policy. It arises from two facts of the international situation. Firstly, that no state is an immured island but a member of a society of states participation of which is inescapable. Secondly, in the international society power is decentralised, that is, distributed among states in unequal measure. Foreign policy assessment of a state includes: (i) a general evaluation of a state's economic, military and international position in relation to other states which may be its neighbours, friends, allies, rivals or enemies; (ii) an appraisal of its capabilities for bold action, caution, self-reliance, isolation, economic ties, or military or political alignment; (iii) developing broad principles of conduct for itself and for international relations generally; and (iv) adopting strategies, tactics and commitments.

On 15th August 1947 India emerged as a new state in the comity of nations and even before on 7 September 1946 as the Vice-President and member-in-charge of External Affairs in the Interim Government, Jawaharlal Nehru, the first Prime Minister of independent India and one of the chief architect of the policy of non-alignment, expressed India's desire to keep away from power politics of groups, aligned against one another. The contradiction inherent in the cold war brought about a situation in which it became essential for the newly independent states to assert their determination to stay independent of either of the two blocs. Alignment with the West was economically attractive but the dependent economic relationship it would have created was perceived by most of the newly independent nations as likely to prevent self reliant growth. Political alignment with the Communist bloc was also not viable option for India which was not prepared for a revolution to restructure its society and economy. In the circumstances India was left with no option but to remain non-aligned in Post-Independence era.

Prevailing Approaches

Traditionally, there are two basic approaches applied to the study of foreign policy since the days of the French Revolution. One is ideological approach, according to which the policies of states vis-à-vis the rest of the world are merely expressions of prevailing political social and religious beliefs. In this category foreign policies are classified as democratic or totalitarian, libertarian or socialist and peace-loving or aggressive. The second approach to foreign policy is analytical. At the heart of this viewpoint is the proposition that policy rests on multiple determinants, including the state's historic tradition, geographical location, national interest, and purposes and security needs. The apparent shortcomings of the psychological or ideological approach, especially in accounting for present day international development made the analytical approach popular and acceptable.

In the early postwar period, it was felt by several western countries that in sphere of foreign policy means, methods, or techniques may have changed, but the interests and objectives have been relatively constant. Gradually, it became obvious in the light of international developments that a foreign policy is nothing more than a by–product of domestic politics could hardly do justice to the elements of continuity in national policy. At some point, it became necessary to recognise that objective requirements of the national interest place certain irremovable limits upon any statesman seeking to formulate foreign policy. Regardless of the intentions, social philosophy or religious outlook of individuals, there are broad strategic interests intimately bound up with a nation's geographic position and international role that must be safeguarded if its independence is to be preserved.

But the prevailing approaches to the study of foreign policy provide no ready –made categories that can be applied to every nation. A state's foreign policy is the course or courses of action that its government adopts in dealing with other states with a view to attaining its national interest, goals and objectives. Nations, at large, differ in national context or elements of foreign policy that are more or less material in character. Some of these are relatively permanent, such as geography and natural resources. Others, like the economic, industrial, and military establishment are more responsive to change and human manipulation. Then there are human factors, largely quantitative in the case of population, and qualitative as regards national character, social structure, national morale, political institutions and experience and an effective tradition of diplomacy.

Every country must have a foreign policy for a fuller and systematic involvement in the international relations. While formulating the principles of its foreign policy a country has to keep its domestic conditions as well as the realities of the external environments. The sum total of the goals and objectives of a nation's foreign policy constitute its national interest as the nation conceives it. It is the concept of national interest that helps the nation decide the order of priorities among different objectives and goals. National interest is a matter of crucial concern in the perusal of any foreign policy, for it is a key factor thereof. Although national interest in its details differs from country to country the core of national interest is the same for different countries. All countries big and small desire and continually search for national security. Security implies, at the minimum level, national independence and territorial integrity.

A state's national interest is rooted in the deepest soil of its consciousness and cultural identity of its people. Its value roots lies in the state's unique historical background, its political institutions, traditions, mass belief, that is, ideologies, economic need, power factors, aspirations, peculiar geographic circumstances and the basic set of values. It has characteristic permanence in a relative sense in as much as a state continues to hold it at least as long as a particular political system endures. Basic conceptions of national interest have, however, to be adapted to changes in world political, economic, technological, military and even ideological conditions.

Case of Independent India

India, on the eve of her independence was ready to formulate a foreign policy keeping in view all these facts in an analytical manner. It is not only the result of the physical environment but also the product of the traditional values of Indian society and the commitment of the Indian national movement during the freedom struggle. India fought a prolonged struggle for freedom. This fight provided some inspiration to the struggle for freedom in other Asian countries too and strengthened the Indian peoples' determination to fight on. India's entire background was consistently anti-imperialist and she necessarily sympathised with the struggle against western colonialism, no matter where it was being carried on. Thus, history, past experience and geography were powerful factors making for a strong independent foreign policy to take shape over the years and for this foreign policy to be mainly anchored to the Asian-African community and the community of the developing countries.

In the meantime, the global strategic environment especially after the World War II, had changed drastically and it projected into the international system two super powers in a total state of confrontation, determined to absorb other countries into their spheres of influence. The situation between the US and erstwhile USSR and the newly independent countries was so asymmetrical, and the pressures so great that the latter were faced with the problem of maintaining their independence. Considering the state of the world at the time intensely bipolar, greatly confliction, sharply ideological and deeply rancorous-the decision to build an alternative model of international relations that deviated sharply from the prevalent one received considerable attention from the international community.

In that very kind of national and international situation; Non–alignment became the logical framework of India's foreign policy. Jawaharlal Nehru, the first Prime Minister of India, used foreign policy as an instrument to defend and strengthen India's newly won independence and to safeguard India's national interests and to develop the self-reliance, self-confidence and the pride of the Indian people even while serving the cause of world peace and anti-colonialism. At the time India's policy of Non-alignment secured a consensus and was taken out of the ambit of day-to-day politics Through the adoption of a policy of independence, support to the anti-imperialist struggles elsewhere and through a policy of promoting peace in the world, Nehru took foreign policy out of the vortex of domestic politics and made it subserve the cause of unification and stability in the country.

Tenets of Non-alignment

India's policy of non-alignment in any case did not mean only to refuge joining any power bloc but a lot more than that. The main objectives of the policy are the pursuit of peace not through alignment with any major group of powers but through an independent approach to each controversial and disputed issue; the liberation of subjected peoples; the elimination of social discrimination; and the elimination of wants, disease and ignorance. India was the first nation to design and articulate a new non-aligned foreign policy framework and was one of the three leading nations, along with Egypt and Yugoslavia, to conceive and project the policy of non-alignment as a transnational subsystem. As it was an attractive model for most developing nations very soon it became a major plank of the foreign policies of third world countries. With India's thinking and cooperation with Nasser and Tito the policy of non-alignment resulted in the emergence of an important movement whose purpose was essentially to make it possible for nations to help each other, and to offer a broad framework for collective dialogue and collective action against the developed countries.

This is the true origin of the concept of non-alignment which germinated in the hells of the United Nations in 1946 and 1947. Hence it is not merely a reaction to the cold war but it has a much wider basis. It was the heartfelt response to the aspiration of the people of newly born democracy of India which was eager to attain the status of equality with other nations of the world. However, Non-alignment does not mean non-involvement in any and every matters. Military pacts and alliances are to be avoided only to maintain peace in the world. It even does not mean passivity or neutrality, when crucial issues are before. In other words it means judging an issue on its merit as made it more clear by Jawaharlal Nehru himself, 'we want to maintain independent opinions, to decide freely and to act as we deem proper. We do not want to be in a position where we should be forced to any decision because of the compulsion of our relationship with other countries'.

As a result of its suitability the policy of non-alignment in foreign sphere became a popular plank of newly independent countries at the close of 1950s and thereafter. Soon it was transformed into a movement and it was created out of the desire to orient India's foreign policy towards the group of newly decolonised states, hoping to create a larger area of peace by fighting common dangers of imperialism and racialism together. Nehru wanted India to be the leader of the developing world, in this way carving out a global role for the country. He also believed that these idealistic broad concepts used in global policy formulation could be used at the micro-level, subject to some minor adjustments. However, the principle of India's leadership was to be based on moral rather than economic power.

A significant milestone in the development of the Non-aligned Movement (NAM) was the 1955 Bandung Conference, a conference of Asian and African states hosted by Indonesian President Sukarno, who gave a significant contribution to promote this movement. The attending nations declared their desire not to become involved in the cold war and adopted a "declaration on promotion of world peace and cooperation", which included Nehru's five principles. His five principles, also called Panchsheel were: (i) mutual respect for each other's territorial integrity and sovereignty; (ii) mutual non-aggression; (iii) mutual non-interference in domestic affairs; (iv) equality and mutual benefit; and (v) peaceful co-existence. These principles, later served as the basis of the Non-aligned Movement whose first Conference of Heads of State or Government was held in September 1961 in Belgrade.

Initial Experiments with Non-alignment

India's relations with the superpowers during the cold war were difficult as its non-aligned status was never really accepted by the US who saw India as being in the Soviet camp. India's desire for economic self-sufficiency also went against the grain of the concept of free market economy, which was being pushed by the western powers. On the other hand relations with the Soviet Union were cordial with substantial trade and barter trade underlying the relationship. However, India never subscribed to the communist world's ideology, trying to combine a socialist economy with a democratic system at home. India refused to be a part of any defence pact or to take sides against either the western powers or the communist bloc. Although the overall policy orientation of India remained in initial years pro-West, Jawaharlal Nehru tried to act as a bridge between the East and the West. In the start and specially during the regime of Stalin, the policy of USSR was not favourable to developing countries because Soviet Russia considered all non-communist nations as anti-communist. In post – 1953 phase India's relations with USSR improved significantly when Pakistan became a member of US-led military alliance, SEATO and US arms supplies began pouring to Islamabad. India despite the charge of pro-Soviet stance continued to work hard to strengthen non-alignment.

The non-alignment policy of India came under severe attack from all corners in the wake of Chinese aggression in October 1962. In one stroke the aggression against India proved to be a rude shock not only to India's international prestige, and morale of the people and armed forces, but also to the policy of non-alignment. Michael Brecher drew two conclusions from what he called, 'non-alignment under stress during 1962 war. For him, India's policy changed (i) from "equidistance" in relation to Superpowers to "equal proximity" to Moscow and Washington; and (ii) "from an active, dynamic involvement in world politics, that is, "neutralism in its original Nehru - Menon conception to a more passive non-alignment". Brecher concluded that non-alignment was almost toppled as the pillar of India's foreign policy. The term was retained but it became an empty shell. But even after Chinese aggression, Nehru refused to give up the policy of non-alignment and argued that India could take economic assistance from both the blocs, not in charity but as loan or on easy payment, only if we remained non-aligned.

After the death of Jawaharlal Nehru in 1964, his successor Lal Bahadur Shastri's regime witnessed a war with Pakistan in September 1965. In the war both USA and China sided with Pakistan which naturally pushed India towards the USSR. In 1966 the sad demise of Shastri made Indira Gandhi the next Prime Minister of India. She remained at the helm of affairs for a long time and tried to reorganise the unity of Afro-Asian countries. Later India's relations with the US became unfavourable and in response New Delhi signed a Treaty of Friendship and Cooperation with USSR in August

1971. The events of 1971 including the Bangladesh was changed the course of India's foreign policy although India's treaty with Soviet Union invited sharp criticism and it was said that non-alignment had been turned into alignment with USSR.

7.2 Foreign Policy through the Ages

With the end of cold war the old framework of India's foreign policy collapsed and further the disintegration of Soviet Union in the following year signified the cessation of existing world order. The formal end of cold war was announced at Malta by US President George Bush and Soviet President Mikhail Gorbachev in December 1989. The new world order had not really emerged at once but the old world order, created after the end of second World War was now no more. It heralded a new era characterised by a highly uncertain world order. The world faced a new situation and so did India. The country had to think afresh and a new.

Re-setting of Perceptions

In the changed circumstances, the Nehru's framework of staying away from bloc politics, of non-alignment, of the quest for world peace, of the struggle against colonialism and racialism, of the maintenance of the autonomy of judgement, of independent development, of cooperation with all the big powers but subject to the preservation of India's interests, security and independence, of unity of action to the extent possible of the non-aligned and developing countries, all this was the conceptual framework answering to the objective situation prevailing in cold war period. And new directions were needed for India's foreign policy.

No doubt, the foreign policy that India formulated, and the international prestige that she rapidly acquired, opened great possibilities for her to obtain concessionary aid from the two competing and opposed blocs that dominated the international system. Undoubtedly, this was a major achievement for India's economic and political diplomacy, since she was the first developing country to benefit from a cold war situation, obtaining meaningful assistance when the other developing countries, who had allied to one bloc or the other, should have been logically the greater beneficiaries of the bipolar system.

At the juncture, the world was in transition from the old order that was dead and gone to a new order that was yet struggling to be born. International relations have frequently been marked by contradictory trends, but rarely was this complexity more evident, demanding more careful examination and analysis as today. However, the change must relate to the actual situation, to the prospects opening before the world, to the geopolitical situation faced by the country, not just to distant rumblings in a far off region, and to the deeper undercurrents of international politics of a particular period.

As the old parameters had to be supplemented with new ones, it was felt that in the new situation foreign policy must advance the economic interests of India. The economic imperative, no less than the security imperative, must govern India's policies. Except in an emergency, like the imminent threat of war, international economic relations must now share the pride of place with the more traditional geopolitical considerations. The regional situation, the threats to India's security, the nuclearisation around India's borders, the state-sponsored terrorism from across the frontiers, all these factors must continue to engage India's concern and prompt India's vigil.

The basic characteristic of the new international phase is the urge for cooperation, mitigating and eliminating conflicts and enmities, regional economic integration and economic development of each country. We have seen that the regional scenes are not alike and artificial transplantation does not work, but trends in the world today interpenetrate in different parts of the planet much more rapidly than ever before. There is need to be alive to them and to promote them whenever opportunity present itself our way.

Globalisation with Policy Inputs

In the context, the most significant and really qualitative leap towards the globalisation of India's economy was taken in 1991 by the then Congress government headed by P.V. Narasimha Rao. The decision to globalise the Indian economy was certainly a defining moment in contemporary Indian history. The 1991 economic reforms saw the birth for a new role for international economic and trade relations. India suddenly had to engage with the post cold war world and reassess its foreign policy priorities. The opening up of the economy to international players also meant that foreign relations had an economic dimension and trade became a foreign policy tool. Leaving *Swadeshi,* economic self-sufficiency behind and engaging in international trade was India's new way forward.

After the Congress lost power the United Front government under Deve Gowda and I.K. Gujral started to focus more on foreign policy and foreign relations. In part this was due to India coming to term with its first coalition government where consensus on domestic affairs was not always forthcoming. The I.K. Gujral peace moves towards Pakistan were a direct result of this–as were Deve Gowda's economic interest in South East Asia and the 'Look East' policy with a clear vision for India's North Eastern states. The 'Look East' policy was a part of India's re-assessment of its role in the wider region, for the first time looking at Southeast Asia as a neighbour which mattered politically and economically. As India was looking for new markets and relations with the US still had not warmed up, a strategic decision to focus on Southeast Asia was taken.

In BJP - led coalition government the vision was one of a multi-polar world in which economic relations were going to be crucial. Regional policy became of prime importance, especially with regard to improving trade and improving the situation in India's border states. The BJP's foreign policy priorities have not been that different to that of Congress. The BJP unlike previous Congress government also saw that there are direct links between foreign policy formulation and domestic policy especially in the economic realm. The then government not only continued but intensified the economic reforms after forming their coalition called National Democratic Alliance (NDA). Their agenda was focused on increased open markets and more trade, internationally as well as regionally.

Simultaneously, a process of introspection was underway in country's social, economic and political structures, which will redefine a vibrant, dynamic and open India, at ease in its interactions with the world at large. Gradually, India's foreign policy has assumed a positive outward orientation with new policy initiatives aimed at consolidating traditional relationships, developing new relationships with countries and regions where it has vital strategic interests.

As a part of this new strategy, relations with the US, Israel and Myanmar were all revived. These were countries India aspired to keep away from for various regions: the US for its imperialistic global bullying strategy, Israel for its war against the Palestinians and Myanmar for its undemocratic government in light of the 1990 elections. The 9/11 war on terror changed relations with the US for good. India saw in this an opportunity to ally itself with the US and portray the Kashmir problem as part of the war on terror. The US was seen as a powerful economic ally holding the purse strings of various international funds. Peace or a dialogue about peace with Pakistan was seen as essential. Peace meant that India would finally be seen as an economically safe region for international investment. The government finally decided to tackle the China factor for the first time. With China increasing as a economic might in the region, India needed to improve relations and increase trade quickly.

India's relations with the United States has expanded remarkably over the last few years on civil nuclear and other strategic issues. The new agenda laid greater emphasis on economic dimension in foreign policy, on the need to revitalise the Non-aligned Movement and to reform and restructure the UN to better reflect the aspirations of the developing countries. At present, these apart, India attaches the highest importance to developing cordial and friendly relations with her neighbour with a view to promote peace, stability, mutual confidence in the region, and for developing strong economic and commercial relations for all-round prosperity. Adjustments on all these fronts were made during the period of post-cold war.

Evaluation

While cooperating with the US for realising these goals, India needs to remain very cautious as regards its commitment towards the policy of Non-alignment as well as that of the movement in order to arouse self confidence among the developing nations and also to win their unflinching support to the goals and ideals of NAM, so that NAM remains united, vigorous and working for achieving its unfulfilled dream of freedom, justice, equity and peace in the world. The changes that took place in international system emphasised the enormity of an event which altered the course of contemporary world balance.

Thus, the changes that have brought the phase of post-cold war to our doorsteps also compel us to examine about the Non-aligned Movement and the foreign policy associated with it. Those who feel that the non-aligned movement is no more relevant fail to realise that logically it will continue to be a force against any global domination–multipolar, bipolar or unipolar. It is a movement against the domination of great powers over the weak powers. Even in the post – cold war period and thereafter any country or group of countries that turn dominating will be opposed by the members of the non-aligned movement. At present India is the most developed among the developing countries and therefore, it should guide if not lead them in the struggle for a new international order based on equality, equity and mutual benefits. The new situation arising due to the end of Cold War and emergence of the United States as a single superpower have presented before us the problem to study India and its policy of non-alignment in the entirely changed context.

7.3 National Interest and Neighbourhood in Globalisation

The new or present day world order is facing challenges in setting up its principles but has a definite prospect in world politics. India, like other non-aligned counties, is trying to face the challenges with its overall prospects in view. The current phase of global politics is more competitive and open in which nations of the world are struggling for their effective survival along with sustainable development. With bright prospect India is trying to minimize its challenges in bilateral, regional and global spheres in the changed global scenario.

Policies outside the Region

Ever since the end of the cold war India has been making a strong bid to reverse its relative decline in the Indian Ocean basin and re-establish its economic and political relevance. With its Look East Policy launched in the early 1990s, India re-established loose cooperation initially with South East Asia and later with Japan, South Korea and Australia. Looking for markets, technology and capital, India was keen to partake in the East Asian economic miracle. This policy soon paid off with India becoming a full associate member of the Association of South East Asian Nations (ASEAN) and a member of East Asian Summit, thanks to strong political support from Japan, Indonesia and Singapore.

Similar dynamism is evident in India's outreach with Central Asia, the Gulf and Africa. As India's economic weight increased from the early 1990s, its economic and political linkages with these regions began to grow rapidly. With its economic development acquiring a new pace, New Delhi got a new interest in ensuring adequate external supplies of energy resources and raw materials. This in turn, meant a strong focus on the protection of sea-lanes and expansion.

Likewise, as India's defence market emerges as one of the largest in the world, it has become an important area of competition for the world's arms manufacturers. This has provided an unprecedented for New Delhi to diversify its sources of supply away from the traditional reliance on Russia. India's new advantages in defence purchases combined with acquisition of nuclear capability have encouraged the country to shift its military doctrine away from traditional obsession with territorial defence. Amid a cold peace with Pakistan and military tranquility on the China border, the army is now beginning to focus a little more on the prospects for developing stronger expeditionary capability and deploying Indian troops beyond the border.

Convergence of Interests with US

Since the international order has ceased to be bipolar, India has to deal with major powers of the world, the US in particular, to advance its national interests. India has been consistently trying to improve its relations with major powers such as, the European Union (EU), Russia, Japan and Australia, etc., ever since the collapse of the Soviet Union. In the case of India–US relations, bilateral ties have improved substantially in recent years as manifested in wide ranging engagement across many fields including defence and security issues, counter–terrorism, science and technology, health, trade, space, agriculture, maritime cooperation and environment.

In the post–cold war period with growing understanding between them on various bilateral, regional and global issues, the US administration has described India as its natural partner.[1] Entering a phase of unprecedented improvement, India's relations with the United States got transformed over the decades. The US is India's second largest trading partner, the predominant destination of India's IT services exports and the major source of foreign investments. India and the United States have established over 15 institutional forums that meet regularly.[2] Circumstances brought India and US closer and it made the US wrap up the nuclear deal on 2 March, 2006 that inspired Indian Prime Minister to declare, "We have made history."[3] India has accepted to be a 'strategic partner' of the United States and an agreement on 'peaceful use of nuclear energy' is foremost on the bilateral agenda of India and the United States. A commentary in August 2007 stated, 'The US-India nuclear agreement has strong symbolic significance for India achieving its dream of a powerful nation.[4] In fact, the purpose of the US to sign a civilian nuclear energy cooperation agreement with India is to enclose India into its global partners' camp.

Barak Obama, the present President of the US has reaffirmed his support to the growing ties. He said, 'Deepening and broadening the friendship between our countries will be a first order priority for me in the coming years. He also admired Manmohan Singh for piloting the civil nuclear cooperation agreement through parliament, the IAEA and the NSG. The investment that both sides have made in the relationship is predicated as much on mutual benefit as on its global significance.

However, the consolidation of India-US partnership depends on addressing four significant issues. Firstly, both sides have to hammer out a legal framework for resuming nuclear cooperation. In India-US civil nuclear cooperation agreement certain controversial issues such as reliability of fuel supply to safeguarded Indian nuclear reactors, reprocessing of spent fuel and the transfer of dual use technology to India have to be clearly tackled. Secondly, India–US defence cooperation has to graduate from military exchanges and expensive joint exercises to actual cooperation in weapons supplies and technology transfer. Thirdly, both sides have to harmonise their interests where they intersect in Asia. While, for instance, both New Delhi and Washington have worked together in Nepal and Sri Lanka they have certain differences dealing with country with Afghanistan, Pakistan, Iran and Iraq. Fourthly, what will be India's status in India–US partnership? New Delhi must find ways to address these issues in India-US relations as also to consolidate its ties with other major powers.

But despite these obstacles, a major strategic shift is clearly evolving one that may finally align the USA and India as equal partners in dealing with the biggest global challenge of today: global economic recession with uneven and fragile recovery and nuclear proliferation in the age of global terrorism.[5] Although the outlines of this new emerging convergence of approach between the two are still indistinct, yet this was on the sidelines of the 2009 UN General Assembly meeting and later in the G-20 Summit at Pittsburg on 24 September, 2009, and again was visible in the G-20 Summit in Toronto on 26 June, 2010.[6] All these have paved the way for a new synergy of cooperation between them.

Themes of India's Policy

The Prime focus of India's foreign policy has always been to maintain good relationship with neighbours. The issues before our policy makers are to satisfy the national needs of peace, security and development and at the same time to face the challenges posed by our neighbours like Pakistan and China. Kashmir problem and border issues are yet to be resolved. Cross border terrorism at the instance of Pakistan and regional imbalance because of China's 'Leap Forward' attempts are, no doubt, matters of great concern for Indian strategic policy and diplomacy. This is why India had to invest a lot in defence cooperation with certain nations. India's internal security is involved in rooting out acts of terrorism throughout the country, combating insurgency in the North Eastern region and naxalite activities in different parts. This factor is playing a crucial role in shaping India's foreign policy.

India's stated objective is to ensure a peaceful, stable and prosperous neighbourhood. Despite being accused of big brotherly attitude, India continues to attach the highest priority to close and good neighbourly relations with its neighbours. India also gives priority to safeguarding its security interests in its neighbourhood. In line, I.K. Gujral spelt out five principles of India's neighbourhood policy in 1996 which include; (i) non-reciprocal treatment (ii) respect for territorial integrity (iii) non-interference in internal affairs, (iv) no use of territory by any state against the interest of another state, and (v) direct settlement of disputes through dialogue. This is known as 'Gujral Doctrine.'

Pursuing its policy aimed at enhanced regional cooperation P.V. Narasimha Rao initiated 'Look East' policy recognising the importance of

South East Asia as fast growing economic region. Atal Bihari Vajpayee started the policy of active engagement and showing strength and capability in economic and technological field. While Manmohan Singh is pursuing the policy of constructive dialogue to resolve problems with neighbours and is effectively dealing with major powers to make India centre of attraction at global level.

Vexed Issues with Pakistan

The biggest challenge for India has been to balance its relations with Pakistan and China. A prospect worthly of realisation remains dissuading Pakistan from using terrorism as an instrument of its foreign policy. Pakistan's needling of India in Kashmir remains a core concern for India. India sought constructive engagement with Pakistan. It aspires for meaningful dialogue to reduce tension. Lahore Declaration, Agra Summit and many such initiatives of composite dialogue were taken by India to achieve this objective. But the peace process produced limited results. Some de-escalation of tensions occurred on the Kashmir and nuclear–risk related agreements were signed between the two countries,[7] but Pakistan did not follow up the Indo-Pak joint statement issued after the meeting between Prime Minister Manmohan Singh and President Asif Ali Zardari on 8 September, 2008. After the terror attacks in Mumbai on 26 November, 2008, India put on pause the institutional dialogue and it took relations to the lowest ebb.

In this context, facts remain standstill as even in today's Pakistan because the army permeates the social political and economic fabric of the nation. Right from its inception Pakistan has been under military for about half a period. Whenever there was civilian rule the army called the shots, 'Throughout the 1990s, a period of nominal democracy, the army still held sway over critical national security and foreign policy portfolios, including the direction of Pakistan's nuclear programme and the management of relations with Jihadi outfits in Afghanistan and Kashmir.[8] Apart from this US blind faith on Pakistan and latter's collusion with China against the Indian interest has been a regular concern for Indian security perception. Washington can win confidence of Pakistan military establishment without accepting its exclusive political authority, and it can help empower civilian leadership without jeopardising the army's core interests.[9] Winning the confidence of army is an essential condition for any success strategy in Pakistan. It has become Pakistan's strongest government institution. It probably is the only force that can deal with wide spread militancy and terrorism in the country. It is in India's interest that there should be a popularly elected government in Pakistan as people–to–people relations are healthy and friendly.

Dangers from China

India-China relations are influenced by too many variables. They have had the longest uninterrupted existence as civilisational nations. They have almost common geographical and human resoures on the planet. There are links between the two nations in cultural, religious and trade. However, Indo-China war of 1962 and China's role in 1965 and 1971 Indo-Pak war again added fuel to make already estranged relations between these two nations more toxic.

After the dissolution of USSR, the whole world became unipolar, with the US enjoying unrivaled supremacy. The pattern of relationship between these two nations was to be viewed through the new prism of emerging world order. Undoubtedly, both India and China are two most important nations in Asia. The role and impact of these two Asian nations can not be ignored in the regional politics of both South Asia and Pacific Rim.[10] Their decisions have influenced international affairs. So naturally to get more importance in world politics, both the nations try to assert their independence from US supremacy.

However, China's growing influence in Burma (Myanmar) in 1996 caused India to take new initiative for making new regional pacts with Bangladesh, Sri Lanka and Thailand to promote regional cooperation in 1997 but it failed to restrict China's ambitions. Now China is much keenly trying to keep control strategically over Nepal, Bangladesh and Myanmar. Its consistent claim on the north-east part of India proved that despite its so called cooperation in United Nations with India, its sole aim is to prevent rising India in regional and global power politics.[11] In fact this strategy proved so successful that some observers feel India is on China's diplomatic radar. This situation induced US to support India get importance in world politics. US-India Civil Nuclear agreement is reported to be testimony to it.

According to John Garwar, 'India–China relationship has, over the years been shaped by deep and enduring geo-political rivalry.[12] He further says that the rivalry is rooted in the decades–long, multi–layered, and frequently in sharp conflict over two states' relations with lands and peoples lying around and between them.[13] This view is supported by Sumit Ganguly who also contends that 'any dramatic improvement in Sino-Indian ties is unlikely and the relations between the two will remain competitive.[14] The fact is that whether India likes it or not, the inherent competition for regional influence and interplay of international forces will always underpin the realities of the relationship and therefore, India needs to shape its foreign policy accordingly.

On Kashmir, China has changed its earlier stand in which it treated the problem as a bilateral issue between India and Pakistan. Recently the Chinese embassy in New Delhi began stapled visas in a separate sheet to applicants from Jammu and Kashmir and Arunachal Pradesh in November, 2009. It denied a Chinese visas to North Command Commander Lieutenant General B.S. Jaiswal, who was nominated by the government to visit China as part of the regular high level exchanges between the defence establishments of the two countries. On the issue Dr. C. Rajamohan, an expert on international politics, felt that China had gone even further than Pakistan in defining the Kashmir issue. He believes, 'While Pakistan insists that Kashmir is disputed territory, Chinese positions have made it clear that Beijing believes Pakistan occupied Kashmir is Pakistan territory, while India's Kashmir is the only part of the province that is disputed.[15] China wants to make Kashmir a trilateral issue and forging majority in favour of Pakistan and keep India in a position of disadvantage.

The US News in September 2010 reported about the Chinese army's presence in Pak–occupied Kashmir. It certainly worried India. China is a belligerent power. It has never been trust worthly and its only aim is to expand its territory through encroaching on others' territories. In addition the increasing influence of People's Liberation Army (PLA) creates potential threat for India. Chinese are way ahead of India in terms of strategic missiles, artillery, development of indigenous military hardware and acquisition.

In October 2010 the Indian Prime Minister Manmohan Singh met his counterpart Premier Wen Jia Bao during the sideline of the East Asia Summit in Hanoi. The two Prime Ministers decided to be 'sensitive to each other's core issues'. The Chinese Premier gave assurance for further discussion and reaching on consensus. Keeping India engaged in endless talks is an old Chinese strategy so that Beijing can continue its work on changing the Himalayan balance decisively in its favour through a greater building up of military power and logistical capabilities.[16] In the meantime, Army Chief General V.K. Singh has rightly described China and Pakistan as two major irritants for India's security and stressed that nation should have substantial conventional war fighting capabilities with the ability to fight in a nuclear scenario.[17] Therefore, we should be vigilant about the danger from China and its intentions.

With Other Small Neighbours

Transformation of idealistic fervour to realistic tone is treated as a challenge for the policy makers. The new leaders of India have adopted some sort of 'Power Politics' and still want to continue with giving due consideration to old traditional norms of foreign policy. India is located in a volatile neighbourhood system where political system is yet to be stable. Sri Lanka, Nepal, Pakistan, Afghanistan, Bangladesh and Myanmar are suffering from internal disturbances. Nepal has come out of the Maoist insurgency, but its political system is still under strain. Although Sri Lanka had got victory against the Liberation Tigers of Tamil Eelam (LTTE) in May 2009 but still the humanitarian crisis is there which caused anxiety to India as coalitional constraints from Tamil Nadu parties bind the option in the wake of ethnic fraternity.

Likewise Afghanistan, Bangladesh and Myanmar are suffering from other kinds of problem. The momentum in India–Afghanistan relations has been maintained in post 9/11 period and several thousand Indians are engaged in development works in Afghanistan. But the deteriorating internal situation and increasing Taliban influence and attack on Indian personnel remained a matter of concern. India's border with Bangladesh creates problems of insurgency and illegal migration. Issues of concern to India include use of Bangladeshi territory by Indian insurgent groups, support for terrorist activities and involvement of Bangladeshi nationals in crimes in India. The status of India - Myanmar relations have remained steady and a cooperative relationship is being built around a commitment to stabilise the area, cooperate in economic projects and create multi-model transport links extending to Thailand and prospectively beyond. With Bhutan and Maldives India has enjoyed a friendly relations.

7.4 Theoretical Challenges of NAM in Post Cold War Era

The current era of post–cold war international order saw various characterisations: unipolar, multipolar and now nopolar. The call for new world order proclamation about the end of history and warning about imminent clash of civilisations had attempted to describe the international scenario during 1990s. In shifting, contemporary situation is being summed up by predicting that the United States unipolar moment,[18] is over, international relations in the twenty – first century would be defined by nonpolarity.[19] Power would be dispersed rather than concentrated, and the influence of the nation–states would decline as that of non-state actors increase. The world would be dominated not by one or two or even several states but rather by dozens of actors possessing and exercising various kinds of power. In contrast to multipolarity that involves several distinct poles or concentrations of power–a nonpolar international system is characterised by numerous centres with meaningful power.

In this context, many consider the resistance to the studied indifference, the turning away from, and denigration of theory–as the most serious inhibiting factor to the development of international relations scholarship in India.[20] Apart from economic considerations, the demise of the Soviet Union presented a predicament to India. Outside the Communist bloc the shock was greater for it because the 1971 treaty had become redundant. India's situation could be understood from the fact that in October 1996 it lost to Japan by 142 to 40 in an election for the non-permanent seat in UN Security Council. Earlier during the heydays of non-alignment, it had served UNSC five times between 1967 and 1992. Forgetting third world or non-aligned solidarity most of the developing nations also toed the US line.[21]

India desired to be recognised in stature on the same plinth with G-7 states and China. Earlier in the direction of attaining its rightful place among world's major powers began after the National Democratic Alliance government came in 1998 which conducted nuclear tests. India's adaptation to the post – cold war world was focused on relations with USA. The subtle policy shift came into open when Atal Bihari Vajpayee announced in his UN General Assembly speech that India and the USA were 'natural allies.[22] Though faced with sanctions, it soon entered into strategic talks with the US administration, Union Minister Jaswant Singh and US Deputy Secretary of State Strobe Talbott had twelve rounds of discussions doing the groundwork for the betterment of Indo-US relations. The shift from estranged to engaged democracy, natural allies and strategic partners was described as transformation.

Regional

The fastest growing region in the world today is Asia and not Europe or America. The rate of growth of Asia over the last 20 to 25 years has been between seven to 10 per cent whereas Europe is growing at the rate of about two to 2.5 per cent, the United States at about three to four per cent, and Japan is not growing at all. So the economic power balance is decidedly shifting towards Asia from Europe and America and the twenty first century is being rightly described as the Asian century. There are tremendous opportunities to redirect our foreign trade to take advantage of this new situation. As a matter of fact, expanding linkages are already being developed between our economy and other dynamic economies of Asia. Market–driven linkages are being established between India on the one hand and Korea, China, Malaysia and Thailand on the other. The rate of growth of our exports to China has been in the range of 25 to 30 per cent, to Korea, ASEAN and Japan taken together by 23 per cent. With these rates of growth of the economy as well as of exports that have continued over the last 20 years, it seems, Asia is going to be the real power centre of the world.[23] And this poses a very big challenge to India's foreign policy.

A major challenge is how to turn the *de facto* linkages that are taking place with other dynamic economies of Asia, into *de jure* linkages or how to give a formal shape to *de facto* linkages that are taking place. The obvious way to give a formal shape is by concluding free trade agreements and comprehensive economic cooperation agreements with these Asian countries. Today, we have concluded or are in the process of concluding agreements with about a dozen countries of Asia. The second thing that we are doing is to nudge these Asian countries to move towards a pan Asian economic grouping. There has been a pan–African movement, a pan–Latin American movement and a pan–European movement. But there has been no pan–Asian movement.

In this background now we are on the verge of a second wave of regionalism. And this regionalism is very much driven by the same forces which are behind the rise of globalisation. This regionalism is competition driven. In order to face competition, countries or groups thereof are seeking larger markets in order to benefit from economies of scale and are pooling resources to be able to invest in science and technology.[24] There is thus a trend towards countries signing bilateral free trade agreements (FTAs) joining or concluding FTAs with existing regional groupings or establishing new groupings. One of the challenges for India's foreign policy is how to place itself in this rise of new regionalism: which country to join; with which countries to sign free trade agreements, with which country avoid signing such an agreement. India cannot remain untouched by this second wave of regionalism because today 70 per cent of world trade is conducted within the framework of free trade agreements and only 30 per cent, according to the rules of the multilateral trading system.

In the post – cold war period the Premiership of Atal Bihari Vajpayee and thereafter, India is gaining increasing recognition from ASEAN, catching the attention of western sponsored alliances–G-4, G-8. Significantly, India, a hub of Asian power, has been pursuing policies to strengthen the spirit and ideology of SAARC due to the challenges of Asian security architecture, fluid situation in the subcontinent in regard to security, stability, cooperation and growth so that peace and development may not remain a far crying for this zone. Pursuing its policy aimed at enhanced regional cooperation, India as chairman of SAARC worked for moving, from a declaratory phase to execution. Coming into force of SAFTA (2006), making operational the SAARC Development Fund, setting up of a South Asian University, and a SAARC Food Bank signify spirit of regional cooperation.

Strategic

Broadly, there are three major sets of challenges ahead for India's foreign policy, namely, meeting strategic challenges, and secondly, responding to the challenges of globalisation and managing critical issues such as human security, water, energy, environment, Weapons of Mass Destruction (WMD), etc. and thirdly evolving a national consensus on what constitutes India's national interest.

As regards strategic challenges, perhaps the most formidable enduring strategic challenge to India emanates from Pakistan and China. Earlier the peace initiative launched by Atal Bihari Vajpayee in January 2004 is continuing despite recurring terrorist attacks. The UPA Government led by Prime Minister Manmohan Singh has gone a step further and has formed Joint Mechanism for dealing with terrorism with Pakistan. This has of course not helped India in tackling the scourges of Islamic fundamentalism. In this context our experience of marshalling our military might Pakistan after the terrorist attack on Indian Parliament shows, a military option is very risky in view of Pakistan's known nuclear capability. The fundamentalism who are in alliance with the Pak Army in pouring venom against India and the Islamic radicals denouncing the US are both extending their constituency in Pakistan.[25] While this is impacting negatively on the domestic situation in that country, it is also coming in the way any initiatives that could be made for developing people to people contacts between the two countries, transcending the political conflicts facing New Delhi and Islamic Islamabad.

As a remedy the prevailing situation calls for an appropriate strategy to be shared by the civilian leadership on both sides-particularly by the civilian leaders of Pakistan, of finding a way of not letting Indo-Pak dialogue be held hostage by the Pak Army. On India's part, the remedy lies in better management of internal security, awakening our sleeping intelligence network, providing them better equipments, giving teeth of anti–terror laws, and above all, political will to give the security agencies necessary autonomy in dealing with the terrorists along with making sincere efforts to address the genuine grievances of the Muslim community.

At the juncture, the international community should encourage the civilian rulers of Pakistan to take courage in their hands, stop being submissive to the Army's mandate and open up avenues for mutually beneficial bilateral cooperation, in areas beyond the hard political disputes.[26] India has, therefore, adopted the strategy of not letting terrorism any chance to be a success on Indian territory.

In line, another difficult neighbour–China, has been posing equally, if not more, formidable challenge for the makers of India's foreign policy. As the gravity of power is shifting to Asia and it is on the top of the power hierarchy in Asia and a significant player in global politics, Beijing resents India's growing weight in the world politics. A few years back when the then Defence Minister in NDA Government George Fernandes said that China was our enemy number one, there was a great furore from a section of the prople and the media alike, but the recent developments in relations between India and China and the Chinese attitude on various issues upholds Fernandes opinion more robustly. Day by day China is becoming more and more hostile towards India.[27] According to strategic affairs expert Brahma Challeney, the rail link to Nyagtri will strengthen China's rapid military deployment capability in the eastern sector and strike at India whenever it wants to.

In case of China, India is using a three-pronged approach to deal with this tough neighbour. Firstly, New Delhi is trying to engage Beijing especially in the economic field. Sino–Indian bilateral trade continues to grow rapidly, with the trade value in the first half of 2008 hitting the dollar-29 billion mark, recording a 69 per cent jump over the corresponding period last year. Secondly, New Delhi is strengthening its ties with other major powers in general and the US in particular to counter–balance China. Thirdly, it is also strengthening its defence modernisation programme. In addition, India should make long–term strategy by forging military alliance with ASEAN nations which are very important for countering China specially in Indian Ocean.

Apart from Pakistan and China, building a strong and enduring partnership with other neighbours too has been a major continuing challenge for India. Without friendly neighbours, India cannot concentrate on socio-economic development, a major (preoccupation) of the Indian political leadership since independence. The country has been engaged in finding a sustainable basis for winning friendship of her neighbours and retaining its political primary in South Asia. Domestic transformations and turmoil in these countries have unfortunately complicated this task. Indian foreign policy establishment must therefore deliberate on how to facilitate stability in these countries and build up interdependent, which not only integrates economies, but also creates stake in each others prosperity and stability.

Challenges in Globalisation

We are living in the era of globalisation wherein liberalisation and privatisation rule the roost. Globalisation, in its different manifestations, has encapsulated almost all aspects of life in the present era. The traditional barriers of time and space have been compressed and the society has expanded its scope to corner the nations and the world. Men have become liberated from the fringes of local and national boundaries because of the amazing developments in the field of communication and information technology, which has digitised the modern world in the real sense.

Amartya Sen defines globalisation as a movement of ideas, people, technology and goods from one region to others benefiting the people at large. Stephen Gill defines globalisation as the reduction of transaction costs, of transborder movements of capital and goods, thus of factors of production and goods.[28] While according to David Held, 'Goods, capital, people, knowledge, communication and weapons as well as crime, pollutaints, fashions and beliefs rapidly move across territorial boundaries, far from this being a world of discrete civilisation, or simply an international society of states, it has become a fundamentally interconnected global order, marked by intense pattern of exchange as well as by other patterns of power, hierarchy and unevenness.[29] It advocates for a global village', 'global neighbourhood' and a world without boundaries.

Globalisation releases enormous opportunities and challenges for developing countries like India. Liberalisation and privatisation are other component of globalisation. This trend is called LPG to which India started in 1991 under the pressure of World Bank and International Monetary Fund (IMF) authorities. Introduction of several economic reforms under the process in India has created a mixed reaction. One reaction being that it is dynamic and development oriented and the other, that it is a destroyer of home economy.

But coming to its implications for our foreign policy, globalisation poses two challenges: the first is how foreign policy can be best conducted to help India link itself with the outside world, with the world economy and those of the major powers. Globalisation has created many opportunities for us. A challenge of foreign policy is to take maximum advantages of these opportunities. This calls for effort to find expanded access to foreign funds for investment in India and enhancing the competitiveness of our economy by importing frontier area technologies. The performance of our diplomats should be judged by the extent to which they have facilitated our availing of these opportunities.

At the 15th Conference of Non-aligned Movement held in July, 2009, while specifying the causes and consequences of this crisis Indian Prime Minister Manmohan Singh said at the NAM Summit, 'The benefits and burdens of globalisation were so unfairly distributed, it would be even harder for the developing economies to cope with the crisis. And if the aftermath of the crisis is not carefully managed and if the abundance of liquidity leads to a revival of speculative activities, we may well see a period of prolonged stagflation.'[30] He added farther that this continuing slowdown will force more and more people from these nations back into poverty, bringing down levels of nutrition, health and education. Further the globe recession has strengthened protectionism in developed countries' markets, drastically reduced developing nations exports and choked credit and capital flow to the Third World.[31] Evidently the developing nations are the worst sufferers of this recession and they immediately need greater resources as loans and further steps need to be taken to ensure foreign investment in the development of their infrastructure so that they may properly address social disaffection and enjoy fruits of development.

Globalisation also casts a darke shadow on the whole social fabric and due to this several forms of terrorism and insurgent activities are taking place. Proper multilateral negotiation among likeminded nations and stern action against terrorist is also an urgent task before India's foreign policy. India stands on the top amongst the nations severely affected by the acts of terrorism of various kinds like state terrorism, state–sponsored terrorism and Naxalism. To defeat terrorist design, the government should make it public that no individual or group can ever stand upon nation's security. All the political parties should have consensus opinion about national security and integrity. To win over the terrorists' motives, the support and enthusiasm of all sections of society is the need of the day.

There is also a NAM–related challenge before the foreign policy makers as to how to accelerate its pace and how make it more efficient and powerful to sort out the problems of member states and to face successfully the critical situation came by power politics at international level. India has proved its strength economically, politically and strategically in the world. Now it has to boost up the moral of NAM so as to make it more pertinent and relevant for a prospective future.

7.5 Perspective and Prospect of Modern NAM

The working of the foreign policy of India since 1990s has resulted in a happy note with the simultaneous expansion of good relations with the all major powers, growing importance in Asia and the Indian Ocean regions and growing importance in international system. India is bound to change according to the world politics milieu and national capability. The country has moved from its traditional pursuit of gaining power to the level of sustaining and increasing power. However, in concentrating on major international issues and regional conflicts, India will have to find ways to fulfil the requirements of national interest. Luckily, the absence of confrontation among important players of power politics, in the last few years, has allowed India the luxury of converting the non-alignment perspective into an independent and pro-active foreign policy. Amidst potential new rivalries among the US, China, Europe, Russia and Japan at international allies so as to become at par with major powers.[32] Having completed decades of its independence, India is mature enough to draft its foreign policy and strategy. India has become self–dependent in many sectors of development with noticeable economic growth and has acquired ability to assume great power responsibility in contemporary world system.

Applied Context

Foreign policy is the extension of domestic policy. While conducting foreign policy, the state makes sense of the scenario, situations itself into it, assesses its capabilities, national interest and priorities; and attempts to realise its goals. Goal realisation includes developing broad principles, adopting strategies and tactics and making commitments.[33] Since 1947 to the present day India's foreign policy witnessed three distinct historical phases. The first phase was the period from 1947 to 1962. It constituted the most idealistic phase of India's foreign policy under Jawaharlal Nehru. During the period India played a significant role in multilateral institutions and particularly in the United Nations. Having emerged as a critical proponent of the non-aligned movement, it contributed towards the process of decolonisation.

The second phase of India's policy of Non-alignment began with its defeat in the 1962 Sino–Indian border war, which marked a watershed in India's, foreign and security policies. It saw a gradual shift away from the early idealism and the adoption of an increasingly self–help' approach to foreign policy while retaining elements of the Nehruvian rhetoric.[34] The post–Nehru era may be characterised as one of 'modified structuralism'. Despite a brief military cooperation with India in the aftermath of the 1962 war, the United States soon disengaged itself from South Asia after the Indo-Pak conflict in 1965 as it became preoccupied with the Vietnam war.[35] Though India emerged robustly confident after the Bangladesh war, during 1970s, its influence remained confined to the South Asian region. The United States forged a strategic relationship with Pakistan almost immediately after the Soviet invasion in Afghanistan.[36]

The third phase began with the end of the cold war. But a more pragmatic foreign policy based on the Principles of Realism was adopted much later. The end of cold war presented India with a stark choice. During much of 1990s, India was yet to come in terms with the emerging realities.

India's core principle of Non-alignment lost practicability in the wake of post–polarity paradigm. During the Gulf war, India's response was based on a faded image of itself as leader of the non-aligned nations. In the year 1996 India's foreign policy calculations again went wrong on CTBT issue and filling five non-permanent seats on the Security Council. While the end of the cold war transformed the political landscape of Europe, it did little to ameliorate India's security concerns. The primary task of Indian foreign policy since 1947 has naturally been to enable the transformation of India's society and economy, restoring traditional patterns of dealing with the world, the building strategic autonomy of choice.

India's approach to the world is naturally a function of our values, our history and geography, and of how we define our interests. Our strategic perspectives in the lost decades have been a product of the historical aberration that was the early twentieth century. Throughout history, India had been a society that was open, pluralistic and intensely engaged with the rest of the world.

India's Adjustment with NAM

Accordingly, Government of India set certain objectives which mention, inter alia, to present the autonomy of the decision making process and to play a pioneering role in the establishment of stable, prosperous and secure global order; and to build an international environment which is supportive of India's rapid economic growth including higher investments, trade, access to technology and strengthening India's energy security. The objectives have been all the same since independence. But there is a sharp difference in the prevailing realities then and now.

In the new world order Manmohan Singh, the Prime Minister of India, expressed the Indian approach to NAM in a statement in which he said, 'Our stand is in full conformity with what our founding fathers would have liked us to do. Non-alignment is a state of mind and ability to exercise an independent judgement on all issues.[37] Defining the role of NAM during the 14th Havana summit on 15 September, 2006 the Indian Prime Minister stated that the aim of NAM was not to divide the world further but to adopt approaches, which will further human civilization.[38] The Declaration on the Purposes and Principles of the Non-aligned Movement in the present international juncture' contains the essence of the decisions at Havana Summit in 18 points as desired of 118-member NAM that thrusts on multilateralism. The NAM is a powerful movement of 'dissent' against hegemonic superpower.

But as the time passed and the global power equations have changed, a sea change has also been taken place in the perception of Indian leadership towards the New International Order. There is reflection of India's attitude of indifference towards non-alignment. The Indian media threw light on such attitude as Shekhar Gupta wrote in *The Indian Express*, 'Also, now anti– Americanism will not be ideological glue that once kept NAM together. You might say that NAM has come of age and emerged as more genuinely non-aligned, obviously because there is no Soviet bloc, whose faithful, tail-wagging shadow it became for three embarrassing decades.[39]

In addition, the perception and interests of the Indian ruling elites, of course, have undergone a sea change because they have equated all the major national goals with the rates of annual growth of Indian economy. On the eve of the Havana Summit our Prime Minister Manmohan Singh stated,' foreign policy is essentially a device to widen our development options.[40] Hence, in order to 'expand economic and other multifaceted contacts with other countries, India has to toss all the balls.' It reflects that Indian foreign policy is driven by economic considerations. Thus, market driven goals have come to dominate the values of Indian elite who looks for benefits from linkages with the global markets. The explanation for India's indifference to the movement of Non-alignment can be found in the new economic orientations. The dominant economic classes are driving the foreign strategic and economic goals because a belief exists among the Indian elite that strategic friendship with western developed countries is the only way to achieve their interest of maximising economic growth rate.

In fact, Indian political elite has somehow come to believe that there is a 'convergence' of interests between the developed capitalist countries and the fast developing capitalism of India. The Indian market and its stock exchanges are rated by global investors including the powerful western banks. United States and other Western countries are enthusiastic about the deepening of their bilateral relationship with India. Even David Cameron, the leader of the British Conservative Party stated, 'in the 21st century, as the world's centre of gravity moves from European and the Atlantic to the South and the East, I believe it is time for Britain and India to forge a new special relationship, to meet our shared challenges in the new era of international affairs.'

India, in its journey of foreign policy through the tenets of Non-alignment has successfully moved from the days of cold war to post-cold war and has reached the stage where it is trying to transform the nation into a great power, at least internationally. We have seen that the NAM without having no political, economic or military strength, successfully resisted the powerful nations including the United States of America and other allied countries. Non-alignment even in days of cold war had meant much more than not being aligned with the two power blocs and the era of post-cold war or globalisation has inherited the basic themes of the policy which it makes today – alive, active and relevant.[41] It is conceived as the voice of the former colonies and poor nations in a world overwhelmingly dominated by the rich Western nations. Over the years another organisation, G-77 has also developed which takes up the cause of the developing countries in international fora on economic and development issues, is complementary to Non-aligned movement. However, in recent decades Non-alignment has been defined in exclusively Indian national terms to enhance its independence or sovereignty and provide room for manoeuvre amidst diverse pressures to promote its ambitions and interests.

The fast changing global scenario of 1990s provided India a more influential perspective to reset its policy preferences especially after the collapse of the Soviet bloc and the initiation of domestically radical economic reforms. The founding fathers of NAM saw the two objectives; national independence and the solidarity of developing countries. But the change over of the Indian perspective on NAM is being seen in the context of its revised foreign policy agenda, almost exclusively focused on transforming India into a big power.[42] The way towards this objective, it is felt, is to start thinking big, join the rich man's club and enter into friendly relations with the rich and powerful nations for economic, high-tech and military benefits and a place at the high table where the great powers decide the fate of humankind. To advance this agenda, friendship with the most technologically and economically advanced and militarily powerful nation, the United States is seen as the most promising path. The real challenge for India, at the juncture, is to maintain this friendship with the "strategic autonomy" to preserve the "strategic space" for itself.

References

1. *India Today* (New Delhi), 16 March 2006, p. 40.
2. *The Hindu*, 1 October 2008.
3. *The Times of India* (New Delhi), 3 March 2006.
4. *Ibid.*, 14 January 2006.
5. Sudhanshu Tripathi, 'India US and NAM–A Fine Balance Needed', *South Asia Politics*, Vol. 9, No. 6, October 2010 (New Delhi : 2010), p. 38.
6. *Ibid.*
7. Sri Prakash Mani Tripathi, 'Emerging Challenges to India's Foreign Policy', in K.C. Choudhary (ed.), *India's Foreign Policy in Contemporary International Scenario*, (New Delhi : South Asian Publisher, 2009), p. 35.

8. Kumari Saroj, 'prospects of India's Foreign Policy in the Twenty – first Century' in *Ibid.,* p. 51.
9. Kenneth Waltz, *The Theory of International Politics* (Boston : McGraw Hill, 1979), as quoted in *Ibid.*
10. G.G. Mirchandani, *India's Nuclear Dilemma* (New Delhi : Popular Book Services, 1968).
11. Kumari Saroj, 'Prospects of India's Foreign policy in the Twenty–first Century,' p. 52.
12. *Asia Age* (New Delhi), 13 September 2006.
13. *Ibid.*
14. Shekhar Gupta, 'NAM Change', *The Indian Express,* 16 September 2006.
15. Awadesh Kumar Singh, 'India: From Non-alignment to Rise to power', in K.C. Choudhary (ed.), *India's Foreign Policy in Contemporary International Scenario,* p. 44.
16. P.R. Chari, Pervaiz Iqbal Cheema and Stephen P. Cohen, *Four Crisis and a peace Process: American Engagement in South Asia* (Washington, D.C. : The Brookings Institute, 2007).
17. Y.C. Halan, 'A Burning Pakistan–Causes and Cures', *South Asia Politics,* Vol. 6, No. 5, September 2007 (New Delhi : 2007), p. 14.
18. *Ibid.,* pp. 15-16.
19. Vivek M. Diwan, 'Perspectives on India-China Relations', *Third Concept,* Vol. 24, No. 288, February 2011 (New Delhi : 2011), p. 7.
20. *Ibid.,* p. 8.
21. John W. Garwar, *Protracted Contest: Sino–Indian Rivalry in the Twentieth Century* (DC : University of Washington, 2001), p. 1.
22. *Ibid.*
23. Sumit Ganguly, 'India–China: Border Issues, Domestic Integration and International Security', in Frankel and Harding (eds.), *The India– China Relationship: Rivalry and Engagement,* p. 103.
24. Vikash Anand, 'China's Hostile Attitudes Towards India', *South Asia Politics,* Vol. 9, No. 10, February 2011 (New Delhi : 2011), pp. 27-28.
25. *Ibid.,* p. 28.
26. *Ibid.*
27. Charles Krauthammer, 'The Unipolar Moment: America and the World', *Foreign Affairs,* 1990/91, Vol. 70, No. 1.
28. Richard N. Haass, 'The Age of Nonpolarity: What Will Follow US Dominance', *Foreign Affairs,* May/June 2008.

29. Suvir Kaul, 'Indian Academic and Resistance to Theory', in Rajeshwari Sundar Rajan (ed.), *The Lie of the Land: English Literary Studies in India* (Delhi : Oxford University Press, 1993), pp. 207-28.

30. C. Raja Mohan, 'Lessons from the Debacle at the UN', *The Hindu*, 2 November 1996.

31. C. Raja Mohan, *Crossing the Rubicon: The Shaping of India's New Foreign Policy* (New Delhi : Viking, 2007), p. 49.

32. Muchkund Dubey, 'Challenges for India's Foreign Policy', in K.C. Choudhary (ed.), *India's Foreign Policy in Contemporary International Scenario,* p. 5.

33. *Ibid.,* p. 4.

34. D.C. Pathak, 'India's Role in the 'War on Terror', *South Asia Politics*, February 2011, pp. 5-6.

35. *Ibid.*

36. Vikash Anand, 'China's Hostile Attitudes towards India,' *South Asia Politics*, p. 27.

37. Globalisation Market, 'Civilisation and Disciplinary Neo-liberalism', Vol. 24 (3), *Millennium*, 1995, pp. 399-423.

38. David Held et al, *Globalisation: Politics, Economics and Culture* (Cambridge: Polity Press, 1996), p. 49.

39. Sudhanshu Tripathi, 'India, US and NAM–A Fine Balance Needed', pp. 38-39.

40. *Ibid.*

41. K.N. Hari Kumar, 'Still Relevant After All These Years', *The Hindu*, 25 September 2012.

42. *Ibid.*

Bibliography

Documents

Administrative Reforms Commission, *Report of the Study Team on Centre-State Relationships*, Vols. I and II (Delhi, Manager of Publications, 1970).

All India Reporter (from 1950 to date) *Constitutional Law Decisions Cabinet Mission Plan (1946).*

All India Congress Committee, *The Background of India's Foreign Policy* (New Delhi, 1952).

Asian Relations Organisation, *Report of the Proceedings and Documents of the First Asian Relations Conference*, March-April 1947 (New Delhi, 1948).

Cabinet Mission Plan (1946).

Constituent Assembly Debates 1947-1949.

Constitution of India (Draft – 1949).

Constitution of India (Text – 1950).

Constitutional Proposals of the Sapru Committee (1945).

Debates in the House of Commons (1945-47).

Debates in the Lok Sabha and *Rajya Sabha* (India) 1950 to date.

Defence of India Act 1962.

Federal Court (of India) Reports from 1937 to 1950.

Foreign Affairs Record, Ministry of External Affairs External Publicity Division (Government of India, New Delhi).

Government of India, Administrative Reforms Commission, *Report of the Study Team on State Administration* (Manager of Publications, Delhi, 1970).

Government of India Act 1919.

Government of India Act 1935.

Government of India's Despatch on Constitutional Reform

India Independence Act, 1947.

Indian Round Table Conference : *Proceedings of Federal Structure Committee and Minorities Committee,* 1932.

India, Muslims in India, Ministry of Information and Broadcasting (New Delhi, 1966).

Montagu-Chemsford Report, 1918.

Memorandum of States Treaties and Paramountcy dated 12 May 1946.

Nehru, Jawaharlal, *India's Foreign Policy: Selected Speeches, September 1949-April 1961* (Publication Division, Ministry of Information and Broadcasting, New Delhi, 1961).

Nehru Committee Report, 1928.

Report of the All Parties Conference, 1928.

Report of the Federal Structure Committee, 1932.

Report of the Joint Parliamentary Committee, 1934.

Report of the Joint Select Committee, 1935.

Report of the Provincial Constitution Committee, June-July 1947.

Report of the Union Constitution Committee.

Report of the Union Powers Committee as Adopted by the Constituent Assembly, August 1947.

Report of Linguistic Provinces Commission (Constituent Assembly of India), 1948.

Report of the Backward Classes Commission, 1955.

Reports (Annual) *of the Commissioner for Scheduled Castes and Tribes* from 1951 onwards.

Report of the States Reorganisation Commission, 1955.

Report of the Committee of Parliament on Official Language, 1958.

Report of the Election Commission of India – First General Elections, 1951-52 and second General Elections, 1957.

Report of the Committee on Emotional Integration, 1962.

State Financial Corporation Act, 1951.

Text of Joint Communiques, Lok Sabha Secretariat, *Foreign Policy of India. Text of Documents 1947-1964* (New Delhi, 1966).

World Press Review (Publication Division, Ministry of Information and Broadcasting, Government of India, New Delhi).

Books

Achin Vanaik, *The Painful Transition : Bourgeois Democracy in India* (London, 1990).

Acimovic L., ed., *Non-alignment in the World of Today* (Belgrade Institute of International Politics and Economics, 1969).

Aiyar, S.P. *Federalism and Social Change* (Asia Publishing House, Bombay, 1961.)

Aiyer, S.P. and R. Srinivasam, eds., *Studies in Indian Democracy* (Allied, Bombay, 1965).

Alam Javeed , *Who Wants Democracy Tracts for the Times* (Orient Blackswan, New Delhi, 2012).

Alexandrowiez, C.H., *Constitutional Developments in India* (Oxford University Press, Bombay, 1957).

Ali, Sadiq, *Towards Socialist Thinking in Congress* (New Delhi, 1960).

Ali, Sadiq, *The General Election 1957 : A Survey* (1959).

Alker and Russell, *World Politics in the General Assembly* (Connecticut University Press, New Heaven, 1965).

Allen, Douglas, ed., *Religion and Political Conflict in South Asia* (Oxford University Press, New Delhi, 1993).

Almond, Gabriel A. and B.G. Powell, *Comparative Politics : A Developmental Approach* (Little Brown, Boston, 1966).

Almond, Gabriel A. and James S. Coleman, eds. *The Politics of the Developing Areas* (Princeton University Press, Princeton, 1960).

Alexander, P.C., *My Years with Indira Gandhi* (Vision Books, New Delhi, 1991).

Apter David, *The Politics of Modernisation* (University of Chicago Press, Chicago, 1965).

Appadorai, A., ed., *Selected Documents on India's Foreign Policy and Relations 1947-1972* (Oxford University Press, Newyork, 1982).

Austin, Granville, *The Indian Constitution : Cornerstone of a Nation* (Oxford University Press, Newyork, 1966).

Ayub Khan, Mohammed, *Friends Not Masters : A Political Biography* (Oxford University Press, London, 1967).

Azar, Edward E., and Chung In Moon eds., *National Security in the Third World: The Management of Internal and External Threats* (Edward Elgar Publishing, Aldershot, 1988).

Bandyopadhyaya, J., *The Making of India's Foreign Policy: Determinant Institutions, Processes and Personalities* (Allied Publishers, Bombay, 1979).

Bailey, F.G., *Caste and the Economic Frontier,* (Manchester University Press, Manchester, 1957).

Bardhan, Pranab, *The Political Economy of Development in India* (Oxford University Press, Delhi, 1985).

Basu, Amrita, *Two Faces of Protest : Contrasting Modes of Women's Activism in India* (University of California Press, Berkeley, 1992).

Baxter, Craig, *The Jana Sangh-A Biography of an Indian Political Party* (Philadelphia, 1969).

Bhambhari, C.P., *Foreign Policy of India* (Sterling, New Delhi, 1987).

Betielle, Andre, *The Backward Classes in Contemporary India* (Oxford University Press, Delhi, 1992).

Bose, Sugata and Ayesha Jalal (eds.), *Nationalism, Democracy and Development: State and Politics in India* (Oxford University Press, Delhi, 1997).

Bowels, Chester, *Ambassador's Report.*

Brecher, Michael, *Nehru : A Political Biography* (Oxford University Press, London, 1959).

__________, *Nehru's Mantle : The Politics of Succession in India* (Praeger, Newyork, 1966).

__________, *The Struggle for Kashmir* (Oxford University Press, Newyork, 1953).

Brown, Michael E. and Ganguly, Sumit, eds., *Government Policies and Ethnic Relations in Asia and the Pacific* (Cambridge, 1997).

Byres, Terence (ed.), *The State and Development Planning in India* (Oxford University Press, Delhi, 1993).

Carras Marry C., *The Dynamics of Indian Political Faction* (Cambridge University Press, Cambridge, 1972).

Chanda, Asok, *Federalism in India: A Study of Union-State Relations* (George Allen and Unwin, London, 1965).

Chaudhuri, Nirad C., *The Continent of Circle : An Essay on the Peoples of India* (Oxford University Press, London, 1966).

Chavan, Yashwant Rao B., *India's Foreign Policy* (Somaiya Publishers, Bombay, 1979).

Choudhury, R.A., Sharma Ghamkar and Aurobindo Ghosh, *The Indian Economy and its Performance since Independence* (Oxford University Press, Delhi, 1990.

Chopra, Pran, *Uncertain India : A Political Profile of two Decades of Freedom* (Asia Publishing House, Bombay, 1968).

Cohen, Stephen P., and Richard L. Park, *India : Emergent Power* (Crane, Russak & Comp., Newyork, 1978).

Cormack, Margaret, *The Hindu women* (Asia Publishing House, Bombay, 1961).

Cressey, George B., *Asia's Lands and Peoples,* McGraw-Hill (Newyork, 1951).

Curran, J.A. Jr., *Militant Hinduism in Indian Politics, A Study of the RSS* (Newyork, 1951).

Damodaran, A.K. and U.S. Bajpai, eds., *Indian Foreign Policy : The Indira Gandhi Years* (Sangam Books, London, 1990).

Dash, S.C. *The Constitution of India* (Chaitanya Publishing House, Allahabad, 1968).

Davis, Kingsely, *The Population of India and Pakistan* (Princeton University Press, Princeton, 1951).

Dean, Vera Micheles, *New Patterns of Democracy in India* (Harvard University Press, Cambridge, 1969).

Derrett, J. Duncan M., *Religion, Law and the State in India* (Free Press, Newyork, 1968).

Dhavan Rajiv and Jacob Alice (eds.), *Indian Constitution Trends and Issues* (1978).

Divetia, Kumud, *The nature of inter-relations of Governments in India* (1957).

Dube, S.C., *Indian Village* (Routledge and Kegan Paul, London, 1955).

Dutta, Palme, R., *India Today* (1946).

__________, *India's Changing Villages – Human Factors in Community Development* (Routledge and Kegan Paul, London, 1958).

Easton, David, *The Political System : An Inquiry into the State of Political Science* (Scientific Book Agency, Calcutta, 1971).

Edwardes, Michael, *Nehru : A Political Biography* (Penguin, 1973).

Edmead, Frank, *Analysis and Prediction in International Mediation* (Unitar, Newyork, 1971).

Embree, Ainslie T., ed., *The Hindu Tradition* (Modern Library, Newyork, 1966).

Erdmann, Howard K., *The Swatantra Party and Indian Conservatism* (Cambridge, 1967).

Esposito, John L., ed., *Islam in Asia : Religion Politics and Society* (Oxford University Press, Oxford, 1987).

Falik, Richard A., *Global Approach to National Policy* (Harvard University Press, Cambridge, 1975).

Frankel, Joseph, *The Making of Foreign Policy : An Analysis of Decision Making* (Oxford University Press, London, 1963).

Friederich C.J., *Constitutional Government and Democracy* (1966).

__________, *Trends of Federalism in Theory and Practice* (London, 1968).

Gaan, Narottam, *Indira Gandhi and Foreign Policy Making : The Bangladesh Crisis* (Patriot Publishers, New Delhi, 1992).

Gandhi, Indira, *Aspects of Our Foreign Policy : From Speeches and Statements* (An AICC Publication, New Delhi, 1973).

Gandhi, Rajiv, *Statements on Foreign Policy : November 1984-April 1985* (Ministry of External Affairs, New Delhi, 1985).

Gangulee, N., *The Making of Federal India* (James Nisbet & Co., 1936).

Ghouse, M., *Secularism, Society and Law in India* (Vikas Publications, New Delhi, 1973).

Ghurye, G.S., *Caste and Class in India* (Bombay, 1955).

Gledhill, Alan, *The Republic of India, the Development of its Law and Constitution* (London, 1951).

Gopal, S., *Jawaharlal Nehru : A Biography* (Oxford University Press, Delhi, 1976).

Gupta, M.G., *Rajiv Gandhi's Foreign Policy : A Study in Continuity and Change* (M.G. Publishers, Agra, 1987).

Gweyer, M., and Appadorai, *Speeches and Documents on Indian Constitution* (Oxford University Press, Bombay, 1957).

Halayya, M., *Emergency : A War on Corruption.*

Harrison, Selig S., *India : The Most Dangerous Decades* (Princeton University Press, Princeton, 1960).

Hartmann, Horst, *Political Parties in India* (Meenakshi, Meerut, 1971).

Hastings James, *Encyclopaedia of Religion and Ethics* (1959).

Hassnain, S.E., *Indian Muslims : Challenge and Opportunity* (Lalvani Publication House, Bombay, 1968).

Hussain, Asif, *Elite Politics in an Ideological State* (Dawson, Folkestone, 1979).

Hutton, J.H., *Caste in India* (Oxford University Press, Newyork, 1963).

International Monetary Fund, *World Economic Outlook : April 1985* (External Relations Department, Washington, 1985).

Irwin, Lord, *Some Aspects of the Indian Problem* (1932).

Israni, Kimat and Haku Israni, *India : A Superpower* (Lancer International, New Delhi, 1989).

Jacob Alice (ed.), *Constitutional Developments since Independence* (1975).

Jackson, Robert, *South Asian Crisis : India, Pakistan, Bangladesh* (Chatto and Windus, London, 1975).

Jalal, Ayesha, *Democracy and Authoritarianism in South Asia: A Comparative and Political Perspective* (Cambridge University Press, Cambridge, 1995).

Jalal Ayesha and Sugata Bose, *Modern South Asia – History, Culture Political Economy* (Oxford University Press, New Delhi, 2005).

Jansen, G.H., *Non-alignment and the Afro-Asian States* (Praeger, Newyork, 1966).

Jennings, Sir Ivor, *Some Characteristics of Indian Constitution* (Madras, 1953).

Kapur, Harish, *India's Foreign Policy 1947-92, Shadow and Substance* (Sage Publications, New Delhi, 1994).

Kavic, Lorne, J., *India's Quest for Security : Defence Policies, 1947-1965* (University of California Press, Berkeley, 1967).

Kohli, Atul (ed.), *Indian Democracy : An Analysis of Changing State – Society Relations* (Princeton University Press, Princeton, 1988).

Kothari, Rajni, *State Against Democracy : In Search of Humane Governance* (Konark, New Delhi, 1988).

Krishnaswami, A., *The Indian Union and the States : A Study in Autonomy and Integration* (Pergamon Press, London, 1964).

Lakdawala, D.T., *International Aspects of Indian Economic Development* (Oxford University Press, London, 1950).

Laxmi, Y., *Trends in India's Defence Expenditure* (ABC, New Delhi, 1988).

Livingston, W.S., *Federalism and Constitutional Change* (Oxford University Press, Delhi, 1956).

London, Kurt, *The Making of Foreign Policy : East and West* (J.B., Lippincot Co., Philadelphia, 1965).

Ludden, David (ed.), *Making India Hindu* (Oxford University Press, Delhi, 1996).

Madan, Gopal, *India as a World Power : Aspects of Foreign Policy* (Saga, Publications, New Delhi, 1974).

Madhu, Limaya, *India and the World* (New Delhi, 1979).

Mallik, Dev Narayan, *Post-war International Politics – A quadripartite Survey* (Veena Mandir Publishers, Muzaffarpur, 1973).

__________, *The Development of Nonalignment in India's Foreign Policy* (Chaitanya Publishing House, Allahabad, 1967).

Martin, Lawrence W., ed., *Neutralism and Non-alignment : The New States in World Affairs* (Praeger, Newyork, 1962).

Mason, Edward S., *Foreign Aid and Foreign Policy* (S.R. Suneja Publications, New Delhi, 1964).

Mirchandari, G.G., ed., *Reporting India 1977* (Abhinav Publications, New Delhi, 1978).

Misra, B.B., *Government and Bureaucracy in India 1947-1976* (Oxford University Press, Delhi, 1986).

__________, *The Indian Middle Classes, Their Growth in Modern Times* (London, 1961).

Mishra, Pramod K., *South Asia in International Politics* (UDH Publishers, Delhi, 1984).

Mookerji, Girija, *History of Indian National Congress* (Meerut, 1974).

Moore R.J., *Tradition and Politics in South Asia* (Vikas Publishing House, New Delhi, 1979).

Morris Jones, W.H., *The Government and Politics of India* (Butchinson & Company, London, 1971).

Munshi K.M., *Pilgrimage to Freedom* (Bharatiya Vidhya Bhawan, Bombay, 1967).

Naik, J.A., ed., *India in Asia and Africa-Documents : 1976-1978* (Avinash Reference Publication, Maharashtra).

__________, The *Great Janata Revolution* (S. Chand and Com., New Delhi, 1977).

__________, *Pak Bomb and Rajiv's India* (National Publishing House, New Delhi, 1986).

Nanda, B.R., *Indian Foreign Policy: The Nehru Years* (Vikas Publishing House, Delhi, 1976).

Narain Iqbal (ed.) *State Politics in India* (Meerut, 1976).

Narayan, Jayaprakash, *A Plea for the Reconstruction of Indian Polity* (Kashi, 1969).

Natarajan, S., *A Century of Social Reform in India* (Asia Publishing House, Bombay, 1959).

Nayar, Kuldip, *The Judgement* (Delhi, 1977).

Nehru, Jawaharlal, *The Discovery of India* (John Day, Newyork, 1946).

__________, *Glimpses of World History* (L. Drummond, Newyork, 1949).

__________, *India's Foreign Policy* (Publication Division, Ministry of Information and Broadcasting, Government of India, 1961).

Nettle, J.P., *Political Mobilisation – A Sociological Analysis of Methods and Concepts* (Newyork).

Overstreet, Gene D., and Marshall Windmiller *Communism in India* (University of California Press, Berkeley, 1959).

Palmer, Norman D., *The Indian Political System* (Houghton Mifflin, Boston, 1961).

Palit, D.K., *War in the High Himalayas : India in Crisis – 1962* (Lancer International, New Delhi, 1991).

Pannikar, K.M., *The Problems of Indian Defence* (Asia Publishing House, 1960).

Park, Richard L., and Irene Thinker, eds., *Leadership and Political Institutions in India* (Princeton University Press Princeton, 1959).

Patel, Surendra J., *Indian Economy : Towards the Twenty First Century* (Universities Press, Hyderabad, 1955).

Pattabhiram, M. (ed.), *General Elections in India 1967 – An Exhaustive Study of Main Political Trends* (Bombay, 1967).

Power, Paul E., ed., *India's Non-alignment Policy* (D.C. Health & Co., Boston, 1967).

Prasad, N., *Change-Strategy in a Developing Society : India* (Meerut, 1969).

Pye, Lucian W., *Asian Power and Politics : The Cultural Dimensions of Authority* (Harvard Universtiy, Cambridge, 1985).

Rahman, M.M., *The Politics of Non-Alignment* (Associated publishing House, New Delhi, 1969).

Rajan, M.S., *Nonalignment : India and Future* (University of Mysore Press, Mysore, 1970).

__________, *India in World Affairs, 1954-56* (Asia Publishing House, 1964).

Rana, A.P., *Imperatives of Nonalignment : A Conceptual Study of India's Foreign Policy in the Nehru Era* (MacMillan, New Delhi, 1976).

Rasgotra M. Chopra, V.D. and Mishra K.P. eds., *India's Foreign Policy in the 1990s* (Patriot Publishers, New Delhi, 1990).

Rasgotra, M.K.,ed., *Rajiv Gandhi's World View* (Vikas Publishing House, New Delhi, 1991).

Rosenau, James, N., *Domestic Sources of Foreign Policy* (Free Press, Newyork, 1967).

Rosen, George, *Democracy and Economic Change in India* (University of California, Berkeley, 1966).

Rosen, Stephen Peter, *Societies and Military Power : India and its Armies* (Oxford University Press, Delhi, 1996).

Roy, S., *Indian Politics and Constitutional Development* (Meerut, 1976).

Rudolph, Lloyd J., Rudolph Hoeber, Susanne, *The Modernity of Tradition – Political Development in India* (Chicago, 1967).

Sharma B.M., *The Republic of India : Constitution and Government* (Asia Publishing House, Bombay, 1966).

Santhanam, K., *Union – State Relations in India* (Bombay, 1960).

Sathyamurthy, T.V., ed., *Region, Religion, Caste, Gender and Culture in Contemporary India* (Oxford University Press, Delhi, 1996).

Sengupta, Bhabani *India: Problems of Governance* (Centre for Policy Research, Konark, New Delhi, 1996).

Shakir, Moin., *Secularisation of Muslim Behaviour* (Minerva, Calcutta, 1973).

Shelat, J.M., *Secularism, Principles and Application* (Tripathi, Bombay, 1972).

Singer, Milton, ed., *Traditional India : Structure and Change* (University of Texas Press, Austin, 1959).

Singer, Jasjit, ed., *Kargil 1999 : Pakistan's Fourth War for Kashmir* (Knowledge World, New Delhi, 1999).

Singh, Maj. Gen. Sukhwant, *India's Wars Since Independence : General Trends* (Vikas Publishing House, New Delhi, 1982).

Singh, Rajkumar, *Less Tasty Indo-Nepal Political Relations, 1947-1997* (Novelty, Patna, 1998).

Singh, Rajkumar, *India-South Asia Minus Congress Regimes* (Novelty, Patna, 2000).

Singh, Rajkumar, *Indo-Pak Nuclear Tension 1974-1998* (Samiksha Prakashan, New Delhi, 2001).

Singh, Rajkumar, *India's Foreign Policy-The First Study in Continuity and Change* (Samiksha Prakashan, New Delhi, 2001).

Singh, Rajkumar, *Past, Present and Future of Kashmir* (Gyan Publishing House, New Delhi, 2008).

Singh, Rajkumar, *India and Pakistan – Social, Political and Military Perspectives* (Regal Publications, New Delhi, 2009).

Singh, Rajkumar, *Global Dimensions of Indo-Nepal Political Relations Post-Independence* (Gyan Publishing House, New Delhi, 2009).

Singh, Rajkumar, *Relations of NDA and UPA with Neighbours* (Gyan Publishing House, New Delhi, 2010).

Singh, Rajkumar, *Contemporary India with Controversial Neighbours* (Gyan Publishing House, New Delhi, 2011).

Singh, Rajkumar, *Ethnic Politics and LTTE in Sri Lanka* (Kalpaz Publications, New Delhi, 2012).

Singh, Rajkumar, *Myth and Reality of Terrorism in South Asia* (Kalpaz Publications, New Delhi, 2013).

Smith, Donald E. *India as a Secular State* (Princeton University Press, Princeton, 1963).

Smith, Wilfred Cantwell, *Modern Islam in India: A Social Analysis* (Ripon Printing Press, Lahore, 1947).

Sobhan, Rahman, *The Crisis of External Dependence : The Political Economy of Foreign Aid to Bangladesh* (Dhaka University Press, Dhaka, 1982).

Srinivas, M.N., *Caste in Modern India and Other Essays* (Bombay, 1962).

Subrahmanyam, K., *Security in Changing World* (B.R. Publishing Company, Delhi, 1990).

Subbarao G.C.V., *Indian Constitutional Law* (1971).

Suri, Surinder, *1962 Elections – A Political Analysis* (New Delhi, 1962).

Thakur, Janardhan, *All the Prime Minister's Men* (Vikas Publishing House, New Delhi, 1977).

Tharoor, Shashi, *Reasons of State : Political Development and India's Foreign Policy Under Indira Gandhi* (Vikas Publishing House, New Delhi, 1982).

Thimmaih, *Union-State Financial Relations in India* (1974).

Thompson, Edward John and Geoffrey Theodore Garratt, *Rise and Fulfilment of British Rule in India* (Macmillan, London, 1934).

Thomas, Raju, G.C. *Indian Security Policy* (Princeton University Press, Princeton, 1986).

Tyagi, A.R., *Rights and Obligations of Civil Servants in India* (1959).

Vajpayee, Atal Bihari, *New Dimensions of India's Foreign Policy* (Vision Book, New Delhi, 1979).

Varadarajan, M.K., *Indian States and the Federation* (1939).

Varma, S.P. and Misra, K.P., ed., *Foreign Policies in South Asia* (Orient Longmans, New Delhi, 1969).

Venkatarama, T.S., *A Treatise on Secular State* (1950).

Venkatarangaiya, M., *Competitive and Cooperative Trends in Federalism* (Gokhale Institute of Politics and Economics, Poona, 1951).

Victor, Cecil, *India : The Security Dilemma* (Patriot Publishers, New Delhi, 1990).

Wattal, P.K., *Parliamentary Financial Control in India* (1953).

Weiner, Myron, *Party Politics in India : Development of Multiparty System* (Princeton University Press, Princeton, 1957).

__________, *Political Change in South Asia* (Farma K.L., Calcutta, 1968).

Zaidi, A.M., *The Annual Register of Indian Political Parties*, Vols. I and II (New Delhi).

Zaidi, A.M., and Zaidi, S.G. eds., *The Encyclopaedia of Indian National Congress* (S.Chand and Company, New Delhi, 1981).

Articles in Books, Periodicals and Newspapers

Abraham, A.S., 'Decade of Turbulence – System Under Growing Stress', *The Times of India*, 21 December 1979.

Agrawal, Arun Kumar, 'Corruption in Historical Perspective - A Case Study of India', *The Indian Journal of Political Science*, Vol. LXIII, No. 2, April-June 2007 (Meerut, 2007).

Aiyar, S.P., 'The Structure of Power in Indian Political System', in Subhash C. Kashyap (ed.), *Union State Relations in India* (The Institute of Constitutional and Parliamentary Studies, New Delhi, 1983).

Alphousal, Maria A. and J. Belphine Prema Dhanaseeli, 'Strategy Against the Threat to Poor', *Eubious Journal of Asian and International Bio-Ethics* (2003).

Amrutkar, Prashant, 'Indian Secularism : Is It a Way Out to Communalism?', *IJPS* Vol. LXXI, No. 3, July-September 2010 (Meerut, 2010).

Ann, Elliot Kimberly, *'Corruption and Global Economy'* (Institute of International Economics June 1997 (Washington, D.C. 1997).

Anand, Vikash, 'China's Hostile Attitudes Towards India', *South Asia Politics*, February 2011

Arend Lijphart, 'Cultural Diversities and Theories of Political Integration', *Canadian Journal of Political Science*, Vol. IV (March 1971).

Balachandrudu, K., 'Understanding Political Corruption', '*IJPS* Vol. LXVII, No. 4, October-December 2006.

Balasubramanian, Dr. R., 'Indian Polity in Transition', Presidential Address, *53 Annual Conference of Indian Political Science Association*, 27-29 December 2006 (Jaipur, 2006).

Banu, Zenab, 'Religion in Indian Politics: Need to be Value Oriented Not Power-Oriented', *IJPS* Vol. LXX, No. 3, July-September 2009.

Behera, Harish Chandra, 'Political System and Governance in South Asia', *SAP*, Vol. 8, No. 11, March 2010 (New Delhi, 2010).

Beloff, M., 'The Federal Solution in its Application to Europe, Asia and Africa', *Political Studies*, 1953.

Beteille, Andre, 'Politics Without Policy', *The Hindu*, 28 June, 2012.

Bhagwan, Vishnu, 'Corruption and Good Governance', *IJPS*, Vol. LXVIII, No. 4, October-December 2009.

Bhatia, Krishna, 'The Ordeal of Nationhood', *Imprint*, November 2007 (Bombay, 2007).

Bhatnagar, Mridula, 'Gender Politics : In the Context of Social Structure and Development', *IJPS*, Vol. LXX, No. 4, October-December 2009.

Biju, B.L., 'Market Preserving Federalism : A Theoretical Hybrid of Liberal Democracy and Global Capitalism', *IJPS*, Vol. lXVIII, No. 2, April-June 2007.

Bjorkman, J.W., 'Changing State/Society Relations : Broad Brush Approaches and Analytical Models', *Administrative Change*, Vol. XXVIII, No. 2, Vol. XXIX, No. 1, January-December 2001 (Jaipur, 2001).

Chandra, Bipin, 'Truth is God', *The Hindustan Times*, 5 April 2002.

Chaturvedi, Geeta, 'Democracy in Global India', *IJPS* Vol. LXIX, No. 4, October-December 2008.

Chaturvedi, T.N., 'Corruption in India : An Overview', in Subhash C. Kashyap (ed.), *Eradication of Corruption and Restoration of Values* (Sterling Publishers, New Delhi, 2003).

Chatterjee, Somnath, 'Parliamentary Democracy and Some Challenges', *The Hindu*, 15 November 2007.

Chawla, Navin, 'Towards a Level Playing Field', *The Hindu*, 5 January 2012.

Chowdary, T.H., 'Ending the Maoist Menace', *SAP*, Vol. 8, No. 7, November 2009.

Chowla, N.L., 'Indian Democracy in Perspective', *The Times of India*, 22 December 1980.

Das, Arvind N., 'India Invented Ostrich Approach to National Unity', *The Times of India*, 19 September 1991.

Das, Ch. Dr. Dibakar, 'Corruption and Society in India', *Third Concept*, Vol. 20, No. 235 September 2006 (New Delhi, 2006).

Das, Gupta S., 'Regaining the Faith', *India Today*, 8 April 2002 (New Delhi, 2002).

Das, Kartick, 'Naxalbari to Today's Maoist : Uprising and Implications', *IJPS*, Vol. LXXI, No. 2, April-June 2010.

Das, Shreeram Chandra, 'Political Relevance in Constitutionalism', in Satya Prakash Das (ed.), *Constitutional and Political Dynamics of India* (Sarup & Sons, New Delhi, 2004).

Das, Satya Prakash, 'Indian Federalism and Distribution of Responsibilities', *IJPS*, Vol. LXVII1, No. 4, October-December 2007.

Deb, Papia, P.K. Sengupta, 'Coalition Politics and the Changing Perspectives of India's Federal Governance,' *IJPS*, Vol. LXX, No. 2, April-June 2009.

Devi, Syamala D. and G. Lakshmi, 'Need for a CMP in Coalition Governments', *SAP* Vol. 6, No. 8, December 2007.

Diwan, Vivek M., 'Perspectives on India-China Relations', *Third Concept*, Vol. 24, No. 288, February 2011.

Dube, M.P., 'Changing Patterns of Centre-State Relations in India', in Hari Hara Das and Sanjukta Mahapatra (eds.), *Centre–State Relations* (Ashish Publishing House, New Delhi, 1986).

Dubhashi, P.R. 'Meaning of Secularism', *The Hindu*, 11 June 2002.

Dubhashi, P.R. Hazare's Fast and Its Aftermath', *SAP* Vol. 10, No. 1, May 2011.

Dubhashi, P.R. End of Anna Team's Fast and Its Aftermath, in Ibid., Vol, 11, No. 5, September 2012.

Dubey, Muchkund, 'Challenges for India's Foreign Policy', in K.C. Choudhary (ed.), *India's Foreign Policy in Contemporary International Scenario* (South Asian Publishers, New Delhi, 2009).

Dyke, Varginia Van, 'Religious Mobilisation and Sadhus in Politics : The Idealized Versus Realpolitik', in Paul R. Brass and Achin Vanaik (eds.), *Competing Nationalism in South Asia* (Orient Longman, New Delhi, 2002).

Elazar Daniel J., 'Federalism and Consociational Regimes', *Publius* Vol. 15, No. 2, Spring 1985 (Temple University, 1985).

Engineer, Dr. Asghar Ali, 'Who is for a Common Civil Code ?', *The Hindustan Times*, 3 August 2003.

Evans, Tony, 'Introduction : Power Hegemony and the Universalisation of Human Rights', in Tony Evans (ed.), *Human Rights Fifty Years on—A Reappraisal* (Manchester University Press, UK, 1998).

Faleiro, Eduardo, 'Reflections on the Republic Day', *SAP*, Vol. II, No. 10, February 2013.

Gamson, William A., 'Experimental Studies of Coalition', in Leonard Berkowitz (ed.), *Advances in Experimental Social Psychology* (Academic Publication, Newyork, 1964).

Gandhi, Gopal Krishna, 'Three Cheers to Parliament', *The Hindu*, 17 April 2012.

Ganguly, Sumit, 'India-China : Border Issues, Domestic Integration and International Security', in Frankel and Harding (eds.), *The India-China Relationships : Rivalry and Engagement.*

Ghose, Moumita, 'Democracy in India-Background and Emerging Challenges', *SAP*, Vol. 9, No. 8, December 2010.

Ghosh, P.S., 'Hindu Nationalism : The Politics of Nation Building and Implications for the Legitimacy of the State,' in S.K. Mitra and D. Rothermud (eds.), *Legitimacy and Conflicts in South Asia* (Manohar Publications, New Delhi, 1997).

Ghoshal, Sarbani Guha, 'Human Rights : Concept and Contestation', *IJPS*, Vol. LXXI, No. 4, October-December 2010.

Gill, S.S., 'Team Secularism', *The Hindustan Times*, 3 March 2003.

Greene, Joseph N., 'Goal of Democracy', in Sardar Patel Institute of Administration (ed.), *Administration and Politics in Modern Democracies* (Allahabad, 1976).

Grodzins, Morton, 'The Federal System', in Aaron Wildavsky (ed.), *American Federalism in Perspective* (Little Brown and Company, Boston, 1967).

Groethuysen, B., 'Secularism', in Edwin R.A. Seligman (ed.), *Social Sciences* (MacMillan Company, New Delhi, 1959).

Gupta, Dipankar, 'Communalism and Fundamentalism – Some Notes on the Nature of Ethnic Politics in India', *Economic and Political Weekly*, Vol. XXXVI No. 11-12 March 1991 (Mumbai, 1991).

__________, 'Flagging India's Missing Freedom', *The Hindu,* 29 September 2009.

Gupta, Shekhar, 'NAM Change', *The Indian Express*, 16 September 2006.

__________, One Dynasty Dimming', *The Indian Express*, 23 February 2013.

Habermas, Jurgen, 'Private and Public Autonomy', in Belgrade Circle (ed.).

Halan, Y.C., 'A Burning Pakistan – Causes and Cures', *SAP* Vol. 6, No. 5, September 2007.

Haqqi, S.A.H., 'The Indian Federal Structure and National Unity', in Subhash C. Kashyap (ed.), *Union-State Relations in India.*

Haass, Richard N., 'The Age of Nonpolarity : What Will Follow US Dominance', *Foreign Affairs*, May/June 2008.

Hazary, S.C., Wither Indian Party System', *Political Scientist* (Ranchi, 1980).

Iyer, V.R. Krishna, 'Needed a Renewed Socialist Concern, *The Hindu,* 4 February 2008.

Jain Girilal, 'Language of Indian Politics : Borrowed Idiom Giving Way', *The Times of India*, 2 April 1980.

__________, 'Gandhiji and Mr. Nehru – Two Different Moral Universe', *The Times of India*, 16 November 1980.

__________, 'Effects of Politicisation – Need to Strengthen Institutions', *The Times of India*, 31 December 1980.

Jain M.P., 'Federalism in India', *Journal of Indian Law Institute,* Vol. 6 (1964).

Jain, R.B., 'The Art of Political Corruption : An Analysis of Some Major Scams Since Independence', in Subhash C. Kashyap (ed.), *Eradication of Corruption and Restoration of Values.*

Jha, Prem Shankar, 'Overcome by a Sense of Betrayal', *The Hindu*, 15 January 2013.

Kalaignar, Karunanidhi M., 'Autonomy for the States, Federalism at the Centre', *The Hindu*, 5 August 2007.

Kapoor, Suneera and Shrawan Singh, 'Gandhi and Nehru on Religion', *IJPS*, Vol. LXVI, No. 3, July-September 2005.

Kashyap, C. Subhash, 'President-Prime Minister Relationship. Dr. Rajendra Prasad's Presidential Years', *SAP* Vol. 8, No. 5, September 2008.

Kashyap, C. Subhash, 'Democratic Governance – Space for the Underprivileged', in *Ibid.,* Vol. 7, No. 8, December 2008.

__________, 'Corruption and Criminalisation of Politics', in *Ibid.,* Vol. 7, No. 9, January 2009.

__________, 'Innovative Federal Structures and Conflict Resolution in India', in *Ibid.,* Vol. 11, No. 3, July 2012.

Katju, Markandey, 'Four People's Principles', *The Hindu,* 11 January 2012.

__________, 'Rid Over Body Politic of Communal Poison', in *Ibid.,* 11 October 2012.

Katju, Vivek, 'Herald a National Vision That Little Resembles the Old', *The Hindu,* 16 November 2012.

Katyal, K.K., 'Coalition Politics: The Latest Phase', *The Hindu,* 17 March 1997.

Kaul, Suvir, 'Indian Academic and Resistance to Theory', in Rajeshwari Sunder Rajan (ed.), *The Lie of the Land : English Literary Studies in India* (Oxford University Press, Delhi, 1993).

Kaviraj, Sudipta, 'Religion, Politics and Modernity', in Upendra Baxi and Bhikhu Parekh (eds.), *Crisis and Change in Contemporary India* (Sage Publications, New Delhi, 1995).

__________, 'The Modern State in India', in Zoya Hasan (ed.), *Introduction: The Political Career of the State in Independent India* (2000).

Khanna, K.C., 'Strong Centre – Weak States – New Problems in Perspective', *The Times of India,* January 1980.

Khare, Harish, 'At 60, the Political Culture Needs Renewal', *The Hindu,* 16 August 2007.

__________, 'Time for House – Cleaning in the Congress', *The Hindu,* 4 April 2012.

Khobragade, Vinod F., 'The Secularisation of Political Culture', *SAP,* Vol. 6, No. 6, October 2007.

Kothari, Rajni, 'The Congress System in India', in *Party System and Election Studies* (Allied Publishers, New Delhi, 1967).

__________, 'Integration Exclusion in Indian Politics', *Economic and Political Weekly,* Vol. XXIII, No. 43 (1988).

Krauthammer, Charles, 'The Unipolar Moment : America and the World', *Foreign Policy,* Vol. 70, No. 1, 1990/91.

Kumar, Arun, 'The Corrupt Rule the Roost', *The Hindu,* 7 January 2012.

__________, 'Why Fears of a Foreign Hand are Real', in *Ibid.,* 22, June 2012.

Kumar, Biju V., 'Post-colonial State : An Overview', *IJPS,* Vol. LXVI, No. 4, October-December 2005.

Kumar, Brijiesh Justice, 'An Appraisal of the Working of the Indian Constitution', *SAP*, Vol. 11, No. 7, November 2012.

Kumar, Ramesh, 'Political Parties in India and the United States: A Comparative Analysis', *IJPS*, Vol. LXX, No. 4, October-December 2009.

Kumar, Suresh, 'Human Rights Protection in India – An Institutional Framework', *SAP*, Vol. 7, No. 3, August 2008.

Kumari, Saroj, 'Prospects of India's Foreign Policy in the Twenty-first Century', in K.C. Choudhary (ed.), *India's Foreign Policy in Contemporary International Scenario*.

Lasswell, H.D., 'The Policy Sciences', in *Encyclopaedia of the Social Sciences*, Vol.2 (MacMillan, Newyork, 1968).

Madhumita, 'Naxalism – Development or Discontent – A Study of Jharkhand', *SAP*, Vol. 9, No. 6, October 2010.

Maheshwari, S.R., 'Political Reforms for Good Governance', IJPS, Vol. XLIV, No. 3, July-September 1998.

__________, Political Corruption its Magnitude and Cure', in Subhash C. Kashyap (ed.), *Eradication of Corruption and Restoration of Values*.

Malhotra, Inder, 'The Changing Face of Parliament,' *The Times of India*, 17 August 1980.

Mathur, A.B. , 'The Indian Polity : A Mild Indictment', *Administrative Change*, Vol. XXIX, No. 2, Vol. XXX, No. 1, January-December 2002 (Jaipur, 2002).

Mavromaras, Marco, 'The Definition of Secularism', *Social Commentary*, Vol. 3, Issue, 5, February 2007.

Mc Garry, John, 'Federalism (Federation) as a Method of Ethnic Conflict Regulation', *Working Paper, Conference on From Power-Sharing to Democracy : Post Conflict Institutions in Ethnically Divided Society*, 9-10 November 2002 (London, 2002).

Mehta, Balraj, 'India : Perspective and Prospectives', *Employment News*, 7-13 April 1990.

Mishra, Vandana, 'Analysing the BJP and Congress', *Mainstream*, Vol. XLII, No. 19, May 2004 (New Delhi, 2004).

Mody, Piloo, 'We Have No Parties – Only Leaders', *The Times of India*, 17 August 1980.

Mohan Raja C., 'Lessons from the Debate at the UN', *The Hindu*, 2 November 1996.

Mohammad, Khai Ali Mia, Yasin and Yasmin, 'Gender Equality – Rhetoric or a Panacea ? : A Review of the Present Concerns', *IJPS*, Vol. LXVII, No. 4, October-December 2007.

Mohanty, Biswaranjan, 'Tackling the Naxal Insurgency', *SAP*, Vol. 9, No. 12, April 2011.

Mohanty, Manoranjan, 'Secularism : Hegemonic and Democratic', *Economic and Political Weekly*, Vol. XXIV, No. 22, 3 June 1989 (Mumbai, 1989).

__________, 'The Contemporary State', *Teaching Politics*, Vol. VIII, Nos. 1-2, 1992.

__________, Party and Polity', in G.P. Deshpande and Alka Acharya (eds.), *50 Years of India-China-Crossing a Bridge of Dream* (Tulika Publications, New Delhi, 2001).

Mukherjee, Aditya, and Mridula Mukherjee, 'Imperialism and the Growth of the Indian Capitalism in the Twentieth Century', *Economic and Political Weekly*, 12 March 1988.

Muhhammad Yunus, 'The Grameen Bank Story : Rural Credit in Bangladesh', in Anirudh Krishna, Norman Uphoff and Milton Esman (eds.), *Reasons for Hope-Instructive Experience in Rural Development* (Vistaar, New Delhi, 1997).

Mukherjee Uddipan, 'Maoism and Its Future in India', *SAP*, Vol. 7, No. 3, July 2008.

Muthamma, C.B., 'Corruption : Causes and Cures – Need for Systemic Change', in Subhash C. Kashyap (ed.), *Eradication of Corruption and Restoration of Values.*

Naidu, Ashok, 'Secularism Reexamined', *IJPS*, Vol. LXVIII, No. 3, July-September 2007.

Naidu, Gurappa Y., 'Globalisation and its Impact on Indian Society', *IJPS*, Vol. LXVII, No. 1, January-March 2006.

Nand, Reena, 'The Dynamics of Indian Political System', *IJPS*, Vol. LXI, No. 2, April-June 2010.

Narain, Iqbal, Arvind K. Sharma, 'The Emerging Issues and Ideas in Indian Federalism – A Post – Fourth General Election Review', in Subhash C. Kashyap (ed.), *Centre – State Relations in India.*

Narud, Hanne Martha, 'Electoral Competition and Coalition Bargaining in Multiparty System', *The Journal of Theoretical Politics* (1996).

Nathan, Dev, 'India : From Civilizations to Nation's', in Kumar Rupesinghe and Khawar Mumtaz (eds.), *Internal Conflicts in South Asia* (Oslo, 1996).

Navlani, Kavita, 'National Integration and the Dynamics of Coalition and Federalism in India', *IJPS*, Vol. LXVII, No. 1, January-March 2006.

Nayyar, Sanjeev, 'Definition of Secularism – A Global Perspectives', October 2003.

Noorani, A.G., 'Anti – Consensus, Pro Hate', *The Hindustan Times*, 21 January 2003.

__________, 'Every Picture Tells a Story', in *Ibid.,* 4 March 2003.

Ojha, A.K. 'Globalisation and Liberalisation – Prospects of New World', *Third Concept*, August 2002.

Pal, Kushal, 'Dynamics of Party System and Formation of Coalition Government in India', *IJPS*, Vol. LXX, No. 2, April-June 2008.

Palanithurai, G., 'Indian Democracy – A Rethinking', *SAP*, Vol. 6, No. 5, September 2007.

Palekar, S.A., 'Federalism : A Conceptual Analysis', *IJPS*, Vol. LXVII, No. 2, April-June 2006.

Panda, Baijayant 'Jay', 'Choosing between Reform and Referendum', *The Hindu*, 11 January 2011.

Parsons, Talcott, 'Political Development : Times Sequences and Rates of Change', in Finkle and A. Gable (eds.), *Political Development and Social Change* (New York, 1971.

Pathak, D.C., 'India's Role in the War on Terror', *SAP*, Vol. 9, No.10, February 2011.

Phukon, Dolly, 'Gender Development Approach and Social Protection : Understanding the Case of Assam', *IJPS*, Vol. LXIX, No. 4, October – December 2008.

Prasad, Ganesh and Anand Kumar, 'The Concept, Constraints and Prospect of Secularism in india', *IJPS*, Vol. LXVII, No. 4, October-December 2006.

Pye, Lucian W., 'Party System and National Development in Asia', in Joseph La alombara and Myron Weiner (eds.), *Political Parties and Political Development* (Princeton, 1966).

Rajarajan, R., 'Secularism in Indian Politics : Theory and Practice', *IJPS*, Vol. LXXIII, No. 2, April-June 2007.

Raman, A.S., 'Revolution in India', *Contemporary Review*, Vol. 233, No. 1352, September 1978.

Rao, P.P., 'Working the Constitution', *SAP*, Vol. 9, No. 6, October 2010.

Rawls, John, 'The Law of People', in Belgrade Circle (ed.), *The Politics of Human Rights* (London and Newyork, 2002).

Rizvi, Md. Mahtab Alam, 'Secularism in India – Retrospect and Prospects', *IJPS*, Vol. LXVI, No. 4, October-December 2005.

Sachar, Rajindar, 'Lokpal Bill 2010 – A Farce on Public', *SAP*, Vol. 9, No. 10, February 2010.

The National Herald (New Delhi).

The Newyork Times (Newyork).

The Patriot (New Delhi).

The Sunday Standard (New Delhi).

The Statesman (Delhi).

The Times of India (New Delhi).

The Times (London).

The Tribune (Chandigarh).

Periodicals

Administrative Change (Jaipur).

American Political Science Review (Newyork).

Eastern Economist (Bombay).

Economic and Political Weekly (Bombay).

Foreign Affairs (Newyork).

Foreign Policy Report (New Delhi).

Illustrated Weekly of India (Bombay).

India Today (New Delhi).

Indian Journal of Political Science (Hyderabad and Meerut).

International Affairs (Moscow).

International Studies (New Delhi).

Pacific Affairs (Newyork).

Political Science Quarterly (Newyork).

SAARC News (Calcutta).

South Asia Politics (New Delhi).

Third Concept (New Delhi).

Time (Newyork).

World Politics (Princeton).

World Today (London).

Index